"We Want Freedom and Citizenship"

Documents of Salish, Pend d'Oreille, and Kootenai Indian History, 1912-1920

"We Want Freedom and Citizenship"

Documents of Salish, Pend d'Oreille, and Kootenai Indian History, 1912-1920

edited by
Robert Bigart
and
Joseph McDonald

published by
Salish Kootenai College Press
Pablo, Montana

distributed by
University of Nebraska Press
Lincoln, Nebraska

Publication of this book was made possible through the generosity of the Oleta "Pete" Smith Endowment Fund of the Montana Community Foundation.

Cover design: Corky Clairmont, artist/graphic designer, Pablo, Montana.
Cover illustration: Mary Lemery. Source: detail from "First Indian Girl to Be the Head of a Tribe," *The Dearborn Independent* (Dearborn, Mich.), July 17, 1920, page 14. From The Henry Ford, Dearborn, Michigan.

Library of Congress Cataloging-in-Publication Data:
Names: Bigart, Robert, editor. | McDonald, Joseph, 1933- editor.
Title: "We want freedom and citizenship" : documents of Salish, Pend d'Oreille, and Kootenai Indian history, 1912-1920 / edited by Robert Bigart and Joseph McDonald.
Description: Pablo, Montana : Salish Kootenai College Press, [2021] | Includes bibliographical references and index.
Identifiers: LCCN 2021007513 | ISBN 9781934594308 (papaerback)
Subjects: LCSH: Salish Indians--Montana--History--20th century--Sources. | Kalispel Indians--Montana--History--20th century--Sources. | Kootenai Indians--Montana--History--20th century--Sources. | Indians of North American--Montana--Government relations--1869-1934--Sources. | Flathead Indian Reservation (Mont.)--History--20th century--Sources.
Classification: LCC E99.S2 W38 2021 | DDC 978.6004/979435--dc23
LC record available at https://lccn.loc.gov/2021007513

Published by Salish Kootenai College Press, PO Box 70, Pablo, MT 59855.

Distributed by University of Nebraska Press, 1111 Lincoln Mall, Lincoln, NE 68588-0630, order 1-800-755-1105, www.nebraskapress.unl.edu.

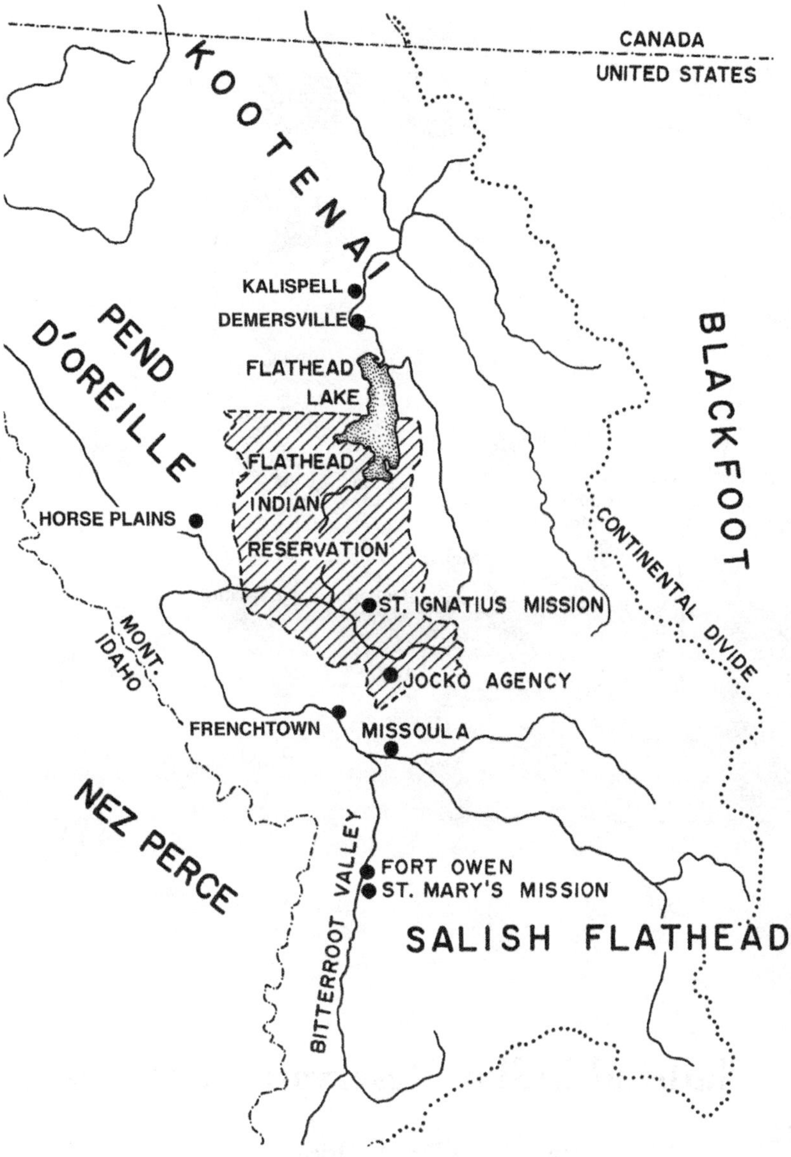

Flathead Indian Reservation Showing Tribal Territories and Surrounding Towns

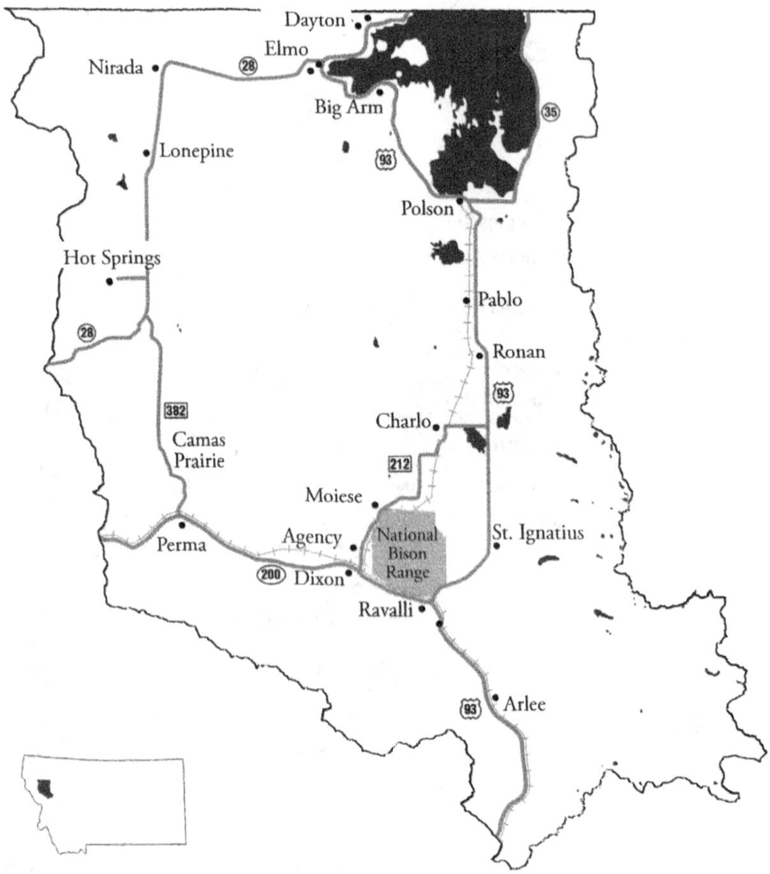

Flathead Indian Reservation, Montana

Map by Wyatt Design, Helena, Montana.

Table of Contents

Detailed Table of Contents

Introduction

"The nine years between 1912 and 1920 were a period of economic and political struggle for the Salish and Kootenai tribes of the Flathead Indian Reservation in western Montana. The Indian people toiled to maintain their economic independence despite the theft of most of their land assets. The new Flathead Irrigation Project destroyed most of the private irrigation ditches tribal farmers had dug over the years. Some tribal members opened businesses and organized rodeos, but many ventures were frustrated by government policies, fire, and drought.

While trying to adapt to the economic impact of allotment, the tribes also fought against paternalistic and exploitive government policies. The Flathead Agency dribbled out individual Indians' funds from leases and land sales, which prevented tribal members from using the money as they chose. Until 1916, half of tribal income from timber and land sales was used to operate the agency and construct an irrigation project that largely benefitted white settlers. During most of the 1912 to 1920 period, Flathead Agent Fred C. Morgan and his allies on the Flathead Business Committee fought the more radical Flathead Tribal Council over agency policies. The Flathead Tribal Council especially fought against congressional appropriations to construct the irrigation project as long as the construction was to be paid for with tribal funds or with liens on tribal allotments.

Government Indian policies in the early twentieth century made little allowance for the best interests of the Indian people and rarely listened to tribal voices and preferences. But against these headwinds the Indian people of the Flathead Reservation refused to be silent. The Flathead Tribal Council was even able to gain access to congressional appropriation committee hearings in Washington, D.C., to fight against the use of tribal assets to build the irrigation system.

Cautions, Biases and Selection Strategies

The documents of Flathead Reservation history in this collection were selected because they offered valuable information about the tribes. However, because they were written records, they also reflect the biases and bigotry of the white men and women who wrote many of the records. Some of the documents in this collection were written by Indian people, but most records that survived give the government's side of the story. The readers need to look beyond the bigotry to see the specific incidents being described.

The editors have given preference to statements by individual Indians or chiefs or descriptions of specific activities. The documents chosen needed to be readable and make sense on their own. Normally historians often rely on many small, short references in diaries or newspaper articles which do not tell a full story.

The documents have not been edited to remove all bigoted words or references. However, an offensive term describing Indian women has been rendered as "s...." An offensive term for Black people has been rendered as "n......"

The editors have tried to use "sic" as infrequently as possible. It is usually only used when we felt the reader might be confused about whether the mistake was in the transcription or in the original manuscript.

The most important sources for tribal history are the oral traditions of the elders. The written sources contribute towards telling history, but they do not give the history. Hopefully, the documents reproduced here will supplement the oral tribal histories currently being collected and written by the Séliš–Ql̓ispé Culture Committee in St. Ignatius and the Kootenai Culture Committee in Elmo, Montana.

Agent Fred Morgan and the Brotherhood of North American Indians

Much of the tribal opposition to Flathead Agency policies took the form of opposition to the administration of Agent, and later Superintendent, Fred C. Morgan between 1908 and 1917. In 1912, a Missoula newspaper reporter wrote a feature describing a day in Morgan's life as agent. (Document 2) Tribal members resented Morgan's efforts to control their personal funds. (Document 28; Document 30; Document 33; Document 46; Document 65) Unfortunately, most of the written sources that have survived give Morgan's side of the conflict. The oral history being compiled by the Séliš–Ql̓ispé Culture Committee should help provide more of the Indian side of the story.

Two of Morgan's most prominent opponents were Henry and Alexander Matt. Morgan wrote a scathing description of Henry Matt's political activity in 1916. No account by Henry has survived to balance the picture. Henry Matt did have legal problems revolving around bootlegging liquor. (Document 65) The Matts were prominent in 1912 in helping organize Flathead Reservation chapters of the Brotherhood of North American Indians. In February 1912,

Alexander Matt wrote an extended report on his trip to a national meeting of the Brotherhood in Washington, D.C. (Document 4) Henry Matt and Chief Martin Charlo organized local chapters of the Brotherhood in various reservation communities. (Document 7) The Brotherhood was a short-lived organization founded by Richard C. Adams, a member of the Delaware Tribe in Oklahoma. Adams had a controversial history which may have included graft. The Brotherhood supported tribal treaty claims in the United State Court of Claims, wanted the Bureau of Indian Affairs to pay out tribal funds as per capita payments, and asked for Indian delegates in the United States Congress. The organization collapsed in 1913. See also the last two documents in volume five of this series covering 1907 to 1911. No written records have survived describing the activities of the Brotherhood on the Flathead Reservation. The Brotherhood may have been involved in the December 1913 complaints about Flathead Agency policies. (Document 41)

The Flathead Business Committee

Early in Morgan's tenure as agent, in 1909, he called a general council of tribal members to elect a business committee to handle tribal business. Duncan McDonald; Mose Delaware; Angus Pierre McDonald; Charles Allard, Jr.; Peter Paul; Eneas Concow; Magpie; Joe Peon; and Chief Martin Charlo were elected to two-year terms on the committee. Morgan and the Indian Office were happy with who were elected and continued the committee members in office until after 1920 without a new election. (Document 130) The Business Committee proposed some policy changes but was mostly willing to work within the framework of federal Indian policy at the time. (Document 28; Document 31; Document 45)

Duncan McDonald

One of the most prominent tribal members in the written documents was Duncan McDonald, half Scottish and half Nez Perce and adopted into the Flathead Reservation tribes. McDonald had long been active as a businessman and spokesman for the tribes. As mentioned above, in 1909 he was elected chairman of the Flathead Business Committee. In 1912, he was selected as a Progressive Party candidate for the Montana State Legislature, but he lost the election. (Document 19)

In September 1912, McDonald was elected as a tribal representative on the committee to appraise the remaining tribal lands that were open to homesteading. (Document 20) The Ronan newspaper praised McDonald on his appointment: "there is not a man in all this section who could or would serve his people better and at the same time do what is absolutely right as he sees it, all the time." (Document 31) However, McDonald and the appraisal committee set the value of the land at its real value which was more than the bargain prices set under the original provisions of Joseph Dixon's 1904 allotment law. White homesteaders were outraged and the newspaper did not repeat its praise of McDonald: "Who wants to pay actual value for the land and use a homestead right besides?" (Document 40)

McDonald was frequently interviewed by Missoula newspapers and in February 1915 gave a lecture on tribal lore and customs at the state university at Missoula. (Document 53) A number of these interviews or historical reminiscences have been reproduced in this collection. (See for example, Document 55; Document 63; Document 80; and Document 109)

The Flathead Tribal Council

Tribal opposition to agency policies continued, and in 1915 and 1916 some tribal leaders relied on "Princess Red Feather" to lobby for them in Washington, D.C. Princess Red Feather was part Cherokee and went by a number of aliases. The Indian Office files contain salacious charges against her, but her side of the story did not survive. (Document 62; Document 71; Document 74) It is not known if her lobbying in Washington and organizing on the reservation was related to the formation of the Flathead Tribal Council in 1916.

Mary Lemery and Max J. Barnaby were the principal organizers of the tribal council in 1916. (Document 130; Document 82) The tribal council wanted dramatic changes in Flathead Agency policies. They especially opposed using tribal money to fund the construction of the irrigation project. The use of tribal funds was ended in 1916 and the construction charges were made liens on the allotments and homesteads. This new policy left tribal members with a crippling debt attached to their allotments. (Document 82) The Flathead Tribal Council delegation to Washington, D.C., opposed any congressional appropriations for the irrigation project that were liens against the land. (Document 84) The tribal council also protested the coerced opening of the reservation in 1910 and wanted legislation to allow the tribes to sue the federal government for failure to fulfill treaty provisions. (Document 85)

The tribal council delegates shocked the Montana political establishment by their opposition to appropriations funding the Flathead Irrigation Project construction. The project funding was part of the political "pork" which Montana senators brought home to enrich western Montana white voters. (Document 86) Senator Harry Lane of Oregon got the tribal council delegates admitted to the Senate appropriation hearings. They were backed financially by Victor J. Evans, a Washington, D.C., attorney. Evans was a wealthy Washington patent attorney who, among other interests, represented a number of Indian tribes seeking redress for government wrongs. (Document 84)

The tribal council lobbying did succeed in getting the irrigation project appropriations greatly reduced, but Senator Joseph Dixon and his newspaper, *The Daily Missoulian*, were offended and outraged. The *Missoulian* thought the Flathead Indians should appreciate everything Dixon had done for them and not be led astray by agitators. (Document 100)

Mary Lemery was remarkably effective in organizing opposition to government policies on the reservation. She was a graduate of the Holy Name College of Oregon, and farmed her allotment near St. Ignatius. (Document 136)

Battles with State Authorities

As a backdrop to the factional battles on the reservation over federal government policies, the tribes had to fight against state and county efforts to tax tribal members. In 1912, the assessors for the local counties were on the reservation trying to force members to pay county taxes. (Document 11) Flathead County assessed Chief Koostatah for his horses and cattle in 1920. (Document 127) In 1915 the federal court affirmed that state fish and game laws did not apply to Indians on the reservation. (Document 64)

Crime and the Courts

As usual, considerable newspaper attention was paid to crimes committed by tribal members. Most of the crime was Indian on Indian, but some involved alleged attacks on white people.

In March 1912, a white man accused Pierre Adams, Jr., of assaulting him. Adams was arrested but released after he produced witnesses who swore he was someplace else at the time of the assault. (Document 9) The next month, an unnamed Indian was charged with attacking a homesteader's cabin near Perma. (Document 12) In May 1912, three Indians accused a white man of stealing $1.50 from them, but the case was dismissed. (Document 14)

Several legal cases arose from the 1912 Arlee celebration. Eneas Grandjo was charged with attacking his wife while drunk. (Document 16) Charges of drinking alcohol and gambling at the 1912 celebration were denied by some Arlee whites. (Document 17)

An Indian policeman killed a prisoner in 1912 during an escape attempt. (Document 25) Henry Matt and Pete Matt were arrested in July 1913 and accused of assaulting Robert Holland, an Arlee merchant. (Document 36) A dying, consumptive Indian was convicted of purchasing alcohol, but he was pardoned by President Woodrow Wilson so he could return home to die.

(Document 37) Leo Barnaby was shot by an Indian policeman in January 1914, during an attempted arrest for a liquor violation. (Document 42) In April 1914, Henry Matt was found not guilty of furnishing whiskey to an Indian. (Document 44)

A number of reservation Indians were arrested for being drunk in Missoula. In July 1914, some unnamed Indians who were in Missoula to perform for the Fourth of July celebration were arrested after a brawl. (Document 47) A number of tribal members in Missoula in August 1914 for the circus were arrested for theft or fighting while drunk. (Document 49) In October 1915, three white men were charged with stealing money from an Indian in Missoula. (Document 59)

Court cases involving Indians continued to feature in the Missoula newspapers during the second half of the 1910s. In February 1920 the Missoula County Sheriff declared war on the town of Arlee in an attempt to clean up the alcohol and gambling offenses there. (Document 125)

Tribal Celebrations

Tribal celebrations continued in 1912 to 1920, and often had numerous white visitors. In 1912, large crowds of white spectators attended the Fourth of July powwow held at the town of Arlee. (Document 15) Agent Fred Morgan wanted the activities moved to the Jocko Agency across the valley. Charges of drinking and carousing were made and denied, but the controversy got caught up in tribal complaints about Morgan's management of the agency. (Document 17)

Chief Martin Charlo and many of the Jocko Valley Indians performed at the 1913 Fourth of July festivities in Missoula. (Document 35) Apparently some of the Arlee merchants resented the loss of business. Henry Matt and Robert Holland, the Arlee merchant, were involved in a fight which presumably resulted from moving the Indian camp to Missoula. (Document 36) A number of tribal elders were welcomed at the June 1915 stampede or rodeo in Missoula. (Document 56)

Two celebrations sponsored by the Flathead Agency drew reporters and crowds of tribal members. In September 1913, Dr. Joseph Dixon (no relation to the Montana Senator) and the Rodman Wanamaker Expedition of Citizenship to the North American Indian visited the Flathead. With great ceremony, patriotic speeches were given to the Indian audience. A declaration of allegiance to the government of the United States was signed by the Indians, and an American flag was given to the tribes. (Document 38)

A similar maudlin affair was held at the Dixon Agency in June 1916 to celebrate Indians who had recently received patents to their allotments and become United States citizens. The ceremony tried to symbolize the Indian men giving up the bow and arrow for the plow. New Indian women citizens received purses in which to save money. (Document 73) Some of the new citizen Indians pressured the government to divide up the tribal funds and assets and pay the money out in a per capita payment. (Document 72; Document 87; Document 99)

Tribal Members Businesses

The period between 1912 and 1920 saw a number of tribal members — primarily mixed bloods — establish businesses on the reservation. In 1912, Richard McLeod operated the Pioneer Pool Hall in Ronan. (Document 6) The August 1912 fire that destroyed much of Ronan burned out businesses owned by Michel Pablo, Andrew Stinger, Edward Clairmont, Crawford & Stinger, and Richard McLeod. (Document 18) Michel Pablo originally wanted to rebuild his Ronan store, but finally decided not to risk the loss from another fire. (Document 22) Harry Burland operated an auto repair garage and a blacksmith shop. (Document 23) In November 1912, John Matt sold 1,000 tons of Jocko Valley hay to buyers in Butte. (Document 24) Julian Courville had a livery and feed stable in St. Ignatius (Document 26), and Edward Deschamp sold cigars, soft drinks, and confectionery in St. Ignatius. (Document 27) Joseph Grenier, Jr., purchased stock in a new St. Ignatius bank in 1913. (Document 39) In 1916, Annie Dupuis sold millinery and ladies' furnishings in a Ronan store. (Document 76) Between 1917 and 1919, Malcolm McLeod sold firewood, ran a harness and shoe repairing shop, and had an automobile bus route from Ronan to Ravalli. (Document 83) Frank McLeod, Jr., ran a vulcanizing shop in Ronan in 1919. (Document 112) Also in 1919, Alex Pablo was a partner in the Central City Auto Company in Ronan. (Document 115) In 1920 one of the McLeod's operated an automobile stage line between Ronan and Missoula. (Document 128)

Between 1917 and 1920, Charles Allard, Jr., managed several rodeo and wild west shows, giving employment to tribal members. He managed the 1917 Missoula Stampede and the 1920 Bozeman roundup. (Document 89; Document 137) He was also sued by the First National Bank in Ronan on an overdue promissory note in 1918. (Document 106)

Other Interesting Glimpses of Reservation Life

The obituaries of three prominent tribal leaders gave some information about their lives and deaths: Judge Louison (Document 13), Michel Pablo (Document 48), and Chief Antoine Moiese (Document 107) A remarkable commentary on Flathead Agency history was provided by Henry Matt's account of Flathead agents from Peter Ronan to Samuel Bellew. (Document 43)

A few other items of interest include a U.S. Army recruitment effort on the reservation in 1917, and Indian purchases of war bonds and volunteer work for the Red Cross in World War I. (Document 88; Document 95) In 1917, Eneas Grandjo was seriously injured by a quack dentist in Missoula. (Document 94) In January 1918, Edward Griva, S.J., published an account of a New Year's celebration he spent with the Kootenai Indians on Flathead Lake. (Document 96) Salish Indians danced in Missoula in 1919 as part of a pageant-masque put on by the State University of Montana Summer School. (Document 116) In September 1919, Chief Big Hawk from the reservation got his first airplane ride. (Document 118) Ominously, in 1920 a special competency board was working on the reservation to select tribal members to receive forced patents for their allotments, regardless of the wishes of the Indians. (Document 131)

Conclusion

The 1912 to 1920 period was a time of struggle and conflict on the Flathead Indian Reservation. The tribes had already been robbed of much of their land through Congressman Joseph Dixon's allotment bill. Now the tribes had to undo Dixon's efforts to use tribal money to build an irrigation system to mainly benefit white homesteaders on the reservation. The Flathead Tribal Council was able to find a sympathetic U.S. Senator to gain entrance to appropriation hearings and oppose further money for irrigation project construction. In the 1910s that was a remarkable accomplishment. The financial mess left by Dixon's funding of the Flathead Irrigation Project with tribal assets to reward white Montana voters was not finally resolved until 1948. The Salish and Kootenai people were a troublesome lot for the federal government. They insisted on voicing their objections to government policies and having their interests respected.

Chapter 1

Documents of Salish, Pend d'Oreille, and Kootenai History Between 1912-1913

Document 1

Indian Policeman Kills Drunken Tribal Member

January 1, 1912

Source: "Full Blood Indian Was Kizer," *The Daily Missoulian,* January 1, 1912, page 10, col. 6.

Editors' note: Michel Kizer was killed by a blow to the head suffered in a fight with an Indian policeman. Kizer was reportedly drunk at the time and attacked the policeman.

Full Blood Indian Was Kizer

Coroner Marsh Has No Jurisdiction and Says Story Told Is Exaggerated.

Coroner Marsh was home yesterday from his trip to the Flathead agency where he was called on account of the death there Saturday of Michel Kizer, death having been the result of a blow which Kizer had received on the head about a week ago at the hands of Baptists Joseph, an Indian policeman. Mr. Marsh found that Kizer was a full-blood Indian and that the trouble between him and the policeman took place on an Indian allotment and therefore the case was entirely in the hands of the federal authorities and his official services were not needed. Joseph had already been arrested by Major Fred Morgan and will be held in custody pending an autopsy which is to be held today.

"It seems that the stories in the case have been greatly exaggerated," said the coroner last evening. From the investigations it appears that Kizer was intoxicated on the night of the trouble and when the officer attempted to get him to go home, Kizer resented the effort and attacked him. The officer admits having struck Kizer on the head and immediately went to the agency and reported the case, securing help to bring the man in. Kizer was left in jail and the following day it was found that he was still unconscious. He received medical attention and was removed to the home of his brother, but never regained consciousness. I examined the body, although not in an official capacity, and instead of it being badly bruised as was reported, there was only evidence of the one blow on the side of the head that probably caused a hemorrhage and resulted in death. Officer Joseph has never denied striking Kizer, but it appears that he did so in performing his duty and in self-defense."

Document 2

Morgan Deals with Indian Protests and Prisoners January 7, 1912

Source: "A Day with the Flathead Indian Agent," *The Daily Missoulian*, January 7, 1912, editorial section, page 1, col. 1-7, and page 8, col. 5.

Editors' note: This feature related some of the details about Agent Morgan's treatment of the Indian policeman who had just killed another Indian, possibly in self-defense. The reporter was impressed with Morgan and the agency employees.

A Day with the Flathead Indian Agent

It is a custom of the Flathead Indians to observe the birth of a new year with a week of celebration, marked by the settlement of debts and scores of every sort. The tribe gathers together at the principal meeting points of the reservation, the bucks smoke the pipe of peace, settle their differences, shake hands and start the new year with a clean slate for the whole world. It was to witness the beginning of such a celebration that the Cub Reporter was sent to the agency on New Year's day. He was expected to come back with a lot of interesting sidelights on the life of the Indian. Instead, he learned little of particular credit to the Indian and a lot regarding the difficulties surrounding the life of the Indian agent and his assistants.

Indian agent has an easy sound about it. It appeals to the imagination and most people think that the berth is a soft one given only to the select and carrying with it little hard work. The Indian agent is virtually an autocrat, and most of us feel that of all jobs that of being autocrat is about the easiest ever. The absolute ruler who would be just, however, has no small job in front of him, and the Indian agent is no exception to the rule.

When the Cub Reporter reached the agency he found that there was to be no celebration at all. Tragedy instead of jollity held the boards. An Indian policeman, Baptiste Joseph, had killed another red man in some sort of a brawl a week before, and until the period of mourning had passed the New Year would not be celebrated, regardless of the calendar. Discontent there was with the mourning. Sons and daughters as they were of men who would have killed Baptiste in atonement for his deed before resting easily, the relatives of the dead man could scarcely restrain themselves from violence, especially since Baptiste was at large. They were gathered at the agency, filled with wrath, to protest to Major Morgan, the agent, that Baptiste should be locked up. The Cub in entering the agent's office ran into two-score of sullen, unsmiling Indians, crowded together, arguing their case before the agent and two of the hereditary judges, John Charlie and Louis Pierre. Stolidly they sat there, smoking innumerable cigarettes, until finally agent and judges persuaded them that since Baptiste had admitted the killing and was anxious for a trial, and since he could easily escape from jail if locked up, it was best that he be allowed his liberty until he could be brought to trial. Assured at last that their leaders were right, the Indians filed past the major, shook his hand, wished him a happy new year, and left.

The major then turned his attention to the Cub. "Wait a minute," he said. "The judges are going to let some prisoners go since it is New Year's day." As he spoke one of the Indian policemen led a file of dirty, disreputable looking Indians into the room and lined them up before the two judges. Major Morgan reviewed the fault of each as he stepped before the judges. This one, he told them, had come home drunk, this one had taken for himself a wife, without benefit of clergy, and this one, a mere boy, would not behave himself properly. There were several drunks, one of whom, the major said in an undertone, had two notches in his stick already. When the prisoners had taken their places the judges began their lecture. Like parents to disobedient children did they speak. They told of the evils of drink to the drunkards, and commanded them to leave the white man's whiskey alone if they wished to keep out of jail. They told the wayward boy that he might go free if he would let the major put him in school. To the young, almost-married man they gave a marriage license.

It is indeed a remarkable court. Chief Justice Duncan McDonald was not present, but John Charlie and Louis Pierre handled things well enough. Old men they are, who have the interests of their people at heart; men of the type which prevailed before the invasion of civilization; men of a far different caliber than the young bucks of today. These three men sit in judgement over all strictly local cases, and they keep their people pretty closely in check. It was easy to gauge their influence by the shamefacedness of the prisoners as they listened with downcast eyes to the arraignment against them and as they humbly wished their judges a happy new year before marching out into the open air. As a race, the Flatheads are almost decadent, but men such as these command anyone's respect.

As the prisoners and the judges filed out Major Morgan sighed with relief. "This is the first let-up all day," he said — it was now late in the afternoon. "This is the way we spend Sundays and holidays here." Then, without stopping to rest, Mr. Morgan suggested a visit to the jail for the instruction of his visitor and led the way toward the old white house which serves as an abode for the wrongdoers of the reserve. A stranger jail would be hard to find. There are three rooms on the ground floor, one for the use of the jailer, one for the women prisoners and the third for the men. There were no s....s in the lockup this New Year's day, but a mattress thrown into a corner and replaced by a few ragged blankets on the floor showed the original Indian of the last occupant as clearly as the multitude of cigarette butts showed the Indian of today. The other room, however, was pretty well filled. Lying about on the floor were half a dozen or more Indians playing cards in pairs, and in the corner, looking on disdainfully, was a fat, harmless looking half-breed, whose crafty, dangerous eyes were almost offset by a stupid face. This man, Lawrence Finley, Major Morgan explained, participated in the killing of a couple of men some 20 years ago. He turned state's evidence and went free, four of his fellows hanging for the crime. Since then he has served several prison terms and is now being held for bootlegging just after having served an 18 months' sentence at Fort Leavenworth. The major shook hands with the prisoners and wished each a happy new year, promising them some apples as a new year gift.

As he went out he introduced the Cub Reporter to the jailer. It was Baptiste Joseph, the man whose killing of another Indian had just caused so much trouble. Baptiste does not look like a murderer. He is big, frank and honest in appearance and a glance at him makes his story of self-defense seem thoroughly dependable. At any rate the confidence of Major Morgan has not been misplaced. Baptiste will honor his parole.

The real pleasure of the whole visit, though, was the evening meal with the men of the Indian service. Courteous, modest, they made the Cub Reporter realize the magnitude of the work which they are doing. Across from him at the table sat a young fellow who was introduced as "Ike, the Terror of the Rockies." Ike is a slender youngster of about 20 who was kidded throughout the meal for an arrest which he made single-handed a few nights before. He spotted a big fellow as a bootlegger as he got off the train at Arlee, it seems, and, following him until sure of the fact, halted him, took his booze away from him and put him in jail. Ike's modesty made him easy meat. His pompadour, the major's coat, another fellow's gun were all given as the real cause of the exploit. The major himself called Ike down. "Think of a fellow who will stop an entire stranger and take his whiskey away from him," he said. "The man told Ike that he had cramps; that he took the whiskey to relieve them and then rubbed the alcohol, which was among the contraband, on the outside. But Ike put him in jail just the same." Next to Ike sat a quiet chap who kept pretty much to himself during the meal. After dinner the major told of how this man walked into Lawrence Finley's house at the mission one day and took out 34 gamblers. That is no small achievement, but it is of the sort which marks the every-day life of these men. A handful of them, together with a few Indian deputies, have charge of the whole broad reservation, and it is to their credit that the reserve has mighty little real trouble. They are busy, fearless, gentlemanly men, and the people who think that they are resting in soft berths are mistaken. They treat a stranger in a way which can't be forgotten, and the Cub Reporter is looking forward anxiously to the time when he can make them another visit.

Document 3

Matt Employee Attacks Family

January 27, 1912

Source: "Negro Runs Amuck in Matt Residence," *The Daily Missoulian*, January 27, 1912, page 12, col. 6.

Editors' note: Yet another variant of a reservation law and order problem that attracted attention in Missoula.

Negro Runs Amuck in Matt Residence

Fred Seal, a negro who formerly lived in Missoula, and Gussie Jones, with whom he was living at the Henry Matt residence near Evaro, furnished the reason for a trip to Evaro last night by Undersheriff Marion and Deputy Sheriff Johnson. Seal, who is working for Henry Matt, ran amuck yesterday afternoon and chased the Jones woman, who is also colored and is known in Missoula's tenderloin as "Midget," up and down the countryside. Later in the day he returned, and, wielding a lamp as a weapon, cut "Midget" badly and ran the Matt family to the woods. A hurry-up call to the sheriff's office sent the local officers to Evaro, but Seal had escaped.

Document 4

Alex Matt Reports on D.C. Trip

February 22, 1912

Source: Alex Matt, "Matt's Trip," *The Daily Missoulian*, February 22, 1912, page 2, col. 5-6.

Editors' note: Alex Matt and other Indians from the Flathead Reservation were anxious to have Washington officials pay attention to their needs and interests. Matt was working through a national lobbying organization, the Brotherhood of North American Indians, to make his appeal. The Brotherhood was founded by Richard C. Adams, a member of the Delaware Tribe in Oklahoma. Adams had a controversial history which may have included graft. See also the 1911 documents about the Brotherhood on the Flathead Resrvation in volume five of this series, 1907-1911.

Matt's Trip

Editor, Missoulian: — I left Arlee on the 10th day of January and arrived in Washington, D.C., on the 15th of January. Upon arrival there we went to the hotel and next day had a visit with the Indian office. In afternoon went in council with the Brotherhood of North American Indians, comprising over 60 different tribes. While in council all matters concerning the Indians were taken up. The following day I visited the Indian commissioners and had a very nice talk with Commissioner Valentine. My treatment from this office was very encouraging. I explained to Mr. Valentire [Valentine] that the Indians were not properly treated; that they were in very poor condition. They all have 80 acres of land, which is naked; the majority of the Indians have nothing to work this land, and have no means of buying the necessary implements for working this land. In the early days it was not necessary; the Indians had considerable hunting ground and could make a living, but since these lands, monies and hunting ground have been taken away from them they are practically left on their own resources with practically nothing for their livelihood. They are now looking to no one but the government for protection. It is a fact also, that the Indian should have taken up their rights a long time ago. In making an address to congress I convinced them of the present conditions of the Indians. Congress was always aware that the Indians were in very good condition, but were very much surprised to hear of the present conditions. All the higher officials in Washington were in sympathy with the Indians, and their talk to me was very encouraging.

In the early days the Indians had a strip of ground which they called their own and was given to them by God. They had a large acreage of their own and lived very happy, but of later years most all this ground has been taken away from them.

The Indians would be very glad to have a little park of their own, where they could fish and hunt without the interference of the white man.

There are at the present time 93,000 Indian voters in the United States, and about 300,000 that are not yet citizens. It is not the policy of the Indians to favor any particular party in politics, but the man that is in sympathy with the just rights of the Indians, regardless of whether he is a democrat or a republican, and if he will give some of his attentions to the Indians, then this man could have all the support of any and all Indians.

I can remember in the early days in the Bitter Root valley when the white people would come to the Indians and ask for land. I at that time was interpreter and know of many instances when old chief Victor would tell them to go and pick out land and use it; and all these white people had the protection of the Indians in the valley; and in later years all the thanks the Indians got was a petition for the removal of the Indians from the Bitter Root to the Flathead country. The Indians remembered these instances and it is one reason they feel down-hearted.

When the Nez Perces came through the valley the Flathead Indians told them to go through, but to not harm even a chicken belonging to the white man.

The Indian made all efforts in the early days to help the whites, but since they have grown poor and become wards of the government they have no recognition from the white people. And they feel that the help they gave the whites in the early days should be returned to them by the whites in time of need, which is the present time.

Speaking of the conditions on the reservation now, there are several sections of land taken from the Indians and sold to the state. These lands are of the very best quality, but were sold to the state at the very lowest price possible. Such matters as these have been taken up through my efforts and I expect that a proper settlement will be made.

There are a great many appropriations being asked for (out of Indian monies) that do not entirely benefit the Indians.

The Indians feel that some of the appropriations asked for should be set aside, and if any is to be made, then let an appropriation be made for the

Indians, whereby they might buy farm implements, horses to work their land and lumber to build their homes. If the whites would look at it from the Indians' side of it and give him a little justice, he would not feel his hurts as he does now. Perfect harmony could exist between the Indians and the whites, if only the whites would jar loose and let the Indian have a few of the rights now held by all whites and some of which are not as entitled to them as lots of our good Indians.

Alex Matt.

Arlee, February 20.

Alexander Matt
Source: Virginia Matt Brazill, Arlee, Montana

Document 5

Indian Dies Without Paying His Debts

March 1912

Source: "Indian's Spirit Stirs Under Pall of Debts He Left; Tells Old Man," *Spokesman-Review* (Spokane, Wash.), March 30, 1913, page 6, col. 1.

Editors' note: Gabriel Na-tah died with unpaid debts and could not find peace after death. Some of the quotes within a quote, within a quote, got a little confused, but they have been reproduced here as they appeared in the newspaper. Years later, Louis Taelman, S.J. related a slightly different version of this story to Verne Dusenberry which was published in Verne Dusenberry, "Gabriel Nattau's Soul Speaks," *Journal of American Folklore*, vol. 72, no. 284 (April-June 1959), pages 155-160. The Dusenberry version of the story gave the date of the vision as March 1912.

Indian's Spirit Stirs Under Pall of Debts He Left; Tells Old Man
Weird Narrative Brought From Flathead by Father Louis Taelman, S.J.
"Have Pity," Says Ghost
"I Have Been Traveling Up and Down; I Suffer; I Burn" —
Relatives Pay for Him.

"While I was at the Flathead reservation to help the superior of St. Ignatius mission, Father de la Motte, in the holy week and Easter services, a curious and interesting story of his experience was told me by an old Indian named Antoine Teheminten (Hammer)" said Father Louis Taelman, president of Gonzaga university, last night. "I was myself head of the St. Ignatius mission for four years and know the Indians well. Antoine is 60 years old and a sober and truthful man. The story was told me in the Indian language and he also told it to Father de la Motte. I offer no explanation of it beyond saying the moral that one ought to pay one's debts if possible before dying seems a good one.

On Way to Pray.

"'Three weeks ago,' said Antoine, 'I was going at dusk to the house where an Indian had died and where, according to custom, the Indians were coming together for the wake, to spend the night in prayer. On my way thither I passed by the house of Gabriel Na-tah, a Spokane Indian, who had died three years ago. I there heard a voice calling me by my name, Antoine.

"'I looked and saw no one. I heard the voice a second time, looked around, passed by the gate but could find nobody. I was going back to the road when I heard a long whistle. I went to the spot whence it came. I knelt down, took off my hat, blessed myself with the sign of the cross and said "Who are you?"

Saw No one.

"'I saw no one, but the voice answered:

"'"I am Gabriel Na-tah."

"'"But you died three years ago," said I.'

"'"Yes, I died and since then I have been traveling up and down. I suffer; I burn."

"'"Why do you suffer?" I asked.

"'"Because I had debts when I died which I did not pay."

"'He then mentioned four persons, the first Sgu-too, a Sioux Indian to whom he owed $2; another Indian to whom he owed $10, a third whom he owed for a horse and a fourth whom he owed for a plow.

"'He added: "Antoine, ko-akankon-eminem Antoine (Have pity on me)!"

"Antoine answered: 'I would pay your debts if I had money, but I have none. You have many relatives who perhaps will pay.'

"No answer.

"Antoine said: 'Have you anything else to say?'

"No answer.

"'Then,' says Antoine, 'I made the sign of the cross and started to go, and as I was starting I saw Gabriel standing before me and perfectly recognized him. Gabriel made for me and touched me on the head and said:

"'"Have pity on me. Tell my relatives."

"By that time I began to stagger and fell to the snow and swooned. I then went to the house where the Indians were gathered for the wake. I walked like a drunken man. One of the Indians says to me: "Are you drunk?" I said "No, I am not! I threw away drinking when I was a young man."

"'This occurrence became known and caused great excitement amongst the relatives of Gabriel. They investigated the matter and found that the statements in regard to the debts were true."

Did Not Know of Debts.

"Teheminten had not known of these debts, and this makes his narrative all the more strange. One of these relatives, a little less poor than the rest of them, undertook to cancel Gabriel's debts. She was in difficulty about the $2 due to the Sioux Indian, who died two years ago. On Easterday, in the afternoon, she came to see Father de la Motte, the superior of the mission.

"'I come to see you about something very important,' she said. 'My grief is exceedingly great.'

"'What is the matter?' said Father de la Motte. 'I want to pay Gabriel's debt. I want to give you the $2 due to the dead Sioux Indian. Take the money. Here it is.'

Give It to the Poor.

"'No,' said Father de la Motte, 'but go and give it to the poorest Indian woman you can find in the camp.'

"This was done, and on Monday morning the poor old Indian woman who had received the money, through gratitude, went to confession and holy communion for the repose of the soul of Gabriel. On Easterday also the same relative found the Indian to whom $10 was due. She gave the money, but the Indian through charity accepted $6 as full payment. Arrangements are also under way to pay for the horse and the plow.

"The event stirred up many people. Chief Baptiste Kai-kai-shee was considerably worried.

Chief Owes Debts.

"He came to Father de la Motte and said: 'I have debts with you and can not pay them. What will become of me if I die without paying them?'

"The father quieted him, saying that if he should die without being able to pay his debts he would call it all square. This promise greatly relieved him. Other Indians also feel the weight of their debts, and will no doubt get to work to straighten out their accounts before they answer the final call.

"It will not be out of place, in connection with the foregoing, to add here another little narrative made on Ash Wednesday to Father Taelman by Helen, an excellent Indian woman of the Calispel tribe, residing across the river from Cusick.

"Her daughter Anne, 19 years old, had died last December a most beautiful and saintly death, full of hope and consolation. The thought of Anne was frequently on the mind of her mother. When on Ash Wednesday she was through with her confession she said to me: 'Some time ago I was sleeping, and in my dream I saw Anne, and she said to me, "You must pray for me."

"'And another time I was asleep, and in my dream I again saw Anne, and she said, "You must pray." And a third time I was not asleep, but awake, and I saw Anne, and she said to me, "Now, you can rejoice."

"Great is the simplicity of many of these Indians, and whatever one may think of their narratives there is no reason for doubting their subjective sincerity and veracity."

Document 6

The Pioneer Pool Hall

The Ronan Pioneer, March 1, 1912, page 4, col. 3.

THE

Pioneer Pool Hall

Is the place to spend your leisure time. Best tables in town. If you come and see us once, you will sure come again.

RICHARD McLEOD

Rooms in Connection

Document 7

Flathead Reservation Indians Join Lobbying Organization March 1, 1912

Source: "Bitter Root Indians to Join Brotherhood," *The Daily Missoulian*, March 1, 1912, page 2, col. 4-5.

Editors' note: As early as 1912, Flathead Reservation Indians were organizing and joining a national Indian lobbying organization to get their grievances heard.

Bitter Root Indians to Join Brotherhood

Henry Matt was in town yesterday. He is preparing for the first meeting of local Indians to organize a branch of the Brotherhood of North American Indians. The meeting will be held Saturday morning at the former residence of the late Chief Charlot. Chief Martin Charlot will preside. There will be other branches organized on the reservation, one each at St. Ignatius, Ronan, Polson, Dayton and Camas. Mr. Matt thinks there will be 1,200 Indians in the local branches and sees in the new brotherhood the means of obtaining all the rights to which the Indian is entitled and is enthusiastic over the prospects. He is one of the salaried officers — interpreter.

Document 8

Tribal Members Have Trouble Selling and Leasing Allotments March 1912

Source: "Rich in Flathead Lands, Entire Family Suffers," *The Ronan Pioneer*, March 8, 1912, page 1, col. 1-3; Excerpt from O. H. Lipps, "Flathead Reservation: Report of Supervisor O. H. Lipps, April 16, 1912, from file 39,847-8/1912 Flathead 320, Central Classified Files, RG 75, National Archives, Washington, D.C.

Editors' note: According to the *Ronan Pioneer,* Mary Howlett, a widow with minor children, could not support her family despite having land holdings. See Lipps report for a different version of Mrs. Howlett's situation. The local newspaper could have desired to get Mrs. Howlett's lands in the hands of white settlers.

Rich in Flathead Lands, Entire Family Suffers

Considerable has been said and written concerning the ruling of the Indian department concerning the manner in which the lands of the wards of the government are being administered on the Flathead reservation. In a general way the statement has been made that from the refusal or neglect to lease and sell certain lands, much suffering has resulted. This fact was true and numerous instances have become known during the past two years in which the same have been pitiful. Heretofore the matter has been treated generally, without going into details, although the names and circumstances could have been puplished [sic] many times. It was thought that, mayhap, the department might change its attitude without specific cases being cited, but such does not appear probable, at this time. To fully substantiate the statement that many of the wards of the government on the Flathead reservation have been allowed to suffer and without any good reason therefor, the following affidavit has been secured and it is published to show the people just what is actually happening here.

This is a case of widow, left with small children, without any means of support, being allowed to eke out an existence by selling a few eggs and the butter from three cows. She and her children have been allotted 680 acres of land and during the present winter have not been sufficiently clothed and only partially fed. Under present conditions there seems no relief for this family for two years yet to come.

It is a shame that people with land rich in soil like these unfortunates have, should be allowed to freeze and starve when so many are seeking the privilege of working the land and would willingly pay a good rental for the chance. It would help in two ways.

One of the children died leaving an allotment, and this should be sold and the money distributed to the heirs, providing them with the ordinary necessities of life at a time when they have no other opportunity of doing so. What will it avail the other members of the family if the land is more valuable after the reclamation project is completed, if they starve and freeze to death waiting its completion?

But read the affidavit of Mrs. Mary Howlett and judge for yourself:

State of Montana, ss
County of Missoula,

Mary Howlett, being first duly sworn, says: that she is of lawful age and is the widow of John Howlett, who died upon the Flathead reservation in November, 1910; that she is a member of the tribe of Flathead Indians and the mother of five minor children, who are now living, and have one deceased child; that she and her children have all been allotted lands upon the Flathead reservation, as follows, viz:

Mary Howlett, age 42, 120 acres
Steve Howlett, age 14, 80 acres
Max Howlett, age 12, 120 acres
Denny Howlett, age 10, 80 acres
Frankie Howlett, age 6, 80 acres
Maggie Howlett, age 4, 120 acres
Theodore Howlett, deceased, 80
Total —— 680 acres

That the eighty (80) acres of land allotted to Denny Howlett was leased to W. H. Krebs in the spring of 1910, for a period of five (5) years. Said Krebs, for the use of the land, agreed to build a small house, barn and granary, and to fence and cultivate the land all of which improvements will amount to about five hundred ($500.00) dollars; that in the spring of 1910, one hundred and sixty (160) acres of the land allotted to the deponent and her minor children, was leased to Charley Quigley and Dwight Large for a period of five (5) years, and, upon the following terms: they were to fence and cultivate the land and build a small house, chicken house and granary and to pay two ($2.00) per acre for the use of the land the last year of the lease.

Deponent further says that at the time of the death of her husband, John Howlett, he was the owner of and possessed practically no personal property and that he left deponent and her minor children without property or means of support except the land allotted to them by the government; that she is about forty-two (42) years of age and that all of her minor children are under fourteen (14) years of age; that none of them are able to work out and earn anything towards the support and maintenance of herself and family and that all her children are dependent upon her for support, clothing and education, and have been ever since the death of her husband; that none of her children have any property other than the land allotted to them and have no income except such as may be derived from the lands allotted to them; that none of said children are able to support themselves or render any material help towards the support and maintenance of deponent and her family.

Deponent further says that all of her time is practically taken up in the care of her minor children and the care of her small amount of stock; that she has no property except three cows, two horses and a few chickens, except the land allotted to her as stated above; that she has no income except such as derived from the cows, horses and chickens and which is derived from the land allotted to herself and family.

Deponent further says that from the leases above mentioned, she has never received a dollar and will not be entitled to receive a single cent for a period of two years yet to come, with which to support, maintain and educate her family, and that unless she receives some income from the balance of the land allotted to herself and family, she will be obliged to clothe, feed and care for them by her individual efforts and whatever she can make out of her three cows and a few chickens.

Deponent further states that she is obliged to depend absolutely on the allotted lands for the support and maintenance of herself and children, and that so far as the matter now stands, for some time yet to come she will receive no revenue from these lands with which to support and maintain her children, and although she and her family are rich in land she is without the means to buy comfortable clothing and nourishing food for herself and children.

Deponent further states that at this time her children are practically barefooted and are scantily clothed; that Max, aged twelve, for the want of something to wear on his feet, severely froze his feet in January of this year while on his way to school.

Deponent further states that at times they do not have proper food to sustain life; that in case of sickness she has no means by which she can get medicine or the attendance of a physician; that it is her desire to educate her children, to teach them thrift and usefulness and become good examples to the rest of the tribe upon the reservation, but that it is almost impossible to do more than keep body and soul together without an income of any sort from the lands owned by her and her family.

Deponent further states that the balance of the land allotted to herself and family, being four hundred and forty (440) acres, can be largely put under cultivation, and that portion which could not be easily farmed could be readily rented for pasture; that from this lond [land] a revenue could be obtained which, with the assistance of the deponent, would be sufficient for the deponent to keep together her family until such time as they might become self-supporting; that she desires to have the balance of the land allotted to herself and family, except such portions as she desires to keep for her own use, leased upon such terms as will insure to her a revenue with which to support and maintain her children; that the leasing of her lands at this time, upon the improvement basis, affords her nothing with which to buy food and clothing.

Deponent further states that it is her desire to have the land of her deceased child, Theodore, disposed of immediately and the proceeds invested for her in equipping some of her land for cultivation and provide a revenue for the support and maintenance of her children; that she desires a patent in fee to her own allotmdnt [allotment] so that she may buy cows, horses, wagon and equipment with which she may earn a living and educate her children.

For all the above sundry requests, deponent urgently asks an early and earnest consideration of your department; that this is a critical time in the life of herself and children and would ask an immediate relief.

(Signed) **Mary Howlett.**

* * * * * * * * *

Flathead Reservation
Report of Supervisor O. H. Lipps.
April 16, 1912.
Section 8: Lease and Sale of Lands.

. . . . .

I heard many complaints while on the reservation to the effect that there were many old and indigent Indians who were suffering for want of the necessities of life and arguments were advanced to support the contention that the lands of these Indians should be either leased or sold, against their consent if necessary, and the proceeds used for their support.

In order that I might know definitely as to the truth of the statements made by these people who complained of the destitute condition of these Indians I sent the day school Inspector, Mr. Brown, to investigate the two cases that were reported to me as being examples of the extreme poverty of these Indians. The results of Mr. Brown's investigation showed that in one case the old Indian was not suffering; that only a few weeks before the Additional Farmer at Ronan had sent him a sack of flour and some bacon, and that a white woman who lives nearby has the old Indian's land fenced and has been using it and paying him from time to time for the use of it. The other case was that of Mrs. Howlit whose husband is dead and who has made application to sell his allotment. She has several small children but she has not been suffering. She has cows, chicken, pigs, etc., and told Mr. Brown that she was not in need; that Mr. Rathburn, editor of the Ronan newspaper, influenced her to make an affidavit to the effect that she was in great need but that he overdrew the matter. It appears that a hearing has been held to determine the heirs of her deceased husband and that some complication has arisen to delay the matter. She is not competent to secure a patent in fee and she does not wish to dispose of any of her lands unless she is assured that all the money will be turned over to her in a lump sum.

From my observations made on the ground I am convinced that these stories of suffering Indians are being circulated by interested whites who want to get hold of the Indians' lands. They are particularly anxious that patents in fee be granted as they will then be able to secure the lands for from 1/3 to 1/2 their actual value. There are a lot of scheming real estate dealers in the Flathead country who are doing every thing in their power to influence the Office and the Department to adopt a more liberal policy in reference to removing the restriction from allotted lands. They pretend to have the welfare of the Indians at heart when in fact they are in no way even remotely considering the future welfare of the Indians. It is the same old story everywhere I go. I meet it on every hand and the annoyance is becoming so great on many of our reservations and allotted districts that the superintendents are working under a constant strain and many of them are now on the border of a nervous breakdown. The Office is right in drawing the restrictions closer and closer for unless we can check the greed of the whites for Indian lands, the poor, ignorant Indian will not have enough land in a few more years on which to pitch a tepee. There is one thing sure, when the land he now has is gone there will be no more land for him. In many instances there is no land now for his children.

It is true that there are many cases where it is advisable for an Indian to sell his land, or a part of it. The regulations provide for this, but as a rule it should be sold only after due advertising and the proceeds should be expended for the benefit of the owner under Office regulations. There are no doubt a number of old Indians on the Flathead reservation who would be benefitted by selling part of their lands, but I know of no way of forcing them to do so.

Respectfully.
O. H. Lipps
Supervisor of Farming.

Document 9

White Homesteader Accuses Indian of Assault

March 1912

Source: "Wounded Man Identifies Indian Charged With Attempt to Kill," *The Missoula Sentinel*, March 21, 1912, page 1, col. 4, and page 2, col. 5-6; "Adams Is Released Has a Strong Alibi," *The Missoula Sentinel*, March 26, 1912, page 2, col. 6.

Editors' note: The white homesteader was positive tribal member Pierre Adams, Jr., had shot him, but Adams had two witnesses who could prove that he was not near the place of the shooting. Adams was released.

Wounded Man Identifies Indian Charged With Attempt to Kill
Jesse Potter Says There Can Be No Doubt That Young Indian Did Shooting.
Was Attacked by Dog
After Shooting Animal, the Sheriff Claims the Indian Returned During the Night and Attempted to Take the Life of Its Master — Potter is Recovering — Sheriff to Find Dog.

"No, I don't want to shake hands with you, for you are the fellow who shot me," was the statement made by Jesse Potter, the homesteader who was shot last Monday night in his tent, when confronted by the Indian, Pierre Adams, Jr., in the room of the wounded man this morning. Adams was arrested yesterday and brought to Missoula by Sheriff Kelley and was eaken [taken] before Mr. Potter by the sheriff and County Attorney Mulroney for identification. Adams is a full-blood Flathead Indian and was in Potter's tent on Sunday night. "There can be no doubt of the identity of the fellow," said Mr. Potter. "I know him well and I recognized his voice."

The sheriff returned late last night with the prisoner and is confident he has a strong case. Pierre Adams, father of the defendant, arrived in Missoula this morning and, with Attorney R. H. Smith, visited the jail, where a long interview with the prisoner was held.

Mrs. Potter was with her husband when the Adams boy was taken to the hospital. Sheriff Kelley tried to keep the young fellow back, but the patient caught sight of the defendant and crief [cried] out to his wife that Adams was responsible for the gun shot.

Wanted to "Shake."

Adams burst into the room and, holding out his hand, asked Potter to "shake." "No, I won't shake hands, Adams; you are a bad egg, and you shot me," was the reply from the sick bed.

According to Sheriff Kelley, on the night before the shooting the Indian came to Potter's tent, where he attempted to gain entrance through the flap. A small bulldog, the property of the white man, sprang out upon the Indian and only at his master's command would he keep away from young Adams.

The following day Mr. Potter went to Arlee for supplies, taking the dog along. During his stay in the town the animal was lost, but believing he would come home, Mr. Potter returned without searching. On the same night Adams is believed to have stolen back and, with a revolver purloined from the tent, opened fire through the canvass upon the unsuspecting inmate.

"There can't be any doubt of it," said Potter. "I heard Adams cry out when the dog attacked him. The same cry came when the shot was fired at me. He is also the only one who knew where I kept my gun and how to gain entrance to the tent. I am as certain as I am here that this young fellow is the one who attacked me.

"When the Indian came to the tent on Sunday he shouted 'Ay! Ay!' The person who came on Monday night attracted my attention with the same call, uttered in the same voice and with the same inflection. When I felt the shot pierce my back I looked around for my revolver and it was not in its accustomed p[l]ace. I believe that Adams stole it and shot me with it. You may rest assured that he is the fellow who is responsible for my condition."

The injured man today asserts that he walked to within a short distance of the Brandt homestead, but, weakening from his exertions and loss of blood, he fell in a ditch and was unable to rise. He shouted for help and these shouts attracted the attention of Mr. Brandt, who carried the wounded man to his house, where he was made comfortable while Mr. Brandt was hitching up a team for the drive to Arlee.

Any cloud of suspicion that may have attached to "Rocky Mountain Bill," another Flathead Indian, has been dispelled by a positive alibi. The Indian is known to have been in bed at the Arlee hotel one hour prior to the shooting and was in bed when the wounded man and Mr. Brandt reached that town.

Sheriff Kelley has gone back to Arlee to locate Potter's dog, either dead or alive.

* * * * * * * * *

Adams Is Released Has a Strong Alibi
Indian Accused of Wounding Potter Was With Horse Buyers at Time.

Louis Adams, the Indian youth who was arrested on a charge of having shot and seriously wounded J. A. Potter, the Arlee homesteader who is suffering from a bullet wound in the ribs at St. Patricks hospital, was released from custody yesterday afternoon, as a result of the story told to County Attorney Mulroney by Gray Scott and Ed Lane, two reservation horse buyers, who were in the city yesterday. Scott and Lane stated that on the day of the shooting they met Adams about 20 miles from Ravalli and rode with him to Ravalli, and that they left Ravalli at 7 o'clock in the evening, and that Adams left them at a point so far away from Potter's camp that it would have been impossible for him to have reached that place and to have done the shooting at the hour it took place. The story proved a good alibi for the Indian, and he was released.

Document 10

Salish Indian Living in Bitterroot

March 23, 1912

Source: "'Indian Jim' Lands Some Free Elk Meat," *The Daily Missoulian*, March 23, 1912, page 3, col. 2.

Editors' note: Nothing much more is known about Indian Jim, but he seemed to have been a Salish Indian who remained in the Bitterroot Valley after 1891.

"Indian Jim" Lands Some Free Elk Meat

Stevensville, March 22. — (Special.) — "Indian Jim," the Flathead who was raised in the Bitter Root, and cannot be contented away from here, is a very tickled Indian tonight. Jim would rather be poor and live in the Bitter Root than to be the owner of all the fine ranches in the Flathead reservation and have to live there. He is one of the very few Indians who never take a drink, and has an unequaled reputation for honesty and loyalty, and counts every citizen in this vicinity as his true friend. Jim was on hand at the unloading of the elk yesterday — how he knew the car had arrived is a mystery — as it was kept as quite [quiet] as possible, but, anyway, he was there, and when the animals that were killed in the transportation were unloaded, Jim furnished a sight that few will ever have the opportunity to see again, in doing the butchering act. In little or no time, he had one of the animals skinned, dressed, quartered and loaded into his buggy, which made such a load there wasn't room left for himself to ride, and joyously started home with real elk meat that will put fat on the ribs of his family so quickly that they will hardly be known when they come to town next time. More than likely the papooses will all be wearing new moccasins made from the hide, but that time, and for some time to come, Jim will inquire from his many friends, "when there will be some more elk come?"

Document 11

Indians Complain About Taxes and Irrigation

April 14, 1912

Source: Martin Charloo, et. al., to Commisioner of Indian Affairs, April 14, 1912, from file 43,057/1912 Flathead 302, Central Classified Files, RG 75, National Archives, Washington, D.C.

Editors' note: Tribal leaders could not see the justification in their being taxed to support local county governments that provided them no services. They also objected to using tribal money to pay for the construction of irrigation ditches without their consent. Some periods have been added for readability.

Apr. 14, 1912

To the honorable commisoner of Indian affairs.

Gentlemen we are writing to you in regards to the Acessor of the three Countys here Missoula, Sanders, and Flathead Countys. Acessors from each County are working here on the resevation, and are trying to force us to be taxed. We refuse to be taxed. the Acessars Claim that they have orders from the head office of each one of these three Countys to tax us. We now Demand of you to notify these three Countys to withdraw their orders and these men from our premises.

We also wish to state in this letter something in regards to all this Ditch expense. We have never order this work done. the people that is at the head of the work promise us that we did not have to pay for the use of the water. We are told that our money is being used to build these Ditches, if so we never have given our consent to have our money used in this manner, and we now Demand our money, so we may to build, and fence land, instead tying our money, in these Ditches that we have never signed for nor Agreed to.

We have search all over our resevation among the three tribes here, the Kootanis Pond Oreilles, and the Flatheads, and will say that we havent found any one that has signed for this Ditch expense or any other expense to piled upon us.

We now beg of you to give this matter your attention, and we hope that our interest will be protected by you.

We Remain the undersigned
Martin Charloo, his x mark
Pierre Big Hawk, his x mark
Baptist Pa-ka tah, his x mark
Joe LaMoose, his x mark
Pierre LaMoose, his x mark
Little Fransaw, his x mark
Charly Cooper, his x mark
John Delaware, his x mark
Hustine, his x mark
Jos R. Blodgett
Adolph Barnaby, his x mark
Macille Wolf Tail, his x mark
Alex Bigknife, his x mark
Sam Reserrection, his x mark
Alex Anselee, his x mark
Basil Rilea, his x mark
Antoine Filex, his x mark
Chas Kickinghorse, his x mark
Pascale Antoine
Tony Delaware
Louie ToKamate, his x mark
Banawa White Rabbit, his x mark
Mr A. Isaace
Mrs A. Isaace
Louis Red Owl, his x
Peter gray Bear, his x

Document 12

Indian Attacks Homesteader Cabin

April 29, 1912

Source: "Big Injun Resents Homesteader," *The Daily Missoulian*, April 29, 1912, page 2, col. 4.

Editors' note: This account is vague and partly based on the reporter's assumptions, but it may indicate tribal resentment over the forced opening and homesteading of the reservation.

Big Injun Resents Homesteader
Fire Water Stirs Up Smoldering Sentiment and Red Destroys Property.

Word was received from Perma yesterday of a little trouble between an Indian and a homesteader, and the story has both a serious and an amusing side. The serious phase of the matter is that the Indian did damage to the white's man property, his act having been prompted by an over indulgence in firewater that stirred within his breast a sentiment that still is smoldering in the tribe — that the whites really have no rights on thier [sic] land and that their presence is an imposition. The amusing features lies in the manner of the Indian's actions and what he did.

Jim, which will answer for the Red's cognomen, as his real name could not be learned, had driven to Plains the night before from his own ranch some distance above Perma and there secured whisky that put him in a meditative mood. As he drove along homeward yesterday forenoon he conversed much with himself and by the time he had reached the white man's cabin he had convinced himself that his was a downtrodden race; that it was time that he should take up arms against the invasion of the land which once the tribe had called home — their happy hunting ground. At about this stage in his train of thought he came opposite the homesteader's cabin-house.

"Whoa!" said Jim. The horse was obedient and Jim stumbled out of his rig and marched with all the dignity of which his condition would allow to the door. He rapped; then rapped again. No response. Then he shoved in the door and surveyed the interior of the cabin with much disgust. A sudden idea struck him. He donned his war paint, figuratively, and made the circle of the room in about the same fashion as in other days he would have ridden the circle of an enemy's camp. Then he made the attack. Jim was brave and not a single stick of furniture in the room escaped him. Chairs, tables, dishes and even the stove followed each other in quick succession through the window. The routing of the enemy was complete. Then he left the cabin, after kicking out the only remaining window light, and once outside made a careful survey of his surroundings. There was nothing left intact except the young orchard. This was easy money for Jim and in a very few seconds he had uprooted the last tree, leaving their upturned roots to bleach in the sun.

Jim could find nothing to make the victory of his raid more complete and went home. There he evidently encountered some objection from his wife for he straightway picked up an overgrown club and swatted her over the off eye, changing its color quickly from copper to black. A neighbor — a white man — was called by the household and sat upon Jim until he sobered up and was penitent. The Flathead agent was summoned to adjust the difficulties.

Document 13

Judge Louison Died

May 17, 1912

Source: "Chief Louison Is Dead," *The Daily Missoulian*, May 17, 1912, page 8, col. 2-3.

Editors' note: Louison was a Nez Perce Indian who married into the Salish tribe. He spent many years as a tribal judge and elder. He was rich in cattle and horses, but Mary Ronan attributed most of his prosperity to his wife's business acumen.

Chief Louison Is Dead

Louison, sub-chief of the Flatheads and for many years judge at the Flathead agency, died yesterday noon at the agency of the infirmities of old age, aggravated by bronchial trouble. The old chief had been failing for a fortnight and his death was expected by his friends.

Louison was nearly 80 years old. He was of Nez Perce blood but was adopted by the Flatheads a good many years ago. When Major Ronan was agent of the Flatheads, he appointed Louison judge and he held that office for years until his infirmities made it impossible for him to attend to the official duties.

He was a good Indian always friendly to the whites and always a good influence among his people. He was not a dominant figure in tribal councils, his nature was not commanding. But he was always a good listener and he reasoned well. His advice was good when he gave it and he didn't give it until he had carefully considered the matter in hand.

"Poor old Louison," said Mrs. Mary Ronan last night when a Missoulian reporter told her of the death of the old chieftain. "He was a fine Indian. I knew him a great many years. My husband, when agent, appointed him judge and he filled the office well. He was not a forceful man, but was careful and thoughtful and always meant well and tried to do what he thought was right. He was living on the reservation when we went there. Soon after he married a woman of Charlot's band, bringing her from the Bitter Root, where Charlot then lived. She was of the royal family — I think a niece of Charlot.

"When Louison brought his wife to the agency, she was rich. She had a good many cattle and was an excellent business manager. She recognized the passive character of her husband and handled the family affairs herself and was successful. She was a vigorous and energetic woman. After awhile, we noticed that she let Louison do some of the business, but it was always under her direction. For his part, Louison never seemed to dislike the role of a bossed husband. He had a comfortable and well-managed home and was always contented.

"I am sorry the old man is dead. He was one of the good Indians. But he had lived a good many years and his time had come."

Judge Louison, Salish
Source: National Anthropological Archives, Smithsonian Institution, Washington, D.C.
photo 03545500

Document 14

Indians Charge White Man with Theft

May 25, 1912

Source: "Disappointed Indians Cause Man's Arrest," *The Daily Missoulian*, May 25, 1912, page 2, col 3.

Editors' note: It was hard to figure out what actually happened here, but apparently the Indians were cheated by a white man and did not receive restitution.

Disappointed Indians Cause Man's Arrest

Poker Jim, his son, Poker Joe, and Joe Pritchard, all Indians from the reservation, swore out a warrant for the arrest of Julius Finske yesterday, charging him with obtaining money under false pretenses. Judge Von Platten heard their story, laughed a bit, discharged the prisoner and sent the Redskins back to the reservation. They came before the judge and claimed that they had given the prisoner $1.50 to go and play poker for them. Instead of playing poker, they insisted he had spent the money over the bar. It developed during the hearing that Finske wasn't the man at all, but that it was a fellow who looked a whole lot like him. It is surmised that the Indians gave the man money to get whisky for them and were then forced to stand outside and imagine the liquor part of their orgy. The judge advised the trio to stampede to its hunting grounds.

Document 15

1912 Arlee Powwow Draws Large Crowds

July 6, 1912

Source: "Indian Dances Start Auspiciously at Arlee," *The Daily Missoulian*, July 6, 1912, page 3, col. 2-5; "Gorgeous Parade Is the Beginning of Indians' Festivities at Arlee," *The Daily Missoulian*, July 8, 1912, page 10, col. 4-5; "Palefaces Watch Flathead Dances," *The Missoula Sentinel*, July 8, 1912, page 5, col. 2; "Reds Are Dancing to Big Crowds," *The Daily Missoulian*, July 9, 1912, page 3, col. 2.

Editors' note: The 1912 Arlee powwow was a big celebration. It was held at Arlee which made it easy for white visitors to take the railroad to Arlee and then walk to the grounds. The reporters described many of the dancers and the occasion seemed to be peaceful. See however the articles from the *Missoula Sentinel* newspaper July 11 and 15, 1912, that painted the celebration in a different light.

Indian Dances Start Auspiciously at Arlee

Arlee, July 5. — (Special.) — The first day of the Indian dancing starts off with delightful weather. There are this afternoon 75 lodges in the circle about the big dance tent and the Indians are in a really frolicsome mood, which forecasts a merry season of dancing. Sam Resurrection is the master of ceremonies this year, taking the place of Big Sam, the veteran chief who led the dances last summer. Sam is a great grandstand player, but he is full of pepper — when he isn't full of booze — and is a popular leader. He is on his good behavior and his old age seems merely to have added picturesqueness to his dancing, which is as vigorous as that of a youth.

The Jocko range of mountains is beautifully green this July and the valley is, like an emerald carpet, furnishing a charming setting for the village of the Indians which is attractively located, here in the midst of Arlee town, convenient for visitors and insuring a good patronage from Missoula on account of the proximity to the railway. The morning train from Missoula reaches here in time to afford opportunity for a stroll before dinner is called at the hotel, where Mrs. William Orvill is making special provision for the days of the dances. It is home cooking, home vegetables and home butter — the whole menu a fine advertisement for the Jocko's productiveness.

After lunch comes the hour of preparation among the Indians. Don't come to the camp with an expectation that there will be a dance pulled of[f] every minute. If you go to the big tent looking for a continuous vaudeville performance, you will have another guess coming, for the Indian doesn't move that way. He requires all the red-tape action of a government officer to make his entrance impressive enough to suit himself.

But if you moved about through the village while the tom-toms are beating in the big tent and the chant of the tribal songs of victory goes on to the steady and monotonous accompaniment of the drumhead orchestra, you will not find the time heavy on your hands. You will see Sam Resurrection in his stately march through the village, calling the braves to participate in the dance, bidding them forth for the glory of their fathers and urging them to make haste.

In every lodge there is a make-up layout and each one is in use at this time; there is a lot of painting and primping; gala attire is donned; gorgeous blankets are brought out; feathers and furs are brushed. These dancers are as vain as chorus girls.

Presently from one of the lodges, walking proudly across the glade, there comes the first dancer. As he enters the big tent and looks about him, the orchestra strikes into a quicker measure; there are encouraging yells and probably the dancer indulges in a few steps as a solo performance. Soon others appear and presently the full corps of dancers is on hand and Leader Sam starts the afternoon performance.

The parade of women is the most picturesque scene of the day and this year it is particularly brilliant. The Indians are prosperous and their prosperity is reflected in the gorgeousness of the robes which their women wear and in the trappings of their horses. The parade is a feature which every visitor should see.

The dancing lasts until midnight. Really, the best dancing is after dark. But it is good any time and it is easy to see it this year.

* * * * * * * * *

Gorgeous Parade Is the Beginning of Indians' Festivities at Arlee

Arlee, July 7. — (Special.) — The beginning of the festivities this morning was a gorgeous parade. It would require an artist and colors to describe [t]he beautiful decorations with which the horses, saddles and riders were adorned. It seems that this year the outfits and costumes are all new, the result of months of patient labor in sewing the feathers, beads, bells and ornaments into designs. There are many small trinkets and souvenirs made besides their own regalias, and they vary from the common brass necklaces and weasel skins to elaborate bone breast pieces, which are used as presents in their gift dances. An especially noticeable dress is worn by Mary Lumphry, is decorated by hundreds of elk teeth. This dress is perhaps the most elaborate in existence and any proposal from the paleface to secure one of the prized teeth is promptly refused, Mary saying she would as soon part with the whole dress as to give away one tooth.

Last night the evening was turned over to the young Indians and women and after arranging many lanterns in the big tent for light the gift dance was indulged in until the early morning hours. The white people joined in the dance and exchanged their good money for the brass beads and weasel skins, satisfied with their share of the amusement and trophies. In the afternoon the old men and the best dancers gave a splendid exhibition. Three Heads flourished a sabre of the very old type that was carried through the Nez Perce war. Old Jim Sappiel used a bowie knife made from buffalo horn. Old Jim is the most grotesque dancer of the whole tribe and by the applause he receives it seems as if he were the most accommodating or willing dancer of them all.

For real grace and vivaciousness, Joe La Moose is the star, and Joe has the facial expression that augments wonderfully his peculiar gyrations.

Among the paleface visitors yesterday were L. Schwiers and M. Keppler, who reached this place just in time to see the big powwow. These gentlemen are walking from Kalispell to New York, 7,000 miles, and at each postoffice they have the postmaster date their record with the official time. They are not trying to make a record for the time, but are walking leisurely and writing their observations, and are seeking the excitement of novelty. They carry a small tent and gripsack and earn their own living as they are not allowed to pay money at comfortable hotels and stopping places.

* * * * * * * *

Palefaces Watch Flathead Dances
W. A. Clark, Jr., Welcomed as Nephew of Mail Carrier of Former Days.
Dress Is Gorgeous

Several parties attended the ceremonial dances of the Flatheads at Arlee yesterday, and the afternoon performance is described as being one of the best dances the Indians have given yet. Old timers say, though, that there seems to be a lack of enthusiasm on the part of the young Indian men and women, and it is not unlikely that this will be the last tribal dance festival ever held by the Flatheads.

W. A. Clark, Jr., headed a party of spectators, including George R. Brown, Sidney R. Inch and W. W. White of Missoula, Robert A. Carnochan and Judge W. I. Lippincott of Butte. H. E. Chaney brought a party by automobile.

W. H. Perrior and sons and Judge J. L. Sloane, with the Misses Sloane and Schlossberg, were present. Another party consisted of David Van Blaricom of Victor and P. T. Wiltse. Deputy Sheriff Johnson who was up near Arlee looking for an escaped horsethief, also watched the dances.

"Joe Clark's Nephew."

W. A. Clark, Jr., was introduced by Michel, the interpreter, as "Mr. Clark, the nephew of Joe Clark who used to carry the mail to the reservation." When the Indians heard that they spread out a special seat of robes for the guest, and Sam Resurrection, master of ceremonies, shooed the s....s and children away to give him a good place to see the things.

The visitors say the dress of the Indians, men and women, is gorgeous, though somewhat scant when in "full dress" for the dance. The young men wear nothing but war paint on their legs, but have elegantly trimmed shirts.

A feature of the dance yesterday afternoon was the old man Three Heads, who flourished a naked sabre which was used in the Nez Perce war. It apparently belonged to a United States cavalryman at some stage, but the scabbard was not there. Jim Sappiel used a buffalo horn bowie knife, which was greatly admired. One of the visitors asked young Charlie Kicking Horse if he worked his 500-acre ranch. "No," said Charlie, "I hire men to work it." Charlie made the best of the gathering to do a little horse dealing, as he has a number of head of good horses for sale.

Young Men Dance.

Saturday night was devoted to the dances of the young men and women, who danced the gift dance until early Sunday night. Some of the pale-face visitors joined in this ceremony, and a number of Indian trinkets changed hands.

L. Schwiers and M. Keppler of Kalispell, who are walking to New York, dropped in and watched the doings yesterday.

One of the most gorgeous dresses displayed is that of Mary Lomparey which is trimmed with hundreds of elk teeth. Mary says she wouldn't part with the garment.

* * * * * * * * *

Reds Are Dancing to Big Crowds

Celebration of Flatheads at Arlee Continues with Great Enthusiasm.

Arlee, July 8. — (Special.) — Yesterday the Indians danced with much more enthusiasm than usual and it was noticeable that the large number of dancers were dressed in new and brilliant costumes. The Reds seemed very happy and there was no intermission until evening, when they abandoned the big tent for supper.

Late in the night the prelude for the scalp dance, which is being given this afternoon, took place. The story of the evening ceremonies was told by half a dozen braves who took an old blanket and, holding it by the corner, visited each lodge. Pounding on the blanket with sticks they gave the warning that warriors were on the path; that the Indians giving the warning would soon disguise themselves by painting their faces; would go out and get a scalp or two and return in the morning to join the forces who would be engaged in the fight that day. So today the scalp dance was the first ceremony of the big fight. Yesterday the old warrior, Moiese, took the seat of honor and gaily dressed in little else than war bonnet, vest and belt, looked pleased as he watched the band performing and doing the work. One Indian, Frank Finley, made the hit of the afternoon by dancing with weasel skins pinned on the skin of his legs. This looked torturous, but perhaps it was accomplished without the pins penetrating the flesh.

Alex Parker was the proud possessor of a costume decorated with about 100 weasel skins, and next to Frank Finley, came in for much applause. Some of the dancers were shy on beads and buckskin and depended on a lavish coat of yellow ochre to make up for beautiful wardrobe.

Big Sam is now master of ceremonies, and is working hard to gain the recognition of the pale-face visitors, who are here today in large numbers. Early this morning autos began to arrive and wagons from all directions trudged in bringing whites and halfbreeds until this afternoon the crowd was enormous.

Document 16

Eneas Grandjo Shot During Arrest

July 9, 1912

Source: "Drops Indian by Remarkable Shot," *The Missoula Sentinel*, July 9, 1912, page 5, col. 2.

Editors' note: Eneas Grandjo was accused of attacking his wife while drunk. Some other sources suggest that the reporter exaggerated the seriousness of the attack and the injuries his wife received.

Drops Indian by Remarkable Shot
Eneas Granjeau, Lately of Missoula County Jail, Tries to Stab Wife.
Has Fight with Deputy

Deputy Sheriff Prize at Arlee furnished a side entertainment to the doings of the day yesterday, when he fired a fusilade of bullets after Eneas Granjeau, who is said to be a bad Indian — his latest offense, as charged by the authorities being an attempt to kill his wife. Granjeau is now in the charge of the government officials, and will await trial on the charge.

Granjeau was released from the Missoula county jail a short time ago, where he was held for a horse stealing charge. According to Deputy Prize, Granjeau has been "acting up" since his release from jail. He has been warned repeatedly.

Attacked S.....

Yesterday, in his manner of celebrating the occasion, he drank one too many and started in on his wife. He slashed most of her clothing away, says Prize, and started on her body, when the deputy arrived. Granjeau started on a run, the deputy after him. He jumped on a horse. Prize caught up with him in time to hit him on the head with a revolver butt. But that didn't feaze [sic] the Indian, and he was off in a jiffy.

At this point Prize started on his sharpshooting. The first shot passed over Granjeau's head. The second hit him behind the ear, grazing the flesh. Granjeau dropped from his horse and the spectators thought him dead. But as Prize ran up he jumped to his feet again. Prize had him by the shoulder and placed him under arrest, despite the protests of Mrs. Granjeau, who begged that her "brave" be released.

Document 17

Alcohol and Complaints at 1912 Arlee Powwow

July 11, 1912

Source: "Charges of Carousal at Arlee Lead to Stopping of Sun Dance," *The Missoula Sentinel*, July 11, 1912, page 1, col. 4-5, and page 5, col. 4; "Charges Against the Indians Are Denied by Arlee Residents," *The Missoula Sentinel*, July 15, 1912, page 1, col. 4, and page 2, col. 1.

Editors' note: These reports made the 1912 Arlee celebration look like a drunken and disorderly affair, but see the other newspaper coverage starting with July 6, 1912, above, and the article in the July 15, 1912, *Missoula Sentinel*. There is no question, however, that the Indians had a number of complaints about Agent Fred Morgan's policies, the opening of the reservation, and the use of tribal funds to pay for agency expenses and the construction of the irrigation project.

**Charges of Carousal at Arlee Lead to Stopping of Sun Dance
Flatheads Petition for Investigation of Agency
Indian to Send Complaint to President Taft and Federal Officials — Agent Morgan and Others Cause Authorities to Stop Celebration This Afternoon on Reports of Drinking, Gambling and Other Disorders During the Big Festivities — Ask Dr. Heidelman's Removal.**

Special to The Sentinel.

Arlee, July 11. — All remaining ceremonies of the annual sun dance and festival of the Flatheads were called off this afternoon, and the Indians will pull the tepees up and go home tonight and tomorrow.

The action was taken by the Indians by order of Deputy Sheriff Swan Johnson of Missoula, owing to complaints made to County Attorney Mulroney of Missoula by Indian Agent Fred C. Morgan and others, who had been present, that the Indians were drinking, carousing and gambling and that disorders had occurred and graver ones were feared.

Petition Indian Bureau.

At the same time a petition has been drawn and signed by a majority of the Indians, in general council, asking that the government right certain alleged abuses under the administration of Agent Morgan, including an accounting for Indian moneys, and the petition says: "We feel that as long as he remains agent the cause of the Indians will not be advanced."

The petition is to be sent to President Taft, Senator Myers, Representative Pray, the bureau of Indian affairs and the interior department, and some of the signers declare that if it does not result in an investigation, further steps will be taken to bring the matters complained of before the government officials.

It has been planned that the big council, held today, would be followed by more dancing and celebration on Friday, Saturday and Sunday.

Residents at Arlee say the calling off of the celebration was due to the fact that the agent wished the Indians to hold it near the agency at Jocko, whereas the Indians decided to hold it at Arlee, where visitors to the reservation could more easily come to view it.

They claim that there has been no disorder except the cutting affair in which the halfbreed, Eneas Grandjo, attacked his wife, and that this row was not due to the celebration. On the other hand, it is said that several other instances of disorder were alleged by the agent and other complainants.

Agree to Stop Dances.

Deputy Johnson conferred with Mr. Holland, other residents of Arlee, and the chief Indians today, and it was generally decided that there was no alternative on the Indians part but to call the celebration off as soon as the council had met.

It was said that Agent Morgan had agreed that if the Indians would transfer the rest of the celebration to any other points that Arlee which we may consider as free from evil influences to the Indians, the dances can proceed to the end. It is not yet decided whether they will be continued at the agency until Monday.

Besides sending the petition to the interior department, it is said that it will be sent to the president, Secretary Fisher and Senator Myers.

The Petition.

The text of the petition is as follows:

"Hon. Commissioner of Indian Affairs, Washington, D.C.,

"Dear Mr. Commissioner: — We, the undersigned Flathead Indians, having met in general council at Arlee, Montana, on July 11, 1912, desire to petition you to assist us in bettering our conditions. Conditions now are such that we are not advancing, the reason being that we require the assistance of an agent who can offer us business ideas and assist us to become more and more self-sustaining.

"Our present agent, Fred C. Morgan, is ignorant as to the requirements of the office he now holds, and we feel that as long as he remains as agent the cause of the Indian will not be advanced. Therefore, we respectfully request that he either be relieved or transferred, and someone sent us to act as agent, who has good business ability and one who can help us to make some headway.

Specific Complaints.

"We respectfully request that you assist us as follows:

"First — Have all moneys in the United States treasury, belonging to the Flathead Indians, distributed per capita.

"Second — That all moneys now in the agent's hands derived from Indian lands leased, be given to the Indians who own the land.

"Third — that all surplus land now on the Flathead reservation, be allotted to children of Indians who have been born since the allotment.

"Fourth — That the price of school lands on the reservation be advanced to $10 per acre.

"Fifth — That the charge of $3 per acre for water from ditches under control of the reclamation service be decreased to $1 per acre.

"Sixth — That all cattle now grazing on our lands be taxed.

"Seventh — That we be advised as to what moneys we now have in the United States treasury, stating the total of same from what source derived.

"Eighth — That the agent of the Flathead Indians be instructed to make a statement, showing what funds he now has belonging to us, stating from what source derived and showing the amount belonging to each individual Indian.

"Ninth — That the present agency physician, Dr. John H. Heidelman, be relieved or transferred at once. We do not call on him for medical treatment, but call for physicians from the outside, who can give us proper care. We understand that his salary of $1,200 per annum is paid from our funds, and if he is to continue as our physician it will be paying something for nothing. Dr. Heidelman, we understand, has not passed the state examination and cannot practice among white people, therefore, why should you force him upon us.

"Tenth — That the agent explain why it is that patents-in-fee are granted some Indians and not granted to others, when some that he has refused patents for their land are now and have been self-supporting, and who have good morals and are industrious; while some that have received patents are not now and never were considered industrious and self-supporting.

Want to Be Independent.

"In sending you this petition, we humbly beg of you to give us all the assistance you can. We need you and your help, and feel sure that you can do some good toward helping us to get a start, whereby we can become self-supporting, educate our children as we should, and be able to mix with the white people who are coming in on our land and wanting to do business with us.

"We want you to help toward getting us an agent who has had some business experience; one whom we can have confidence in, and not continue to force the present agent upon us, who, honestly, is a 'joke,' and you would so consider him if you should have an occasion to meet him and see the manner in which he tries to conduct our business. We are not children, and we do not want a child for our agent.

"We also request that you help us toward cutting down the great expense that is eating up our funds, and assist us in finding out our exact condition, and as to what we may expect in the way of assistance from the government.

"Anything you may do for us in this matter will be appreciated by not only us, who have signed this petition, but by hundreds of others who will remember you as an Indian remembers a friend."

* * * * * * * *

Charges Against the Indians Are Denied by Arlee Residents
Many Who Witnessed the Dances of the Flatheads Declare Better Order Than Ever Before Was Maintained — Government Detectives Failed to Make a Single Arrest. Arlee People Say There Was No Ground for Charges of Drunkenness and Gambling.

Many Missoula people who witnessed the Flathead Indian dances at Arlee last week declare the Indians have been maligned in the charges that drunkenness, gambling and disorder were rampant during the big gathering of the redskins. Many say the ceremonies were never attended with better order, that the dancing grounds and the camps of the Indians were policed by government detectives who did not make a single arrest. The only arrest made during the entire celebration was by a deputy sheriff, who promptly suppressed the only case of disorder during the gathering.

Indians Angered.

The Indians are said to be considerably wrought up over the enforced curtailing of their program, and agreed to close their councils earlier than they had planned only in the hope that they would secure a government investigation of conditions on the reservation.

The following letter from R. J. Holland, a merchant of Arlee, sets forth the views of the residents of that town with regards to the celebration:

The Letter.

"Editor Missoula Sentinel, Missoula, Montana.

"Dear sir: Attention has been called to an article in the Missoulian under date of the 12th instant, wherein it is stated that the Indian's dance and celebration was stopped on complaints from the agency and Arlee people; that the Indians were continually drinking, gambling, etc.

"This complaint was not made by any people living in Arlee, but I have been informed that it was made by the Indian agent, Fred Morgan, and it was made more from a personal grievance against the merchants in Arlee than from facts.

Free From Drinking.

"The citizens of Arlee desire to go on record as saying that this celebration has been more free from drinking and disorder than any celebration given by the Indians in the last 10 years. For the last three days not a drunken man, with the exception of one, has been on the grounds, and he was properly taken care of by Deputy Sheriff Price.

"No gambling of any description has taken place during the entire celebration.

"The poolhalls have been closed during the entire celebration.

"There was not any cutting affair as alleged, but Eneas Grandjo was struck over the head by Deputy Price while he was trying to arrest Grandjo for assaulting his wife. Enemies of the celebration tried to make it appear that the woman was cut to pieces and Grandjo shot by the deputy, both of which statements are false.

Government Detectives There.

"The government has had whisky detectives here day and night and, as far as we know, not an arrest has been made. At other celebrations arrests were made every day and the dances were held under the protection of Fred Morgan and his Indian police, assisted by whisky sleuths, whose salaries are based, so I am informed, upon the number arrested. This year they were absolutely starved out as far as Arlee was concerned.

"Any claim or statement that the Indians were gambling, drinking and disturbing the peace is absolutely false, and any person making it knew it was false, and he also knew that it was made because the Indians refused to allow him to select the place for the celebration, where he could be pointed out to visitors as the "majah" of the Indians.

"Hundreds of visitors from Missoula were here, many staying two and three days; they can state facts in regard to the truthfulness of the complaints, and the citizens of Arlee ask the public to take their statement as a statement of the actual truth.

"This statement is made and sent in by me at the suggestion of citizens of Arlee.

R. J. Holland."

Document 18

Ronan Fire Burns Many Tribal Member Businesses August 24, 1912

Source: Excerpts from "Ronan Business Section Is Almost Entirely Destroyed, Loss $350,000," *The Ronan Pioneer,* August 30, 1912, page 1, col. 1-6, and page 2, col. 4-6.

Editors' note: The August 1912 fire which burned most of the Ronan business district was one of the most cataclysmic events in the town's history. The detailed account of the fire named many Ronan businesses owned by tribal members. Not all of the tribally owned businesses were able to reopen after the fire. See the list of businesses destroyed and their losses in this story.

Ronan Business Section Is Almost Entirely Destroyed, Loss $350,000

History of Ronan will date hereafter from August 24, 1912, the date of the big fire. On that day at between 2:30 and 2:45 p.m., the exact minute being in dispute, a fire was discovered in the automobile garage of Crawford & Clairmont, in the alley to the rear of the Hart pool hall. By the time any one was on the ground the flames were eating their way into the icehouse of the Glacier Drug company and into Dr. Fuhrer's garage and the pool hall. One of the fiercest winds of the season was blowing at the time, and it simply forced the fire ahead at a rate never before witnessed in the burning of a town or city. From the pool hall the flames extended to Dr. Sheen's dental office, in the Clairmont & Crawford building, and across the alley to the Bell Telephone company's exchange. Willing hands were ready to fight progress of the fire, but there was simply nothing to fight it with. The chemical engine was not charged and before it could be half the town was in ashes and the remainder beyond hope of saving. From Dr. Sheen's office the flames extended to the shoe repairing shop of Morris Flatman, the real estate office of Crawford & Clairmont, the real estate office of Brower & Hollingsworth, the Ronan State Bank, on the south, and Dr. Fuhrer's office and hospital and the Glacier Drug company to the west. On the north the Pablo hotel, a two-story building, was soon enveloped in flames and the Ritter building was next to go. Abe Meilleur's blacksmith shop, M. J. Benedict's general store, Richard McLeod's pool hall, recently leased to J. C. Moore, Lemire Bros. general store, James H. Bonner's new store and hall building and the harness shop followed in order.

Next was the tinshop of A. L. Miller, and this practically wiped out the whole block, with the exception of the empty pool hall owned by W. H. Smead adjoining the Pioneer office, which was the last building to catch fire in the block in which the fire started.

The flames swept across the street to the east from the Hart pool hall and the barber shop of Spencer Powell was soon ablaze. A heroic effort was made to stem the progress at this point, a hose having been connected with Stanley Scearce's tank and a stream of water was played on the buildings. It had no more effect than to make a little steam to mix with the dense smoke. From here the fire divided, going both north and south, and the big store of Stanley Scearce was doomed. In an incredible short time the whole building was consumed, the recently built concrete fire walls being of no service whatever. The tailor shop of Ernest Kering, the Chinese restaurant, the Big Store garage, and Cash Coutler's blacksmith shop being as quickly destroyed. The Reservation Land & Lumber company lumber yard and offices on the northeast corner of the same block met a like fate. Dr. Hall's office and residence, Pablo & Potvin's store and barn with icehouse, on the southeast corner were next. From the big store the fire jumped across the street south, the first building to catch on fire being the office building of A. Sutherland, unoccupied, and from there to the Central hotel, owned by Andrew Stinger. After the hotel building was aflame the fire jumped back again and took in the barber shop of J. D. Glathart, the meat market of H. M. Gehlert, Dr. Putney's office, the Bradley jewelry store and music room of Whitney Bros. The opera house was in the Central hotel building, across the street to the east of Pablo-Potvin's general store. The fire caught in the Fred Potvin residence and spread to The Lumber company's office, the B. H. Denison residence, the Reservation Land & Lumber company's implement warehouse, the Chinese laundry, William Engle's residence, Andrew Stinger's residence and barn and the residence of Robert Watson, occupied by Curtis Jeffries and wife.

Before the Big store was on fire, the wind had carried a blazing sheet of rubberoid to the government mill, over a quarter of a mile away, and it was soon a mass of smouldering ruins. About the last building to catch was the Smead building, just east of the Pioneer building, and it being back of the wind instead of in front, burned much slower than any of the others. This was a plastered building and to this fact probably more than to any other can attach the reason why The Pioneer building is the only one on three and one-half blocks to be saved. . . . .

The loss is difficult to compute at this time and only an estimate can be made.

[The Ronan Pioneer *article gave a full list of businesses and losses. Only those owned by tribal members are listed here:]*

Pablo & Potvin, loss $35,000, insurance $1,000.
Andrew Stinger, loss $20,000, insurance $2,500.
Edward Clairmont, loss $5,000, insurance unknown.
Crawford & Clairmont, loss $1,200, insurance $700.
Richard McLeod, loss $3,000, insurance unknown.
Government saw and flour mill, loss $30,000, insurance unknown.

Document 19

Duncan McDonald Selected as Progressive Candidate September 6, 1912

Source: Excerpts from "Progressives Foil Plan of Amalgamated Parties," *The Daily Missoulian*, September 6, 1912, page 1, col. 1-2, and page 5, col. 1-5.

Editors' note: Duncan McDonald was a delegate to the 1912 Missoula County Progressive Party convention. He addressed the convention and was selected as a Progressive Party candidate for Montana State Legislature in the upcoming election. Unlike many other tribal members, McDonald supported Dixon despite Dixon having forced through the opening of the Flathead Reservation without informed tribal consent.

The results of the November 5, 1912, election, however, were a disappointment for McDonald and the Progressive Party. McDonald received 1238 votes for the Montana House of Representatives, but six other candidates received more votes for the five available seasts. Only one of the winning candidates for Missoula Conty seats in the Montana House was a Progressive, J. B. Henley, who received 1294 votes.

Progressives Foil Plan of Amalgamated Parties
Bull Moose Convention Indorses Wayne by Nominating No Opponent for Him.
County Ticket of Splendid Men Is Named

The progressives of Missoula county met in convention yesterday, holding their sessions of the day in the county courthouse and spending the evening at the Harnois theater, where they listened to an address by Senator Dixon. They nominated a county ticket yesterday, a ticket that is as free of corporation taint as was the convention that made it. There were no bosses in yesterday's convention, a circumstance that makes it a gathering unique. . . .

Duncan McDonald.

There was a delay in the reporting of the committee instructed to map out the convention's business. So the chairman asked Duncan McDonald of Ravalli one of the tribal judges of the Flatheads and a delegate, to address the convention. The response was characteristic:

THE CANDIDATES

Legislative—L. N. Simons, Dr. W. M. Hall, J. B. Henley, Duncan McDonald, W. R. Glasscock.
For sheriff—Dr. Sanford H. McCall.
For clerk of the district court—H. A. West.
For county clerk—Clifford C. Perry.
For county treasurer—Paul H. Gerber.
For county auditor—C. A. Harnois.
For county commissioner—George Briggs.
For county assessor—John R. Latimer, Jr.
For county superintendent of schools—Miss Hattie Hord.
For public administrator—Harry J. McBride.
For county surveyor—E. S. Hatheway.
For county coroner—Ed Rohkramer.

"In the days of my boyhood we chased the buffalo with bows and arrows. I crossed this stream here in 1858 with Major Owens and my father on horseback. I've seen the day when I wheeled my friend, Mr. Kline, and Judge Woody in baby carriages.

"When we saw the dragon coming, we fought with bows and arrows for liberty. Washington fought for liberty; Lincoln did the same thing. Now we've come down again to the same thing. Teddy Roosevelt has done more for the country and the people than anybody. He can do more. What do I care for Roosevelt and Joe Dixon and their petty troubles? I care for the nation. I don't want back-room talk. I'm proud to say that I am sent by the Bull Moosers of Ravalli. It's not a Roosevelt fight or a Dixon fight, but a people's fight. No man's done more for the people than Teddy Roosevelt. There's not a man in this state who's done more for this state than Joe Dixon.

"I am only sorry they called the other party an elephant, instead of a coyote. I pledge myself that I'm going to defend that young Bull Moose all I can, so that the coyote won't get him."

This set the delegates wild. They applauded much and were not satisfied until Mr. McDonald had faced them again. He promised the party a moose head — one he has at Ravalli.

The chairman asked P. J. Kline to talk. "I'm no talker," answered that old-timer, "Duncan has talked for me." . . . .

Contests.

There were no contests until the office of auditor was reached. Charles Hedger was nominated by Fred Zeh and Theodore Lentz presented C. A. Harnois. Mr. Harnois was nominated, 64 to 16.

Six candidates for county commissioner brought four ballots. The final choice of the convention was George Briggs. Fred Jamieson of Cold Springs nominated W. P. Maclay of Cold Springs; L. N. Simons nominated George Briggs of Missoula; James McConnel of Ronan nominated Duncan McDonald of Ravalli; W. W. Adams of Saltese nominaed W. H. Dillingham of Saltese; P. J. Kline nominated August Hollensteiner of Lolo; D. H. Ross nominated J. R. Latimer, Sr., of Flint.

The first ballot: Maclay, 11; Briggs, 32, McDonald, 9; Dillingham, 1; Hollensteiner, 12; Latimer. 15.

A rule that the low man be dropped on each successive ballot was made. The second ballot was taken after Duncan McDonald had withdrawn. It resulted as follows: Maclay, 11; Briggs, 37; Dillingham, 1; Hollensteiner, 19; Latimer, 16.

The third ballot: Maclay, 11; Briggs, 39; Hollensteiner, 16; Latimer, 15.

The fourth and final ballot: Briggs, 43; Hollensteiner, 22; Latimer, 17.

Mr. Briggs made a rattling good talk of acceptance.

Legislative.

There were seven candidates for the five positions on the legislative ticket: L. N. Simons, W. R. Glasscock, Dr. W. M. Hall of Ronan, J. C. Clemmons of Frenchtown, Ben H. Chaffin, J. R. Henley, Duncan McDonald. The vote that selected Messrs. Simons, Hall, Henley, McDonald and Glasscock, follows:

Simons, 59; Hall, 48; Clemmons, 33: Chaffin, 43; Henley, 49; McDonald, 59; Glasscock, 54.

Duncan McDonald was the only one of the five successful candidates who was called on for a speech. He said:

"I guess I have enough copper in my skin that I don't need any more. I believe you've made a bad selection in me, but that you'll know afterward. I'm going to work for a principle and not for copper. I will do my best." . . . .

Document 20

Duncan McDonald Elected to New Appraisal Committee September 9, 1912

Source: "An Indian Council Is Held," *The Daily Missoulian*, September 9, 1912, page 2, col. 1.

Editors' note: Duncan McDonald's election to serve on the committee to appraise the remaining tribal lands opened to allotment led to some ruffled feathers. McDonald and the other appraisers tried to value the land at its real value, much to the disappointment of the white homesteaders who wanted to get it for the prices charged for discounted government land. A second committee, with Alphonse Clairmont as the tribal representative, was to look into the old irrigation ditches owned by tribal farmers that were destroyed in the construction of the new irrigation project. The affected tribal farmers did not think it was fair to have the new project destroy their old ditches and then charge them for water from the new ditches.

An Indian Council Is Held
Duncan M'Donald Appointed to Act on Appraisement Committee by Reds.

Major Morgan and other officials of the Flatheads met with the Flathead Indian council at Ronan last week to consider some reservation matters. Of the session the Dixon Herald says:

"Messrs. Morgan, Salzman, Heidleman and Allen, all reservation officials, passed through St. Ignatius Thursday on their return from Ronan, where they attended a council meeting of the Indians. The principal matter of importance was the appointing of a committee of three to appraise the unappraised land on the reservation. Duncan McDonald of Ravalli, was appointed as a representative of the Indians on the appraising committee.

"The other matter attended to was that of appointing a committee to look into the matter of old ditches across different allotments on the reservation, as well as land belonging to white settlers. It appears that certain ranchers on the reservation had put in irrigation ditches of their own long before the reclamation service was ever heard of in these parts, and now that their ditches have been cut across by the government ditches, they want to be recompensed in some way or other for the damage. The committee appointed will look into this matter and have it straightened out. Alphonse Clairmont of Ronan was appointed to represent the Indians on this committee.

"This council was called by Major Morgan and is just another evidence of the sincere interest he takes in the welfare of the Indians and all matters under his charge.["]

Document 21

Nine Pipes Seeks Runaway Wife

September 27, 1912

Source: "Nine Pipes Loser Is Better Half," *The Daily Missoulian*, September 27, 1912, page 2, col. 2.

Editors' note: Nine Pipes' domestic difficulties were made fun of in Charles Hall's letter, but Nine Pipes had been seriously grieved at the loss.

Nine Pipes Loser Is Better Half

Indian Brave Comes to Missoula to Seek Answer to Domestic Problem.

Nine Pipes is sick at heart. His wife has been stolen. He wants her back and yesterday he came to town from the reservation to see what he could do about it all. His domestic tragedy overshadowed everything and his state of mind showed through the stoicism that Cooper and a lot of writers since his time have wished onto the noble red man as a dominant characteristic. Nine Pipes upset the dope; he was worried and he didn't care who knew it.

He found a friend and this friend gave Nine Pipes the following letter:

Mr. W. L. Kelley, Sheriff — This letter will be handed you by my friend Nine Pipes, who is accompanied by his friend, Francois Samonso. Some bad man has stolen Nine Pipe's wife, and, as he only had one, he feels that he has been grievously wronged. He was in search of his friend the game warden, W. W. McCormick, but, McCormick being out of the city on official business, I feel that you as a friend of all those in disertess [sic], would be interested in doing what you could to restore to Nine Pipes his better half. Failing in that, it occurred to me that perhaps you might have an extra one or two in your custody at this time, in your official capacity, of course, and, perhaps, you might relieve Nine Pipes by staking him to a newer and gentler wife than the one who has taken French leave. I have seen Deputy Sheriff Hugh Kelley on the street a number of times lately with a female dressed in light tan and a large willow-plume. If she is unattached, perhaps she would not object to sharing with my friend, Nine Pipes, the 80 acres of land which our generous friend,

Uncle Sam, has recently allotted to him. Any favors you can show Nine Pipes will be most worthily appreciated.

Yours truly,
Charles H. Hall

September 25, 1912.

Document 22

Michel Pablo Decides to Close His Ronan Business October – December 1912

Source: "Pablo & Potvin to Build Brick Store," *The Ronan Pioneer*, October 4, 1912, page 1, col. 3; "Will Quit Business on January First," *The Ronan Pioneer*, December 27, 1912, page 1, col. 5-6.

Editors' note: Michel Pablo originally wanted to rebuild his merchandize business in Ronan after the August 1912 fire, but finally decided that, without an effective system to fight future fires, continuing the business would only result in further losses.

Pablo & Potvin to Build Brick Store

It is authoritively announced that Pablo & Potvin will rebuild their store on the site of the one burned, at an early date. They announce that brick will be the material used and that the new store will be much larger in every way than the old one.

As a business firm Pablo & Potvin have been known to Ronan and reservation people ever since there has been a town here, and they are to know more of them in the future than in the past.

They are now using the building lately erected, until the new one can be made ready, after which it will be used as a warehouse. They are receiving new goods now every day.

* * * * * * * * *

Will Quit Business on January First

It has been authoritively announced that the firm of Pablo & Potvin will quit business in Ronan on January 1. This course has been decided upon by the senior member of the firm after considerable hesitation. The fire of August last destroyed their large stock of goods and the building which has been accumulated and built during the past two years and being without insurance was practically a total loss. This loss was close to $25,000 and represented money invested and made by the firm during the time it has been in business here, and not wishing to re-invest any sum again M. Pablo has decided to retire from active business in Ronan.

Mr. Pablo is amply able, financially, to again build and restock an equally large establishment but does nat [not] seem inclined to do so.

Mr. Potvin has not definitely decided just what he will do, the probabilities being he will remove from Ronan, a fact which many friends regret.

One of the members of this firm said the other day, in conversation with the Pioneer, that it was the lack of fire protection as much as anything which decided Mr. Pablo to not rebuild. He thinks that without a system of water works to combat a fire with, that no matter how much of a fire proof building he might build, a recurrence of last August's catastrophe would wipe them out again. This is probably true. The town needs a system of water works and after discussing the matter with a number of the business men it seems to be the general opinion that they would much rather pay a greater tax to maintain such a system than to pay it to insurance companies in premiums and eventually take big losses. If the matter of building a system could be hurried along it would be a grand thing for Ronan.

Document 23

Harry Burland Builds a New Garage in Ronan

October 1912 — May 1913

Source: "Will Build a Garage in Ronan at Once," *The Ronan Pioneer*, October 11, 1912, page 1, col. 2; "Ronan Is Revisited by Fire," *The Daily Missoulian*, December 14, 1912, page 12, col. 5; *The Ronan Pioneer*, January 3, 1913, page 4, col. 1; *The Ronan Pioneer*, May 23, 1913, page 4, col. 2.

Editors' note: In October 1912, Harry Burland announced plans to build a new garage in Ronan to service automobiles, despite the recent fire in the town. In December 1912, another fire started in Henry Burland's blacksmith shop and automobile garage. A tribal member, Andrew Stinger, lost a new automobile which had been parked in the garage. In 1913, Burland was working to build yet another garage.

Will Build a Garage in Ronan at Once

Harry Burland announces that he will build a garage in Ronan at once, believing that the demand for such a business is urgent here at the present time. He will build it on his lots on the east side, in Smead addition and says it will be of sufficient capacity to take care of the business here at present and for sometime to come.

Auto owners are experiencing the drawbacks attendant upon lack of facilities to repair their cars and will welcome the establishment of a public service garage, and a competent mechanician.

— October 11, 1912.

* * * * * * * * *

Ronan Is Revisited by Fire

Three Buildings Destroyed by Blaze Which Starts in Blacksmith Shop.

Henry H. Burland's blacksmith shop building and garage at Ronan were destroyed by fire about 2 o'clock yesterday morning. Shortly after the disastrous fire which visited Ronan during the summer Mr. Burland erected a building. His blacksmith shop adjoined this on one side and on the other he constructed a garage. The fire is said to have originated in the blacksmith shop, and it had gained such headway that by the time it was discovered there was little chance for the citizens to extinguish it. There was little insurance on the structures. The loss is estimated at $3,000.

Andrew Stinger, who came to Missoula on Thursday, lost a new Ford touring car, which he purchased recently. Mr. Stinger had run his new car but 500 miles and carried no insurance on it. He was called to Missoula Thursday and started to drive his own car down. He stopped at Burland's garage to put on chains. Just then the automobile stage passed and the driver called to Mr. Stinger and told him he had better ride down on the stage, as it looked like snow and he might have trouble in getting his car back. Mr. Stinger left his car in the garage and took the stage. He was called up yesterday and told that it had been destroyed.

— December 14, 1912.

* * * * * * * * *

Harry Burland has his new blacksmith shop almost enclosed and roof will be on in a day or two. It is being built on the site of the one burned down on the east side. It will be larger than the old shop and built more modern.

— January 3, 1913.

* * * * * * * * *

Harry Burland announces that he will shortly commence the erection of a substantial garage and repair shop for automobiles, with the latest equipment. It will be built on the old Central hotel corner this side of the bridge.

— May 23, 1913.

Document 24

John Matt Sells Jocko Valley Hay

November 22, 1912

Source: "John A. Matt Makes Big Sale of Hay," *The Ronan Pioneer*, November 22, 1912, page 1, col. 6.

Editors' note: This sale of 1,000 tons of hay by John Matt involved hay raised by his white and Indian neighbors in the Jocko Valley.

John A. Matt Makes Big Sale of Hay

The Sentinel says that the largest deal in hay in this part of the country has just been turned by John A. Matt, a merchant and rancher of Jocko. Matt returned from Butte Nov. 15, where he sold 1,000 tons of timothy to be shipped at once. Although he did not make public the price, Matt declates [sic] that it was a good one.

The sale will be good news to the residents of the reservation, as the hay that was sold is the output of nearly all the white and Indian ranchers in the vicinity of Jocko.

Document 25

Indian Policeman Kills Prisoner During Escape

December 7, 1912

Source: "Policeman's Bullet Kills an Indian," *The Daily Missoulian*, December 7, 1912, page 10. col. 5.

Editors' note: Apparently Joe Finley shot Sineyau rather than chase the escaped prisoner.

Policeman's Bullet Kills an Indian
Sineyau Attempts to Escape From Officer at Arlee and Is Shot.

Arlee, Mont., Dec. 6. — (Special.) — Joe Finley, Indian policeman at Arlee, shot and killed a full-blood Indian named Sineyou [sic] here this evening. The shot was fired by Finley as his prisoner attempted to escape after having been placed under arrest. Sineyau had been drinking and according to the reports here was wanted at the agency. Finley arrested Sineyau and had him in R. J. Holland's store. Sineyau asked Finley to come outside with him as he had something he wished to tell him. They went outside and Sineyau offered Finley $1.50 and a steer if he would let him escape. Finley said there was nothing doing and that he intended to hold him until the police arrived from the agency. Just at this time the policeman from the agency appeared and Sineyau wheeled and ran. Finley called to him to stop, but he only ran faster. Then Finley shot. The bullet struck Sineyau in the back and he died within a few minutes. Finley claims that he tried to shoot the fugitive in the legs. Coroner Marsh and Under Sheriff Marion came up on No. 5 to investigate the shooting.

Document 26

Julian Courville

The Daily Missoulian, December 15, 1912,
Reservation Valleys Section, page 7, col. 5.

Julian
Courville

St. Ignatius, Mont.

LIVERY
and FEED
STABLE

Hack line to Ravalli.
Livery teams to Ronan.

Special Attention To
Commercial Travelers

Document 27

Edward Deschamp

The Daily Missoulian, December 15, 1912,
Reservation Valleys Section, page 7, col. 4-5.

Edward Deschamp

Dealer in

Cigars, Soft Drinks and Confectionery

Pool Room in Connection. Also Dealer in Cattle, Horses, Hogs, Hay and Grain.

ST. IGNATIUS, MONTANA

Document 28

Delegation to Monument Ceremony

February 16, 1913

Source: "Proceedings of a General Council of Indians of Flathead Agency," February 13, 1913; Martin Charlo, et. al., to Commissioner of Indian Affairs, February 16, 1913; and Fred C. Morgan to Commissioner of Indian Affairs, May 3, 1913, from file 20,951/1913 Flathead 056, Central Classified Files, RG 75, National Archives, Washington, D.C.

Editors' note: The controversy surrounding the selection of a Flathead Reservation delegation to the laying of the foundation stone for a Washington, D.C., memorial to the American Indian reflected the factionalism on the reservation and opposition to Superintendent Fred Morgan. See the documents under date of March 3, 1913, relative to the reservation matters brought up by the delegation while in Washington.

Flathead Indian Reservation, Montana.
(Ravalli, Montana,
February 13, 1913.

Proceedings of a general council of Indians of Flathead Agency, Montana, called for the purpose of ascertaining whether expenses of delegation visiting Washington, D.C., to attend laying of corner stone to monument of American Indians, should be paid from tribal funds. Called in compliance with Office telegram of February 12, 1913.

Council convened by Supt. Morgan at 6:00 P.M. February 13, 1913.

Duncan McDonald and Louie Pierre selected to act as interpreters during council by the Indians.

Telegram from Commissioner of Indian Affairs, dated February 12, 1913, read to council, as follows:

> "Washington, D.C., February 12, 1913. Morgan, Supt., Arlee, Montana. If council consents to payment of expenses from tribal funds and two typical Indians of good physique with an interpreter to be selected by you can attend laying of corner stone to monument of American Indians have them report in Washington by February nineteenth, bringing full Indian

regalia. If council authorizes you to come at tribal expense at same time to take up important tribal matters pending you are also authorized to come. Wire answer.

(S) Abbott, acting commissioner."

Zeb Gebeau moves that tribal funds be used to pay expenses of two Indians and one interpreter to represent Flathead Indians at laying of corner stone of monument to American Indians at Washington, D.C.

Seconded by Angus McDonald.

Council voted unanimously to send two Indians and one interpreter to Washington, D.C., at tribal expense, to represent them in laying of corner stone of monument to American Indians.

Mose Auld moved that Supt. Fred C. Morgan be sent with the representatives of Flathead reservation and that his expenses be paid from tribal funds.

Seconded by Angus McDonald.

Motion unanimously carried by council.

Supt. Morgan selected Louie Pierre and John Charley as representatives, and Alex Matt as interpreter.

Mose Auld moved that Angus McDonald be sent as an additional interpreter, to represent the Kootenais of the north part of the reservation.

Seconded by Duncan McDonald.

Council unanimously voted that Angus McDonald be sent as an additional interpreter at tribal expense.

Council unanimously approved selection of Louie Pierre and John Charlie as representatives, and Alex Matt as interpreter.

Supt. Morgan requested that all the Indians who had matters to take up with the Department present them to him so he could know what matters to take up for them; also requested that they make their wishes known to the representatives and interpreters.

Council adjourned at 11:30 P.M.

We, the undersigned, certify that we were the interpreters at the council held at Ravalli on February 13, 1913; that we truly & correctly interpreted from English into Indian and from Indian into English; and that the above is a correct transcript of the proceedings of the council and the action taken by the council.

D. McDonald
Louie Pierre

I certify that I was present at the council held at Ravalli, Flathead Reservation, Montana, on February 13, 1913; and that the foregoing is a true and correct record of the business transacted at said council.

H.S. Allen
Chief Clerk.

I certify that, in compliance with instructions in Office telegram of February 12, 1913, I called a general council of the Indians of Flathead Reservation for the purpose of acting on the matters referred to in said telegram; that the council met at Ravalli, Montana, Flathead Reservation, on February 13, 1913; and that the above and foregoing is a correct report of the business transacted by said council.

Fred C. Morgan
Superintendent.

* * * * * * * * *

Feb. 16, 1913.

Hon. Commissioner of Indian Affairs,
Washington.
Sir:

We, the undersigned Flathead Indians, do hereby enter a protest concerning the manner in which the delegation of four Indians, (who are now enroute to Washington, accompanied by Superintendent Morgan), were selected.

The council was attended by only 32 Indians, most all of whom being friends of the Superintendent.

We hereby enter our protest against the payment of their expenses from Indian monies; we protest anything that may be said or done by them towards continuing Superintendent Morgan in office.

The Indian Office should soon realize the fact that the Indians on this reservation are not advancing as we should, and we insist, and will continue to do so until redress is given us, that Fred C. Morgan is not competent to attend to our affairs as Superintendent, for the reason that the tribe, as a whole, is at a standstill, and has been so since he was placed in charge of us.

Before he was appointed we can't find where he ever showed any business ability, and since then he has showed less.

[Signed by x marks for Martin Charlo, Antoine Moiese, and 41 other Indians. The names were all written in the same handwriting.]

* * * * * * * * *

Department of the Interior
United States Indian Service
Flathead Agency, Jocko, Montana,
May 3, 1913.

Protest against
delegation.

The Honorable
Commissioner of Indian Affairs,
Washington, D.C.
Sir:

Referring to Office letter of April 2, 1913, enclosing for consideration and report a copy of a petition protesting against the delegation of Indians who visited Washington for the purpose of attending the laying of the cornerstone of the monument to the American Indians, I have the honor to advise that under date of February 12, 1913, your Office wired as follows:

> "If council consents to payment of expenses from tribal funds and two typical Indians of good physique with an interpreter to be selected by you can attend laying of cornerstone to monument of American Indians have them report in Washington by February 19th, bringing full Indian regalia. If council authorizes you to come at tribal expense at same time to take up important tribal matters pending you are also authorized to come. Wire answer."

Your Office will appreciate the fact that if the delegation was to be in Washington on the 19th it would be necessary to leave here on the 14th or not later than the morning of the 15th, and this made it necessary to call the council on the 13th — the day after Office telegram was received. I immediately notified the farmers in the different districts by phone, and also notified many of the Indians, in addition to having all the Indian police start out at once to notify the Indians. So that all who could get away might have an opportunity to attend it was necessary to hold the council at some more accessible place than the agency, for if held here the attendance would of necessity be limited to the Indians of the Jocko Valley, while if held at Ravalli, the point selected, not only the Jocko Valley Indians could attend, but an opportunity would also be given those of others districts to be there.

Among the Indians attending the council were the following: Moses Auld and Alex Andrew from Polson, about 35 miles north of Ravalli; William Gird, of Camas, from the western part of the reservation; Angus McDonald, from the Little Bitter Root, north-western part of reservation; Eneas Concow, Charlo

Bigjohn, from Ronan, about 23 miles north of Ravalli; Louie Pierre from Camas Prairie, south-western part of reservation; Modeste Pichette, Lomay Joseph, Sam Bellmont, Peter Inime and Fred Normandin of St. Ignatius, six miles north of Ravalli; Duncan McDonald, Ravalli; Martin Charlo, Andrew Many Bear, Antoine Moiese, Sam Resurrection, Michel Kyser, Michel Parker, Alex Matt, Louie Pellew, Louie Pierre, John Charley, Zeb Gebeau, Louis Adams, Pierre Joseph, Joe Lamoose, Philip Cullooyah, Marceal Three Heads, Joe Pierre, Paul Antoine and Big Hawk, of Jocko Valley.

While there were not so many present as I would have liked to have had, yet it can be seen that the Indians attending represented the entire reservation, while those who seem to have protested *are all* from the Jocko Valley, some having attended the council and all could have done so had they so desired.

It is noted that all signatures are by mark. Louie Antoine, Louie Cullooyah, Peter Stevens, Antoine Delaware, Gabriel Sapiel, Eneas Three Heads, Peter Vanderburg, Adolph Ninepipes, Adolph Lumpry, Zeb Gebeau and perhaps three or four others of the forty-three Indians whose names appear by mark *sign their own names*. Some of these are not yet of age.

Martin Charlo, Antoine Moiese, Pierre Big Hawk, Joseph Lamoose, Paul Antoine, Sam Resurrection, Three Head, Zeb Gebeau (Yahean), whose names are attached to the protest, attended the council against which they appear to be objecting.

Louie Ashley did not attend the council, nor do I think he was present to attach his signature by mark to this protest, for the only Louie Ashley who has been on the rolls of this agency died on April 17, 1910.

John Fisher, who also appears to have signed the protest, is an old Indian about 70 years of age (allottee 1632) who has been so badly afflicted with paralysis for the past two years that it has been almost impossible for him to leave his home.

I do not think that it is necessary for me to make a lengthy report on this matter, as the protest itself, with the facts I have given above, in my opinion clearly show that it is purely an attempt of some white busybody to try and create a little dissension among the Indians, but in concluding I wish to state that from the information I have it appears that the whole protest was engineered by one Hollard, who runs a small store at Arlee and is also the owner of a pool hall, in which the "council" protesting against the delegation was held. It seems a few Indians did attend, and that after the "proceedings" were over they remained the rest of the night gambling. I am also informed that there was another big gambling game at the same place a night or two later, during which Michel Kizer, a full blood Indian, is reported to have lost the proceeds he received from sale of a cow, a saddle and two horses. I have also been informed that at the time of the "council" quite a few Indians were intoxicated from the drinking of lemon extract. Adel Gebeau, wife of Zeb Gebeau (Yahean), one of those whose name appears on the protest, at the time reported to Mr. Lewis, lease clerk, that "they" were getting Zeb drunk, and wanted them arrested. She advised Mr. Lewis that John Lumpry was giving Zeb whiskey, but upon investigation it appears that Zeb had secured from some source lemon extract. The information secured was given to the U.S. Attorney, but he decided there was not sufficient evidence to secure a conviction.

I have been informed several times by Indians that they have no trouble securing lemon extract and Jamaica ginger from the Holland store, and respectfully suggest that if a special officer who is not known to the Indians or the people in this vicinity could visit Arlee quietly for a week or so he would have no trouble in securing sufficient information to put a stop to this extract and ginger selling to Indians, and also, by reporting to proper state officials the evidence he secures regarding Indians gambling at Arlee, he can break that up to such an extent that a great deal of property now being gambled away by the Indians — property which they are greatly in need of — can be saved for them.

Respectfully,
Fred C. Morgan
Superintendent.

Document 29

Complaints Raised by 1913 Delegation to Washington, D.C. March 3, 1913

Source: Memo relative to Alex Matt about taxes, March 3, 1913, from file 28,088/1913 Flathead 302; Conference transcript with, Angus P. McDonald, Alex Matt, Louis Pierre and John Charlie Qualchinee, March 3, 1913, from file 20,951/1913 Flathead 056, Central Classified Files, RG 75, National Archives, Washington, D.C.

Editors' note: Members of the 1913 Flathead Reservation delegation to Washington, D.C., expressed their concerns about county taxes, payment of lease money, the need for allotments for the babies born to tribal members after the rolls were closed, problems with the survey of the southwest boundary of the reservation, and the lack of justice for Indians killed while hunting in the Swan Valley in 1908. Many tribal members resented the bureaucratic control of individual Indian monies by the local agency.

Department of the Interior
Office of Indian Affairs
Washington
March 3, 1913.

Alex. Matt, an Indian of the Flathead Indian Reservation, Montana, complains that the County authorities are trying to collect taxes on land which belongs to the Indians as wards of the Government. The cattle belonging to the Indians and their horses are grazing on this land which is held by the Government for 25 years in trust for its wards, and he believes the County authorities should not be allowed to collect taxes so long as the land is owned by the Government, and held in trust for the Flathead Indians, its wards.

He says that Senator Dixon's bill when the reservation was opened to settlement, provided that the lands should be held in trust for the Indians for a period of 25 years.

Make answer to *the delegation* & send Matt a copy.

[Illegible initials of writer.]

* * * * * * * * *

Conference held in the Indian Office on March 3, 1913, between Acting Commissioner Abbott and a delegation from Flathead consisting of Angus P. McDonald, Alex Matt, Louis Pierre and John Charlie Qualchinee, with Superintendent F. C. Morgan.

Louis Pierre, through Angus P. McDonald, interpreter. I want to know, have we any money, because we are all saying we have plenty of money.

McDonald. He means the tribe.

Louis Pierre. When we lease our land to white men we understand the money comes here. The money doesn't seem to get back to us fast enough.

Mr. Abbott. Does he mean the leases for allotments or grazing?

Louis Pierre. Leasing the allotments. Why is it that it takes so long for the money to go back for the allotments we have leased?

John Charlie Qualchinee, through Angus P. McDonald, interpreter. I would like to know something about that money, the same thing. Also I would like to have you help this Agent to get money for the Bitter Root land.

Mr. Abbott. Mr. Morgan, what does he mean by the money for the Bitter Root land?

Mr. Morgan. Some thirty odd years ago the Indians were removed from the Bitter Root country, where they had resided. Certain ones had allotments which they relinquished and moved to the Flathead reservation. They have not been paid for all the land that has been relinquished for various reasons. Some was homesteaded and abandoned. These are some of the records that I expect to take up day after tomorrow.

Mr. Abbott. Is it anything that has to go before Congress for approval.

Mr. Morgan. No.

Mr. Abbott. Just the question of collecting the money for lands that have been relinquished to white men?

Mr. Morgan. Yes.

John Charlie Qualchinee. Some of those owners are very old and poor and they need the money for this ceded land in the Bitter Root. That is all.

Louis Pierre. I wish that you could assist my country so that it would have a good forward movement. I wish it would have good Government, — so that it would not be imposed upon by settlers etc.

Mr. Abbott. As to your money from leasing of lands: those funds are placed on deposit to the credit of the individuals, but before that money can be turned over to the individual or expended for his benefit there must be time for the Superintendent to send a request to the Office here in Washington. After that request is signed it goes back and the individual gets the money or gets something purchased for him from that money. I have made all of these requests special as they come to the Office. I have hurried them here so that now these authorities are going back very promptly after the Superintendent sends them in here. I want every able bodied man who is capable of taking care of himself, who is working on his allotment, who is doing his very best to make a living, who is honest, who is taking care of his family and does not drink, — I want to give him his lease money just as quickly as possible. I want him to make his home better and his land better for him to live on. Now in the case of those Indians who are so interested in their families and their homes that they use this money that they get to buy horses or agricultural implements or houses for their land instead of spending it for things to eat up or perhaps for drink, — all of those cases I want to help and I am glad to hear of those cases when they come in. While Mr. Morgan is here I am going to go over all of these questions with him and I am going to go just as far as I can under the rules and regulations to make the money that these people have available for them to use to make their allotments more productive. I am going to try and have a little more money than they have there now to loan to certain Indians who have not enough to help themselves. I am going to ask Congress to let me have it and let Mr. Morgan use it for that purpose. I have heard good things about both of these full blood men here. I hear that they work hard and don't drink, raise crops and spend their money wisely. I am glad to hear that. After you go back I will send you a copy of what you have said and all that I have said and anything further that I can say after going into these matters with Mr. Morgan, so that you can show your people what you have tried to do for them down here.

Louis Pierre and John Charlie Qualchinee. Thank you! Thank you.

Mr. Abbott. I want you to tell your people to stand together. Your only salvation is to work hard, cultivate your allotments, raise crops, and above all let whisky alone. That is the worst enemy of all. Show your people that they can't get along if they use whisky. While I stay here I am going to do all I possibly can to get money to help them to help themselves.

Louis Pierre. We are very proud and thankful. I can face my friends with a clear heart and shove ahead to work.

Alex Matt. The babies, they have no land. We have lots of forest. The Government is selling the big timber. We would like to have the babies allotted. There is a big forest reserve and lots of rolling hills. If those babies could have a little land as long as it is in charge of the Government.

We are pretty well mixed up with white people and there are always white people following the Indians. There are always white men trying to get the Indians to sign petitions. A good many sign against their wishes. We do not want any attention paid to these petitions. If any petitions are made by the full blooded Indians, it is only right that this Office pay attention to them. That is all.

Mr. Abbott. I want to say to you that it is good policy to take any petitions that you may have to your Superintendent. You may not always agree that his views are right, but he is an honest man and you owe it to him and to the Government to talk these things over with him and deal straight with the Government with him. If you have anything against his views, advise your people to say it to him and send it through him. If you will work together through your Superintendent it is very much easier for you to help yourselves and get regulations and laws which will help you than when you oppose the Superintendent. If a tribe does not try to follow the ways that the Superintendent shows for their betterment, the Department watches very carefully before it takes off the strings from any moneys that they have. The more you let outside matters alone and attend strictly to using such means as you have to improve your lands the better it will be for you. You men know that. I am going to do all I can. I am going to take up with Mr. Morgan, all of these things. If I can make any changes that will help you I want to do it.

Angus P. McDonald. I would like to call your attention to the southwest corner of our reservation. There seems to be a dispute over our reservation lines. We think that the State has taken in more of our lands than it is entitled to. We called this to the attention of former Commissioner Valentine. He agreed in the presence of our Senator Dixon that he would send someone to investigate. I don't know whether it has been done or not. I would like to have an investigation if possible.

Mr. Abbott. I will have Mr. Morgan look that up so that I can make an answer in writing.

Mr. McDonald. I have already talked to a man in the Office about another matter. There were four Indians killed in what is known as Swan River. One was killed by a deputy game warden and some other settlers with him and we think it was in cold blood and uncalled for. We thought the Indians had a right to hunt from the treaties. We want an investigation. One of the men who committed the crime was killed.

Mr. Abbott. Has this matter been investigated by the District Attorney?

Mr. Morgan. No, sir. I have investigated it myself some since I came to the Flathead. I think the Office recommended that the matter be turned over to the prosecuting attorney, who failed to act in the matter. We were talking with Mr. Francis the other day and he suggested that the matter be again taken up. Perhaps it might be well to turn it over to the Attorney General for action.

Mr. McDonald. As it stands, the Indians to this day, or some of them, have ill feelings. Families of these that were killed are not in the best of circumstances. The State is to blame, not the Indians or the Indian Department.

Mr. Abbott. I will look the matter up and make a reply also to that, Mr. McDonald.

Mr. McDonald. That is all we have to say.

Document 30

Tribal Members Oppose Agent Morgan's Policies

April 28, 1913

Source: "Indians Decide to Call on Morgan; Ask Resignation," *The Missoula Sentinel*, April 28, 1913, page 1, col. 1-2.

Editors' note: Many Indians opposed Agent Fred Morgan's administration of the agency and federal policies regarding government control of proceeds from renting allotments.

Indians Decide to Call on Morgan; Ask Resignation
Pow Wow at Arlee Attended by 400 Representatives of Over 1,000 Redskins. They Have Made Many Complaints. Morgan Refuses to Resign, Followers of Old Chief Moiese Decide to Bring Suits for Accounting Against Him. Effort to Make Protests Appear As Part of a Political Plot Against Indian Agent Frowned Upon By the Reds. Tribesmen Will Also Appeal to Washington.

Associated Press.

Arlee, April 28. — At one of the greatest Indian councils ever held on the Flathead reservation, 400 Indians, among them many chiefs and subchiefs representing over 1,000 Indians of the reservation took steps to secure the resignation or removal of Indian Agent Fred Morgan. The Indians decided to go directly to the agent with their complaints and to serve notice upon him first handed [sic] and in person that they desire his withdrawal. If their demands are unheeded, the chiefs have decided to employ legal aid and will bring civil suits against Morgan to secure an accounting of the monies held in trust for them by the agent.

[Illegible line] Steps will also be taken to bring the whole matter before the Indian office at Washington. The Indians charge that Agent Morgan has abused his discretion in withholding from them large sums of money which should be turned over to them.

The decision to take action was reached by the Indians after a council which lasted all day, and did not conclude until a late hour last night. The meeting was presided over by old Chief Moiese. He called on a number of subchiefs, who presented the protests of many individuals. There were no arguments, but as is customary, the various subchiefs made specific complaints and demands. These were concurred in by the rest of the Indians through rising votes.

To Call on Morgan.

The Indians decided to lay their complaints before Agent Morgan at the Jocko agency today or tomorrow. They ridiculed a report that they simply represented one faction of the reservation, but insisted that nearly all of the Indians on the reservation were represented. They admitted that Morgan may be vested with authority from the Indian department to withhold their moneys, but they claimed that he has used no discretion and has forced many of their number to the verge of starvation, even though they have large sums in his hands to their credit. The Indians have made no demands as to a successor to Morgan. They declare that they are simply dissatisfied with Morgan's manner of handling their money and they believe he should resign.

George Grover of Frenchtown, whom friends of Morgan are accusing of being behind the movement to oust the present agent, denied today that he had anything to do with the matter. He insisted that he is not seeking Morgan's job and was emphatic in his declaration that he would not take it, if offered to him.

Fred Morgan, Flathead Agent/ Superintendent, 1908-1917
Source: *The Daily Missoulian*, Dec. 12, 1915, ed. sec., p. 1, col. 1-7.
Thanks to Frank Tyro, SKC Media.

Document 31

Business Committee Endorses Public Auctions

May 30, 1913

Source: "Indian Business Council Adopts Resolutions," *The Ronan Pioneer*, May 30, 1913, page 1, col. 2-3.

Editors' note: Apparently the Flathead Business Committee endorsed public auctions for selling the allotments of dead Indians. The white settlers were in favor of any actions that brought more Indian land into white ownership. Note the complimentary comments about Duncan McDonald. The compliments were not repeated after McDonald supported higher appraisements of tribal lands.

Indian Business Council Adopts Resolutions

The business council of the Indians met in St. Ignatius last Saturday and Inspector Lipp was present to advise with them. While it has been impossible to secure a copy of the resolutions they adopted, it has been learned that many of the resolutions adopted by the joint meeting of commercial clubs held in Ronan on the 16th inst. were approved and recommended for adoption by the department in the administration of affairs on this reservation.

The council was emphatic in recommending that dead Indian lands be sold at public auction, and the inspector informed them that the law as now applicable allowed this manner of disposing of such lands. It is proposed now that these lands be offered for sale both at public auction and by sealed bids, the bids to be opened after the auction and should it be found that the sealed bid is highest than the land goes to the highest bidder. By this method it is possible for a person to purchase the land and not be present at the time of sale.

It is gratifying to know that the Indians approve the interest taken by the white men of the reservation in an effort to remedy the drawbacks in the development of the whole country. It shows that they are working in harmony, which is not often found on Indian reservations where the interests conflict more or less. The matters complained of by the Ronan meeting of commercial clubs was as much to the benefit of the Indian as anybody else and to have them see it in that light may aid in securing some of the reforms demanded.

* * * * * * * * *

Duncan McDonald of the board of appraisers and classifiers now at work on the reservation, is also a member of the business committee of the Indians. He occupies a peculiar position being selected as a member of the tribe and also for his insight and knowledge of affairs concerning the reservation. Born and raised on the reservation, he knows it better than a book and his judgment is always sought in matters of this kind. Being a man of upright character, he endeavors to do what the he considers right by everybody. This fact sometimes brings him in conflict with the members of the tribe who accuse him of working in and with the white man, and on the other hand, he is censured as being all for the Indian by the white men. The Pioneer has known Mr. McDonald during all the time it has been published and feels that there is not a man in all this section who could or would serve his people better and at the same time do what is absolutely right as he sees it, all the time. He has become a citizen, is well informed on all the questions of the day, being a constant reader and student, and is an example of what others could be with a determination upon their part.

Document 32

Domestic Difficulties Result in Gunfire

June 13, 1913

Source: "Indian Woman Shoots Rival," *The Ronan Pioneer*, June 13, 1913, page 1, col. 3.

Editors' note: Violence in the Indian community attracted the attention of the local newspaper.

Indian Woman Shoots Rival

Monday evening Mrs. Antoine Finley fired eight shots from a 22-calibre rifle at Catherine Eneas, one of which took effect in the abdomen causing only a slight wound, but which looked like a serious matter. The shooting took place southeast of town about five miles and was caused by jealousy, Mrs. Finley taking exception to the too devoted attentions of her victim toward her husband, Antoine Finley.

It seems Mrs. Finley met Miss Eneas coming from the Nine Pipe reservoir and when about two hundred feet distant opened fire on her, firing eight shots altogether only one of which took effect. Mrs. Finley evidently shoots like a Mexican soldier, as W. G. Brown says, or else her hind sight is bad.

Dr. Hall was summoned and upon examination found that the bullet had not penetrated the abdomen but had passed between the skin and the lining of the stomach, coming out directly opposite the point it entered, which to the inexperienced looked like the bullet had passed through the body.

In company with Dr. Heidleman, he returned next morning to see her again and she was found outside the teepee quietly combing her hair and not much the worse for the wound.

Both are full blood Indians. Mrs. Finley will be taken to the agency and an investigation held.

Document 33

Inspector Reports on Complaints of Indians

June 16, 1913

Source: Excerpt from Oscar H. Lipps to Commissioner of Indian Affairs, June 16, 1913, from file 83,479/1912 Flathead 154, Central Classified Files, RG 75, National Archives, Washington, D.C.

Editors' note: Inspector Lipps presented his views on problems with the 1912 Fourth of July Powwow at Arlee and complaints about Agent Fred Morgan's administration of reservation affairs. According to him alcohol and the avarice of the white settlers were at the root of most of the problems on the reservation. Many tribal members may have seen the situation differently.

United States Indian Service
Flathead Indian Agency,
Jocko, Montana.
June 16, 1913.

Complaints of
Flathead Indians.

The Commissioner of Indian Affairs,
Washington, D.C.
Sir:

In compliance with Office instructions dated May 24, 1913, relative to a communication addressed to Hon. William H. Taft, President, under date of August 22, 1912, purporting to be a petition signed by Indians of the Flathead jurisdiction, I have to advise that I have inquired into the matter and submit my report relative thereto as follows:

Last Fourth of July there was a big Indian celebration on the townsite of Arlee, 4 1/2 miles from the Agency. When the matter of holding this celebration was under consideration, Superintendent Morgan advised the Indians to have their celebration nearer the Agency and on Indian land where he would be in a position to protect them and maintain order. The Indians, however, were persuaded to ignore the Superintendent's advice and they established their camps on the Arlee townsite. The result was that the crowd became very disorderly and the celebration a vertiable drunken orgy. The Sheriff of Missoula County sent out a deputy and broke up the celebration. The Indians and their so-called white friends blamed Superintendent Morgan for this and they immediately set about getting up a petition asking for his removal. Supervisor Charles F. Pierce was here at the time and he told me about it in Washington last fall. Back of the affair were two or three white men who wrote the petition and signed many of the Indians' names to it. One in particular, Mr. Bob Holland, was very active in the matter. Holland was at one time clerk at this agency and later licensed Indian trader here. He now runs a store, pool hall and gambling joint at the town of Arlee. Three pages of the signatures to the petition are in his hand writing. Many of these Indians who are purported to have signed by mark are educated and write their own names. Such a petition is not worthy of serious consideration.

As to the charges made in the petition they are absolutely false and they were framed up by disreputable white men who are in the habit of using the Indians as instruments of their own nefarious designs. Superintendent Morgan in [is] absolutely honest and is one of the most vigilant, industrious and conscientious Superintendents I have ever known. He may not be a man of wide business experience but he is an intelligent man and tries to do his duty. In his efforts to protect the Indians from the greed and avarice of the whites he has incurred enmity of a number of unscrupulous men and through their influence the enmity of some of the Indians.

As to the agency Physician, Dr. John H. Heidleman I know positively that the Indians do call upon him constantly for his services. He is now out on a 40 mile drive visiting sick Indians. He is a member of the State Medical Association and I have been informally advised that Dr. White of the Public Health Service stated last year that he found the work of Dr. Heidleman very efficient and satisfactory. I deem it unnecessary to make further comments regarding this petition.

I inclose herewith a copy of a letter written by the County Attorney of Missoula County to the Sheriff, also a copy of a letter written by Superintendent Morgan to the Office relative to the last Fourth of July celebration for your information.

As to the inclosed letter from Frank C. Bailey, U.S. Commissioner, Polson, Montana, addressed to Senator Walsh, dated April 23, 1913, and inclosing a letter written by an Indian named Joseph Bonapart, I have to advise that I called on Mr. Bailey at Polson last Friday and I also met Joseph Bonapart on the same day. Mr. Bonapart was drunk when I saw him and I told him I would see him at his mother's house the next morning. The next morning I went over to this mother's cabin, which is in the heart of the town of Polson, and in that cabin I witnessed a scene the equal of which I have never before witnessed since I have been in the Indian Service. Joseph was not there, evidently having sobered up somewhat and ashamed to meet me. The woman he is living with (not his wife) was lying on the floor in a drunken stupor. An empty whiskey bottle lay by her head. Joseph's mother, Mrs. Angelic Michell, had been drinking also. There were four children in the house one of which was a bright, intelligent, educated girl of about 17 years of age. An old gray haired white man and a white boy was also in the house. There was every indication that the previous night had been spent in a drunken revel. I can not put in writing a full description of what I saw there. It would be a violation of the postal laws to do so. I was told that this was no uncommon occurrance and that Joseph Bonapart was never known to work or do anything for the support of himself or his family. He is a degenerate of the worst type among Indians and the complaints made in his letter are wholly without foundation in fact and are not worthy of serious consideration.

The Flathead Indians are seemingly going from bad to worse. Few of them will work and practically all of them including the women, are drunkards. Conditions on this reservation are the most discouraging of any Indian reservation in my jurisdiction and it is due largely to whiskey. The Indians are dissatisfied and claim the white man has taken their country from them against their wishes and they seem to have lost all of the nobler qualities usually ascribed to their race. In all of my experience I have never on any other reservation seen more fully and truly exemplified — with the possible exception of on the White Earth reservation — the sentiment expressed by a noted orator of 50 years ago who said:

> "The Indian of the falcon glance and lion daring, the theme of the touching ballad, the hero of the pathetic tale, is gone, and his degraded offspring now crawls upon the soil where he walked in majesty to remind us how miserable is man when the heel of the conqueror is on his neck."

A few years ago a Supervisor who was visiting this agency on official business remarked that he was tired of hearing so much about drunkenness among Indians; that during his ten years experience in the Service he had not seen ten drunken Indians. The next day 22 drunken Indians were hauled to the agency in wagons and placed in jail. He was called to witness the scene and after he had viewed 16 of them stretched out in deadly drunken stupor he turned away and refused to look at the remaining six. I am told that there is not a policeman on the force here who will not get drunk whenever the opportunity presents. In fact they have to be guarded constantly when they are taken to Helena as witnesses in court.

As to the complaints made by Joseph Bonapart I have to advise as follows:

> 1. There is no money due him for right of way for a public road through his allotment. There was a road applied for through his allotment and $90.00 has been paid to the Superintendent for the right of way pending the approval of the Department. However, since that time the Reclamation Service has constructed a reservoir which covers a large portion of the allotment and Joseph will have to take his allotment elsewhere and he has made application to do so.
>
> 2. As to the wood and posts sold to settlers, the proceeds derived therefrom are deposited to the credit of the tribe as Indian Money, Proceeds of Labor.
>
> 3. As to the day school plant near Polson, this is now used as headquarters for the farmer in that district, the school having been discontinued on the recommendation of Supervisor Peairs for the reason that all Indian children in that community are now provided for in the public schools.

As to the other charges, I pass them by as unworthy of notice. The Business Committee for the tribe has already taken up with the Office a number of important matters which were transmitted by me under date of June 5, 1913. I can see nothing to be gained by sending an official here to call a general council of the tribe at this time.

And now I come to the consideration of Mr. Frank C. Bailey, U.S. Commissioner, Polson, Montana. I had two or three interviews with Mr. Bailey and he expressed the opinion that the affairs of these Indians were not being handled properly; that he would do things differently, especially in regard to the sale of their lands and the payment of the proceeds to the Indians. He believes that the Indian should be permitted to make his bargain with reference to the sale of his land with the white man direct; that he and the white man should then go before the Superintendent, execute the deed, have it approved by the Department and the money immediately paid over to the Indian without restrictions. He also believes the Government should make a big annuity payment to the Flathead Indians in order to prevent their starving to death.

Mr. Bailey, in common with the majority of the white people who have settled on this reservation, offers no solution of the vital problem in which we are most interested, viz., the problem of making the Indian an industrious and intelligent worker and a sober, self-respecting and self-supporting citizen and a useful member of society. He poses as an adviser and friend of the Indian and often gives them legal advice, for a literal consideration I am informed, which legal advice is very frequently not legal at all. I do not consider him a vicious man, or one who would deliberately take undue advantage of the Indian, but he is not capable himself of doing business properly and I soon observed that he is not well posted in matters pertaining to Indian affairs and that he is not competent to give the Indians legal advice. I was informed by one of the leading citizens of Polson that Mr. Bailey is a candidate for the position of Superintendent of the Flathead Agency. This may account, in a measure, for his active interest in behalf of the Indians.

This is my seventh visit to the Flathead jurisdiction since last November. I have been watching conditions here closely in the hope that I might be able to make some definite recommendations looking to the advancement of these Indians. It is the most difficult problem I know of among the Indians of the Northwest. The chief cause of the whole trouble is the liquor traffic and the men who wish to take advantage of the ignorance and weakness of the Indian to secure his property at less than its fair and full value. Public sentiment is against the Indian, locally here, and not satisfied with the thousands of acres of the fine lands they have already acquired at a mere fraction of its true value, the avaricous [sic] white people will never rest until they have secured by some means the remaining lands belonging to the tribe. It has even been suggested that the Government sell the lands of all Indians who are not actually engaged in farming their allotments, colonize the Indians, invest the proceeds derived from the sale of their lands and use the income for their support. . . . .

Respectfully,
Oscar H. Lipps
Supervisor.

Document 34

McNickle Family Turmoil Lands in Court

June 1913 — October 1914

Source: "Witness Is Held on Perjury Charge," *The Daily Missoulian*, June 17, 1913, page 5, col. 5; "M'Nickle Family Once Again in Court," *The Daily Missoulian*, October 21, 1914, page 3, col. 6.

Editors' note: Confederated Salish and Kootenai Tribes author D'Arcy McNickle got caught up as a child in his parents' domestic difficulties.

Witness Is Held on Perjury Charge
Two Unexpected Developments in M'Nickel Divorce Case in Court.

There was an unexpected turn in the divorce case of Philomene McNickel against William McNickel in the district court yesterday afternoon and as a result a compromise was affected concerning the custody of the children and the plaintiff was granted her divorce. There were other unexpected developments in the case yesterday. During the trial George Marlowe, one of the witnesses for the defendant, testified to certain relations that had existed between himself and the plaintiff. Later in the afternoon, when the trial was concluded, an effort was made, so Marlowe says, to have him admit that he had perjured himself when he gave this bit of testimony. Upon his denial of this accusation a complaint was filed against him by Deputy County Attorney Marlowe, with Mrs. McNickel as complaining witness, charging perjury. The accused was taken to the county jail until his bond was fixed by Justice Small. The bondsmen were secured last evening and Marlowe gained his liberty.

The McNickel Compromise.

Under the terms of the McNickel compromise the three children are placed in the Sisters' school, where they can be visited occasionally by either parent. During the summer months and the Christmas vacation the father gets the custody and control of the oldest daughter, Florence. The wife gets the custody of the boy, Dorsetts [D'Arcy]. Ruth, the youngest child, will spend half the time with her mother and the remaining time with her father.

The McNickel case was heard on Saturday in closed chambers. The couple were married in Missoula May 1, 1898. They lived at St. Ignatius, the husband spending part of his time in ranching, but for some time he has been employed as engineer at the Mission.

Mrs. McNickel is a half-breed, while the husband is white.

****

M'Nickle Family Once Again in Court

The domestic troubles of the McNickle family from the reservation were being aired in the district court again yesterday and in connection, an attack has been aimed at the Indian school at Chemawa, Ore.

The case was the continuation of the divorce action of Philomene McNickle against William McNickle, a decree of divorce having been granted more than a year ago. There are three minor children and twice before the decree has been changed in regard to their custody. The last court order placed all three of the children in the Chem[a]wa school. Several months ago William the oldest boy, ran away and came home to mother, near St. Ignatius. When the father insisted that he be sent back to the Oregon school, the mother protested. To settle the matter the action was brought in the district court. It was opened before Judge Duncan yesterday morning and took up the whole day.

Among the many witnesses summoned, most of whom came from the reservation, where the McNickles are well known, was H. E. Wadsworth, superintendent of the Chemawa school. It was alleged by the mother that the children did not receive proper treatment there. Such charges were very energetically denied. Testimony was also introduced in an attempt to show that the mother is not a fit and proper person to have the care of the children.

After a whole day had been spent in hearing testimony Judge Duncan issued an order giving the custody of the boy, William Dorthy McNickle, to Flathead Agent Morgan, and instructed him to select the school which he thought the lad should attend and to see that he remains in school. Both mother and father will be privileged to visit him.

Document 35

Indians at Missoula Fourth of July Celebration

June – July 1913

Source: "Chief Describes Indian Dances for Fourth," *The Daily Missoulian*, June 29, 1913, page 2, col. 2; "Indian Department Says Flatheads May Come," *The Daily Missoulian*, June 30, 1913, page 8, col. 3; "Great War Drama Will Be Given by Indians," *The Daily Missoulian*, July 3, 1913, page 9, col. 1-2; "Flatheads Are Dancing Before Big Crowds at Park," *The Daily Missoulian*, July 6, 1913, page 4, col. 2-5.

Editors' note: In 1913 Missoula recruited many of the Jocko Valley Indians to celebrate in Missoula rather than in Arlee. The performance included a sham battle as well as a variety of dances. The change in venue probably contributed to the altercation between Henry Matt and Robert Holland, Arlee merchant, soon after the celebration ended. See the next document.

Chief Describes Indian Dances for Fourth
Through Interpreter Charlot Tells of Exhibition to Be Given by His Tribe.

Further assurances have been received from the reservation and it is now a certainty that the Indians will be here in full force on July 4. Chief Martin Charlot has promised that the best dancers from the reservation will be in Missoula on that day and advices received from him would indicate that the Indian village to be erected at Riverside park will contain more than 30 tepees. The dances will be held on July 3, 5 and 6. On July 4 the Indians will be in Missoula for the big morning parade. There will be no dances on the Fourth. A prize has been offered for the best dressed Indians and the best dressed s.... in the procession. As a consequence it is believed that the Indian section will be a big feature of the Friday morning program.

Chief Martin Charlot recently visited Missoula for the purpose of making the final arrangements for the coming celebration. The chief was enthusiastic over the celebration and the parade features struck him as being particularly good. Through his interpreter, Henry Matt, the chieftain declared his intention of making the trip to Missoula a big success. With great eloquence he addressed the committee and it was evident from his gestures that he was making some reference to clothes. The interpreter translated the harangue as follows: "You won't know him when he comes down here on Fourth of July," through his interpreter, says the chief. "He will wear his best Indian clothes and war bonnet. He won't look like he does now."

From a description of his dolled-up appearance on July 4, Charlot swung into a recitation of the dances the Indian are to give in Missoula. Translated from the Indian it sounds prosiac, but it was far from that delivered by the old chief in his gutteral language. Interpreted from the original it ran something like this:

"The order of our dances will be as we used to have them. First will come the general parade. This means the preliminary to going out to fight. Just like before taking the war path. All the Indians will have on their war paint. This is followed by the womens' parade led by the chief. Then comes a beating of drums and the Indians go into their dance house. The women now have a dance which tells of the great deeds done by their husbands. Each dances to say what he has done to make him great and her proud of him. Then there is the giveaway dance in which the dancers give away Indian things and are given something in return."

War dance, dog dance and marriage dance follow the other dances described by the chief. All of them are truly interesting and portray the old customs of the tribe. The Indians have agreed to pitch their camp at Riverside park and will build it according to the plans of their ancestors. They will construct their dancing lodge of boughs in the center of the village. The picturesqueness of the park will add greatly to the general attractiveness of the encampment and it is believed that the three days' dance in addition to the big dress parade of the Indians will prove an unusual feature for the entertainment of Missoula's visitors.

* * * * * * * * *

Indian Department Says Flatheads May Come
Morgan's Consent for Redmen to Come to Dance Approved in Washington.

When the chamber of commerce asked Superintendent Fred Morgan of the Flatheads to allow the Indians to come to Missoula for a big dance on the Fourth of July he granted the request subject to the approval of the commissioner of Indian affairs at Washington. Yesterday Secretary Ferguson of the chamber received a letter from Major Morgan with which was attached the approval of the commissioner of the plan. The two communications, which are self-explanatory, are as follows:

Mr. William G. Ferguson, Secretary Chamber of Commerce, Missoula, Mont.

Dear Sir: Referring to your request for permission to secure some of the Indians of this reservation to take part in your Fourth of July celebration at Missoula, I have to advise that copy of your request, with copy of reply I made to you were forwarded to the Indian office at Washington and I am just in receipt of a letter from the commissioner, copy enclosed, which is self-explanatory.

Trusting this will be satisfactory to you, I am respectfully.

Fred C. Morgan, Superintendent.

The Commissioner's Letter.

This is the commissioner's letter to Major Morgan:

Mr. F. C. Morgan, Superintendent Flathead School.

Sir: Your letter of June 12, 1913, relative to the proposed Fourth of July celebration to be held in Missoula, Montana, under the auspices of the Missoula Chamber of Commerce, has been received.

For the reasons given in your letter your action in acquiescing in the request of the Missoula Chamber of Commerce that the Indians of the Jocko valley be permitted to hold their Fourth of July celebration and dance at Missoula is approved.

The office wishes you to co-operate as fully as possible with the citizens of Missoula in restraining the Indians from indulgences in excesses of all kinds at the celebration and a report is desired giving the result of this experiment.

Respectfully,

(S.) **F. H. Abbott**.

Acting Commissioner.

* * * * * * * * *

Great War Drama Will Be Given by Indians

Program of Dances Will Depict Stirring Scenes of Battle Preparation.

The big band of Indians who will take part in the Fourth of July celebration descended upon the city after their trip from Arlee last night and made their camp near the old circus grounds on the west side of town. At 7 o'clock this morning they will fold their teepees and continue to Riverside park, which is to be the scene of their dancing. They will arrange their lodges in regular Indian village style with a large dance pavilion in a central spot. The program of dancing is arranged to commence this afternoon and to be continued on Saturday and Sunday. During the periods between dances the humdrum existence of the everyday Indian may be observed in the camp, a sight which for many will be nearly as interesting as the exhibitions of tribal customs.

The whole program of dances for the three days will depict the preparations for battle, from the courage-breeding war dance on tomorrow afternoon to the highly dramatic rushing dance on the eve of battle. Between the first and last acts of this unique drama are intermediate scenes portraying the different happenings before the warriors leave for the fight, and all with a deep meaning to the Indians. Some of the other dances are in the nature of between-the-acts specialties and their meaning is apart from the general story of the impending conflict.

The dancing lodge will be ready this afternoon for the first of the dances. At 3 o'clock the warriors who compose the standing army of the tribe will dance the war dance which is deeply characteristic of the battle spirit. Following this dance, which lasts for two hours, the s....s will dance the give-away ceremony at 7:30. The idea of this dance is the same that is seen when civilized women give little articles for personal comfort to their departing soldier husbands.

There will be no dances or other exhibitions at the camp on the day of the celebration. All the Indians will come to the city to take part in the parade. Some of the younger bucks expect to enter the bucking contest, and also to give an exhibition of fancy riding at the university campus in the afternoon.

Dances Continued on Saturday.

On Saturday, at 3 o'clock the battle drama will continue with a general scalp dance by the women which will be the only exhibition in the afternoon. The evening's entertainment will commence with a parade of all the Indians arrayed in their most gorgeous habiliments. The scout dance, one of the most spectacular of the program, follows this grand entry. The warriors mounted, leave the camp or rather, get behind the scenes. Then as the scouts sight the approaching enemy they dash into the village and pick up the women and old men to carry them out of danger. While the fighting men are away from the camp, the women prepare the moccasins and accoutrements of war.

On Sunday afternoon the first dance is the dog dance, a sort of comic supplement to the more serious ceremonies. An old man of the tribe who has dedicated his life to some cause, makes the rounds of the camp and collects food and blankets which have been left outside the tepees for him. After this the main drama is concluded with the thrilling rushing dance. The warriors, who have left the camp during the dog dance, return in a headlong rush. Their faces are blackened and with wild abandon they circle the camp just before leaving for the battle.

Another war dance and a big parade on Sunday evening will end the Indians' stay at the park. Besides the dances which have been outlined, a number of other exhibitions will also be given.

* * * * * * * * *

Flatheads Are Dancing Before Big Crowds at Park

There is no admission fee in connection with the Indian dances at Riverside park. There was a misunderstanding about this yesterday and many went expecting to pay. But the attraction is free. It is a part of Missoula's Fourth of July celebration and costs not a penny.

****

At Riverside park yesterday Chief Charlot and his band of dancers entertained nearly 2,000 people during the afternoon and evening. The Indians had their camp all completed yesterday before noon and have a dancing pavilion that is conveniently arranged for the accommodation of a big audience for each dance. The reds are entering into the dancing with great enthusiasm. Old-timers who have witnessed their celebrations on the reservations say that it is the best dancing they have witnessed by the tribe in a dozen years. All of the real dancers are here and they seem to appreciate the inquisitiveness of the whites and take a pride in showing to the best advantage possible.

Beautiful Gifts.

Two of the dances yesterday were especially interesting and pleasing to both evening and afternoon crowds. These are known as the gift dances, one in which the s....s step into the crowd and select a white partner and the other in which the bucks choose white women partners. At the conclusion of the dance the Indians bestow presents upon their partners. They have come to Missoula well supplied with beautiful bead work presents, some of them extremely valuable and yesterday they gave these with a lavish hand. These dances will be given again today and it has been tipped off that some especially beautiful presents have been reserved for the Sunday crowd. Among those from the city upon whom the s....s bestowed gifts yesterday were Charles H. Hall, D. R. Beck, Thomas J. Farrell and others. The moving picture man, who was also honored, is making some choice films of the dances.

The street railway company has made special arrangements to handle the crowd which will go to the park this afternoon and evening. Dancing in the afternoon will begin at 2 o'clock and the evening's entertainment will start at 7 o'clock. After 12 noon today there will be a 20-minute service on the Bonner line, the specials to run in a two-car train. This service will be continued all day and as late as necessary at night.

"We expect tomorrow to be the biggest day in the history of the street railway service," said Superintendent Bickenbach last night. "On this account we have arranged a service which, we think, will be sufficient to prevent delays to any one who wishes to make the trip during the afternoon or evening. The

Indians are behaving splendidly and they seem to be taking a great interest in their celebration."

Historic Relics.

The Indians have taken special pains to inject everything they have of historic interest into the dances. There are many old war-time trophies exhibited by the dancers as they circle the big pavilion to the music of the s....s and the tom-tom. The tom-tom used at this celebration is itself one of the sacred relics of the tribe. It has been in the Flatheads' possession for generations. It is the old, original war-dance drum and has been preserved with great care. It has not been used before by the tribe since Garfield came from Washington to call the tribe in council to enact the Flathead treaty.

Document 36

Altercation in Arlee Result of Indian Dances

July – August 1913

Source: "Holland Accused of a Serious Offense," *The Daily Missoulian*, July 8, 1913, page 10, col. 4; "Arlee Troubles heard by Small," *The Missoula Sentinel*, August 7, 1913, page 2, col. 2.

Editors' note: The altercation between Henry Matt and Robert Holland, the Arlee merchant, seemed to have been fallout from the loss of many Jocko Valley Indians to the Missoula Fourth of July celebration in 1913.

Holland Accused of a Serious Offense
Henry Matt Claims Arlee Merchant Assaulted Him with a Gun.

When Henry Matt, who was partly responsible for the Indians from the reservation when they were in Missoula for the celebration and dancing, reached Arlee last evening he stirred up a mess of trouble that caused his arrest last night and will porbably [sic] result in Bob Holland, well known Arlee merchant, being landed in jail today. Henry Matt says that he had some words with Holland about the Indians as soon as he reached town and that Holland was still "sore" because the Indians had been allowed to come to Missoula instead of remaining at Arlee and calling the crowds there. One word led to another until, Henry says, Holland hit him over the left eye with a heavy six-shooter and ran. Then Pete Matt, Henry's cousin, heard of the trouble and went over to Holland to ask what was the trouble. John Matt, Henry's brother, was a witness to this act when he says Holland struck Pete in the jaw and then pulled a gun on him and called for him to be arrested. Holland complained to a man named Price, a special deputy appointed to go to Arlee and prevent the Indians from becoming too boisterous in their celebrating — it having been anticipated that they would probably get hold of some booze — arrested Henry Matt at Holland's request and brought him to the city. Pete Matt came in to see the case through and when he reached the jail he was also put behind the bars at the instance of the special officer who left immediately to return to the reservation. Holland was not arrested last night.

Upon furnishing satisfactory bail the two Matts were released from jail shortly after they had been locked up. They alleged partiality shown by the officer in the arrest because Holland was the man who had used all the violence. They are ready to swear out a complaint against Holland this morning for assault.

****

Arlee Troubles Heard by Small
Court Discharges Peter Matt; Case Against Brother Under Advisement.
Holland Had a Gun

After hearing the evidence in the disturbance case brought by R. W. Holland of Arlee against the Matt boys, Justice Small dismissed the case against Peter Matt and took the case against Henry Matt under advisement. The court will render an opinion inside of 48 hours.

A charge of exhibiting a deadly weapon, brought by the Matt boys, is still hanging over Holland. At the conclusion of today's trial Attorney Edward C. Mulroney, counsel for the Matt boys, agreed to submit the case against Holland on the testimony in the Matt cases. Deputy County Attorney Marlowe refused to enter into such agreement, declaring that he wanted some time to think the matter over.

The trouble between Holland and the Matt boys has been of long standing, it is said. It reached a climax a few days after July 4, upon the return of the Indians to Arlee after a trip to Missoula.

The evidence showed that Holland had a revolver, and that he struck both the Matt boys. Holland himself admits that he left his store with a revolver in hand, but insisted that he hit the Matt boys with his fists and not with a gun.

Holland testified that after the Indians returned to Arlee Henry Matt, while under the influence of liquor, paraded in front of the Holland store, boasting that he could lick any man on the reservation, especially Bob Holland.

The case against the Matt boys will cost the county from $60 to $75 in mileage for witnesses, and the taxpayers will have to pay a similar amount if the case against Holland is tried.

"I don't see why this case was not brought at Arlee. There is a justice of the peace there," declared Justice Small at the conclusion of today's proceedings. "Why these witnesses should be dragged all the way from Arlee at the expense of the taxpayers when the case could have been tried where the trouble occurred is beyond the court's comprehension."

Document 37

Consumptive Indian Pardoned

August 16, 1913

Source: "Indian Is Released from Jail to Go to Ronan Home and Die," *The Missoula Sentinel*, August 16, 1913, page 1, col. 1.

Editors' note: Alex Ainsley purchased alcohol from a white man, but he may have planned to use it for its medicinal properties to treat his tuberculosis.

Indian Is Released from Jail to Go to Ronan Home and Die
Humane Office of E. C. Mulroney Enables Flathead to Spend Last Hours with People.
Presidential Pardon
Continued Imprisonment Would Have Meant Early Death, Argument That Won.

Dying of consumption and with only a few months to live, Alex Ainsley, a full-blood Flathead Indian, has been released from the county jail and rushed to Ronan on the reservation, there to spend his remaining few days with his wife and child. The dying Indian owes his release to Attorney Edward C. Mulroney, who, through the good offices of United State Senator Myers and Congressman Evans, secured a pardon for him from President Wilson.

On April 8, last, Ainsley was convicted of perjury in the federal court, in connection with his testimony in the case of Harry Anderson, on trial for selling liquor to Indians. Judge Bourquin sentenced Ainsley to six months imprisonment and a fine of $100 and costs. Ainsley was confined in the Helena jail until July 14, when he was transferred to the county jail in this city.

A few days ago Attorney Mulroney happened to be in the county jail on some legal business, when his attention was called to the dying Indian by County Physician Fuller and Sheriff Kelley. In the last stages of the white plague, and scarce able to move, the Indian was suffocating by breathing the stuffy air of the jail, and forced to mingle with the 20 or 40 prisoners that crowd the jail daily. At night he was forced to occupy a cell with another Indian.

Prompted solely by a spirit of humanitarianism, Attorney Mulroney took up the case of the poor Indian. he secured affidavits from County Physician Fuller and Sheriff Kelley to the effect that Ainsley will never live to serve out his sentence. Attorney Mulroney himself swore to an affidavit setting forth the unfortunate Indian's plight and mailed them with an application for a pardon to President Wilson. At the same time he enlisted Senator Myers and Congressman Evans in the cause of Ainsley.

So urgent was the case that Attorney Mulroney urged that the pardon be telegraphed, fearing Ainsley would die before its arrival, should it be sent by mail.

President Wilson evidently was as much impressed with the unfortunate condition of the poor Indian as was Attorney Mulroney, for a few hours after the application reached Washington Sheriff Kelley was notified by wire that a pardon had been granted.

County Physician Fuller believes that on account of his release Ainsley may live a short time longer, but he is certain it will not be much more than six weeks or two months. The dying Indian is 35 years old. Unable to talk English and so weak he could hardly move Ainsley through gestures thanked Attorney Mulroney as he was liberated.

Document 38

Ceremony Promotes Patriotism

September 20, 1913

Source: "Indians Swear Allegiance to Flag," *The Daily Missoulian*, September 20, 1913, page 1, col. 1, and page 6, col. 2; "Indians on Warpath Great Flag's Stolen," *The Daily Missoulian*, April 23, 1917, page 5, col. 3.

Editors' note: The visit of the Wanamaker expedition to the Flathead Reservation was a maudlin affair that did not address the serious problems of government failure to support Indian efforts towards self-determination and economic independence on the reservation. The symbol of the American flag did little to compensate for the loss of tribal assets and land.

Indians Swear Allegiance to Flag
Picturesque Ceremony Takes Place at Historic St. Ignatius Mission.
Scene Is Impressive
Twenty-Four Prominent Men of the Flathead and Kootenai Tribes Grasp Halyards and Hoist the Banner of the Nation —
Is Part of Campaign Being Conducted by Dr. Dixon.

Twenty-four prominent men of the Flathead and Kootenai Indian tribes pulled the halyards yesterday that raised to the peak of the flagstaff at St. Ignatius mission the American flag, thus symbolizing their sworn allegiance to the United States. The banner used was the same flag that was hoisted by 35 chieftains from tribes in all parts of the United States at the dedication of the monument to the North American Indian at Fort Wadsworth, N.Y., last spring, and the ceremony yesterday was a partial, although faithful repetition of that momentous event. Dr. Joseph Kossuth Dixon, director of the Rodman Wanamaker Expedition of Citizenship to the North American Indian, and his party conducted the services which bound the red-skinned Flathead and the white men in sincere brotherhood.

Following the flag raising the assembled Indians gathered about a large flag, each grasping the banner, and Dr. Dixon dedicated to them the faith of the white man and in turn received their allegiance to the flag and the nation. It was a solemn and impressive scene as the Indians bent over the flag and kissed the banner that is now their own. They betrayed a strong sense of patriotism — patriotism in-born, but heretofore crushed by their white brothers.

The flag was presented by Dr. Dixon to the Indians and will be their memento of his visit and the sign of what they may hope for when Mr. Wanamaker's plans of citizenship for the Indians are fulfilled.

The ceremony at the mission was concluded with the signing of the declaration of allegiance to the government of the United States. This declaration was inspired by the chiefs present at the Fort Wadsworth ceremony and was signed by them then. It is now carried by the expedition to all the reservations and representatives of every tribe and [add] their signatures. It was this voluntary pledge made by the Indians in their newfound country that attracted the most general attention at the dedication services. It will be placed in the Fort Wadsworth museum.

Is Making of History.

The coming of the Wanamaker expedition to the Flathead is very significant in the history of the relation of those Indians to the white man. It seems that they have pledged themselves in solemn faith to the white man's government, and it also means that they will be helped to attain an equality in citizenship in the nation. The purpose of the expedition is not simply to thrill the Indian with patriotic fervor, however, but is to interest him in better farming, education and to encourage him to high ideals of citizenship. Mr. Dixon has high hopes for the future of the northwest Indian. He believes that the time is coming when cheap foreign labor now doing work through this part of the country will be replaced by the native American. And the Indian, he says, will have a valuable interest in the country's development that is entirely lacking in the Italian and Bulgarian.

Dr. Dixon and his party, traveling in their workshop, the Pullman sleeper Signet, were in Missoula last evening on the train carrying them to eastern Montana Indians. The director has been a close student of the American Indians for 15 years and has a great faith in them and a sympathy for their welfare — a fitting leader for so momentous an expedition. He was very much pleased with the spirit shown by the Flathead Indians and spoke warmly of the assistance in the ceremony given by Major Fred Morgan, Angus McDonald, Alex Matt, Louis Pierre and John Charlie, who composed the delegation to the dedication services at Fort Wadsworth.

Indian Has Sentiment.

Dr. Dixon approached the Indian by appealing to his sentiment, but sentiment he considers as sense. "The Indian needs sentiment as well as the white man," he asserted. "He lives absorbingly in a mystic land and he finds rest in communion with the great mystery. But there has been much to deaden every sensibility of the Indian and to crush the ardor of his spirit. He is a man without a country; he does not own an American flag and never did own one. On the reservation you will find a flagstaff and a government official raises the flag at sunrise and lowers it at sundown. Is it any wonder that those 32 chieftains who raised the flag at Fort Wadsworth on the spot where a memorial is to be erected to their race, declared, 'We never before felt that we were a part of the country, we now feel we are the white man's brother, and our desire is to live for the flag?'"

This demonstration was what prompted Rodman Wanamaker to finance the expedition which is visiting every tribe of Indians in the United States and repeating before them the services at Fort Wadsworth. The same flag and the same ropes that were used then will be used at the ceremony on each reservation and to each of the tribes Mr. Wanamaker also presents a large flag for their own. When the expedition finishes its great mission every American Indian will be linked hand-to-hand around the stars and stripes.

American Flag Is Eternal.

"Do you know," said Dr. Dixon, "that the flag of the United States is really the only eternal flag? That may be a new thought, but it is our password to the Indians. It is easy for him to grasp the idea of everlasting in the white stripes, because, when untouched by the despoiler, he follows the trail of purity from his own tepee to the throne of the great mystery. The red stripes are a shade of his own color — they represent life, blood — he is told that brave men have defended it with their blood and now is the time for him to show his valor to the flag by deserting his old ways and striving for the white man's ideals of citizenship. The field of blue which holds the stars will be familiar to him. He has his love star, his peace star and his war star, and now we tell him to follow his stars of peace and love towards his brothers, the white men, and his war star against all that hinders him in his upward climb."

The ceremony of raising the Fort Wadsworth flag and the signing of allegiance to the government is made as solemn and sacred as when the priests of old bore the ark of the covenant into the temple enclosure. Dr. Dixon told of scenes among the Indians of New Mexico, reached by expedition on horseback, where the tribes had never seen an American flag and some of the men were over 100 years old. When they bent over the flag and kissed it they betrayed emotion that was an awakening of the deepest patriotism.

Every Tribe Will Be Reached.

The expedition which Dr. Dixon is now leading is the third to be sent by Mr. Wanamaker since 1909. Before returning to New York they will have traveled 22,000 miles and the flag will be given to 320,000 redmen in 169 tribes, the whole number of present-day Indians. Photographs will be taken in every tribe of typical men, costumes and institutions and these will be placed with the oath of allegiance in the Fort Wadsworth museum.

The first stop made by the expedition was at Muskogee, Okla. From there the trip was made across Colorado, New Mexico, Arizona, Lower California, then up the Pacific coast and over Washington, Idaho and Montana. The next Indians visited will be on the Crow reservation and from there to northern Montana and through the Sioux country in the Dakotas, concluding with Minnesota, Wisconsin and the New York state reservations.

* * * * * * * * *

Indians on Warpath Great Flag's Stolen
Banner Presented by Wanamaker Expedition Taken from St. Ignatius.
Was Highly Prized
White Population Angered by Theft and in Search of Guilty Parties.

St. Ignatius, April 22. — (Special.) — The Indians of the Flathead reservation are on the warpath today as they never were in the early days. They are aroused against whites, yet fighting for the American flag.

Somebody has stolen from St. Ignatius the great American flag which was presented to the Flatheads two years ago by Rodman Wanamaker expedition. The presentation was accompanied by an impressive ceremony which the Indians greatly enjoyed. They regard the flag as something sacred and are profoundly stirred by its loss.

The Wanamaker expedition, it will be remembered, visited all of the Indian tribes of the United States, representing the white citizenship and bearing messages of good-will and instruction in patriotism. A flag was presented to each tribe, and the Indians kissed the banner as evidence of their loyalty

Now someone has stolen the flag which the Indians regarded as a sort of sign of their part in national affairs. White and reds have joined in a search for the thief.

Document 39

Joseph Grenier, Jr., Bought Stock in Mission Bank October 1913 – March 1914

Source: "New Bank Planned by Mission People," *The Daily Missoulian*, October 26, 1913, page 2, col. 3; "New Bank to Open at St. Ignatius on Flathead," *The Daily Missoulian*, March 24, 1914, page 3, col. 1.

Editors' note: Joseph Grenier, Jr., was one of the tribal members who invested in local businesses on the reservation.

New Bank Planned by Mission People

St. Ignatius Is to Have a Financial Institution with A. P. Morse as Cashier.

Carl H. Drews of The Missoulian's circulation department, returned last night from a trip over the lower end of the Flathead reservation country. He says the region has the look of prosperity everywhere, and that during the trip he saw some of the finest farms he ever set eyes upon. "St. Ignatius is specially good," said Mr. Drews. "There were scores of farmers in town this afternoon, and they all seemed to be doing business. It was as lively in St. Ignatius as it used to be in the old days on the occasion of an Indian celebration. But it was a different kind of activity. There is considerable building being done this fall in St. Ignatius. Most of it is in the new townsite on the hill. There are two or three more stores nearly finished, and stakes have been driven for the erection of a new bank building. The Mission State bank has just been organized. Colonel Morse of Drummond and his son, A. P. Morse, of Missoula, are the only outside capitalists. All of the rest of the stock has been subscribed in St. Ignatius. Joe Grenier, the Beckwiths and others of the local business men have subscribed the entire amount and more could have been sold, but the capital, I was told today, has been fixed at $20,000. A P. Morse will be the cashier, and has started a residence. As soon as his house is finished he will move to the mission."

****

New Bank to Open at St. Ignatius on Flathead
"Mission State" Is Name of Institution Capitalized at Twenty Thousand.

Andrew Beckwith, well-know[n] merchant at St. Ignatius, arrived in Missoula yesterday on a short business visit. He brought word of the incorporation of a new bank at St. Ignatius, the Missoula [Mission] State Bank, which is to open for business at once. The institution is capitalized at $20,000 and the stock, issued in shares of $100 each, is fully subscribed. At the meeting of the directors held yesterday the following officers were elected: G. H. Beckwith, president; Joseph Grenier, Jr., vice president; A. P. Morse, cashier.

The following stockholders attended yesterday's meeting: A. P. Morse, G. N. Beckwith, Joseph Grenier, Jr., A. K. Lusk, A. J. Brower, George Broughton, I. M. Brandjord, A. W. Hollingsworth, W. E. Moore, Joe Buckhouse and Andy McGee.

Document 40

Homesteaders Complain About Re-Appraisements November – December 1913

Source: "Missoula Receives the Re-Appraisement Plats," *The Ronan Pioneer*, November 21, 1913, page 1, col 6-7; "Settlers Protest Against the High Appraisement," *The Ronan Pioneer*, December 5, 1913, page 1, col. 6-7; "Commissioner Tells How and Why It Happened," *The Ronan Pioneer*, December 13, 1913, page 1, col. 1-3.

Editors' note: Duncan McDonald was the tribal representative on the re-appraisal commission. When the commission set the land prices at the market value of the land rather than the bargain appraisals of the first commission, white homesteaders were outraged. According to *The Ronan Pioneer*, "Who wants to pay the actual value of the land and use a homestead right besides?" The newspaper did not repeat its praise of Duncan McDonald's fairness which had been included in the article reporting his appointment to the commission in May 30, 1913.

Missoula Receives the Re-Appraisement Plats

The plats from the general land office have been received at the Kalispell land office showing the re-appraisement and classification made by the board of appraisers which has been at work on the Flathead reservation during the past two years. This work was done to make available for entry such lands as were not on the schedule at the time of the opening and which have been applied for since August 26, 1910, the date of the commissioner's letter making such unappraised lands subject to settlement. This was the now celebrated letter of Commissioner Dennett opening to settlement and entry all unreserved and unappropriated lands, on the schedule or otherwise. On June 14, 1911, this letter was recalled and such lands as were not applied for between August 26, 1910, and June 14, 1911, which have been applied for since the latter date have been rejected, and all applications made between those dates have been suspended.

The commissioner of the general land office notifies the register and receiver at Kalispell that all suspended filing will be adjudicated promptly, but that all rejected homestead applications will have to be made again, or that the land embraced in such entries will be subject to entry by the first applicant applying therefor. This method of proceedure is bound to cause much confusion, as many of those who have applied for the lands are now living on the same and have a squatters right, which is paramount and superior to any other application. Parties who may apply for any of the lands on the new list may find the same occupied and partly improved when they come to investigate, and that their rights are subject to the squatter. A squatter has ninety days after the land is available for entry within which to make his filing and make his payment.

The new appraisement of the land is in many cases higher than the original valuation fixed for the land and range in price from $1.50 to $30 per acre. The latter price being for a 40 acre tract near the town of Polson. In addition to the price of the land, where there is any timber thereon, the timber is appraised separately and must be paid for in cash at the time of making entry.

The filing of these plats and the adjudication of the claims of those who have made selections of the land will be of much benefit to the country as it will permit those who desire the land to know whether or not they are to get it. Quite a number are interested and it will be glad news to all of them.

Later —Since the above was put in type, word has been received in Ronan that the plats have been filed in the Missoula land office. From all reports received, the Missoula office is instructed in accordance with the Kalispell office as to the disposal of the land.

* * * * * * * * *

Settlers Protest Against the High Appraisement

At a meeting of the executive committee of the Homesteaders' Protective Association held at the office of the secretary in Polson, Montana, on the 29th day of November, 1913, the following resolutions were unanimously adopted:

Whereas, the commission appointed to appraise and classify the unappraised and unclassified lands of the Flathead Indian reservation has completed their work and made their report to the Hon. Indian Commissioner, and

Whereas, the report of said commission is entirely unsatisfactory to a large majority of the settlers upon said lands, and

Whereas, the prices placed upon almost of the said lands are far in excess of the prices placed upon similar lands by the first commission, and

Whereas, the settlers upon the unappraised lands have borne the hardships and privations of a frontier life in equal proportion with those upon the appraised lands, for an equal length of time, and have equally aided in increasing the value of the whole country, therefore be it

Resolved, That we strongly condemn the appraisal made by this last commission the same being wholly and unjustifiably unjust.

Resolved, That we ask the Honorable Secretary of the Interior to cause a re-appraisement of these lands, that justice may be had, and that all action in regard to requiring the initial payments on these lands, be suspended until such time as the values can be properly adjusted.

Resolved, That the Acts of congress and the president's proclamation opening this reservation contemplated that **all** of of [sic] the unappropriated lands therein should be opened to settlement and entry at the same time, and the settlers accepted the inducements upon the same promulgated basis.

Resolved, That we ask that none of the unappraised lands at the time of the opening be appraised at more than the maximum appraisement by the old commission, namely, seven dollars per acre. The same rule should apply now as at the beginning, for the reason as above stated, the settlers on the unappraised lands have lived upon said lands as long a time, and have done as much to improve the whole country as those who have been living on the appraised lands.

Respectfully submitted,
W. H. Sabin,
Nathan Hart,
C. M. Mansur,
Committee.

The executive committee requests that like organizations at St. Ignatius, Dixon, Ronan, Big Arm and Dayton, and other localities, unite in a co-operative movement with the aim of getting this last appraisement properly reconciled and adjusted.

The executive committee has called another meeting to be held in Polson on December 6, 1913, at 1 o'clock, probably at the Masonic hall, at which time it is desired that people and representatives from all parts of the reservation will be present.

Respectfully,
J. A. Trow, Sec'y.

* * * * * * * * *

Commissioner Tells How and Why It Happened

Below will be found a letter addressed to Hon. John M. Evans, one of Montana's representatives in congress, from Hon. Cato Sells, Commissioner of Indian Affairs, in which it is told how it all happened that so much of the Flathead lands were unclassified and unappraised at the time of the opening of the reservation to homestead entry. The commissioner has his dates a little mixed, especially when he says the reservation opened to homestead entry in 1909, as there are too many of us still here who know that it was in 1910 that the actual opening took place. Aside from this, and a few other discrepancies, it tells some things which have been bothering a large number of people for quite awhile. But if the general history of the how and the why of it is not any more accurate than the things which we know have become confused, there will be a great many people read the letter who will have a hesitancy in taking it as being literally true.

The letter referred to reads:

Washington, Dec. 11, 1913.

Hon John M. Evans,
House of Representatives.
My dear Mr. Evans:

Referring to your inquiry regarding the disposal of the surplus lands within the Flathead Reservation, Montana, and particularly the appraised value, as shown by the schedule recently approved by the Department, the following is submitted:

After the completion of the allotment work in the early of 1908 a commission was appointed to appraise the surplus lands within the Flathead Reservation, in accordance with the provisions of the Act of April 23, 1904 (33 Stats. L., 302). This work was completed in the latter part of calendar year 1908. The lands were not opened, however, until the summer of 1909 and between the completion of the apparaisement work and the opening of the surplus lands to entry a large number of Indian allotments were changed, due to the fact that withdrawals had been made for power and reservoir sites and that a number of Indians had been allotted lands which they claimed not to have selected. When the original commission was at work the lands allotted to Indian[s], of course, were not appraised but changes in allotments made after appraisement work had been completed did leave within the reservation vacant unallotted, and unreserved lands which had not been classified and appraised.

Under authority of Section 29 of the Act of June 25, 1910, (36 Stats. L., 863), and of June 6, 1912 (37 Stats. L., 125), a board of appraisers, consisting of Fred C. Morgon [sic], Superintendent of the Flathead Indian School, John C. Van Hook, a representative of the Surveyor General's office of the State of Montana, and Duncan McDonald, a representative of the Flathead tribe, was organized for the purpose of appraising the surplus lands within the Flathead Reservation not heretofore appraised, and reappraising those tracts shown to have been erroneously appraised in the first instance.

Some time was consumed in this work as the various tracts of land to be viewed aggregated 30,000 acres scattered over different parts of the entire reservation but the schedule submitted by this board was approved by the Department a few weeks ago. Numerous complaints are now being received that the price fixed by this board is greatly in excess of the actual value, or at least the price per acre is many times that placed on land of a similar character by the original board appointed for the purpose of appraising the surplus lands within the Flathead reservation.

You will readily understand that when the first board was convened to appraise these lands, the reservation was unopened and it was practically uncultivated virgin soil and the general outlook for agricultural development at that time may not have been very promising. The schedule of prices fixed by the first board ranges from ten cents an acre for barren, burned-over land to $7.50 per acre for what was designated as first-class agricultural land.

As previously stated, the reservation was opened in the summer of 1909. Four years have transpired since that time, during which considerable development has taken place. Railroads have been constructed, towns built up, the farming industry developed, and conditions now are entirely different from those existing four years ago. Aside from these facts the price of land per acre has increased slightly over the entire country generally. The members of the recent board convened for the purpose of appraising the tracts heretofore unappraised and to re-appraise those tracts wherein claim was made that the original appraisement was erroneous, were under obligations to perform their duty faithfully and it is presumed that the schedule submitted by them is the result of careful examination and a joint conclusion as to the value of the lands as they now stand.

It is regretted that settlers who located or attempted to locate on these unappraised lands three or four years ago should now be required to pay a greater price per acre than their neighbors who settled on lands appraised by the original board, yet it would seem that they should be willing to pay a fair average price per acre for these lands according to their present value. It has been reported here that the State of Montana has sold some of the lands granted to it by the Act of April 25, 1904, falling in sections 16 and 36, or their equivalent, as school land, for a price per acre as high as $60.00. If this be correct, it is not seen why an Indian should be expected to part with good agricultural lands for a nominal sum per acre.

Senator Myers called at the office on December 8 with several telegrams received by him from business men in Polson, protesting against the high appraisement placed on these lands, and I have recently requested the commissioner of the general land office to withhold further action in this matter until an opportunity could be given to persons desiring so to do to file protests, statements of facts, and arguments in support of a request for re-appraisement should they deem the present prices excessive.

Should you have any views to submit with reference to this matter it would be appreciated if they are presented at an early date.

Very truly, yours,
(Signed) **Cato Sells**,
Commissioner.

As to the claim made by the Hon. Commissioner of Indian Affairs in respect to the value of the land and what the state has sold lands for, a little explanation will be timely. There may have been some pieces of sate land sold for $60 per acre, but as to that the Pioneer is not able to state. This paper never heard of the circumstance. But in case it is all true, there is a vast difference between buying state land and having 20 years to pay for it in, and homesteading a tract, being compelled to reside upon the land and improve it, making final proof and not getting a title in 20 years. Who wants to pay actual value for the land and use a homestead right besides? That it [is] just what it amounts to where one pays the price fixed by the late commission.

In a number of cases where the land has been appraised above the maximum fixed by the original commission, some startling circumstances seem to have governed the late commission in fixing the new valuation. The person who has a suspended entry has lived upon and improved the land, built houses and barns, fenced the land, plowed and cultivated and really made the land valuable. In many instances he has done so much and expended so much time and money that he cannot quit now, and this fact seems to have been the guiding instrument in fixing the valuation. Is that treating the entry-man fair?

The trouble is that the commission appointed to make the classification and appraisement did not enter upon their duties with minds absolutely unprejudiced and unbiased. It was composed of officials who should never have been appointed. They had all the work they could do aside from this duty, and being in the employ of the government in one branch or another, should have been allowed to attend to duties already provided. A fair way would have been to have appointed civilians who were unbiased and then the charge of unfairness to the homesteader and too much friendliness to the Indian could not have been made.

The facts are that much of the land is appraised at a greater value than patented lands can be bought for in the immediate vicinity of the land. This tells the whole story of the fairness or the unfairness of the appraisement. There are a number of suspended applications which will never be completed owing to this fact. As an example, it can be stated with all truth, that on the big flat south of Ronan several 80 acre tracts have been sold as low as $800, or ten dollars per acre, and the new appraisement of lands in that locality range from $10 to 18 per acre. This should answer the Hon. Commissioner's statement that the land was appraised according to what other lands in the vicinity were worth.

Duncan McDonald
Source: Photograph Archives, Montana Historical Society, Helena, Montana, photo 943-624

Document 41

Tribal Complaints to United States Government

December 25, 1913

Source: "Complaint Filed by Flathead Tribe," December 25, 1913, from file 17,099/1914 Flathead 056, Central Classified Files, RG 75, National Archives, Washington, D.C.

Editors' note: This manuscript summarizes the complaints of the Flathead Reservation tribes. It includes the failure of the government to fulfill the promises made in the treaty and later agreements, agency control of Indian money from leases and timber sales, and other concerns. This copy of the complaints did not have signatures attached.

St. Ignatius, Montana.
December Twenty Five
Nineteen Thirteen.

Complaint Filed by Flathead Tribe.

To the Honorable
Franklin K. Lane,
Secretary of the Interior.
Honorable Sir: —

We are hereby summoned to answer the complaint in this action. You will please take notice that pursuant to and for the reasons stated in the attached affidavit and in accord with this notice of our deposition of our country by the Flathead Indians, and by the old people of the tribe.

To show the honor the Flathead Indians have for the whites, we took the best of care of Louis [sic] & Clark (a hundred years ago) and his clients to which they gave their robes to cover, for they were the first white men they had seen, and they treated them like Lords. We are to show you citizens you have never treated us the same, and the thanks we have gotten is to be "turned down." If you see a full bearing cherry tree you will clean it up and keep it clean and trim it down — it looks too good, and therefore you are to return us a favor and give us a square deal in all our accounts of the past.

This is one of our complaints: —

Complaint No 2.

A treaty was taken between the Flathead, Kootenay and Upper Pend O'Relles in the year 1859 [sic] and was established by a council, and the records of these people and all in the treaty was never paid in full, and for that reason we want a full settlement of that treaty, which was established by Governor Stevens.

Complaint No. 3.

This treaty of Garfield was taken in 1878 [sic], promising to the Flathead, Kootenay and Upper Pend O'Relles of building houses and cows given and money for the term of twenty (20) years and these promises were never fulfilled, for also moving the Flatheads of the Bitter Root Valley by disagreement, to make a new boundary line from Evaro to Flathead lake and dividing waters, and since that time in this treaty of Garfield's, there was land taken away from their boundary line and dividing waters; also a promise of a hospital, flour-mill, blacksmith-shop, and the best of schools has never been fulfilled.

In the battle with the Nes Perce in 1877, more or less, by that time we had saved the Whites of Montana citizens; we have never gotten credit for this and the thanks we gave to the white citizens charmed them like little chickens and saved their lives and no favors given to us except that they took our country.

Complaint No. 4.

The opening of the Reservation. In the bill which was passed by Congress, through our Senator Joseph Dixon, has never been filled out according to his bill. Indians were to get paid in full in five years, annually payments. We have never seen it yet. We also want a general settlement of this bill which was passed through Congress — for you will reach over your capacity of limits, gone by eight years now.

Complaint No. 5.

We have a better view for our conditions to begin a new rule as to ask you to let us open a bank of our own, so we can lend our own money on interest on good security, but not to let other banks make our profit, for we need all the interest — for the Tribe needs it; also, we ask you for a Government man to manage our Bank, and also Indian Directors for same.

Complaint No. 6.

We wish any Indian to have the right to sell their timber those who have timber allotments; they are poor, and also to find a buyer and to be b[r]ought before the Agent and to sell his timber right not less than $4.00 a thousand. This will help the poor Indian to live. This money to be deposited to his credit in the Indian Bank and to let him use his money as he wishes. This would save trouble to the Agent and the Indian and to the Commission[er] of Indian Affairs.

Complaint No. 7.

We wish the Indian to have the right to lease their land either cash rent or share of crop, to whom they wish. Let the Agent have the power to pay the Indian at the time of the transaction. This would save trouble for the Agent, Indian and Commission of Indian Affairs.

Complaint No. 8.

We do not wish to sell dead allotments on sealed bids. Would recommend that buyer be brought to the Agent [and] settlement made.

Complaint No. 9.

We wish to have the power to rent our children's land also; if in timber, and see fit to sell the timber to the betterment of the children money to be placed to the credit of the children, and the parents to draw the interest for children's keeping. If a forest fire comes the poor children will be at a loss. If any parents are capable to put the money in good investments, to be allowed to do so, upon the recommendation of the Agent.

Complaint No. 10.

We wish to sell the Polson Falls to some big concern or the Government for water power, but we reserve our water right; we wish to sell the Mission Falls and reserve to [the] water.

Complaint No. 11.

A bill was passed by Senator Dixon to the Reclamation Service to complete all ditches on this Reservation in five years — it is now eight years. You are not doing justice to us in this matter. If we had put it on bids we would have had it completed by this time; we do not wish to pay out of the Indian funds; for mules, harnesses, frenos, steam-shovels, etc., used by the Goernment [sic] on the ditches. We want the cost of all implements, etc., returned to the Indians in cash.

Complaint No. 12.

We wish to sell all timber on the Reservation to big corporations or Government, but want the right to get our wood, poles, posts and logs to build stables and houses. This to be sold at $4.00 or more a thousand. If a forest fire comes the poor Indians will be at a loss. Contracts shall be made before the Agent and Indian Council and a Government's Special Agent.

Complaint No. 13.

Please let us have our Agent to have all power, as the above complaints, which may be done and to make this as a law it would save trouble between the Indian Agent and Commission of Indian Affairs.

Complaint No. 14.

We want to have the right and the say when we reach Washington, D.C., as to what we believe and to be looked after with all privileges and our interests and the Government.

Complaint No. 15.

We wish to have a bill passed to give us the right to put an elevator for grain and get the best of prices for our grain and to not let big corporations have the advantage of us. We also ask for sheds to put our hay in.

Complaint No. 16.

We also ask the Government to build us an Indian Corporation store; to get their goods at cost prices. We want this to be governed by Government care and also Indian Directors; and to have the right to retail to whom they please; for to make their interest and profits divided, after all bills are paid, among the Indians.

Complaint No. 17.

We wish a full general settlement of all accounts of the Reservation up to date, and if any money is to be paid, give each Indian his individual credits to his bank account and for the Indian to know what he has got. If a full settlement, we also want to reserve one-fourth (1/4) for the new generation born.

Complaint No. 18.

We wish a Business School (boarding). We are away behind times for you have never built us a good school in this Reservation; give us the chance as a White Man's chance will soon civilize with our education, if kept down we cannot make good.

Complaint No. 19.

We do not wish to move the Agency, for it takes out of our Indian funds $47,000, and we do not wish this, but to leave it as it is, for this we want as a memory of our forefathers, which was established by treaties.

Complaint No. 20.

We had a council at St. Ignatius Mission and there was a promise to give the new born land where it can be found on this Reservation. This promise was made four years ago.

Complaint No. 21.

We are not to be taxed. A bill has been passed by Senator Dixon Indians to hold good for 25 years, which we do not think is right, for the twenty-five years has not elapsed. You are to wait until we become citizens.

Complaint No. 22.

If any old people who are feeble, let them sell their land to their tribe or relation, or to whom they please.

Complaint No. 23.

Indian Councils are not consent to the surveying of this Reservation for the white people opened it and not according to any agreement with the Indians. Also for allotments — do not which to pay this, or for the appraisement of the Reservation and timber, And, all state lands we want the cost of what it is appraised for, and also town-sites and the buffalo park.

Established by the Council of the St. Ignatius Indian, this 25th day of December, 1913, and approved by the undersigned: —

[There are no signatures on this copy of complaints.]

Chapter 2

Documents of Salish, Pend d'Oreille, and Kootenai History Between 1914-1915

Document 42

Indian Policeman Shoots Man During Arrest

January 23, 1914

Source: "Shooting Affray at St. Ignatius," *The Ronan Pioneer*, January 23, 1914, page 1, col. 4.

Editors' note: Violence between tribal members and Indian policemen made the local newspapers.

Shooting Affray at St. Ignatius

Word was received Tuesday morning from St. Ignatius telling of a shooting affair in that town. It appears that Leo Barnaby was creating a disturbance and Henry Moss was sent to arrest him. Some difficulty arose between them, resulting in Moss shooting Barnaby through the left lung and into the stomach, causing a wound which at last accounts was considered very dangerous.

A later account says Moss arrested Barnaby for boot-legging and was going to take him to Polson for trial. Barnaby resisted the arrest and Moss struck him with his handcuffs and then pulled his gun. The Indian continued to fight and during the struggle put his hand over the end of the gun. Moss fired, blowing half the hand away. As the Indian backed away the officer fired a second time, the bullet passing under Barnaby's left arm, close to the heart.

Moss at once sought Deputy Ramsey and another officer named Arnold. These men put Moss in custody and assumed charge of the case. There was but one witness of the shooting, Constable Fred Normandin.

County Attorney Hefron has decided that the county has no jurisdiction in the matter and the sheriff's office made no move.

Document 43

Henry Matt Looks at Flathead Agents

January 26, 1914

Source: "How Former Agents Looked After Their Indian Charges," January 26, 1914, newspaper clipping from unidentified newspaper, possibly *St. Ignatius Post.* Copy in Henry Matt probate file, number 325, Flathead Agency Records, U.S. Bureau of Indian Affairs, Pablo, Mont.

Editors' note: This article gave one tribal member's evaluation of the different Flathead Indian agents. Henry Matt supported the Brotherhood of North American Indians in trying to influence federal Indian policy and described his trip east to attend a national meeting of the Brotherhood.

How Former Agents Looked After Their Indian Charges
A Short History of the Superintendents Who Have Had Charge of the Flathead.

The following interesting history of the Agents who have had charge of the affairs of the Indians of this reservation was written by Henry Matt of Arlee. Mr. Matt has spent his entire life in this section and speaks from personal observation of the different officials, as he was employed by nearly all of them during their terms in office.

Major Peter Ronan

was superintendent over our people for eighteen years, which was the longest in point of service of any man in the United States. He was kind and attentive to all the Indians, and did everything that lay in his power[.] He was especially kind and looked after the interests of the old Indians. Every New Years day there was a great feast given by him which was always attended by all the Indians in the valley. Major Ronan's wife was a great help to him in taking care of "his people." She was always on the watch for any of them that needed assistance, and especially if they were sick, when she herself would nurse, feed and care for them, and see that they had medicine and food. There seemed to be nothing on earth that she was not ready and willing to do. She was worth much to our people and none of us will ever forget such a blessed woman. Major Ronan did everything in his power for any and all of our people that was proper and right and he also will never be forgotten by them.

Mr. Robert Irvine

better known as "Bob Sub Agent," was appointed by Major Ronan especially to see that the old and infirm Indians had all that they needed and he looked after them with great care. He did his duty faithfully and was the right man in the right place.

Mr. Charles Gardiner

who had lived among the Indians around Dayton creek for fifty years was Sub-agent and Boss Farmer. He was a right man also and did everything in his power for the Indians. He was a good hearted, whole-souled fellow and was well liked by all.

Major Joseph Carter

was the next agent and general superintendent and he followed out as far as possible Major Ronan's method of dealing with the Indians. He was also a great worker himself, and he did not ride around and mislead his people in any way whatever. He taught them how to farm, and would take up the pick and shovel himself and show the Indians how the work should be done, and they would then take hold and work themselves. He encouraged and showed them how to plant their gardens and raise a little wheat, and when Mr. Indian would bring his little handfull of wheat to the mill to get it ground into the staff of life Major Carter would compliment him on doing so well and encourage him to keep on trying, instead of discouraging him, and by so doing he started many of the Indians supporting themselves by the "sweat of their brow." He helped many, among them myself, to build their houses, do their fencing and dig their ditches, and showed them how they could become independent citizens.

When the inspectors from Washington came around, he would take them to see the poor Indians, who needed help, so they could see for themselves what the Indians needed. He evidently thought that the competent Indians who had good homes and could look after themselves did, not need any inspection, but that the poor and infirm were the ones, so he took the inspectors right to their homes in broad daylight. He always taught the Indian that he had every right to push ahead and make a citizen of himself and be an independent man, this not only in our breeds but to the full bloods. Major Carter was a good man and a good agent.

Major W. H. Smead

was also a good man, but he had different ideas. He thought the opening of the reservation was in the best interests of the Indian, which it was not. This was against the Indians will, and through it we lost most of our best chiefs, who really died of grief. They were, first, Chief Chalkan Maschel, Pondera; second Chief Charlos, Kootenai [sic], and third Chief Isica. They all grieved themselves into a "bed of sod" over the loss to their people, which we are sorry to say but which, however, is true. Major Smead was well liked by all the Indians, and they never blamed him for this thing as all believed he thought that it was really for the best interests of all. At the time Mr. Dixon was congressman and then after he was made senator and he introduced the bill that opening the nation, which was very wrong for the Indians, for now their lands are sold and they have nothing left, and many of them are destitute, and they can get nothing that is coming to them, and which they need very badly.

"Old Man" Major Bellow

was a first class superintendent. He was next to Major Ronan. He never allowed any of the Indians to suffer, neither among the young or the old. He took great interest in their behalf and the only fault ever found with him was that he was a little too old to get out and look after them but when he did he went to the nidians [sic] that needed help. He also took the inspectors to see the poor Indians, the sick, the old and infirm and those that were destitute. He did not take them to see the houses of the ones who were able to support themselves and thus have the report go into Washington that everything was all right. When these inspectors come around they should be shown not only what the "poor Indians" need, but what the "poor white homesteader" needs, instead of being shown the people who are getting along so good, and that is what the agents who were liked by the Indians used to do, and it should be done now.

Henry Matt

the writer of this article, was born in the year 1872 at Stevensville, Montana, in the Bitter Root, where I lived until I was 23 years of age. I went to the Carlisle, Pennsylvania school, and I thank hte [sic] government for the slight learning they have given me. In 1912 I was a delegate to Washington with Chief Moise, Chief Kaka and Chief Antiste, and another interpreter, nd [sic] while there I met head men and chiefs from 40 different tribes. They had fine lawyers with them, graduates of our own blood Indians, and it made me feel mighty cheap to find out how far behind the times our whole tribe is in education. We have no schools here, we are neglected, we are sorry to say, and we feel pain in our hearts when we realize what a bad position we are in.

Under Commissioner Valentine gave us a fine lecture advising us to make up a petition by council for all of the Indians to sign those complaints of their wants and conditions. He said he would like to come here and see all the Indians, he wished he could have the right to do so, and help them to have their rights and justice, as he would do that he could do for them. He was very sorry to learn of such a state of affairs, and said he wished that some of the nIdians [sic] could represent themselves in congress.

I am glad I went to Washington. It was quite an education for me. I am a full-fledged North American citizen, and I hope all the citizens will believe and take an interest in what I have said, and join in the movement to help the people of this reservation get what is only justice to them. I have attempted to tell nothing but the truth, and it would be possible to say a great deal more than I have but did not deem it necessary, but I will vouch that every word I have written is the truth.

Henry Matt.

Henry Matt
Source: Virginia Matt Brazill, Arlee, Montana

Document 44

Whisky Charge Against Henry Matt Dismissed

April 10, 1914

Source: "Henry Matt Freed by Federal Jury," *The Daily Missoulian*, April 10, 1914, page 10, col. 4.

Editors' note: Whisky on the Flathead Reservation in 1914 was common and federal charges were brought against those accused of supplying the alcohol.

Henry Matt Freed by Federal Jury
Reservation Resident Is Acquitted on Charge of Selling Whiskey to Reds.

After being out but a short time the jury in the United States district court found Henry Matt not guilty of furnishing whisky to Indians.

The trial of the case occupied only a little time, the state calling only a few witnesses directly interested in the events supposedly connecting Matt with the crime of which he was charged, while the defense merely used a few business men and prominent Indians in order to establish Matt's good reputation.

From the evidence it appears that on June 27 Alec Matt, father of the defendant, gave a dance near Arlee. Shortly before the festivities began, the old man told his son that several Indians had secured liquor and were drunk. He asked Henry to get the booze and destroy it. With Felix Barnaby, Henry Matt went out to look for the liquor. They found a jug in the grass some distance from the Barnaby home, but instead of destroying it, took it to Barnaby's and there drank some of it. Henry Matt then went to the dance to play in the orchestra. Later he invited Mary Louise Ashley, a young Indian girl, to the Barnaby house to get some of the booze. Felix Barnaby and his wife were already drinking. They say that Matt gave the Ashley girl a drink of whisky. Upon this act the prosecution laid particular emphasis.

The whole case hinged, practically, upon this single point and upon the transfer of the booze from the field to the Barnaby house. If Matt carried the jug, the court explained, he was guilty of introducing liquor into Indian country. If Barnaby carried it Matt was not guilty. Again, if Matt gave the Ashley woman a drink of whisky he was guilty of giving whisky to an Indian. If, however, he merely participated in a general drinking bout with the other three he could not be called guilty.

The case went to the jury at about 4:30 o'clock.

Document 45

Business Committee Asks for Changes in Government Policies May 24, 1914

Source: Duncan McDonald, et. al., "Resolutions Adopted at a Meeting of the Business Committee of the Flathead Tribe of Indians Held at St. Ignatius Montana on the 24th Day of May, 1914," from file 70,964/1913 Flathead 054, Central Classified Files, RG 75, National Archives, Washington, D.C.

Editors' note: The Flathead Reservation Business Committee noted continuing problems associated with the new allotment policy forced on the tribes, and requested that the government look out for the interests of tribal members. The erroneous survey of the southwest boundary of the reservation after the 1855 Hellgate Treaty had still not been addressed.

Resolutions Adopted at a Meeting of the Business Committee of the Flathead Tribe of Indians Held at St. Ignatius Montana on the 24th Day of May, 1914.

1. Whereas, it appears that there are numerous cases on the Flathead Indian reservation where allotments have been selected and made for orphan children and for incompetent and other Indians who were disinterested in the selection of their allotments on the tops of high mountains and hills and on land unfit for either agriculture or grazing purposes, we respectfully request that the Indian Office and the Department of the Interior take such action as may be necessary to permit the exchange of such allotments for other lands belonging to the Flathead Tribe of Indians and which are suitable for agricultural purposes. The Tribe still owns much valuable agricultural land which has been classified as forest land, land reserved for reservoir and power purposes and later found not to be required for the purposes for which reserved. It appears that many of the allottees whose original allotment was relinquished and the land reserved for reservoir and power purposes, did so with the understanding that in case such land would not be required for those purposes, such allotments would be restored to the original allottees. Instead of such Indians getting back their original allotments, white men have squatted on those lands and are now in possession of them. This we consider manifestly unjust and unfair. The last and only hope of our people rests in the securing of a piece of land on which they

may maintain a home and make a living and unless the Government rectifies some of the errors that have been made in the allotting of a number of our people many of them will be without a home on which it will be possible for them to eke out an existence.

2. Whereas, the Act of Congress, approved June 6, 1912, providing for the reclassification of the Flathead Tribal timber lands where such lands are claimed by white settlers to be more valuable as agricultural lands than as timber lands, resulting in numerous applications being filed with the Department of the Interior for reclassification and that it has opened a new way for the white people to acquire additional large areas of our most valuable timber lands, we respectfully request that said law be amended so as to more completely protect our interests. We entertain grave fears that if this law is allowed to remain in full force in its present form, in a few more years the Flathead Indians will have no forest lands left of any value.

3. Whereas, there are a number of aged men and women who are too old to work and have no means of support but who have good allotments, we urge that in all such cases where the Indian refuses to sign a lease on his land, that the Superintendent be authorized to sign such leases and to use the proceeds derived therefrom for the support of the allottee. We urge that the Superintendent be given more authority in reference to the handling of Individual Indian Money. We further request and recommend that the Superintendent be authorized to conduct the next land sale at public auction instead of by sealed bids and if the method proves satisfactory that it be adopted. We believe land sold at public auction, and on the deferred payment plan, will result in more active bidding and better prices.

4. Whereas, an error was made in the Survey of the boundaries of the Flathead Indian Reservation as described in our treaty made in 1855 with Governor Isaac I. Stevens, we respectfully request that this matter be brought to the attention of Congress with the view of having this just claim of many years standing referred to the United States Court of Claims for proper and equitable adjustment. We urge on behalf of our people that this matter receive prompt and careful attention.

5. Whereas, a board consisting of the Project Engineer of the Flathead Reclamation Service, the Superintendent of the Flathead Reservation and one member of the Tribe have been appointed to adjust the water rights of Indians owning irrigation ditches before the Reclamation Service constructed its system, we urge that this board be instructed to proceed with their work of adjustment as soon as possible.

6. Whereas, our people have recently received their allotments and many of them being poor and too old to perform hard labor and are without the

necessary funds or means of improving these allotments and establishing homes thereon and whereas all the money derived from the sale of our surplus lands are under the present law used to pay for constructing an irrigation system from which the white settlers receive the same benefit as ourselves, many people find themselves at a time when they are most in need of assistance totally without funds or resources and unable to earn their support on a bare piece of land without buildings, tools or any means of providing the simplest comforts of live [life] we humbly ask that Congress be requested to advance to the Flathead tribe of Indians the sum of $500,000.00, the same to be repaid from the sale of their tribal timber, said sum to be paid to them per capita or deposited to their individual credit in bank and expended in improving their homes and farms.

The foregoing resolutions have been carefully considered by the business committee of the Flathead tribe of Indians and it is believed that they contain only fair and reasonable requests when considered in connection with the laws that have been imposed upon us without our consent and against our wishes and in view of the present condition of our people. In making these requests we are acting in good faith and in consideration of the best interests of the Flathead people we trust that these requests will not be passed upon lightly or without a careful consideration for our welfare but that they will receive most careful consideration and be presented to the Honorable Secretary of the Interior who will in turn present them to Congress with appropriate recommendations.

Duncan McDonald, Chairman
Charles Allard, Secretary
John Matt
Enase Michel
Angus P. McDonald
Peter Magpie, his mark.

Witnesses to all signatures:
H. S. Allen, chief clerk, Jocko, Mont.
Isaac Hawley, Stenographer, Jocko, Mont.

Document 46

Agent Morgan's Defense Against Criticism

June 12, 1914

Source: Fred C. Morgan to Commissioner of Indian Affairs, June 12, 1914, from file 62,878/1914 Flathead 723, Central Classified Files, RG 75, National Archives, Washington, D.C.

Editors' note: This letter gives Agent Fred Morgan's defense against charges made by Martin Charlo, Antoine Moiese, Eneas Grandjo, and Henry Matt. It is only one side of the story, and unfortunately no record was made of the Indian version of events. Apparently the "troublemakers" opposed Morgan's efforts to closely control tribal money and activities.

Department of the Interior
United States Indian Service
Flathead Agency, Jocko, Montana.
June 12, 1914.

The Commissioner of Indian Affairs,
Washington, D.C.
Sir:

Referring to Office telegram of June 8, 1914, as follows:

> "Chief Martin Charlo and Antoine Moiese wired as follows:
>
> > 'An old lady died from starvation and three more old ladies. Ignace Grandjo have money for buying horses and implements. Morgan won't let them have it. Buying horses for Indians are crippled.'
>
> Consult with Indians named and take prompt steps to relieve suffering. Report fully by letter."

I have to advise that after receiving the above quoted message, I went to Missoula for the purpose of interviewing Martin Charlo and Antoine Moiese whom, I understood at that time, were in Missoula. Upon my arrival there I visited the several Indian camps which were immediately west of Missoula on the commons, and learned that Moiese had left for the reservation but that Martin Charlo, in company with Henry Matt, were in Missoula or vicinity, having frequently been around the Indians camps. From a reliable Indian woman and her son I learned that Martin Charlo and Henry Matt had been drinking during the past two or three days. I then returned to the Agency and sent for Moiese and Martin Charlo to come to the office in order that I might interview them regarding the statement contained in their message.

Since I was busy in the field on the 10th I did not have an opportunity to see Antoine Moiese, who was waiting for me, until about 9:15 that evening when I returned to the Agency. Owing to the lateness of the hour I did not get a statement from Moiese but questioned him in the presence of Clerk Lewis Main and John H. Heidelman, Agency Physician. I told him that a message signed by he and Martin Charlo had been forwarded to me from the Commissioner of Indian Affairs and I would like to have him inform me who the four old Indian women were who died from starvation. Moiese seemed very much embarassed and he evaded the question by stating that he had been in town visiting Senator Dixon and had not said that four old Indian women had died from starvation but did say that one old woman named Mary Ann Pateenitz was found dead near her cabin during the last summer.

I further questioned him regarding the statement in his message of my refusing to purchase horses and implements for Ignace or Eneas Grandjo. He said he did not know anything about it, had never heard of it before and did not say anything about that matter. I then asked him if he knew of any horses that had been purchased under the supervision of this Agency for the Indians that were crippled before purchase, to which he replied that he knew nothing about it and had said nothing about this matter in his message or to the interpreter, Henry Matt who, while Moiese would not admit it, in my opinion wrote the message.

The old Indian woman Mary Ann Pateenitz, referred to by Moiese, was found dead last July (21st) 1913 on a trail leading from the river to her cabin, she evidently having been to the river for water. This old lady has drawn rations ever since I have been in charge of this Agency and the statement that she starved to death is absolutely false and untrue. I am inclosing a death certificate signed by John H. Heidelman, Agency Physician, which shows that this old woman had been a constant sufferer from heart trouble during the past four years which, no doubt, was the direct cause of her death.

Moiese, however, stated that he paid two dollars for sending the message and did not know it contained anything else than a reference to the old woman, Mary Ann Pateenitz, starving to death. He further stated that he did not sign the message, and that Henry Matt acted as interpreter at the telegraph office when the message was sent.

I failed to see Martin Charlo the same evening, so sent for him to call the next morning. Upon his arrival at the Office I questioned him regarding the statements contained in a message signed by he and Moiese whick [sic] I read to him.

I am inclosing his statement which was made through an interpreter and was made of his own free will and accord, and from the statement the Office will note that Martin Charlo denies any knowledge of the message whatever. He also stated that Moiese was Angry at him because he would not take a hand in sending the message.

From the questioning of Charlo and Moiese it appears that they know very little of the contents of the message and it appears to me that Henry Matt who acted as interpreter is responsible for all contained in the message, excepting the statement made by Moiese relative to the old Indian woman being found dead.

Under date of January 15, 1914 there was sold a tract of land allotted to Antoine Grandjo, the deceased son of Eneas (Ignace) Grandjo and Isabel Grandjo, who were the sole heirs to this allotment, the same being sold on application approved by the Department. Prior to the time this sale was approved and the money deposited to their individual credits, Eneas Grandjo and wife made one or two visits to this office for the purpose of obtaining a portion of the money. When Grandjo and his wife were told that any money paid them would have to be expended under the supervision of this office, under instructions from the Office, and that any goods, cattle or horses purchased could not be sold by them without permission, he began to scheme to get the money so as to use it without the supervision of this office.

First they desired to purchase a house and lot just over the reservation boundary line on the road leading from Missoula to the reservation.

Eneas Grandjo is one of the smoothest bootleggers that we have had to contend with and has served two terms for the introduction of liquor onto the Flathead Reservation and will, without doubt, be indicted by the next Federal Grand Jury which convenes at Helena, Montana within the next few days, for a like offense. For this reason and the reason that the property, if purchased, would become a half-way house for bootleggers, I told Grandjo and his wife that I could not recommend that they be allowed to purchase this house and lot, and for the further reason that they had plenty of land on which to build, providing they desired to build a house, other than a good log house which they now have on Eneas's allotment.

Grandjo and his wife then wanted to purchase a team of ponies and was advised that ponies were too small for farm work and that it would be more profitable if they would purchase a team of mares of sufficient size to work their allotments and be in position to increase their stock. They were further advised that it would be to their interest to purchase a few cattle which they could care for and which would increase.

Since this conversation I have seen nothing of them with reference to purchasing stock or equipment and they have spent practically all their time in or around Missoula which has been one of Grandjo's frequent haunts.

I have never refused to purchase horses, cattle or other equipment for them or any other Indian, but have insisted on them purchasing the right kind of stock and equipment, at the same time informing them it would be under the supervision of the United States and they would not be allowed to sell the same without permission. This I deemed advisable for the reason that I knew Grandjo would be inclined to dispose of his property at the first opportunity if he realized that strict supervision would not be exercised over same.

Grandjo is a relative of Henry Matt, hence the apparent interest of Matt in presenting the matter in a telegram signed by Moiese and Martin Charlo.

The fact that Alex Matt, father of Henry Matt, has tried on two different occasions to sell horses to the Indians whose moneys were being expended under the supervision of this office, may have prompted the statements in the message which, without doubt, he is responsible for.

On one occasion Alex Matt offered to sell to Louie Spokane, whose money was being expended under supervision for equipment, a team of horses, which Mr. Corrie Hiatt, Farmer who assists the Indians in purchasing horses for farm work, would not approve of for the reason that the team was a pair of geldings and had the reputation of being balky. On another occasion he tried to sell a pony to Jerome Lumpry, another Indian whose money was being expended under supervision, asking this Indian $75.00 for the pony and upon not receiving the approval of this office he took the horse to Arlee, and it is reported that he sold it for $50.00, a difference of $25.00 in the price which he asked the Indian and the price he sold it to a white man.

The statement which neither Martin Charlo nor Moiese admit as theirs — that I am buying crippled horses for the Indians — is absolutely false and in my opinion is a wilful and malicious misstatement.

Henry Matt's feelings towards this office is perhaps not of the best for the reason that during the last term of the Federal Court held in Missoula, Montana during the month of April, 1914, Henry Matt was tried on the charge of having introduced liquor into the Indian country. This, with two cases against James Matt, a brother of his, for introducing, and one against Eneas Grandjo a relative, perhaps has affected Henry's judgment as to just what has taken place.

In connection with the above I respectfully call your attention to my letter of April 9, 1914, (Ed.–Law & Order, 28053-14) which report is in regard to a team belonging to James Matt, a brother of Henry Matt, having been seized for introduction of liquor into the Indian country.

In conclusion I desire to state that I have at all times since I have been in charge at this agency, endeavored to see that the old Indians were properly cared for, and the field employees are frequently instructed by letter and verbally to ascertain and report if any of the Indians are in need, and such cases reported, are immediately given prompt attention.

I am, inclosing statements made by John Charley and Louie Pierre, Judges of the Indian Court, and of Mr. Omer D. Lewis, Lease Clerk at this Agency, who attends to the issuing of rations to the old and indigent Indians.

Very respectfully,
Fred C. Morgan
Superintendent.

Eneas Granjo
Source: Carling Malouf Papers, MS 640, Toole Archives, Mansfield Library, University of Montana, Missoula, box 79, folder 7

Document 47

Indians Drunk in Missoula

July 7, 1914

Source: "Indians and Booze Prove Unwieldy Mixture," *The Daily Missoulian*, July 7, 1914, page 10, col. 4.

Editors' note: Of all the events that occurred while the Indians were in Missoula for the 1914 Fourth of July celebration, this violent brawl made it into the newspaper.

Indians and Booze Prove Unwieldy Mixture
Red Men Hit John Barleycorn with Sad Results and Celebrate in Jail.

Though peaceful and sober enough while in camp at Riverside park, where they have been dancing for the past three or four days, the Indians who took so prominent a part in Missoula's celebration of the Fourth of July, hit Missoula and John Barleycorn yesterday with sad results to the city and themselves.

The red men are passing through the city towards the reservation for another year of home life. Unfortunately, not all of them could resist the city's temptations any more than some of the Missoula saloon keepers could resist the temptation to peddle illicit liquor to the government's wards. Yesterday half a dozen of the Indians got their hides so full of whiskey that the attention of the city police became necessary.

The most serious fracas of the day occurred when the better half of the Gebeau family found her husband walking down Higgins avenue with Baby Rose, a s.... who is said to be the Vampire of the reservation. Baby Rose and her fatal beauty have caused endless trouble on the reserve. Yesterday the fair redskin added another notch to her gun, to say nothing of several nicks to her own head. When Mrs. Gebeau discovered her husband walking with Rose she went on the warpath. She manhandled her rival and gave her husband a good beating before Sheriff Kelley could interfere. All hands were locked up, to rest until sober.

Document 48

Death of Michel Pablo

July 12, 1914

Source: "Michel Pablo Dies Suddenly at Ronan," *The Daily Missoulian*, July 12, 1914, page 1, col. 5-6; "Funeral of Pablo Is Attended by Hundreds," *The Daily Missoulian*, July 15, 1914, page 1, col. 4.

Editors' note: The death of Michel Pablo was front page news around the state. He left a large estate and a going cattle ranch.

Michel Pablo Dies Suddenly at Ronan

Ronan, July 12. — (Sunday.) — Michel Pablo, one of the oldest residents of the reservation country, died shortly after midnight this morning. He was stricken suddenly about 3 o'clock Saturday afternoon while working at his farm above here. All that was possible was done for his relief, but the stroke was fatal. Whether it was induced by the heat or not is not known.

Mr. Pablo was one of the best-known men on the reservation. For years he had been a successful farmer and stockman. He was associated with the late Charles Allard in the ownership of the famous buffalo herd that was afterward sold to the Canadian government for the Banf national park.

In this connection Mr. Pablo acquired international fame. Scientists and hunters came from many regions to witness the loading and transportation of the large herd of buffalo. Old as he was, Pablo directed the handling of this herd personally; he was in the saddle with the young men of the reserve. Riding hard and managing the business, he won the admiration of visitors. He was a picturesque figure always.

As a citizen and a father, Michel Pablo was a high-class man. The Indian in him was good Indian and his white ancestry had left him the heritage of a gentleman by breeding. He was highly esteemed and will be greatly missed.

* * * * * * * * * *

Funeral of Pablo Is Attended by Hundreds

St. Ignatius, July 14. — (Special.) — Michel Pablo, who died early Sunday morning at his ranch on Mud creek, between Ronan and Polson and who is mourned by hundreds of friends throughout the reservation, was buried here today. This morning at 10 o'clock there was a service at Ronan with requiem high mass and a funeral sermon by Rev. Father O'Mally. Then the funeral procession formed and came to St. Ignatius. There were more than 50 carriages in line on this drive. At 2 o'clock prayers for the dead were said in the mission church and then fully 300 people followed the remains to the Indian cemetery where internment took place. The pallbearers were William Irvine, Angus P. McDonald, Duncan McDonald, Pat Normandeau, Fred Lachambre and Joe Bouchard.

Besides his wife, Mr. Pablo leaves three sons, Louis, Joe and Alec, and three daughters, Mrs. Dupuis, Mrs. Tony Barnaby and Mrs. John Ashley, all well-known residents of the reservation.

Michel Pablo was a wealthy man but it is stated that he left no will and made no preparation for the division of his property. The estate is variously estimated from $250,000 to $300,000. This is in land and cattle and cash, the sale of the famous Pablo buffalo herd having brought him a large sum a year ago.

The Indians of the reservation are making plans to hold a big funeral feast at the Pablo ranch in about 10 days. It is expected that this gathering will eclipse even the feast which was held by the Indians at the time of the death of Mr. Pablo's former partner, Charles Allard, this having been considered one of the largest gatherings of its kind the Flatheads ever held.

Michel Pablo
Source: Photograph Archives, Montana Historical Society, Helena, Montana, photo 944-242

Document 49

Indians Visit Missoula for Circus

August 1914

Source: "Plenty of Booze Makes Indians Troublesome," *The Daily Missoulian*, August 5, 1914, page 3, col. 1; "Thanks the Judge for Six Months in the Pen," *The Daily Missoulian*, August 6, 1914, page 4, col. 4.

Editors' note: The circus brought a crowd of tribal members to Missoula for the show. Most returned peacefully to the reservation, but some used the occasion to celebrate with alcohol.

Plenty of Booze Makes Indians Troublesome
Come to See the Circus and Then Make Show of Themselves and Get Pinched.

There is just one thing the Indian likes more than he likes a circus. That one thing is booze. When he can get the circus and the booze together, he is having the time of his life.

And there were about 50 of the representatives of the Confederated Tribes, who had the time of their aboriginal lives circus day.

The police headquarters yesterday looked like a section of the Flathead reservation. There was a motley throng in the bull pen. Night Sergeant Therriault had sold space until there was not even standing room and the overflow had been sent to the county jail. All upper and lower berths were sold early in the deep in tiers.

The most sensational performer of the day was Joe Baptiste. He had been on the outside of the circus tent with a fine souse. When the Indian music started inside, Joe proceeded to put on a wild-west show of his own. He gave three of the strident notes of the war cry of his fathers, shot his revolver three times, and then dashed into the steps of the Flathead war dance. One of the s....s in his train had the presumption to laugh at Joe's performance. She told him it was more like a tango than a war dance. Joe, forthwith, beat the dramatic critic. And then Jack Rice showed up. Joe, having beaten the woman, thought he could lick a policeman. That was the mistake of his life. When the mixup ended, the features of this native son were spread all over the north end of town and the rest of him was on the way to jail.

Mose Big Sam, son of a line of chieftains, fell to Officer Lease. Mose weighs 250 pounds without a load. He carried excess tonnage last night and Lease had about 375 pounds of Indian and whiskey to handle. It was a night and the aisles were used until the soaked reds were stacked up four *[missing text]* tough job, but Lease landed Big Sam's big boy in the calaboose.

Of course Sam Resurrection was in the crowd. Sam had no distinction in his debauch. He was just spiflicated. But, as usual, he had done that much well and thoroughly.

Alex had stolen a blanket. Jerome Valkenburg had been guilty of using profane and abusive language around the circus. Charles Red Crow had been drunker than the average.

Nancy White Bull, Selish belle, had been toasted too often in the fiery sheep dip and was so much the worse for wear that a kindly policeman took her to the county jail to sleep off her woes.

These were the stars of the aggregation. There were 40 or 50 others with neither the pride of ancestry or the possession of individuality in their carousal to make them worthy of special mention. They sobered up at intervals from 5 to 10 o'clock this morning and were sent back to the reservation in charge of friends. Mose Big Sam followed a mite of a woman as meekly as a trained elephant.

* * * * * * * * * *

Thanks the Judge for Six Months in the Pen

Bad Injun From Reservation Escapes When S.... Reverses Story.

"That's all right. I thank you, judge. That's easy."

In very good English Baptiste Joseph spoke these words yesterday in the court of Justice Phil Gagnon. The remarks were addressed to the justice who had just sentenced the Indian, declared by the officers to be the most dangerous red of the whole reservation tribe, to serve six months in the county jail.

On Monday Joseph was arrested for beating and robbing an Indian woman, Adelaide Michel. At that time Adelaide told the officers that the buck took $10 of her money. Yesterday the s.... changed her story and said that she ran away with Joseph to come to the circus and that the money he took was some he had given her. Joseph's father, the officers believe, appealed to the woman to change her statement and so save his son from going to the penitentiary.

The first complaint against Joseph was for robbery. After the s....'s refusal to stick to her first story, this had to be changed to assault and to this charge Joseph was pleased to plead guilty, his only excuse being that he was drunk. He said he gave a white man $3 for booze which brought about his downfall.

That Vest Recovered.

Baptiste Joseph's father's name is Pierre Joseph. Yesterday he brought a tale of woe to the officers and lodged a complaint against Antoine Pasquale, charging the latter with having robbed him of his beautifully-beaded vest — a vest of many colors and valued at $25. Pasquale's arrest followed. He had "soaked" the vest with a barber for 50 cents. This morning the vest was recovered and Pasquale was fined $5.

Barber Wins.

The barber, however, made money on his four-bit investment. He got his money back and collected $1.50 witness fees for appearing at the trial.

Document 50

John Matt's House Burns in Fire

November 13, 1914

Source: "John Matt's House Is Destroyed by Fire," *The Daily Missoulian*, November 13, 1914, page 3, col. 3.

Editors' note: John Matt suffered a tragic loss when his house burned down from a chimney fire.

John Matt's House Is Destroyed by Fire
Reservation Farmer, Is Here with Sick Wife, Gets Shock When the News Comes.

Hard luck has been coming in bunches this year for John A. Matt, a well-known resident of the Flathead who operates a 200-acre ranch near Jocko. Last June his store at Jocko was destroyed by fire and was a complete loss. Yesterday his ranch home burned to the ground. It was uninsured and the building and furniture had a valuation of about $1,000.

Mr. Matt was eating his supper in a restaurant here last evening when Pete Stevens, a neighbor, walked into the place.

"How long have you been in town," Mr. Stevens asked him.

"I have been here two days. My wife is sick and today I had to take her to the Sister's hospital," answered Mr. Matt.

"Did you know that your house burned down at 9 o'clock this morning?"

Mr. Matt dropped his fork. It was the first word that he had received and it was a severe blow.

On leaving home Mr. Matt left a cook and a hay-baling crew behind, as he was in the midst of his hay "preserving" when Mrs. Matt took ill. According to the word brought by Mr. Stevens, the fire started from the stovepipe up stairs and the glames [flames] spread so quickly that practically nothing was saved.

"I carried no insurance," said Mr. Matt and the house and everything we had will be a total loss.

Document 51

Duncan McDonald Approved of Paxson Paintings November 20, 1914

Source: "Duncan Visits," *The Daily Missoulian*, November 20, 1914, page 10, col. 2.

Editors' note: Duncan McDonald's visits to Missoula always provided some great newspaper coverage. He was generally pleased with the historical accuracy of the new Edgar Paxson paintings in the Missoula County Courthouse.

Duncan Visits

Duncan McDonald came in from his home at Ravalli yesterday on a short business and pleasure trip. During the afternoon he called at the courthouse and spent an hour about the various offices, talking with officials, discussing the recent election and joking with the various candidates over their success or failure at the polls. Beneath Mr. McDonald's stolid exterior there lies a rich vein of humor and the boys at the courthouse are always glad to have him call and they enjoy his visits. While at the courthouse Mr. McDonald made his first inspection of the new Paxson paintings. Perhaps there is no man living who knows the Indian history of western Montana more thoroughly than does Duncan McDonald, and his criticism of the panels from their historical standpoint is worthy of careful consideration. That he was generally pleased with the paintings is no small compliment to the artist. "There is just one thing that looks strange to me in this panel," said Mr. McDonald when viewing the early transportation scene in Hell Gate canyon, showing an old-time stage coach and the Indians moving camp. "Here is depicted the travois in use by the s....s to carry luggage and children," he said. A travois is the carry-all contraption of two trailing poles from a horse's back, with a cross section of skins for luggage. "These were not common on this side of the range because they were too slow. The Indians here always had plenty of horses and because of danger of pursuit the women and children were always mounted on the best horses and the luggage was packed on other animals. Of course this is a true picture of general Indian ways but it looks rather strange to me. Perhaps this is because we did not see many of them in use here."

Document 52

Angus P. McDonald Rides Spirited Horse

November 28, 1914

Source: "Angus McDonald," *The Daily Missoulian*, November 28, 1914, page 10, col. 2.

Editors' note: Angus P. McDonald was a prominent reservation rancher and political leader on the Flathead Reservation in 1914. His experience while in Washington, D.C. for the presidential inaugural added color to the history.

Angus McDonald

For the first time in several months, Angus McDonald is a Missoula visitor. In fact, this is the first visit Angus has paid us since his return trip from Washington, when he headed the procession of the Indian warriors at Wilson's inauguration. There was one incident connected with Angus' participation in the last inaugural parade that never got into print. Good horses are always at a premium in Washington on that occasion. It takes several hundred animals to furnish proper mounts for the various visiting governors and their military staffs, not counting the various civilians of higher or lower degree, that participate in the parade. Any old kind of a plug commands a fabulous price for the day. When it came to mounting the visiting Indian chiefs and warriors, who had come down to assist in giving the proper stage setting to the great occasion, the inaugural committee had run short of horses. Angus assured the committee that he could ride anything that even looked like a horse, so they turned over to him a sleepy looking equine that had done duty on a red clay Virginia farm in his earlier years and had then gone into retirement as the property of a colored hack driver. Anyway it was a case of Hobson's choice with Angus; so donning his war bonnet and arraying his steed with the proper accoutrements befitting an Indian chief he mounted and rode to the head of the procession. To the surprise of everyone the newly found Bucephelus bestrode by the Flathead warrior capered and pranced to the delight of the crowds that lined the sidewalks. Angus himself was a little astonished at the spirit of his steed. That night, when he turned the animal over to the colored chambermaid at the local livery stable, commenting on the vivacity of his steed, the colored gentleman in removing the saddle blanket discovered the cause. "No wonder dat ole hoss showed so much spirit today. Look at dis here cuckleburr stuck to his blanket."

Document 53

Duncan McDonald Gave University Lecture

February 1915

Source: "Duncan M'Donald Will Lecture on Race," *The Daily Missoulian*, February 17, 1915, page 10, col. 5; "Duncan, All Indian, Charms His Hearers," *The Daily Missoulian*, February 23, 1915, page 10, col. 3; "Duncan McDonald Pleases Large Crowd," *The Montana Kaimin* (University of Montana, Missoula), vol. 13, no. 3, (February 26, 1915), page 6, col. 3.

Editors' note: Duncan McDonald made quite an impression with his historical lecture at the University of Montana. The full text of the speech has been published in Robert Bigart and Joseph McDonald, *Duncan McDonald: Flathead Indian Reservation Leader and Cultural Broker, 1849-1937* (Pablo, Mont.: Salish Kootenai College Press, 2016), pages 191-206.

Duncan M'Donald Will Lecture on Race
Famous Indian Leader Will Speak at University on Customs of People.

Duncan McDonald, tribal judge of the Selish nation and undoubtedly the most remarkable man the Montana Indians have produced, will lecture at the University of Montana next Monday evening on "Customs and Legends of the Indians."

No one who has ever spoken with Duncan or has heard him address a white audience will miss the lecture Monday. Those who have never heard the old judge speak, cannot afford to forego that pleasure when it is offered them.

Stored in his alert, highly-imaginative mind, Duncan carries a treasure of Indian legend, heard from his mother's lips before the white man's coming had crushed and bewildered Indian life. The wonderful myths and folk tales of his race have all been preserved in Duncan. He tells them wonderfully, when he will.

Duncan's mother told him of the coming of Lewis and Clark. Through her eyes and his own the wise, understanding man has seen the whole history of the white in Montana from that first day to this.

In love of his people and grasp of their problems, Duncan is no less wonderful than in personal accom- accomplishment [sic]. As head of the hereditary tribal court, he has had a tremendous influence over the Flatheads, and the influence has always been good and wise. Equally well does Duncan understand the problems of the state as a whole. He is well educated and has a splendid natural intelligence. Two years ago he was a candidate for the state legislature on the progressive ticket.

Duncan McDonald's lecture Monday will be a regular number of the university's course. It is quite the rarest of the whole program. Duncan talks seldom of his people and their legendary history. The few speeches he has made before white audiences have been on other subjects. His university lecture will be unprecedented, and is certain to be a treat not to be passed by.

* * * * * * * * *

Duncan, All Indian, Charms His Hearers
Indian History, Mythology and Stories by Noted Character Please

Duncan McDonald was all Indian last night. That fact added charm to his talk before a large audience in University hall. The Scotch of the man didn't show. He was, as he declared, "just a savage."

It was characteristically Indian that he should preface his talk with an introduction which seemed wandering, but which led right to where he wanted to begin. The introduction, too, served Duncan the means for a plea for his people which was eloquent and earnest. He hit straight from the shoulder. He told of the taking of the Indian lands by the whites; he told of the breaking of treaties by the whites; he told of all the wrongs his people have suffered at the hands of the paleface — and then he said: "And now they want to get our mythology. When they get that, what will we have left?"

But he was willing, he said, to give up the mythology. He said it was like the credit which the government has established for the Indian by depositing the proceeds of the sale of Indian lands. The Indian has a credit of millions of dollars, but that won't feed him and he is starving to death.

Then Duncan started with the narrative of some of the legends of The Coyote. These stories were charmingly told. Duncan, as has been said, was all Indian, and he told the stories with characteristic Indian gestures and with the intonation of the "real American."

After he had repeated the tale of the death of the dragon of the Selish at the hands of The Coyote, Duncan sang the Song of The Lark, which was sung after Coyote had slain the dragon and liberated the animals.

There was also the story of how the salmon came to be in the lower Columbia, but not in the upper streams. There was the story, too, of the killing of the Indian Lorelei maidens by Coyote.

Perhaps the most interesting of all was the story of the Quaking Asp, which is the sequel to the death of the Lorelei maidens, and the significance of the name, Missoula, which was given to this stream when the Quaking Asp was made from the shells of the Lorelei girls and which means "Sparkling Waters."

Duncan closed with a brief story of his experience as a newspaper man. This, he said, was "not myth — not a newspaper story; but a fact."

The largest audience of the winter greeted the speaker of last night and the talk was thoroughly enjoyed.

* * * * * * * * *

Duncan McDonald Pleases Large Crowd
The Indian Lecturer Tells of Indian Mythology.
Scorned Our Cult.
Injustices to the Red Race Recalled on the Lecture Platform by Talker.

The largest crowd that the assembly hall has held for some time was afforded an especial treat Monday night, in the person of Duncan MacDonald, Scotch and Indian by birth, but Indian by preference.

He is a man of wide reading and high intelligence, but his peculiarity of utterance made the attention somewhat difficult. As announced by Professor Stone, who introduced the speaker, he attempted to cover a part of the history of the redman. He told of the treaties and the taking of their lands, and of the gradual starving out of the Indians. "And all we get for it is credit," he said, "millions of dollars worth of credit. The only thing we have left is our mythology, and now you want that."

He was scornful of what he called "high culture." He told a little incident of how Dr. Elrod came out into the hills and filled his pockets with "bugs and little flowers, and every kind of thing. With all his knowledge Mr. Elrod would starve up there in the hills while I got fat, because I know which of these plants are good to eat."

But evidently the "high culture" had some appeal to him, for he spent almost a half-hour reading from Professor Stone's "Following Old Trails," the very stories that he had told to the professor "when they chatted together in front of a campfire."

A few legends, however, he told which were not in the book. He related them in true Indian fashion, and in telling them he seemed to lose all consciousness of his surroundings. These legends of The Coyote were intimately connected with the history of Missoula and the invasion of the Bitter Root valley, and were especially enjoyed.

The majority of his hearers were sorry that the only opportunity they had of seeing this man was on the platform, and everyone knew that there was a great deal more he could have told if the time had been longer and the occasion a little less formal.

Document 54

Indian Woman Died of Burns

March 15, 1915

Source: "Firewater Death for Aged Indian," *The Daily Missoulian*, March 15, 1915, page 3, col. 1-2.

Editors' note: The profit motive of white men and the thirst of an Indian woman had a tragic consequence.

Firewater Death for Aged Indian
Mrs. Antoine Julian Dies of Burns Sustained
After Consumption of White Man's Gift.

Dixon, March 14. — (Special.) — Bent and wrinkled with age, with one hand and part of one side of her body burned to a crisp, an aged Kootenai woman was last Tuesday brought by her husband to the Flathead emergency hospital for treatment. Suffering indescribable agony from the time of the injury, she passed away yesterday afternoon, her suffering ended, her scarred form waiting for Mother Earth to hide it.

Mrs. Antoine Julian was a full-blood Kootenai Indian woman and the wife of Antoine Julian, one of the fine old type of Indian men. Antoine, being thrifty, but with nothing to do, pitched his tepee near Somers at the head of Flathead lake, where he could fish and his wife tan buckskin and make moccasins and gloves for sale.

Julian left his tepee and wife early in the week to spend the afternoon fishing. While he was gone, so told Mrs. Julian to the agency officials, there came to the tepee a wh[i]te man with whisky. Two drinks she said she took from his flask, and then remembered no more until she awakened, burned and scarred from the tepee fire into which she fell and where she was found by one of the Indian men returning home.

Base might have been the motives of the white man who would visit the tepee of an Indian and give to his wife the accursed firewater. The government officials should spare no pains in trying to ascertain the guilty party, and there is no sentence too severe to be meted out to the villainous culprit.

Firewater has certainly left its mark upon the small band of Kootenais who are allotted on the north end of the reservation. It is no uncommon sight to see Indians with broken legs, arms, scarred faces, and in some cases eyes gone. This is the tribute the white man's firewater exacts from its Indian victims. One who is forced to witness the frequent scenes can readily understand why there is a wave of prohibition sweeping over the United States.

Document 55

Duncan McDonald Tells of Indian-White History March 6, 1915

Source: "Duncan McDonald Tells of Early Days in the Northwest," *The Kootenai Times* (Libby, Mont.), March 17, 1915, page 1, col. 3-5, and page 3, col. 5.

Editors' note: Duncan McDonald complained about the problems he encountered in trying to correct a popular account of an Indian-white conflict on the Thompson River in 1867.

Duncan McDonald Tells of Early Days in the Northwest

Ravalli, Mont., Mar. 6, 1915.

Kootenai Times:

Sirs — You have requested me to say something about the old times. It was with pleasure that I sat down and read the articles in the Times written by the old-timers. Such men as Cowley, Elliott of Walla Walla, Meyers, Campbell, D. McLaughlin — I was well acquainted with them all. Also Joe Herren.

Bear in mind I am of part Indian blood, born six and one-half miles north of St. Ignatius, Mont., called Flathead post, as we used to call it, by the Hudsons Bay company. I was born in 1849.

My father, Angus McDonald, is the gentleman that Mr. Campbell mentions in his articles to your paper. He came from Scotland, and landed in North America, at York Factory, in 1838. I am here now only a few miles from the place where I was born in 1849, 66 years ago.

I was recently invited to talk by the professors of the University of Montana regarding the history of the Indians, their myths, legends, way of living, customs, etc., which I did on February 22. I had never thought of being in such a position, standing before a full house of highly cultivated people, any more than I had thought of flying. I did talk for half an hour, but there were many experiences and facts which I could not tell for lack of time.

It puzzles me, though, how I could be believed by the whites, even when I tell the truth, against a bad white man. If you have a well balanced mind you will recognize the fact that there are black sheep in both races, white or red men. I must say, in the name of justice and humanity, don't put on the red man all the black spots, and the bright ones on the white man. I am burdened quite a lot by writers today, and will say from actual experience that they would not believe if I did write, as I have tried it before.

For instance, in reference to an Indian war at Thompson's river, near Thompson Falls, in May, 1867. I saw a long write-up in the Anaconda Standard several years ago how that great man by the name of Panama Pat stood his ground against several hundred Indians, and how he escaped. I wrote an article regarding this trouble to the Standard. I was telling the truth but for reasons unknown to me they never printed the article or my answer to Panama Pat. A man by the name of Miky Hunt was killed by an Indian named Madace, and an Indian by the name of Chiri-ax-mi was killed by this great "hero" and defender of Christianity and civilization.

I remember well the time of the trouble, because we arrived at the battle ground, as he calls it. My father, Angus McDonald, of the Hudson Bay company, Rev. Father Van Gorp, Rev. Cataldo, myself and number of whites stood and looked at the dying Indian with nine holes in him. Rev. Van Gorp went to the body of Hunt, about one-half mile from the battle ground, and buried him. Rev. Cataldo attended to the dying Indian, and my father, stopped a row among the whites, as there was quite a number coming from California into Montana, as placer mining was booming.

We were coming from Fort Colville and the two priests were with us. As soon as we heard of the trouble the travelers had a council of war, and decided upon Angus McDonald for a leader of the party coming in from the west, as he was considered one of the most influential men among the Indians west of the Rocky mountains.

Our party was indeed angry against the whites who started the killing, as they were trading whisky to the natives. Among the leaders was Panama Pat. This man had such a fine story, and so aggravating to parties who knew about the circumstances, that I started to write against him, but my article was denied print. Rev. Cataldo is alive and I think he is in Lapwai, Ida. He can tell about it, as he was there on the battle ground.

I sincerely wish to let the public know that dead Indians are not the only good ones, as General Sherman said. Now, let us see. I will write a little about him: Mrs. Sherman received a letter from a woman who was in distress and wanted help, saying that her husband was dead, but she could not bury him because she had nothing. She begged for help. Mrs. Sherman went to her, taking along a young officer. They found the woman, a most pitiful looking creature, and her dead husband was in a box coffin. Mrs. Sherman gave her $20 in cash and bade her good-bye.

After leaving, Mrs. Sherman discovered that she had left one of her gloves in the room occupied by the dead man and sent the young officer back for it. He went in without knocking and to his surprise the dead man was sitting up in the coffin counting the money that Mrs. Sherman had given to the distressed widow. I would like to ask General Sherman if that was a dead Indian.

I appreciate your kindness in opening your columns for me to write, but I am sorry to have to decline, for the simple reason that the public will ask who the writer is, and when they find out that I am an Indian my articles would be called fakes. Siding, of course, with the red man, I would be termed a liar, as not one of them is supposed to be good while alive. We are defenseless and cannot be believed, as we are savages[.] I feel helpless to try and tell some true facts which are unknown to the public. What is the use of writing?

I belonged to the Hudson Bay company, in charge of Flathead post from 1867 to 1872, when it was abandoned, the United States having bought their rights in the latter year. I was the last in charge. Angus M. Donald resigned. He thought this country good enough for him.

I don't think Rev. Cataldo will refuse to tell what he knows of the Indian war at Thompson. This I am sure, will clear up the smoke hanging over the Indian.

You mention that the three men killed on Fisher river were killed by Flatheads. No, that is a mistake; they were Kootenais, five in number, and two of them did the killing. Andre, one of them, was hung by Sheriff Huston. The Ramsdell posse hung the other. These were the leaders. The other three were turned loose, because, as I understand, they were young lads.

Thanking you again for past favors, I remain,

Yours truly,

Duncan McDonald.

PS — Remember, my father was a white man and I have a right to defend him as much as my grandmother, an Indian of America. I stand between them for justice and humanity. My father used to say that we have a bible and churches to teach Christianity. The red man is an ignorant savage. True enough, he never was a savage until he was made one by the bible man. Look at that fellow killing an Indian at Bonners Ferry, with a big family, just for luck. Panama Pat's son-in-law had a pull in politics. No doubt this has a weight with the Anaconda Standard.

Document 56

Tribal Elders to Attend Missoula Stampede

June 30, 1915

Source: "Patriarchs Coming Full of Old Memories," *The Daily Missoulian*, June 30, 1915, page 3, col. 4.

Editors' note: This article gave a few tidbits of information about Flathead Reservation tribal elders in 1915.

Patriarchs Coming Full of Old Memories

O'Brien Signs Aged Indians to Be True Part of Days They Portray.

Searching for something new is the plan of life for most of us, but P. J. O'Brien of Montana has just finished a search for something old — and he found it. The motive was the big parade of the Stampede and the cause was the float committee of the Knights of Columbus which has planned a two-float display, something good, something timely and yet historical. One float is to represent the Indian as he was in the beginning of things when the white man knew him first; the second float to be typical of the present state of civilization.

So Mr. O'Brien went to the Flathead for material and returned with the job well done, for he found and received the promises of men so old that they know not their own ages, that they will be in Missoula for the celebration and will ride on the float of a perished generation.

Mr. O'Brien was not looking for the stripling of eighty or the youth of ninety, but the original of the old man with snow white hair and beard, who wept because his grandfather had spanked him, and among the old men, the wrinkled great-great grandfathers of the young bucks of the Flatheads, but of the worn buffalo tepees of a forgotten race, those who can count one hundred years at least and forget the balance above the century mark will come to Missoula, journeying back to the entrance to the Bitter Root valley, the old home of a great and good tribe.

The most honored of all these centenarians is Francois Saxa, who remembered a hundred springs when the bitter root was good to dig, and a hundred falls when the fat deer were good hunting, and then he counted no more, so no one knows just how old he really is. But he does know that he is a direct descendant of the great Iroquois of the Five Nations and that his tribe knew the meaning of Christianity, and it was he who, after three expeditions of Flatheads had failed in their trips east to get the "Black Robes" to come to the Flathead tribe to teach them Christianity, went on the fourth trip to St. Louis and persuaded the priests that they must come to the Bitter Root valley. It was in St. Louis that he was baptized into the Christian religion, and it was he who guided Father DeSmet over the long and dangerous trip westward to the shelter of Mount St. Mary's in the Bitter Root valley. So as a venerable monument of human accomplishment and longevity Francois Saxa is deserving of all the homage Missoula can give.

There is Louis van Denburg, too, who was in his prime when he had seen twelve hundred moons grow big and wane. He was one of those who received Father DeSmet in 1841 in the Bitter Root and who learned and profited by the ways of the white teacher, and was also a friend of Father Ravalli's. Louis was in some doubt whether the levity of the Stampede was appropriate to one of his years and descretion, but Mrs. Siawashie, his daughter, urged him, for she is proud of the generation her father stands for and would have the world, or that part which attends the Stampede, see the old warriors and remember that there is one of the great Flatheads of all times.

Big Sam, a cutup of ninety-five years, will be in the parade and he, too, was one of the reception committee which greeted Father DeSmet, as did Big Hawk, a mere infant in arms of eighty odd years, who will surely be on the float.

Chief Charlos, son of the famous chief of the Flathead tribe, the greatest undoubtedly of all western chieftains, will come to Missoula for the celebrations and will camp Thursday west of the city. On Sunday the old men will come and, with due respect for their welfare on the day of the parade, will appear as planned above. Any inclemency of weather which would be detrimental to the health of these old chiefs would be cause for their non-appearance, but it is safe to say that they will strain a point so that the public will not be disappointed.

Document 57

Boy Killed Girl by Accident

July 8, 1915

Source: "Six-Year-Old Boy Kills a Girl by Accident," *The Daily Missoulian*, July 8, 1915, page 4, col. 4.

Editors' note: The tragic shooting of a neighbor girl by the six year old son of John Matt marked a sad day for two families.

Six-Year-Old Boy Kills a Girl by Accident

Youngest Son of Mr. and Mrs. John Matt of Arlee Plays with a Rifle.

A six-year-old boy, a 22-calibre rifle and little playmate standing near, made the elements of a sad tragedy at the home of Mr. and Mrs. John Matt at Arlee Tuesday afternoon. The Matt family had been in Missoula to attend the Stampede, leaving a man in charge of their place at Arlee. The man had left a loaded gun on the table in the living room of the house. When the family entered the room, the little boy, youngest son of Mr. and Mrs. Matt, picked up the gun and with childish interest in its workings, pulled the trigger. A little girl, daughter of neighboring homesteaders, who had been living at the Matt home during the winter and attending the Catholic Sisters' school at St. Ignatius, happened to be in the way of the shot, which pierced her right lung.

Dr. T. A. Fitzgerald was summoned at once from Missoula. When he left the Matt home at 1 o'clock yesterday morning the little girl was still alive, but a telephone message about noon told of her death. An order for a casket was received in Missoula at the same time, but no notice of funeral arrangements was given.

Document 58

Reservation Indians Visit Missoula

August 22, 1915

Source: "The Red in Town a Study for Tourist," *The Daily Missoulian*, August 22, 1915, page 2, col. 1-2.

Editors' note: The newspaper reporter described the Indians he saw in town. This was the view by an outsider observing Indian visitors to Missoula. The writer had not talked to any of the Indians to get their viewpoint.

The Red in Town a Study for Tourist
Odds Are the Tenderfoot Meets Romantic Disappointment Here.

The easterner in Missoula on his first western trip would probably see his first Indian. At least, he would see an Indian, and he would probably know no more about the red man's habits and ways than he did about those of the natives of Ting-a-Ling. Leaving probabilities aside, he would be sure to learn things about the Indian's way of living and of spending his time. Returning to suppositions, he would probably be disillusioned.

The fact is, Indians of western Montana do not spend their time in hunting the buffalo, in trapping the muskrat, in making paints for the cuticle and arrows for the bow, or, if "civilized," in tilling large tracts of maise and wheat. Observation of the red man and his s.... in Missoula alone would hint to the easterner that such was not the case, and a questioning of some of the "old timers" would confirm the inkling.

The first impression the tenderfoot would receive would be that Indians spend most of their time in the general practices of strolling on the hot sidewalks and standing on the street corners. This would be all that would impress him unless he were interested and observed considerably farther. Then he would see that the red man spent a considerable part of his time in the investigation of alleys for bright objects and a deal of it striking friends for loans and that he exercised even more diligence in the seeking of the coveted "firewater."

The means of entry to "town," for the Indian are two. He either comes in on the Northern Pacific train No. 42, or he "rides" in on his pony. When accompanied by his s.... he employs the same means, or drives a spring wagon. Rarely does he bring the younger members of his family, unless it be for a large celebration.

Always the Same.

Arrived, the Indian will take his pony or wagon to the back of the sign board on the Higgins lot and there fasten it, or, if he came by rail, he wanders into the station and asks they ticket agent when the next train returns. Both acts are well nigh unvaried in their regularity, although the informant may have asked the agent the same question a score or more times before, or the Higgins lot may be no more convenient than any other vacant lot in the city.

An Indian's sojourn in "town" usually lasts from one to three days. Sometimes he will bring his wigwam and pitch it on the outskirts of Missoula. Otherwise he spends the night at some cheap lodging house. Sometimes he will come on business, this meaning that he has berries to sell or elk horns to vend. Usually he comes to borrow some ready cash, to have a quiet and good time, with a half a pint or more of whiskey, or just to enjoy the sights of the main streets.

The old appeal of the trinket and colored clothing has not been lost. An Indian will sell almost anything he has for the wherewithal to enter the five and ten cent stores for purchases. He does not need this wherewithal to enter, however, for he will walk in and inspect the attractions if he can't buy.

An Indian will ordinarily average a comfortable dozen of friends and acquaintances, in spite of his reticence and lack of volubility. These he will visit in regular order and approach for money. A clever enough story will elicit the desired simoleon or two, although the lender may never hope of seeing it or its equivalent again. There are in Missoula persons who are regular patrons of their particular Indian proteges.

Alleys Well Tramped.

Few alleys and byways go untoured during the week. Articles of food which have not lost their savory smell or inviting appearance are removed from their receptacles. Shoes, hats and other clothing left there may some day be found by their former owners decorating the pedal extremities of an old s... or the capital extremity of a handsome buck.

In leaving the city by wagon or pony, the Indian will often ride the greater part of the night and may be seen plodding along at a late hour, straight and silent on the back of a horse, or leaning forward immutably on the wagon seat, with the faithful s.... at his side.

In departing by the train, Indians often sit for hours in the station waiting for the next one home. At least one train a day must be counted on as sure to be missed by the Indians. Many of the red people come down to the station an hour after the last train has left, or in spite of their patience in the depot will wander off down the street in time to return with it gone.

One old woman is known at the Northern Pacific station to come into town regularly and to appear at the waiting room in a day or so in the best of spirits, speaking literally. She tells everyone she meets: "I going to Arlee. I going to Arlee."

Of course, not all Indians are seemingly so content with a life of nothingness and there are a great many of the race who have attained to some degree of education and prosperity. When these come to Missoula they are greeted as any other newcomer and transact as much actual business. The number is small, however, and our easterner would probably go back without meeting many of this type.

Document 59

White Men Steal Indian's Money

October 2, 1915

Source: "Meet Indian; Take Dollar; Plead Guilty," *The Daily Missoulian*, October 2, 1915, page 1, col. 6, and page 5, col. 1.

Editors' note: This case of three white men stealing Peter Vanderburg's money made it into the newspaper. Fortunately, the thieves were caught.

Meet Indian; Take Dollar; Plead Guilty
Three Wise Men Have Clever Game, but Pull It Off in Front of Wrong Audience.

Will the first-year class in crime please come to order?

Young gentlemen:

> When robbing an Indian never, never use a weapon. You can take the beads from the red man's moccasins, yea, even the Bull Durham from his shirt, simply by assuming the crafty attitude of the fly-cop. For deep in the aboriginal consciousness is the illusion that every white man is a detective. Every time an Indian sees a white collar he expects to be tapped about the hip pockets; habit forces him to submit to explorations for red-eye by every curious white man.

All save Freshmen in Highway Robbery possess that precious bit of information. James Walker, Harry Larson and W. T. Hayes had known it for years, of course, for they were Affable Fair Visitors, and Affable Fair Visitors are old-timers in the graduate school.

When the three saw Peter Vanderberg, an Indian, standing in a dark street Thursday night they wept for joy. There were but two men in sight and they were deep in conversation. All day had the three labored in barren fields. Fat pocketbooks had eluded them, and the natives to whom they whispered hot tips on the races had scorned them. It was night, and none of them had dined or lunched or even breakfasted.

Assuming the dark dignity of detectives they advanced upon Peter.

"I am a policeman," said Hayes. "I saw you buy a bottle of the old stuff from those two guys down the street just now. Come clean or I'll pinch you."

Peter sighed, vastly, with the patient sorrow of generations and extended his arms to permit a search.

Hayes patted the Indian's hip pocket, felt his shirt bosom and then pulled a pocketbook from his coat. In it were a few dollar bills. The detective riffled through them, palmed one, and slipped the others back.

"All right," he said to Peter, "you can go."

The three were just leaving a restaurant half an hour later when Larson nudged Hayes.

"Here come the guys you said the Indian bought whiskey from," he said. "Duck!"

But he was too late.

"My Indian friend down the street tells me you are detectives," said one of the strangers.

"If we are," said Hayes, "it's lucky for you we didn't find any . . . ."

"Oh, that's all right," said the stranger. "I just wanted to meet you, that's all. My name's Glenn. I'm a special officer in the Indian service. And my friend here is called Held. He's a policeman."

Yesterday afternoon the three appeared before the Justice of the Peace Gagnon and were bound over to the district court for trial after they had admitted taking Peter Vanderberg's money. They claim Peter gave them the money and asked them to buy whiskey with it.

Document 60

Indian Exhibits at Western Montana Fair

October 3, 1915

Source: "With But Five Years of Experience Indian Farmers Make Great Exhibit," *The Daily Missoulian*, October 3, 1915, page 2, col. 1-3.

Editors' note: Many tribal members had started farms long before the reservation was opened in 1910. The fair exhibits showed how successful tribal farmers were in 1915. Some typesetting errors have been corrected in this text.

With But Five Years of Experience Indian Farmers Make Great Exhibit

Among the many splendid exhibits at the Western Montana fair was the Indian exhibit from the Flathead reservation. Since remote days, when he made his living solely by hunting game of the forest and the fish of the stream, and digging and drying the roots and berries of the prairies and mountains, there has been a wonderful change in the life and mode of living of the Flatheads.

In the Indian exhibit at the fairgrounds can be seen the result of the civilization the white man has brought, and the efforts of the employes of the government officials, whose duty it has been to interest the red man in the white man's way of the tilling of the soil for the sustenance of life.

Many of the Indians from the reservation came to the fair to see how their exhibits compared with those of their fellows and with the exhibits made by the citizens of western Montana. Not a little credit is due the Indians of the Flathead, especially when it is remembered that is only five years since the Flathead reservation was opened to settlement.

Good Grain.

Fine sheaves of wheat, oats, barley, flax, millet, samples of forage crops and other farm products compare favorably with those exhibited by the white man. The fruit display is very creditable, striking proof of what the Flathead country will produce along these lines. One side of the booth is given up to grains, forage crops, fruit, corn and vegetables, while the other side has exhibits of old Indian handicraft, such as tanned buckskin, bead work, furs and fancy work.

Fresh Strawberries.

Particularly interesting was an exhibit of strawberries, freshly picked, also a strawberry plant in a box which has on it blossoms, green and ripe fruits.

Another novelty was an egg plant recently transplanted from the garden, which was heavily laden with fruit.

Indian buckskin, bead work and novelties was exhibited by Mrs. Cecille Tellier of St. Ignatius, Mrs. Mary Finley of St. Ignatius, Patrick Bigbear and Mary Onickcanilseet of Elmo, and Oyama of Ronan exhibited bead work and buckskin articles. Mrs. Cecile Tellier and Oyama of Ronan, dressed in their Indian costumes, were present in the Indian booth each day of the fair and cheerfully explained to interested spectators the method of making and the use of many of the articles exhibited.

Among other contributors of products for the Indian exhibit were James Hawk of Dixon, a full-blood Indian, who had a good exhibit for which the judges gave several prizes. A large pumpkin and Soudan grass nine feet tall attracted a great deal of attention. Joseph Wilson, better known as "Spokane Joe," a full-blood Indian from Camas Hot Springs, secured the prize for the best general display of farm products. Mrs. Maude Larrivee of Dayton, had a very creditable exhibit of grain, corn, vegetables and canned fruits.

Charles Allard of Polson, had perhaps the largest and best exhibit of grain and vegetables, showing about 30 different [v]arieties. He received several prizes, among them first first [sic] on English garden oats. Alice Dupuis and Mrs. Cora Harwick of Polson had a fine display of canned fruits. Mrs. Therese Felsman of St. Ignatius also had a splendid exhibit of canned fruits and farm products and succeeded in carrying off first prize on canned fruits.

Mary Cramer of Polson displayed several varieties of fruit and received several prizes. Joseph Allard of St. Ignatius exhibited apples and vegetables. Mrs. Alma Glover of Polson had a fine display of grains and vegetables.

Felix Barnaby of Arlee, exhibited fine bead work, grains and grasses. Martin Charlot and John Charley, full-blood Indians of the Jocko valley, also had good exhibits of grains and grasses.

Pictures Tell More.

Two large pictures in the exhibit gave an excellent idea of the grain and hay fields of the reservation. One showed a grain field just south of Polson covering an area og [of] 1,200 acres every rod of which was covered with grain in the sheaf. Another picture showed a hay field on the William Irvine ranch west of Polson. This field produced timothy and red top hay which yielded four and one-half tons to the acre.

Every nook and corner of the Flathead reservation was well represented by sheaves of grain, fruit and vegetables and it was the opinion of all of the many visitors that the soil and climate of the Flathead must be well adapted for the culture of these products.

Governor Sees It.

Superintendent Fred Morgan of the Flatheads, was in charge of preparing the exhibit and was superintendent of the department at the fair. He was ably assisted by Karl Knudsen, forest guard in the Indian service, stationed at Polson. Mr. Knudsen has been especially active and had the exhibit well in hand here. Secretary Lawrence of the fair worked, in conjunction with Major Morgan, in interesting the Indians and the government officials are much pleased with the success that has been made at both the state and local fairs.

Among the distinguished visitors who inspected the Indian exhibit were Governor S. V. Stewart; Seth Maxwell commissioner of agriculture and publicity; Secretary Snelson of the Montana State Fair association; Senator H. L. Myers. C. B. de Fine Olivarnes who is connected with the department of justice of Denmark, and who stopped here one day on his trip across the country, was an interested visitor in the Indian department. Of the whole fair with which he was much pleased he said that he thought the Indian department the most unique.

The Awards.

Those receiving prizes, were as follows:

Best display of fruit on plates, five specimens to the plate — Alice Dupuis, first; Joseph Allard, second; Cora Hardwick, third.

Best exhibit of vegetables and roots by male Indian — Joseph Wilson, first; Joe Irvine, second; Henry Minesinger third.

Best exhibit of grains in sheaf and threshed by male Indian — Charles Allard, first; Mrs. Maude Larrivee, second; James Hawk, third.

Best exhibit of hand work in manual art by male Indian — Irving Allard first.

Best exhibit of farm products by female Indian — Mrs. Charles Allard, first; Mrs. Maude Larrivee, second; Mrs. Henry Felsman, third.

Best exhibit of bead work, moccasins, by female Indian — Mrs. Cecile Tellier, first; Isabella Pierre, second; Mrs. Modiste Finley, third.

Best exhibit of bead work other than moccasins, by female Indian — Mrs. Cecille Tellier, first; Mrs. Modiste Finley, second; Maggie Adams, third.

Best exhibit of fancy work other than bead work, including baskets, sewing, knitting, embroidery and art work of any description, by female Indian — Emma Marion, first; Mrs. [Theirs?] Lucier, second; Mrs. I. J. Delaware, third.

Best display of canned fruit — Mrs. Henry Felsman, first; Mrs. Agnes Dupuis, second; Mrs. Maude Larrivee third.

Best Indian costume, female — Mrs. Cecille Tellier, first; Mrs. Modiste Finley, second.

Best Indian costume, male — Modiste Finley, first; Cecille Tellier, second.

Special for best exhibits of farm products by full-blood Indians — James Hawk, first; Joseph Wilson, second.

Special Prizes.

Superintendent Fred C. Morgan's special prize for best sheaf of oats by a full-blood Indian, awarded to Patrick Bigbear.

Miss Mary Cramer of Polson, received first prize and also a special prize for Bradshaw plums.

Awards of merit were made to the following Indians who exhibited products:

Dayton district — Chief Koostahtah, John Couture.

Polson district — Olive Dupuis, Margaret Morin.

From Jocko district — Martin Charlo, Moses Bigsam, Joseph Kyser, John Charley, Louie Pierre, Felix Barnaby, Louie Cullooyah, Pete Matt.

Camas Prairie district — Pierre Paul, Curley, Dominick Rattlesnake, Andrew Tesco, Jack Ballantine.

Ronan — Lucy Oyama Finley, Fred Houle, Antoine Morigeau, John Valley, Antoine Finley, Malcolm McLeod.

St. Ignatius — August Ducharme, Sam Finley, Theodore Tellier, Lena Palin Hodgson, George McDonnell, Napoleon Pluffe, Marion Deschamp, August Ashley.

Ravalli — Maggie Adams and John Morigeau.

Document 61

Tribal Members Haul Liquor to Reservation

October 1915

Source: "Bootleggers Driven Over Steep Grade," *The Daily Missoulian*, October 6, 1915, page 1, col. 2; "Joe Pablo Caught with Wet Goods Near Ronan," *The Daily Missoulian*, October 7, 1915, page 4, col. 3; "Pablo Says Blame Was Another Red's," *The Daily Missoulian*, April 14, 1916, page 2, col. 2.

Editors' note: Tribal members showed their entrepreneurial skills obtaining liquor to sell on the reservation. The risks were high, but the payoff must have been generous.

Bootleggers Driven Over Steep Grade
Louie Pablo Tries to Smuggle Liquor on Reservation in Automobile and Is Chased Into Ditch.

Monday Louie and Joe Pablo, Indian wards of the United States, conceived the magnificient [sic] idea of beating the reservation whiskey embargo with automobiles.

Last night Louie Pablo's car lay at the foot of Evaro hill, wrecked by a wild tumble from the high mountain road along which bootleggers and Indian agents raced madly Monday afternoon and Joe Pablo's machine was being hotly chased across the reservation by special officers. Louie and five companions had been placed in custody; their booze soaked into the side of Evaro mountain, and the machine had been libelled by the United States.

Glenn Outwits Indians.

Special Agent Glenn broke up the clever scheme of the reds. He heard Monday morning that Pablo and his friends were going to take an automobile load of whiskey to the reservation and when they started was close behind in a machine of his own.

The two automobiles raced madly for the reservation. Pablo's big car made remarkable time, but when the road left the valley and started its climb over the long mountain, speed wasn't so easy. Yet Pablo drove hard, rounding the dangerous curve on the grade without slackening speed. Near the middle of the grade he hit a ditch. The car swerved, left the road and rolled down the hill.

The machine twice turned completely over before it stopped, but six passengers miraculously escaped without a bruise.

To Prosecute Pablo.

Among the wreckage Officer Glenn found evidence that the bootleggers had left Missoula with a full load of whiskey, wine and beer. The uninjured booze was seized, and the riders brought to Missoula.

Louie Pablo is the only one to be prosecuted. His companions will be held as witnesses against him. They are Charles Couture, Charles Hunter, Lawrence Prichett, Miss Frances Rochell and F. W. Balkow, who was driving the machine. Couture and Hunter are Indians; the others, whites. Couture was at liberty under a suspended sentence for bootlegging. He is to be sentenced for an earlier offense on January 1, 1916.

Balkow, the chauffeur, was released yesterday under $200 bonds to appear as a witness when the case against Pablo is called.

After Second Car.

While Glenn was chasing Louie, Deputy Special Officer Ramsay and Andrew Gilbeau, of the Indian police, were hot on Joe Pablo's trail. Joe had reached the reservation and was sighted by the officers near St. Ignatius.

****

Joe Pablo Caught with Wet Goods Near Ronan

Indian Officers Capture Second of Automobile Whiskey Smugglers.

Joe Pablo, the second of the Indian family to fail at smuggling whiskey to the reservation in automobiles, was caught near Ronan with a cargo of booze yesterday by Deputy Special Officer Ramsay and Joe Gilbeau of the Indian police.

Late yesterday afternoon he was brought before Judge George Bourquin of the federal court, a suspended sentence for bootlegging was executed and he was taken to the county jail to begin the service of a five-months' term, at the end of which he is to pay a fine of $100.

The pursuit of Pablo began Monday. Special Officer Glenn got word of the proposed automobile raid by Louie and Joe Pablo. He chased Louie with a machine and drove thim [sic] into a ditch on the Evaro grade. Ramsay and Gilbeau were set on Joe's trail, but the Indian eluded them and struck across country in his car, a new, powerful Hudson "Six." Not until yesterday was he caught.

Frank Woody, assistant district attorney, appeared before Judge Bourquin and asked that the suspension of sentence against Joe Pablo for a previous offense be revoked. The judge granted the motion and sentenced Pablo to serve five months in the Missoula county jail and pay a fine of $100.

* * * * * * * * *

Pablo Says Blame Was Another Red's
Indian Charged with Bootlegging Seeks to Shift Responsibility.

Either Lawrence Pritchett or Joe Pablo, both of whom are Indians, salted the whole southeast corner of the Flathead reservation with whiskey last fall.

The United States government declares that Pablo did it; Pablo insists that Pritchett is the man; both produced evidence which showed that during the months of September and October, 1915, apparently unlimited quantities of whiskey could be taken from haystacks and thickets all about Arlee.

The prosecution was based on three charges: That on September 5 Joe Pablo gave Lawrence Pritchett, Henry Matt and Frank Kirkpatrick three bottles of whiskey from a cache under a haystack at the home of his grandmother-in-law, Blue-Eyed Mary, near Arlee, that on September 6 he gave Lawrence Pritchett several drinks from a quart bottle of whiskey at the Indian hand-game near Arlee; that on October 5 he brought from Missoula by automobile a number of bottles of whiskey.

Pablo was arrested on October 6 after he had been chased across country by Andrew Gibeau, an Indian officer, and Special Officer I. W. Ramsey. Gibeau testified that he followed Pablo's automobile in which were Pablo, his wife and children and Phil Howell, a chauffeur, from St. Ignatius toward Ronan and, suspecting they had liquor with them, tried to make them halt. Instead of stopping Gibeau said, Pablo turned his car from the road and fled across the prairie toward the timber. Gibeau fired at Pablo, but failed to stop him. Gibeau drove to Ronan, where he picked up Ramsey, and then followed Pablo's trail. Along the road, both officers said, broken bottles bearing whiskey labels were found. Eventually Pablo was arrested in Ronan and brought to Missoula. He was then under suspended sentence for bootlegging.

Pablo, on the stand, denied the government's charges. He admitted drinking whiskey on the earlier occasions, but blamed Pritchett for producing it. When he was chased in October, he said, he had no whiskey at all. He turned from the road, he said, because of Gibeau's shots, which he did not understand.

The case went to the jury at 4 o'clock. A sealed verdict will be returned to be opened in court this morning.

Document 62

Antoine Moiese and Princess Redfeather Complain October 12, 1915

Source: Fred C. Morgan to Commissioner of Indian Affairs, October 12, 1915, from file 97,278/1915 Flathead 155, Central Classified Files, RG 75, National Archives, Washington, D.C.

Editors' note: Antoine Moiese, accompanied by Princess Redfeather, complained about Agent Fred Morgan's effort to control Moiese's allotment and the income from it. Princess Redfeather was an Oklahoma Indian newly arrived on Flathead. She and Moiese left no papers giving their side of the story. See Inspector C. M. Knight's June 1916 report on Redfeather for a much more detailed, but still one sided, description of her activities on the Flathead Reservation.

Department of the Interior
United States Indian Service
Flathead Agency, Dixon, Montana.
October 12, 1915.

The Honorable,
Commissioner of Indian Affairs,
Washington, D.C.
Sir:

Replying to Office letter of September 13, 1915, in which it is stated, "Chief Antoine Moease and Princess Red Feather, Flathead Indians, now in this city, have complained that their allotments are leased; that they do not know the amount of rental to be paid and that they can get only a few dollars from the Superintendent. Please report the facts in the case." I have the honor to state that Antoine Moiese is Flathead allottee No. 1573. On January 25, 1910, lease of his allotment for five years, from January 1, 1910, to December 31, 1914, was approved by your Office, the consideration being improvements, and $50 cash per annum, payable semi-annually. This lease was to Logan and Worth. Moiese well knew the terms of the lease, and the lease was signed by him. On January 14, 1911, this lease was cancelled, and a new lease, in favor of Simon R. Logan, covering the unexpired term, for the same consideration, was approved by your Office on January 14, 1911. Moiese was fully aware of the transaction, and signed the substitute lease. Three payments of $25 each were made on the lease by Logan and Worth, and these amounts were promptly paid to Moiese. On the lease to Simon R. Logan six payments of $25 each were made, and these amounts were promptly paid to him. On February 5, 1913, the lease to Simon R. Logan was cancelled, and a new lease, to William E. Long, for the unexpired term, at the same consideration, was approved on February 5, 1913. On this new lease four payments of $25 each were made, and these amounts were promptly paid to Moiese. This lease expired December 31, 1914, since when the land has been idle, as Moiese refused a good offer to re-lease, and will not work the land himself.

As to "Princess" Red Feather, I have to advise that she is not a Flathead Indian, does not belong here, and has no land here. She first appeared here about a year and a half ago, since which time she has been obtaining money from Indians on various pretexts, has held meetings with a few Indians at different points, there nearly always being more or less liquor at these gatherings. She was arrested by Special Officers Glenn and Ramsey on a charge of introducing and giving liquor to Indians, and was convicted before the United States Court on eight counts. Regarding this woman I respectfully refer your Office to my reports of April 12, 1915; March 12, 1915; March 13, 1915; February 15, 1915; December 11, 1914; and October 11, 1915, L-C 97278-15, RJH.

Respectfully,
Fred C. Morgan
Superintendent.

Document 63

Duncan McDonald Complains About White Hypocrisy November 1, 1915

Source: "White Man's Ways Puzzle Indian Leader," *The Daily Missoulian*, November 1, 1915, page 2, col. 1-2.

Editors' note: Duncan McDonald complained about the dishonesty of cultured white people. The exacting honesty of the Salish Indians before the white settlers arrived had been testified to by the early white fur traders in the area. McDonald also commented on the Indian place names for features in western Montana.

White Man's Ways Puzzle Indian Leader
Duncan McDonald Compares Present Day With That of His Youth.

The white man's dishonesties and evasions and lack of faith are bitterly criticized by Duncan McDonald, hereditary judge of the Selish tribes in an interview quoted by the Kalispell Interlake. The interview shows the Indian point of view in an unusual way; cites some interesting Indian customs and reveals some of the forgotten Indian place names, interest in which has been revived by the newly organized Montana Geographic society. Duncan McDonald is quoted as follows:

"Sixty-seven years ago I was born at Post creek, and my father was a Scotchman and was in charge of the Hudson Bay trading station at that time. My mother was a full blooded Iroquois Indian, a number of this tribe following the traders from the east and locating here.

When Stealing Was Unknown.

"I have asked a great many wise men what culture is, but have been unable to receive a reply that will satisfy. Of course I am a savage, and may not be able to understand, but I can remember in my boyhood days that stealing was unknown. When the Indians were traveling the chief led the procession, his family following, and often the line of march extended several miles. If anything was lost it was picked up by the first one who saw it and on the first day of camp it was handed to the chief, and there was a man in the party who acted as a sort of auctioneer or crier, called out the name of the article that was lost, and whoever owned it recovered it. No reward was offered for the return of any article. When the first white men came to the Indians they were required to do as the Indians did, and we had no stealing but soon the missionary, the Bible, the whiskey and the dollar, and the scapegoat came, a great many of these men had escaped the clutches of the law in the east, came among us. It was not a good thing for the Indian. He was quick to pattern after the white men in his devilment, and thieving soon became a custom with some of our Indians. I can well remember when we didn't know what is was to watch anything. When the first miner came the latch string was hanging on the outside. Anyone was welcome to help himself and generally one found a pot of beans ready for the hungry traveler. He would eat the beans, and while he was resting would cook another pot of beans and leave them for the miner when he returned, but when more cultured men came it was necessary to lock the cabin with heavy padlocks, and then Yale keys, and have a secret cache in the woods. I and other savages were puzzled. Was it culture that caused the suspicion? Why, there isn't two men in the lobby that would think of sleeping together. They would each be afraid of the other. Afraid that he would steal his money or his watch, and yet you are all cultured. I can remember when the white man kept his gold dust in tin cans. There was honor among those men, and the one who did steal, soon felt the rope necktie.

Destroyed Shed for Lumber.

"In the early days I was prospecting on Iron mountain and to follow in the footsteps of the white man, I built a necessary outbuilding. My wife becoming lonesome, we made a short trip to visit our savage relatives. While I was away the cultured white men tore down my outbuilding because it contained smooth lumber, and they had use for it and stole it. Was that culture?

"Several years ago I wrote a letter to the land office in Washington. After waiting two years for a reply I went to Washington and made inquiries for the letter. A beautiful pink cheeked, golden haired, cultured gentleman at the desk yawned and said: 'We received your letter, but were too busy to answer.'

Is Bull Moose.

"I don't blame the white man living on the reservation becoming disgusted with the treatment he receives from the land office. Now that I have become a citizen of the United States, even though the savage blood still runs in my veins, I am a Bull Moose, and if we could get Joe Dixon to be secretary of the interior, I think a great many things would be changed.

Flathead Wrong Name.

"I often think that I should bring a suit for criminal libel against the United States for calling us Flatheads. The Indian word is 'Scketcomchindt,' meaning broadwater, and was named after the big lake, as that was the largest body of water we knew of. I don't believe that there are many people who know how

Wild Horse island got its name. An Indian by the name of Shilchilconkan went alone to where the Blackfeet Indians were camped and stole a mare and a colt and a yearling. The water was exceedingly low at that time and he swam them to the island. He never went after them and it was a number of years before anyone visited the island, and then they found between 1,000 and 1,500 horses, all beautiful black animals in the island. This rather disproves the theory that inbreeding is detrimental to stock, because a finer drove of horses could not be found anywhere.

"It is a shame to take away the old Indian names from mountains and ranges and rivers and lakes. Mission range used to be called Sinyealimin. Now see how smooth that sounds, and means so much more than Mission range. The same as Sailish, the original name for the Flathead tribe. I hope something can be done to get the old Indian names back again, but this is a long way from answering my question, 'What is culture?'"

Document 64

State Control of Reservation Hunting Rejected

November 22, 1915

Source: "Indian Is Immune from State's Laws," *The Daily Missoulian*, November 22, 1915, page 8, col. 4.

Editors' note: In August 1910 the State of Montana had moved to control hunting by tribal members on the reservation. Indian leaders complained vigorously. Finally, in 1915 the courts agreed that the state hunting laws did not control on-reservation Indian hunting.

Indian Is Immune from State's Laws

Red Man May Hunt or Fish on Reserve as Pleases His Savage Fancy.

Though rod and gun clubs tear their hair and game wardens curse, the noble red man is privileged to fish and hunt on his native heath after the efficient but (to the white man) unsportsmanlike and uneconomic manner of his fathers.

So the courts of the land have decided after considering the case on Antoine LaRose, a Flathead Indian who was arrested on the reservation for spearing fish. LaRose was tried and found guilty in the courts of Justice of the Peace Phil Gagnon, and was fined $25.

LaRose objected. Through District Attorney Wheeler, one of whose duties is the protection of the government's Indian wards, LaRose petitioned Judge G. M. Bourquin of the federal court for a writ of habeas corpus. In granting the petition Judge Bourquin said:

"The United States has exclusive jurisdiction over his Indian wards, and their acts, within the Indian reservations. The Indians are there subject to only the United States and the Indian laws. State laws do not there apply to them.

"If the Indians' acts there are not offensive against Indians or the United States they are not offensive at all, and are not offensive against the state."

LaRose has been out of jail on his own recognizance since the petition was first submitted to the court and will therefore not be compelled to serve out the jail term imposed upon him by the Missoula justice of the peace.

Chapter 3

Documents of Salish, Pend d'Oreille, and Kootenai History Between 1916-1917

Document 65

Henry Matt Complains About Agent Morgan

March 11, 1916

Source: Fred C. Morgan to Commissioner of Indian Affairs, March 11, 1916, from file 22,020/1916 Flathead 154, Central Classified Files, RG 75, National Archives, Washington, D.C.

Editors' note: Henry Matt was obviously a thorn in the side of Agent Fred Morgan. Unfortunately, we do not have Matt's side of the story. Matt opposed federal policy regarding controlling the money of Indian wards and Morgan's application of this policy on the Flathead Reservation.

Department of the Interior
United States Indian Service
Flathead Agency, Dixon, Montana,
March 11, 1916.

The Honorable,
Commissioner of Indian Affairs,
Washington, D.C.
Sir:

Receipt is acknowledged of Office letter of March 2, 1916, with enclosure of copy of a letter received from Hon. H. L. Myers, United States Senate, quoting from a letter received by him from Hon. S. V. Stewart, Governor of Montana, in regard to complaints made by Mr. Henry Mack, of Arlee, Montana, and two other Indians. Replying, I have the honor to advise that Henry "Mack" is Henry Matt, Flathead allottee No. 325, a mixed-blood Indian about 43 years of age, who was granted a patent in fee under date of October 10, 1910, patent No. 156693.

The matter about which he complained to Governor Stewart has been previously reported on in full to your Office. See Office letter of February 27, 1915, Ed-Ind 21913-15, and my reply of March 20, 1915; my telegram March 30, 1915; my letter March 30, 1915, 21913-15; and Office telegram of March 31, 1915, 37332-15.

The agency reserve at Jocko has an area of 111.60 acres. The Catholic Church at Jocko was given 8.40 acres, and patent No. 164726 was issued for this on December 8, 1910. I respectfully refer your Office to the records showing the lands set aside for the agency reserve at Jocko, and the lands given to the church, from which it will be noted that the church lands are entirely surrounded by the agency reserve lands except on the short south line; and that there is $^1/_8$ mile of agency reserve between the church lands and the land allotted to Mary Finley, Flathead allottee No. 1222.

The allotment of Mary Finley, No. 1222, is described as the S$^1/_2$ SW$^1/_4$ SE$^1/_4$, SE$^1/_4$ SE$^1/_4$ NW$^1/_4$ section 16, T. 16 N., R. 19. W., and the S$^1/_2$ SW$^1/_4$ section 32, T. 20 N., R. 20 W., Flathead Reservation, Montana.

Isabel Charlo is Flathead allottee No. 1546, whose allotment is described as the W$^1/_2$ NE$^1/_4$ section 16, T. 16 N., R. 19 W., Flathead Reservation.

Christine Louison is Flathead allottee No. 1627, whose allotment is described as the SE$^1/_4$ NW$^1/_4$, S$^1/_2$ NE$^1/_4$ NW$^1/_4$, E$^1/_2$ NE$^1/_4$ SW$^1/_4$, section 16, T. 16 N., R. 19 W., Flathead Reservation, Montana.

A reference to the records at your Office will show that the Isabel Charlo and Christine Lousion allotments do not touch the church land; that the Isabel Charlot allotment does not touch the agency reserve, nor the 30 acres allotted to Mary Finley in this section, township and range; also, that the allotment of Christine Louison is separated from the Mary Finley land by the allotment of Christine's deceased husband, Judge Louison. It will also be noted that no lands allotted to any of the Matts join any of the lands above referred to.

A reference to the records at your Office will show to what extremes Henry Matt will go in his statements in endeavoring to further his own ends. Isabel Charlo (the woman referred to by Matt) was living on the 30 acres allotted by Mary Finley, and the lands given the church were in no way involved.

I had not assumed charge at this agency when the agency reserve at Jocko was set aside, the lands given to the church, and the allotments made to these Indians, but there is no question but that the church was given the lands made use of by them, as the church buildings and cemetery are located on the lands given them; also, from the irregular descriptions of the allotments of Christine Louison and her husband it would seem that they secured the lands selected by them; and this would also seem true with regard to the lands of Isabel Charlo and her husband, Chief Charlo, which are adjoining. It therefore appears that Christine Louison, Isabel Charlo and Mary Finley received in allotment the lands selected by them, and the church was given the lands on which the church buildings and cemetery were located. As above stated, there is $^1/_8$ mile of agency reserve between the church lands and the allotment of Mary Finley.

The files above referred to, as stated, give the information relative to this matter. In connection with this I desire to state that the grand-son of Isabel Charlo, Paul Charlo, assisted in moving her from the allotment of Mary Finley,

Fred Morgan, Flathead Agent/ Superintendent, 1908-1917
Source: *The Daily Missoulian,* Dec. 12, 1915, ed. sec., p. 1, col. 1-7.
Thanks to Frank Tyro, SKC Media.

and that Paul Charlo, at this agency, on February 23, 1915, in the presence of Mr. C. E. Dunston of your Office, made a statement of what had occurred.

It will be noted that in my letter of March 30, 1915, I stated that the suit against Mr. Hiatt had undoubtedly been brought by some of the mixed-bloods, annoyed by enforcement of the liquor laws and observance of the rules and regulations relative to expenditure of individual Indian money by the Government officials; and that *Henry Matt*, who tomorrow (31st) had a hearing before the U.S. Commissioner on a charge of giving liquor to Indians attempted to serve the papers on Mr. Hiatt.

Since my report to your Office of March 30, 1915, Christine Louison has stated that Alex Matt (father of Henry Matt) had told Isabel Charlo that if she moved into the house on the agency reserve that Mr. Hiatt had prepared for her that she, Isabel Charlo, would have to pay him, Matt. rent.

As stated previously to your Office, Mary Finley had leased her allotment. Isabel Charlo, who was residing thereon, at first agreed to move, and Mr. Hiatt had fixed up a cabin on the agency reserve for her use. When he went to assist her to move she had changed her mind, and refused to move into the cabin on the reserve, but went to her step-daughters to live. There is but little doubt that this was due to what had been told her by Alex Matt.

In order that your Office may understand the motive which caused Henry Matt to visit Governor Stewart (also why he happened to be in Helena), to take up this matter, and his deliberate falsehood to the Governor as to Isabel Charlo being moved off the perpetual site of the church, I wish to give a brief history of some of the scrapes he has been into:

About Christmas, 1908, Henry Matt had a quantity of liquor at the Catholic Mission at St. Ignatius. He became intoxicated and quarrelsome, engaged in a fight with Immaneul Curley, an Indian, whom he beat up terribly. Curley was in bad shape for a long time. For his offense he was tried by the Indian Court, which gave him a sentence of only 30 days. Special Agent Thomas Downs, who was at Flathead at the time, presided at the Indian Court when Matt received this small sentence. After Matt had served his time at the agency jail he immediately began an active campaign against the Special Agent, whom he stated he was going to have "fired" for permitting the Indian Court to sentence the "leading man" of the reservation.

Matt is one of the smoothest bootleggers this reservation has to contend with, and his offenses are frequent. In June, 1913, he introduced a quantity of liquor, went to the home of an Indian, and got several drunk. For this he was indicted, and was tried in the spring of 1914 before the Federal Court. Just a short time before his trial he went to Missoula, taking Martin Charlo with him, and sent a telegram to your Office requesting Inspector or transportation [for?] three Indians to Washington. See Office telegram to me dated March 19, 1914, and my reply of March 20, 1914. The same reason that prompted him to send that message is responsible for his present complaint to Governor Stewart — an attempt divert attention from his own wrong-doing.

During the spring of 1915 Henry Matt was again arrested by Special Officer Glenn, on the same old charge of giving liquor to Indians. This case was lost because of perjured testimony by the Indians.

During December, 1915, Henry Matt introduced a quantity of liquor on the reservation and gave liquor to several Indians. Matt and some of his

Henry Matt dancing
Source: Lee Ann Hunter Matt, Arlee, Montana

drunken companions went to the home of Tony Barnaby, where they got into a fight during which some of Barnaby's furniture (chairs) were used as weapons and broken. Barnaby finally was able to eject them from his house. Later Matt came back, looking for trouble, and attempted to break into Barnaby's house. After Barnaby had told him several times to go away, and Matt was trying to break down the door, Barnaby shot at him through the glass in a window with a shot gun. Some of the shot and glass scratched him up a little, and it appears he was further damaged by running through a barb wire fence in getting away.

For his latest offense he was arrested by Special Officer Glenn and given a hearing before the U.S. Commissioner at Missoula, who held him for action of the Grand Jury. The Federal Grand Jury which convened at Great Falls during February indicted him on five counts. Matt entered his plea at Great Falls on February 19th, I think. To go to Great Falls it was necessary for him to change trains at Helena, which I think accounts for his presence in Helena at the time he saw the Governor. His purpose in making the complaint in my opinion was solely for the purpose of trying to create the impression he is someone of importance, and attempting to cover his own crime.

Henry Matt often poses as an attorney, and notwithstanding the fact that he has very little education he has informed clerks in the office that he has been admitted to the bar, and has a complete library of "laminated" law books. He frequently mixes up in bootlegging cases by attempting to influence the testimony of Indians. One such case was that in which an Indian, Alex Ainsley, gave testimony at the Grand Jury, and then at the trial gave an entirely different story. He was arrested for perjury, and plead guilty. He stated he had perjured himself because Henry Matt told him what to say.

For the information of your Office I am enclosing a few clippings from our files regarding Henry Matt. I respectfully request that the same be returned to this agency in order that they may be placed in the files.

Also, I am enclosing affidavits of Joseph Lumpry and his daughter, Adel, who came to the agency on the 8th instant and made complaint regarding John Matt, a brother of Henry. These are self-explanatory. This matter I, of course, intend to take up and there is no doubt but that when I do so John or Henry or Alex Matt will imagine they should be permitted to do with the Indians, and the Indians' property, as they please and without molestation; and will try to resort to their usual practice in such cases of attempting to cause trouble for the Government officials and agency employees by circulating falsehoods and making unfounded complaints.

Respectfully,
Fred C. Morgan
Superintendent.

Document 66

Elderly Indian Killed Cow

March 17, 1916

Source: "Aged Indian Is Charged with Butchering a Cow," *The Ronan Pioneer*, March 17, 1916, page 1, col. 3.

Editors' note: Antoine Hammer's side of the story was not given in this newspaper article. Some of the friction between Indians and homesteaders made it into the courts.

Aged Indian Is Charged with Butchering a Cow

Antoine Hammer, a full blood Indian about 70 years of age, living southeast of Ronan, according to a complaint filed in U.S. Commissioner Bailey's office signed by Ben Mendenhall, is charged with killing a cow belonging to the latter. The offense is said to have been committed on or about March 10, while the cow was feeding at a straw pile in Mr. Mendenhall's field. The cow was a full blood Durham, gentle and had a young calf by her side. The head and off-fall was found by Mr. Mendenhall and he at once notified W. G. Brown, sub agent at Ronan, and the latter after as short search located the carcas in the possession of Antoine Hammer.

Mr. Mendenhall then swore to a complaint charging Hammer with killing the cow. In accordance with the rules of the government Mr. Bailey has forwarded the complaint to the district attorney for his approval, and if approved by that officer a warrant will issue for Hammer and he will have to stand trial in the federal court.

Cattlemen on the reservation it is said, have been heavy losers of stock in this way and they have determined to put a stop to it one way or another. If the accused happened to be a white man there be little doubt as to the outcome, but offenses committed by the Indians are a different matter — the federal authorities preventing their being tried in the state courts on the grounds that they are wards of the government. However, there should be some way by which the cattlemen can secure protection for their stock, be the offender Indian or white man, and the approval of the complaint in this case and its prosecution by the district attorney, should lead the way to the protection desired.

Document 67

Indians Visit Missoula for Stampede

April 6, 1916

Source: "Got Booze Easily During Stampede Indians Say," *The Daily Missoulian*, April 6, 1916, page 10, col. 3.

Editors' note: A black woman, Hallie Goldsmith, was tried for selling alcohol to Indians in Missoula during the Stampede celebration. Several young tribal members testified against Goldsmith in the case.

Got Booze Easily During Stampede Indians Say
Boys on Witness Stand Tell of Getting Liquor During Celebration.

The Missoula Stampede of 1915 was described as a refreshing wet "spell" by Indian witnesses, testifying in the federal court yesterday during the trial of Hallie Goldsmith of Missoula on charges of selling liquor to Indians.

"Sometimes I have trouble getting booze; sometimes I don't," said Oscar Luddington, an Indian boy of 21. "Usually it depends on who I see, but last Fourth I didn't have trouble. I could get anything I wanted."

The trial was not completed yesterday. The government rested just before adjournment. Oscar and two other Indians — Marion Deschamps and Albert Tellyer — testified that during the night of July 3 they were served several drinks of beer at a house of prostitution conducted by Hallie Goldsmith, colored. The boys' stories differed in some details but agreed in the statement that beer was served by Hallie Goldsmith. Deschamps testified that he paid for a bottle of beer which the woman gave into the hands of his companion, a white man named Poindexter.

Special Officer John Glenn told of the woman's arrest. He was called, he said, after Deschamps and Poindexter had been caught with their bottle of beer. Deschamps led Glenn and his deputy, Officer Sweeney, to the Goldsmith woman's place. When she was told that she was under arrest the woman said, according to the witness, that she knew she would get into trouble if she let breeds into her place.

Officer Sweeney corroborated the testimony of his chief.

At 5:30 the case was continued to 9:30 this morning, when the case of the defense will be heard.

Document 68

Indian Woman Guilty of Alcohol Violation

April 6, 1916

Source: "Verdict of Guilty Against Dupuis Woman," *The Daily Missoulian*, April 6, 1916, page 3, col 1.

Editors' note: Marie Dupuis was born on the reservation, but she operated a rooming-house in Missoula when charged with furnishing alcohol to Indian customers.

Verdict of Guilty Against Dupuis Woman

Jury Finds Missoula Rooming-House Keeper Sold Liquor to Indians.

To the crammed and hectic career of Marie Dupuis 12 good men and true yesterday added a lurid chapter — a verdict declaring her guilty of violation of the federal law against selling liquor to Indians.

Marie Dupuis is only 27 years old but since her birth in an Indian home on the Flathead reservation she has lived completely. At 27 she has put matrimony aside after a ten-year trial; has borne six children; has suffered neglect and want; has tried with poor success to conduct a rooming-house of whose numerous laxities the one concerning the sale of booze to Indians finally attracted destruction. The woman was tried and found guilty before Judge George Bourquin in the federal court.

A year ago, not long after divorcing her uncaring husband, Marie Dupuis took over the management of a rooming-house at 117 East Main street. Among the attractions she used on prospective customers was a willingness to supply dry Indian throats with irrigation.

Famed Abroad.

Marie didn't advertise this charm of her establishment, but news of it spread so rapidly on the reservation that to quote one of the patrons, "all the s....s got booze there" and "everybody in Arlee talked about Marie Dupuis."

At any rate, the reputation of the Dupuis institution for illicit hospitality was soon so firmly established in Arlee that when Adele Lumphry, an Indian woman with a love of bright lights and brightening liquor, contrived to get $5 from her father for a pleasure trip to Missoula, she went straight to its doors.

Marie gave her visitor beer at a dollar a bottle and whiskey at 25 cents a glass until she was, as Adele herself expressed it, "pretty full."

With the Goods.

During the afternoon Adele paraded about town and was seen by Special Officer John Glenn, who is engaged in the suppression of the liquor traffic among Indians. Glenn learned from Adele where she had secured her liquor and when he saw her re-enter the Dupuis place that evening he followed. He found Adele, Marie and an Indian boy named Pritchett seated about a table, drinking beer.

Glenn, Police Megistrate [sic] Johnson, who accompanied the special officer on the raid, and Adele Lumphry were put upon the stand by the government. Their stories agreed in every essential detail.

The defense called no other witnesses than the defendant. The Dupuis woman ingeniously attempted to build an alibi by declaring that she opened a bottle of beer just before Glenn and Johnson entered and that the Indians poured drinks for themselves as the officers came into the room. An effort was made by the defense to prove that Glenn "framed up" the whole affair.

The jury was out less than half an hour. Sentence will be passed at 9:30 this morning.

Document 69

Indian Charged with Alcohol Offense

April 7, 1916

Source: "'Frame-Up' Hinted by Indian on Stand," *The Daily Missoulian*, April 7, 1916, page 8, col. 2.

Editors' note: James Grinder, a mixed-blood, disputed the federal charge of having furnished liquor to other Indians on the reservation.

"Frame-Up" Hinted by Indian on Stand

James Grinder Intimates That Special Office was Vengelful [sic].

James Grinder, "half Indian and half Irish," on trial in the United States district court on charge of selling liquor to Indians on the Flathead reservation, intimated from the witness stand yesterday afternoon that Special Office Ramsey arrested him in revenge for his failure to "squeal" on a white man.

Grinder testified that Ramsey approached him some time before his arrest and asked him to give evidence against the owner of the Flathead lake steamer "Klondike," was [who] was suspected of selling liquor to Indians. Ramsey told Grinder, the latter said, that if Grinder would testify against the boat's owner the vessel could be sold by the government. Grinder refused to "squeal," and now attributes his subsequent arrest on what he calls false charges to the special officer's anger.

Grinder took the stand in his own defense late yesterday afternoon and denied all of the allegations of the government. Federal witnesses, most of them Indians, had told of getting beer and whiskey from Grinder at Arlee during the Indians' big hand game there in July. The government witnesses were explicit and emphatic in their statements.

Grinder denied that he was in Arlee for more than one day at the time of the game, which lasted for more than a month, and declared that he had no liquor at that time. He said that he had twice served time in the state penitentiary for violations of the state laws.

Grinder was the first witness called by the defense, and the court adjourned at the conclusion of his testimony. The trial will be resumed at 9:30 this morning.

Another case against Grinder is next on the court's calendar.

James Grinder
Source: Photograph Archives, Montana Historical Society, Helena, Montana, photo PAc 85-91.02548

Document 70

Alcohol Offenses Occupy Federal Court Session

April 14, 1916

Source: "For Introducing Liquor Federal Court Convicts," *The Ronan Pioneer*, April 14, 1916, page 1, col. 5.

Editors' note: Flathead Reservation Indian alcohol cases kept the federal court occupied in the spring of 1916.

For Introducing Liquor Federal Court Convicts

The April term of the federal court has been in session in Missoula for the past ten days, its time being principally taken in the trials of men and women charged with selling liquor to Indians, introducing or attempting to introduce liquor on the Flathead reservation. As usual, during a session of the federal court, the reservation country has been more or less depopulated, each case demanding a large number of witnesses. Out of all the whiskey cases tried, only one defendant escaped — a case from Camas. Those convicted and sentenced are:

Mary Dupuis, 60 days in jail and $100 fine.

Hallie Goldsmith, 100 days in jail and $200 fine.

James Grinder, 130 days in jail and $100 fine.

James Murtaugh, 100 days in jail and $100 fine.

Louis Pablo, found guilty of taking whiskey onto the reservation. Sentence will be given later.

Henry Matt of Arlee was tried and acquited on a charge of giving liquor to another Indian.

William Moore, colored, found guilty of giving whiskey to Indians.

Joseph Bonaparte, bootlegging, case postponed until Oct. 9.

Doris Hand, found guilty of bootlegging, sentence postponed until Oct. 9.

Alex McLeod entered a plea of guilty on the charge of introducing liquor on the reservation and sentence suspended until Oct. 9.

Document 71

Indians Oppose Policy of Flathead Agency

April 1916

Source: S. M. Brosius to Commissioner of Indian Affairs, April 17, 1916, and John S. Glenn to Commissioner of Indian Affairs, April 18, 1916, from file 20,153/1916 Flathead 175, Central Classified Files, RG 75, National Archives, Washington, D.C.

Editors' note: The Indian Rights Association and officials in the Indian bureau objected to the activities of several Indians and their white supporters who opposed federal Indian policy on the Flathead. Tribal members complained about tribal money being used to fund the irrigation construction and agency operations. There were also tribal claims resulting from unfulfilled treaty promises. It is hard to tell from the surviving evidence, just how honest Princess Redfeather was in advocating for tribal complaints. Senator Harry Lane of Oregon was sympathetic to the complaints from Flathead and gave the opposition access to Congressional hearings and other support. Lane was senator between 1913 and 1917. A progressive Democrat, medical doctor, and former mayor of Portland, Lane was a member of the Senate Committee on Indian Affairs. Unfortunately, no documents have survived explaining the side of Senator Lane, Princess Redfeather, or others who promised to assist opponents of Flathead Agency policies. See the June 26, 1916, report by Inspector C. M. Knight giving the government's views about Redfeather.

S. M. Brosius, Agent
Indian Rights Association
Washington, D.C.
April 17, 1916.

Honorable Commissioner
of Indian Affairs.
Sir:

Information has quite recently come to me regarding the work of one Perry Kennerly and a "Princess Red Feather" within the Flathead Indian Reservation, Montana. I think the reputation of Perry Kennerly is quite well known to you, as it was made a matter of publicity in the newspapers two or three years ago.

The information I have comes from a reliable source, my informant being one who is specially interested in the protection and betterment of the Flathead Tribe. I quote from a statement made by my informant in this case:

> "We have a mixed-blood Indian by the name of Perry Kennerly, representing himself to be an attorney, and an accomplice who calls herself "Princess Red Feather," on this reservation several times during the past year. They have been telling the Indians that they would help them get their moneys for them from Washington. I understand that the Indians, mostly full-bloods, have been sending them money, $300.00 in the past six months, at No. 64 Pennsylvania Ave., Washington, D.C., some of the letters that go there are addressed to "Pat. Harvey," which I think is fictitious. This "Princess Red Feather" is here now with a petition which the Indians say is to "get some of the Indian officials at Washington and also throughout Montana out," so they will be able to get their money.
>
> This man Perry Kennerly is from the Blackfeet Reservation, Browning, Mont. His record is not good. You may be able to get his past record from the Superintendent at Browning, Mont.
>
> "Princess Red Feather" was convicted and served a sentence at Missoula, Mont., last summer for giving liquor to Indians, and was also convicted and served sentence at Missoula under the "Rooming-house Act" about the same time."

While I have no personal knowledge regarding the work of the parties referred to among the Flatheads, I have no doubt that the situation is as appears in the foregoing statement. It occurs to me that it is possible to interest the Secret Service of the Post Office Department in this matter, so as to punish any parties who may be guilty of violating the laws and to give proper protection to the ignorant Indians who are possibly being duped by the representations of this class of persons.

Trusting that you will take proper steps to protect these Indians from being overreached in this manner, I am,

Very respectfully yours,
S. M. Brosius
Agent, Indian Rights Association

* * * * * * * *

Department of the Interior
United States Indian Service
Missoula, Montana April 18th, 1916.

Hon. Cato Sells,
Commissioner of Indian Affairs,
Washington, D.C.

Through H. A. Larson,
Chief Special Officer,
Denver, Colorado.
My dear Mr. Commissioner: —

There is a woman operating upon the Flathead Indian Reservation under the name of Princess Red Feather, alias Mrs. C. A. Hines, who claims that she is now working for Senator Lane, and that she will, in a short time, after getting the signatures of three fourths of the indians on the Flathead Reservation, secure them their sums of money. She also states that she is going to do away with the Superintendent of the Flathead Reservation and that she, with two indians whom she will select, take charge of the office and run the affairs as the indians want it.

This woman has secured vast sums of money from various incompetent indians on her scheme, and as late as February 29th of this year she secured $300.00 in one sum from one of the indians of the Flathead tribe.

She is a woman of very bad character. I had occasion last year to arrest her for selling whiskey to indians both on and off the reservation, and after a trial by a jury she was convicted on nine counts and sentenced to serve ninety days in the Missoula County jail and to pay a fine of $100.00 and costs on each count, but the Court instructed that the sentence be served concurrently. The night before her trial at Missoula she was arrested by the police authorities of Missoula, Montana, for violation of the rooming house ordinance, and she was fined $25.00 and given a thirty day sentence in the Missoula County jail. She paid her fine and was later released from jail. She returned to the Flathead Reservation and remained there a few days then in company with Antoine Moiese and Maud S. Finley, left for a trip to Washington, D.C. Moiese and Finley later returned, Finley stating that as soon as they arrived in Washington the Princess left them and did not go to the Indian Office with them for some reason or other. At the time of her departure she secured $400.00 from Antoine Marcielle under the pretense that she was going to get them all the money that belonged to the Flathead tribe of indians. She stayed in Washington several months, and while there she received various sums of money which was sent to her by P.O. money orders, and in a very confidential way I have secured the numbers of the post office money orders, the dates and the amounts, and I have also secured the numbers of registered mail sent to her. She is causing no end of trouble among the ignorant class of indians on the Flathead Reservation, and she is being supported by a few who are allotted upon the Flathead Reservation, and who are in fear that something will come up relative to their being allotted upon this reservation. Such people as the Lemery's, whom, it has been reported to me, secured their allotments by false means. Some of these indians claim that if it is investigated by the Government authorities their contention that the Lemery's secured their allotments by fraud will be sustained.

It has been confidentially reported to me that one Dougal McCormick, of Missoula, Montana, and his brother Washington J. McCormick, an attorney in Missoula, are behind the movement of this woman Princess Red Feather. I am inclined to believe that there is something to this rumor, as when Princess Red Feather was arrested by me last fall for selling whiskey to indians she was arraigned before the United States Commissioner and required to give bond in the sum of $500.00. She was not in jail five minutes until she was released on a bond of $500.00 signed by Dougal McCormick and one George Grover, a saloon man of Missoula, and a friend of the McCormick's.

If you have any wishes in regard to this woman if you will make them known to me I will gladly investigate this matter thoroughly, and see if we cannot prosecute her for obtaining money under false pretenses. I would say confidentially my idea would be to secure permission to use an indian to write her a decoy letter that we may obtain necessary evidence against her to substantiate the verbal testimony of indians.

She further claims that she has had a talk with Senator Lane and that he is going to have all of the indian officers fired at this coming session of congress, and she is promising all kinds of positions to her followers.

Please advise me at your earliest convenience relative to the above matter.

Very truly yours,
John S. Glenn
Special Officer.

Document 72

Citizen Indians Want Share of Tribal Funds

June – October 1916

Source: "Indians Ask for Tribal Money," *The Ronan Pioneer*, June 9, 1916, page 1, col. 3; "Flatheads to Get Tribal Money Presently," *The Daily Missoulian*, October 9, 1916, page 8, col. 3.

Editors' note: Before 1916 tribal money from sale of timber and other sources was being used to fund the construction of the irrigation project and to pay the expenses of running the Flathead Agency. In 1916 the money for irrigation construction was returned to the tribal account and the construction costs were levied on the irrigated lands. Some of the money could then be paid to tribal members as a per capita.

Indians Ask for Tribal Money

The Indians on the Flathead reservation who have been granted patents in fee for their allotments, want a division of the tribal funds and a distribution of the money. They argue that by issuing them their patents for their land and the subsequent granting of citizenship, they should be entirely separated from their old affiliations and given their share of the tribal money held by the government.

In support of this contention a meeting was held at the Dixon agency last Thursday, at which time a committee was appointed to solicit signatures to a petition asking for this action. The committee has issued the following address and ask that all interested present themselves and sign the petition:

Flathead Indian Reservation Montana, June 1, 1916.

To the Honorable, The Secretary of the Interior, Washington, D.C.

We, the undersigned, members of the Flathead Indian Reservation, Montana, all of whom have been granted patents in fee to our allotments, hereby respectfully petition that the pro rata shares in any tribal moneys belonging to the Flathead Indians be paid to those members of the Flathead Indian Reservation to whom patents in fee have been issued; and in the event that any Indians to whom patents in fee have been issued be deceased, that the shares of such deceased Indians be paid to their heirs. We also request that where any Indian to whom patent in fee has been issued may be an heir of a deceased Indian that the share of such deceased Indian be paid to the heir who has received patent in fee.

Inasmuch as we, by receiving our patents in fee, are citizens of the United States, we desire to receive, at the very earliest date possible, the entire share in which we may be entitled from any funds that may accrue to the credit of the Flathead Indians; and as these tribal funds are derived from the sale of tribal timber, lands and other tribal property, we hereby respectfully petition that legislation be enacted providing for the payment to the tribal fund by the government of the appraised value of the tribal timber, lands and other tribal property. This would permit the payment to us of the entire sum to which we would be entitled from the tribal funds, and the government would be reimbursed for the timber, lands and other property as the same were disposed of by the government.

Respectfully submitted,
Jos. Grenier, Jr.
Eli Morigeau.
Donald McDonald.
Alex Beauvais.
Henry Burland.
Telesphore DeMers.

Committee representing Flathead allottees who have received patents in fee.

* * * * * * * * *

Flatheads to Get Tribal Money Presently
Indian Petitioners Receive Reply from Commissioner at Capital.

Flathead tribal funds will presently be distributed, according to a letter from E. B. Merritt, assistant commissioner of Indian affairs, received by Joseph Grenier, Jr., of St. Ignatius, in answer to a petition from Grenier and other Indians who have received patents in fee to their allotted lands. The petition asked that the Indians receive their share of the tribal funds which accumulated while the property was held in common. About 2,310 Indians are to share in a fund of $253,000, which will be prorated. The letter follows:

"The office is in receipt of your letter of June 1, addressed to the superintendent of the Flathead agency, submitting a petition signed by Indians who have received patents in fee on your reservation, requesting that the tribal fund now deposited to the credit of the tribe be pro-rated and paid to those entitled to participate therein.

"This matter was referred to the comptroller of the treasury for a decision as to the legality of pro-rating the funds, and on July 28, 1916, the comptroller rendered a decision in which he holds that funds accruing to the credit of the tribe under the act of May 8, 1916, are available only for expenditure for the benefit of the tribe as congress may hereafter direct, and that the same are not subject to discretionary expenditure by the secretary of the interior as are other tribal funds. However, it has been decided that the fund, 'Proceeds of Flathead Reservation, Montana,' amounting to approximately $253,000, which was provided by the ace [act] of April 23, 1904, (33 Stat. L. 305), which act was subsequently amended by the act of May 29, 1908, (35 Stat., 448), should be prorated and if the Indians on your reservation will make application through the superintendent's office on proper blanks furnished by him, the same will receive due consideration when submitted to this office with the superintendent's report and recommendation in each case.

"Your friend,
"**E. B. Merritt.**
"Assistant Commissioner."

Document 73

Government Celebrates Indians Who Became Citizens June 11, 1916

Source: "Indians Made American Voters," *The Daily Missoulian*, June 11, 1916, page 1, col. 1, and page 3, col. 1-2.

Editors' note: The maudlin ceremony described in this newspaper article celebrated the "emancipation" of these Indians from federal supervision. The views of the new American citizens about losing their tribal membership and becoming citizens were not described in the article.

Indians Made American Voters
An Account of Ceremonies by Which Selish Become Citizens.
New Independence of Indian People
Reds Shoot Arrows as Emblems of Old Life and Take Plow as New.

Almost exactly a quarter-century ago, on October 17, 1891, old Chief Charlot led a little band of Selish from the Bitter Root valley, the home of his fathers, to the reservation on the Jocko. It was a woebegone procession and it marked a brave old Indian's resignation to the fact that deceit and subterfuge controlled the world.

"I will go — I and my children," he had said to the leaders of the whites. "My young men are becoming bad; they have no place to hunt. My women are hungry. For their sake I will go. I do not want the land you promise. I do not believe your promises. All I want is ground enough for my grave."

So ended the first independence of the Selish.

The New Independence.

Last Thursday afternoon Major James A. McLaughlin, United States Indian inspector, conferred upon eight women and 12 men of the Selish nation the rights of American citizenship. Upon the campus of the Flathead Indian agency near Dixon the 20 Indians received patents in fee to their allotments and symbols of their right to participate in the government whose wards they had been.

"And now beneath this flag I place upon your breast the emblem of your citizenship," said Major McLaughlin to the Indians. "Wear this badge of honor always: and may the eagle that is on it never see you do aught of which the flag will not be proud."

So begins the new independence of the Selish.

Great Crowd Attends.

All morning the white road from Dixon to the agency was kept clouded with dust. Automobile loads of curious white people whirled past long plodding caravans of bedraggled cayuses and creaking buckboards, loaded to the limit with decked-out Indians. At 2 o'clock, the hour appointed for the ceremony, the agency was crowded. There must have been nearly 400 people, not counting the droves of wiry youngsters and flea-bitten hounds who chased each other about the grounds, yapping and yelling and paying no heed to anything at all but each other.

The agency, ordinarily business-like and unexcited, was like a circus ground. Only the Indians appeared calm. They squatted on their heels on the river bank, stolidly watching the Caucasian uproar. An Indian would doubtless be unmoved by a sudden appearance of the Angel Gabriel. He wouldn't change the expression of his face or hurry the puffing of his cigarette. But he would put on his brightest blanket and paint his cheeks. For the Indian reveals in his dress the emotions expression and demeanor never reveal.

The importance of this citizenship ceremony was manifested in the gay clothing of the Indian spectators. Bits of gaudy finery ordinarily reserved for dances and hand-games were on display.

A plow and a table were placed on the river bank, and presently Superintendent Morgan, Major McLaughlin and Major Small appeared, bearing a great silk flag and armfuls of packages.

Like an Indian Council.

The gathering might have been a council. It had all the deliberate stateliness and dignity of a powwow. The Great White Father was about to elevate a chosen few of his red people. It was an important hour. Few functions of their government are better calculated to tickle the pride of white citizens than these vanishing dealings with the Indian. There is an imperial flavor about them that isn't often found in a democracy. The conquering Anglo-Saxon and the proud, unbending Indian of 50 years ago exist again in the pomp of these meetings.

But here was a difference. This day the Indian was not to be forced to swallow the terms of his conqueror; he was to be granted freedom and equality. And equality is the death of pomps.

"Felix Barnaby!" Major McLaughlin called.

Most of the white spectators, catching the ancient quality of the ceremony must have expected one of the painted, blanketed braves to answer the call. Instead there stepped from the crowd a man who would have passed unnoticed at a grange meeting. He wore the clothes and the carriage of an American farmer. Only his swarthy face and inevitable black peaked hat marked him as an Indian.

Similar were the other men called before the table. Not one of them had even so much as a gay scarf. Some of them, indeed, would have passed as white men; light-haired, blue-eyed farmers. One even had a sandy moustache!

When at last they all stood before him — Felix Barnaby, Samuel Bellman, Newman Blodgett, Orson Dupuis, Frank Ducharme, Joseph Dumontier, Gallatin Ducharme, Adolph Lozeau, Jr., Batiste Matt, Isadore Sorrell and Elmer Turnage — Major McLaughlin spoke.

"The president of the United States has sent me to speak a solemn and serious word to you," he said, "a werd [word] that means more to some of you than any other that you have ever heard. He has been told that there are some among you who should no longer be controlled by the Bureau of Indian Affairs, but should be given their patents in fee and thus become free American citizens. It is his decision that this shall be done, and that those so honored by the people of the United States shall have the meaning of this new and great privilege pointed out by symbol and by word, so that no man or woman shall not know its meaning. The president has sent me papers naming those men and women, and I shall call out their names one by one and they will come before me."

The Last Arrow.

As he called Felix Barnaby before him again, Major McLaughlin picked up a bow and arrow and directed the Indian to shoot.

It became evident that Barnaby had forgotten the ways of his people as well as the garb. He knew no more about the higher uses of the bow and arrow, handled often enough, no doubt, in dances and festivals, than the grocer Knight Templar knows of the fundamental purpose of the sword he swings on parade. His fingers become thumbs as he tried to pull the bow.

"Many the white man you've killed with one of those, Barnaby," shouted some one. The crowd roared with delight.

Barnaby at last achieved a shot, the arrow flying about as far as the 12-pound shot McDonald, the young Indian from Ravalli, threw at the inter-scholastic meet last month.

Eleven demonstrations of Caucasian safety from Indian bow-and-arrow attacks were made. Then the major, handing to each man the flint-headed arrow he had shot, said:

"You have shot your last arrow. That means that you are no longer to live the life of an Indian. You are from this day forward to live the life of the white man. But you may keep that arrow, it will be to you a symbol of your noble race and of the pride you feel that you come from the first of all Americans."

The White Man's Burden.

He turned to the plow. "Take in your hand this plow," he said to the Indians.

The old Indian was above such earthy, sweaty things as plows. They were truck fit only for s....s and white men. But these new Indians grasped the handles gladly, happy to find that one part, at least, the ceremony wasn't devised to make them ridiculous in the eyes of their old men. They had handled plows before, these Indians.

"This act," said Major McLaughlin, "means that you have chosen to live the life of the white man — and the white man lives by work. From the earth we all must get our living and the earth will not yield unless man pours upon it the sweat of his brow. Only by work do we gain a right to the land or to the enjoyment of life."

Then to each man he handed a leather purse, stamped with the arms of the United States. "I give you a purse," he said. "This purse will always say to you that the money you gain from your labor must be wisely kept. The wise man saves his money so that when the sun does not smile and the grass does not grow he will not starve.

"And now I give into your hands the flag of your country."

An Impressive Ceremony.

Cheap claptrap? Under other circumstances, perhaps, but not here. This was no ordinary ceremony. It symbolized the enfranchisement of a race; the elevation of the Indian to equal footing. Here was citizenship after the old Roman notion, dignified and desirable. And the sharpest street-corner orator could hardly have scoffed.

"This is the only flag you have ever had or ever will have. It is the flag of freedom, the flag of free men, the flag of a hundred million free men and women of whom you are now one. That flag has a request to make of you: that you take it into your hands and repeat these words."

The Indians moved forward, touched the flag, and slowly repeated after Major McLaughlin:

"For as much as the president has said that I am worthy to be a citizen of the United States, I now promise to this flag that I will give my hands, my head and my heart to the doing of all that will make me a true American citizen."

From his table Major McLaughlin took a dozen label [lapel] buttons, emblems of citizenship. giving one to each man, he said:

"And now beneath this flag I place upon your breast the emblem of your citizenship. Wear this badge of honor always and may the eagle that is on it never see you do aught of which the flag will not be proud."

Eight Women Citizens.

Christina Hostetler, Mary Jovin, Felicite Matt, Lucy McDonald, Mary C. McDonald, Esther LaRose Ray, Mary Michel Worley were called forward. They looked less like Indians than their men, for it is a farther way from s.... to white woman than from buck to farmer, and these were white women in all save color. They wore shirtwaists and button pumps. Two had on motor veils. Thus does the world move!

To the women, Major McLaughlin gave leather workbags and purses.

"This means," he said, "that you have chosen the life of the white woman — and the white woman loves her home. The family and the home are the foundation of our civilization. Upon the character and industry of the mother and home-maker largely depends the future of our nation. The purse will always say to you that the money you gain from your labor must be wisely kept. The wise woman saves her money, so that when the sun does not smile and the grass does not grow, she and her children will not starve."

Three Cheers for Themselves.

The oath of citizenship was administered. Then Major McLaughlin grouped all the new citizens together and turning toward the crowd, said: "I want you all to join me in three hearty cheers for these new citizens."

The cheers were given, and they were not spoiled at all by the fact that the new citizens joined in them as heartily as the next.

The Old and the New.

On the station platform at Dixon late that afternoon old Indian and new stood together waiting for the train. Old Louis Pierre, a stern patriarch, immensely concerned with his people's welfare, was talking with one of the new citizens, a woman who might just have left a Ladies' Aid society meeting, Louis Pierre is a tribal judge, a monitor of his nation. Evidently he was advising the woman. She paid scant attention. On her shirtwaist glittered a badge of citizenship. She was a freeholder, a voter. What right had this fussy old Indian to talk to her? So spoke her attitude. So, no doubt, the sputtering Selish she uttered. The old man was obdurate. At length the woman turned her back on him and began to read to herself out of a gray, business-like pamphlet she carried.

That pamphlet was a publication of the Child Welfare Bureau of the United States government. It was entitled "Pre-Natal Care."

Lo, it is a new day!

Document 74

Government Agent Makes Charges Against Princess Redfeather June 26, 1916

Source: Excerpts from C. M Knight, "Report on Investigation of Princess Redfeather, June 1, to 26, 1916," from file C. M. Knight, June 26, 1916 Flathead 150, Central Classified Files, RG 75, National Archives, Washington, D.C.

Editors' note: Inspector C. M. Knight claimed he had documentation to back up the charges against Princess Redfeather included in this report. Whether Redfeather really wanted to help the Flatheads or was taking advantage of them could not be evaluated without having Redfeather's side of the story.

Report on Investigation of Princess Redfeather, By Inspector C. M. Knight.

Princess Redfeather, alias, Allie Palmer, alias, Mrs. C. A. Hines, alias, Christine Hines, and alias, Mrs. Wallace Niles is, according to her own testimony and statements made by her to Indians and white people on the Flathead Reservation, Montana, a half breed Cherokee Indian born in Oklahoma in a little town called "Little Green Town," her father being Chief War Eagle and her mother a white woman. She was given the name of Princess Redfeather by her father; was educated at the Sherman Institute and the high school at Plattsburg, Nebraska; was married to C. A. Hines in Vancouver, B.C. Hines dying about eight years ago. She claims to have gone to the Crow Indian Reservation in Montana about ten years ago and was adopted by the Crow Indians and about three years ago came to the Flathead Indian Reservation, Montana, and was adopted into this tribe.

Wallace Niles, a half-blood shoshone Indian who has since married a Flathead Indian woman and is now residing with her near Arlee, Montana, told me that during the spring or early summer of 1913, he met Princess Redfeather in a restaurant in Helena, Montana. . . . .

At the Fourth of July celebration at St. Ignatius, Montana in 1914, many Indians became acquainted with Princess Redfeather. She was pointed out to Mack Couture by Ovilla Courville (at whose place she had stopped in Missoula) "who told him she was a sporting woman and for him to get busy," but he told

Courville he might get into trouble and was afraid. Later, in fun, he pointed her out to Baptiste Finley, a Flathead Indian, and told him she was all right and needed a partner. He later saw Baptiste with her and states that Baptiste lived with her for two months.

During July 1914 Princess Redfeather went to Polson, Montana on the Flathead Reservation and engaged room and board at the Central Hotel which was being run by Mrs. Mary R. Sawyer. She told Mrs. Sawyer her name was Princess Redfeather or Allie Palmer; that she was a Government employee sent out from Washington to investigate the troubles of the Indians and that she received sixty dollars per month from the Government, which amount was sent quarterly. On the strength of this she was allowed to stay there until October 1st, and still owes Mrs. Sawyer for board. While there she brought a sick Indian, by the name of John Gingras, to the hotel, produred [procured] a room for him and treated him, and still owes Mrs. Sawyer for his board.

Shortly after this she went to see Mr. W. A. Gregg, of Polson, a real estate dealer, and wanted to rent a house. She told him she was a Government employee, but he became suspicious of her and would not rent her a house, but she succeeded in renting a house from another party and the bill for rent was turned over to Mr. Gregg for collection. She lived in the house for sometime with Baptiste Finley and Mr. Gregg still holds her suit case for the bill. Among other articles in the suit case was Baptiste Finley's bank books.

About the middle of October 1914, Princess Redfeather met Mr. William H. Feddersen, who was then Government Farmer and stationed at Polson. She asked him to have the Mary Stasoo allotment lease changed from improvements to a cash basis. She told him she was an officer sent by the Department at Washington to investigate the condition of the Indians. He told her it would be necessary to see the lessee.

Prior to this meeting Mr. Fedderson had seen Mary Stasoo and her husband, Antoine, and knew they wished to have the lease changed and at the time had the matter under consideration and was of the opinion it would benefit them on account of the physical condition of Mary Stasoo.

As a result of this information Princess Redfeather went to see the lessee and the next day went to the Farmer's station with Antoine Stasoo and saw Mr. Feddersen. She asked him if he had learned anything more about the lease and he told her no, but was of the opinion that Mary Stasoo would be allowed a cash settlement. The Princess then told Mr. Feddersen that she had spent a lot of money looking after the Indians and that she should be allowed a part of this money for her services. He told her that could not be done. She then stated that if the lease went through this way the Indians had promised to give her $100, and that she would give him one-half of it. Some time later Mr.

Feddersen made inquiry of Antoine and Mary Stasoo as to whether or not they agreed to pay the Princess $100. They would not tell him they had but from their actions he believed they agreed to.

At the same time the Princess talked to Mr. Feddersen about the Stasoo lease, she wanted to know if it could not be arranged to have the timber on John Gingra's [sic] allotment sold, as he was sick and owed her money for taking care of him. This John Gingras is the same Indian the Princess took to the Central Hotel.

Shortly after this Thomas Antiste, an old Indian, went to Mr. Feddersen to make application for a cash settlement instead of improvements in his lease. Antiste would not tell him who sent him but he is of the opinion that Princess Redfeather did as she had been seen with him.

On February 4, 1915 Special Officer John S. Glenn, after securing what he deemed sufficient evidence to convict Princess Redfeather of introducing liquor onto the Flathead Indian Reservation, proceeded there for the purpose of arresting her. Upon his arrival he was informed that she had recently held a meeting at Arlee and had made a speech in which she claimed she was going to Dixon with a band of Indians and would personally throw Superintendent Morgan out of office. He met her later on the road about three miles west of Arlee in company with four Indians, Big Knife, Joe Pierre, Alex Ashley and Antoine Moiese, all riding horses. At first she refused to leave her horse, claiming she would report to the Agency whenever she felt so disposed. After a few minutes talk he could see she intended to resist arrest so he took her off the horse and put her in the automobile he was driving and made the Indians ride ahead down to the agency where he locked the Princess, and the Indians, up and about twelve o'clock that night released the Indians and ordered them to return to their homes.

The next day she was arrainged [sic] before United States Commissioner Whiteman at Dixon, Montana upon complaint filed against her for violations of the liquor laws. At her arraignment she entered a pleas [plea] of not guilty and in default of bonds she was committed to jail. She was given permission to consult her attorney, Mr. William F. Wayne of Missoula, Montana and Mr. Wayne appeared at the Preliminary hearing at Dixon in her defense. At the conclusion of the hearing Commissioner Whiteman remanded her to jail at Missoula, Montana to await the action of the Federal Grand Jury which was to convene at Great Falls, Montana during the same month. She remained in jail but a short time as Mr. George Grover and Mr. W. W. McCormick appeared before United States Commissioner Wallace P. Smith at Missoula and qualified as bondsmen and had her released.

She returned to the reservation and took up quarters at Alex Ashley's house near Arlee, Montana where she remained until the time of the Grand Jury at Great Falls. She appeared in Great Falls and while her case was being presented to the Grand Jury she was bold enough to accost the witnesses in the hallway of the Federal Building and proceeded to tell them what to tell when they were called into the Grand Jury room. This was overheard by Special Office Glenn who immediately took her into custody and placed her in jail until her case was presented and an indictment secured. When she was released she appeared in Court, entered a plea of not guilty and her trial was set for the April term of Court at Missoula, Montana.

During the time between her indictment at Great Falls in February and the time of her trial at Missoula in April, she spent some time on the Flathead reservation, going around to see the witnesses trying to intimidate them and taking up collections.

On the 24th day of March, 1915, she was arrested in Missoula, Montana by Sam Pulliam, a police officer, on complaint sworn to by him for wilfully and unlawfully disturbing the peace and quiet of the neighborhood of the Northern Pacific Depot in the city of Missoula and of Northern Pacific Passenger train No. 1, standing at the depot, by drunkeness and by loud and offensive talking and by tumultuous conduct. For this act she was kept in jail one night, brought before the police Court, lectured for her bad conduct and discharged.

Again on April 8, 1915, she was arrested for wilfully, and unlawfully soliciting and using a room for the purpose of prostitution and assignation. For this offense she received a sentence of thirty days and a fine of twenty-five dollars.

The arrest for this last act took place the night before her trial in the Federal Court, and the court was compelled to wait the next morning for the Marshall to go to the city jail and get her.

She was duly tried in the Federal Court and the jury returned a verdict of guilty as charged in the indictment of eight counts for selling and giving liquor to Indians and for introducing same on Flathead Indian reservation. The Court passed sentence on her giving her ninety days on each count, the sentence to run concurrently and to pay a fine of one hundred dollars and costs, which amounted to $465.45. She was committed to the Missoula County Jail at Missoula, Montana.

While serving her sentence in jail it has been said that she became familiar with one of the trusties at the jail and was caught in the act of having sexual intercourse with him through the bars. I can only report that Mr. R. J. Whitaker, Sheriff, in a letter to me states that he had at the time two trusties working around the jail and one told him he witnessed Princess Redfeather having intercourse through the bars with the other but that very little reliance could be put in any stories emanating from such sources.

After serving the sentence imposed by the United States Court, Princess Redfeather was released August 13, 1915 after taking the pauper's oath. Immediately after her release the City authorities of Missoula took her into custody for the offense that had been committed on the night before her trial in the Federal Court and were going to compel her to serve thirty days in jail and pay a fine of twenty-five dollars. Miss. Marie Lemery of St. Ignatius, Montana, however, came to her rescue and supplied her with money to pay her fine. She paid the fine and on recommendation of the City Commissioner the jail sentence was suspended on her promise to leave the city of Missoula.

After her release she again returned to the Flathead Indian Reservation where she proceeded to hold councils among the Indians, circulate petitions without headings and collect money, and sometime during the fall, in company with Modeste Finley and Antoine Moiese, went to Washington evidently for the purpose of putting their petition in the hands of some official. As near as I can find out the Princess claimed the petition was some sort of a power of attorney for her to act for the Indians and get their money for them. Evidently considerable money was raised for her as Modeste Finley states that Chief Kakashe placed $400 in his and Antoine Moiese's hands for their expenses and that after they got to Washington he saw Princess Redfeather with a large roll of bills. After getting to Washington these Indians saw very little of the Princess and claim they did not know what she was doing. After Finley and Moiese were there for nine or ten days they got tired and came home, but the Princess stayed and wrote a number of letters to Marie Lemery asking for money, and Marie Lemery sent her the following Post Office Money Orders from St. Ignatius, Montana:

October 1, 1915, Serial No. 17867. $30.00
Nov. 3, 1915, Serial No. 18217. $100.00
Nov. 3, 1915, Serial No. 18218. $50.00

Besides this I have been told, confidentially, that numerous registered letters were sent to Princess Redfeather containing money.

About February 16, 1915 [1916], Charlie Gabe, a full blood Flathead Indian, went to Washington to bring Princess Redfeather back. This Charlie Gabe is a disgruntled Indian was a confessed perjurer in the trial of Princess Redfeather before the United States Commissioner at Dixon, Montana. While he was in Washington with the Princess, at least one letter was written to Indians on the reservation asking that money be sent them. I am submitting with this report, this letter, and wish to call particular attention to it. The Princess Redfeather writes it to Marie Lemery asking her to go to old man

Marceal and get $300. for them. Marceal is a Flathead Indian about seventy-five years old. He has been led to believe in Princess Redfeather and I have found it impossible to get any information from him as to whether or not he has given or loaned Princess Redfeather any money. However, I am of the opinion this $300. was gotten from him and was sent to the Princess by Marie Lemery as on February 29, 1916 three Post Office Money Orders for $100. each from St. Ignatius, Montana were sent, the serial numbers being 19,401, 19402, and 19,403.

Sometime in March the Princess returned to the Flathead reservation and spread broadcast on the reservation she was going to hold a big council at Chief Kakashe's house at St. Ignatius on Easter Sunday, April 23, 1916, that she expected to take up a collection among the Indians to enable her to have Congress defeat the Reclamation appropriation bill. She further claimed that Senator Lane was behind her movement and that Senator Lane had a bill in Congress which would pass, provided she secured a sufficient number of signatures from the Indians, which would give them all of their money and that Senator Lane was going to fire Commissioner Sells and all of the employees of the Indian Service and that she and two other Indians would have charge of the Flathead Indian Reservation and would run the affairs as the Indians wanted them.

This meeting was held and I have been informed that about 150 Indians were present. Special Office Glenn and Deputy Ramsey, together with several others, broke up the meeting but the Indians refused to give up the Princess, harbored her and one Indian told them they would be shot if they attempted to take her, and, I have been told, she stood behind the door with a gun and said she would kill the first officer who came in. The officers thought it would be better to wait and arrest her later, and for some little time [she] kept in hiding, being harbored by the Lemery family living near St. Ignatius. Shortly after this she left the reservation in company with Caville Dupuis, Victor Dupuis, and Mary Lem[e]ry, for Washington. I have tried to get statements from Chief Kakashe, Charlie Gabe and numerous others, but they will give me no information; they believe in her and follow her directions. . . .

Document 75

Indians Arrested for Killing a Steer

July 7, 1916

Source: "Arrested for Killing a Two Year Old Steer," *The Ronan Pioneer*, July 7, 1916, page 1, col. 2.

Editors' note: The article only gives one side of the story, but does illustrate the type of crimes that irritated Indian-white relations on the reservation in 1916.

Arrested for Killing a Two Year Old Steer

Deputy Sheriff Wm. Engle and W. G. Brown, government farmer, arrested Antoine Finley and an Indian named Fatty Eneas last Sunday evening, charged with killing a two year old steer belonging to the Sisters at St. Ignatius. They were taken before U.S. Commissioner John N. Bailey Monday and both plead guilty to the complaint and waived examination. They were taken to Missoula Monday and are now in jail awaiting the action of the federal grand jury.

The officers learned of the killing and visited the scene of where it was reported to have taken place and some good detective work was done by them in uncovering the evidence. The hide, head and feet had been thrown into a pot hole and Deputy Sheriff Engle waded around in the water at times up to his chin before he recovered the hide. After securing this evidence the home of Finley was visited, where much of the meat was found, and upon being pressed for an explanation the suspected men acknowledged their guilt.

Document 76

Closing Out Sale

The Ronan Pioneer, July 21, 1916, page 2, col. 4-5.

Closing Out Sale

Millinery and Ladies' Furnishings

Having purchased the stock of Millinery and Ladies' Furnishings owned by Mattie I. Hull and desiring to use the building for other purposes, I will close out the entire stock at greatly reduced prices.

This stock is new and up-to-date and contains many articles of women's wear suitable for summer which will save many dollars. Buy early while the stock is complete.

This is a genuine Closing Out Sale and the stock will not be replenished.

ANNIE DUPUIS.

MATTIE I. HULL, Agent.

Document 77

Indians Sentenced to Work on Rock Pile

August 14, 1916

Source: "Intoxicated Indians Must Now Break Rock Says Chief Houston," *The Daily Missoulian*, August 14, 1916, page 8, col. 2.

Editors' note: The Indian offenders in Missoula were sentenced to work on a rock pile. Sheriff William Houston had been sheriff in the early 1890s and in 1916 was Missoula Chief of Police. In 1920, Houston was elected to a second term as Missoula County Sheriff, but after eleven months he was removed from office for incompetence and working with bootleggers. Presumably, he did not have to break rock as a punishment.

Intoxicated Indians Must Now Break Rock Says Chief Houston

"We have an Indian in jail today," said Chief of Police Houston, "and tomorrow he goes to work on the rock pile. This is the best way to cure them. I'll never forget the time when I put young Joe Blodgett to breaking rock for the same reason. His s.... went down and watched him work for a while, then she went back to town. Soon she returned with Missoula's entire Indian population. They sat there and watched Joe work all day. After that I never had any trouble with him. I tried the same cure on several others and soon noticed that there was a great falling off in Indian law-breakers. Major Morgan told me that it was the best and only way to cure them."

The unfortunate red man who goes to work this morning will be the first to suffer that penalty since Mr. Houston was last at the head of the police.

Document 78

Duncan McDonald Visits Ronan Newspaper Office September 15, 1916

Source: *The Ronan Pioneer*, September 15, 1916, page 2, col. 3.

Editors' note: Duncan McDonald was always willing to share his opinions and reservation news.

Duncan McDonald of Ravalli, made the Pioneer a pleasant call Wednesday. With his wife and a cousin, Daniel McDonald of Middletown, Conn., he is taking an outing in the mountains east of Ronan this week. His cousin made the trip from Connecticut to Montana by auto and is now camping out to get the real local color. Duncan says that Mose Deleware, Angus C. McDonald, Jim Raymond and Ran Roberts have completed the construction of a trail up Mollman creek to the top of the mountains east of town and are now engaged in making the trail down the east slope. This will afford a new passage over the mountain from Ronan to Swan river and it is said to be of easy passage. While here Duncan talked politics, game laws, names of local streams, explained the working of the fish law, whereby the little ones are killed off and the big ones protected, and left the force in better humor than before he came.

Document 79

Indian Exhibits Win Prizes in Fair

October 1916

Source: "Exhibits by Indians Reveal Advance of Race Under Eye and With Aid of Uncle Sam," *The Daily Missoulian*, October 6, 1916, page 10, col. 3-4; "Flathead Exhibits to Be Sent to St. Paul," *The Daily Missoulian,* October 9, 1916, page 3, col. 6-7.

Editors' note: The quality of the Flathead Reservation exhibits at the fall fair probably showed more about the industry and intelligence of the Indian farmers than the agency officials. Many tribal members were making good progress in farming during the 1910s when rainfall and markets were favorable.

Exhibits by Indians Reveal Advance of Race Under Eye and With Aid of Uncle Sam

Surprising evidence of the progress made by the Indians on the Flathead Reservation under the guidance of the government is afforded by the Indian exhibits in the hall under the grandstand at the Western Montana fairgrounds.

There are collected the exhibits which won three silver cups and a number of important individual prizes at the Montana state fair in Helena last week, greatly outclassing entries from the five other Indian reservations [in] the state.

Agricultural products of all sorts compose the bulk of the exhibit. They are arranged with taste and skill and cover a remarkably large field.

Showing Important.

While some of the sheaves of grain and some of the choice vegetables in the display are unsual [sic] enough to attract general attention, it is as a whole that the Indians' showing is most noteworthy. As a whole it demonstrates clearly the fact that the Indians being prepared for citizenship by the government which first conquered and then uplifted them are already industrious and capable farmers. Any ranch in western Montana would be proud to claim the products shown by the Indian farmers.

Upon Superintendent Fred C. Morgan, superintendent of the reservation since it was opened to settlement and the Indians were allotted land, the exhibit reflects great credit. It shows how careful and honest must have been the guidance of the government's wards, for only thorough and persistent education and encouragement could have developed the half-wild tribesmen sent to the reservation less than a quarter-century ago into the farmers who have produced grains and grasses and fruit and vegetables fit to be entered in open competition at any fair.

The exhibit shown at the Western Montana fair won, in Helena, three of the four silver cups offered in the Indian division. And it is noteworthy that the one class in which the Flatheads were surpassed [w]as that of curios, excellence in which indicates a persistence in traditional living rather than the desired acceptance of the white man's ways.

In addition to the principal awards given the Flathead exhibits, individual entrants won many important prizes. All of these displays are included in the showing at the fairgrounds.

* * * * * * * *

Flathead Exhibits to Be Sent to St. Paul
Remarkable Displays by Indians Will Be Shown by Northern Pacific.

The remarkable exhibits shown at the Western Montana fair by Indians from the Flathead reservation will be taken to St. Paul for display by the Northern Pacific Railway company. Immigration Agent Bricker of the railroad yesterday asked Karl Knudsen, the government farmer and collector of the exhibit, for permission to show it in the east.

With the farm products will go the beautiful collection of reservation pictures which was a feature of the booth at the fair grounds.

The exhibit attracted much attention. It reflects great credit upon the Indians themselves and upon Superintendent Morgan and Mr. Knudsen who have directed the education of the government's wards in farming.

Some of the prizes awarded in the Indian division at the fair were printed with the general list in Sunday morning's paper. The following additional awards came too late to be listed with the others:

Best display of fruit on plates — Adeline Allard, Leon, first; Therese Felsman, St. Ignatius, second; Peter Dupuis, Polson, third.

Best vegetables and roots — Henry Minesinger, Polson, first; Mitch Michel, Polson, second.

Best exhibit of beadwork — Mary Polson, Polson.

Best display of canned fruit — Alice Dupuis, Polson.

Best Indian costume (female) — Angeline Michel, Polson, first; Mrs. Pete Finley, Polson, second.

Best Indian costume (male) — Joseph Bonaparte, Polson.

Best pencil sketch — Mary Houle, Polson.

Document 80

Bison Range Herd Increasing

December 28, 1916

Source: "Buffalo Are Increasing," *The Daily Missoulian*, December 28, 1916, page 10, col. 5.

Editors' note: As Duncan McDonald got older, he liked spending the cold winter weather in the steam heated accommodations of a Missoula hotel. He was pleased with the growth of the buffalo herd on the new Bison Range on the reservation.

Buffalo Are Increasing

Reserve Herd Makes Satisfactory Increase, According to McDonald.

Duncan McDonald is spending a few days in Missoula as there is not much work at present on the ranch and the facilities for keeping warm are a little better here. Duncan McDonald is always a welcome visitor, for while, as he says, his friends are thinning out, occasionally one of the "newcomers" — in so far as Duncan is concerned — is able to get a true insight into Montana as it was through conversing with him.

"You say the Flathead is going to be a fine country?" asked Duncan. "It's fine right now. It's just going to get a little better."

The conversation drifted around to the buffalo reserve and Mr. McDonald told of the fine growth which the herd was making. "The way it is increasing now," he said, "there is little doubt but that the buffalo will never be entirely extinct. When I think of that little bunch in there, though, and the multitudes I have seen on the prairies of eastern Montana it makes you wonder how they could have killed them off so fast. That is, you would be surprised unless you knew the slaughter as it used to be.

"I wintered in 1875 in Saskatchewan at old Fort McCloud. The mounted police estimated that winter that 100,000 buffalo were killed within a radius of 10 miles. This accounts, of course, for their rapid disappearance."

Mr. McDonald felt a great personal loss when Judge Woody died. There are only a few of what he calls the "old-timers" left, but those who are able to talk intelligently over the days gone by are on his calling list when he pays his infrequent visits to the city.

Document 81

Business Committee vs. Tribal Council

January 6, 1917

Source: Duncan McDonald, et. al., Flathead Business Committee meeting, January 6, 1917, from file 1,438/1917 Flathead 056, Central Classified Files, RG 75, National Archives, Washington, D.C.

Editors' note: The Flathead Business Committee headed by Duncan McDonald opposed the Flathead Tribal Council led by Marie Lemery. The Business Committee worked with Fred C. Morgan, the Flathead Superintendent, while the Tribal Council wanted to change agency policies, especially those related to the funding of the Flathead Irrigation Project. The competition continued throughout the rest of the 1910s and resulted in competing Flathead delegations heading for Washington, D.C.

Flathead Indian Reservation.
St. Ignatius, Montana.

The Flathead Business Committee met at St. Ignatius on January 6, 1917, at eight P.M., with the following members present:

Duncan McDonald, Chairman;
Charles Allard, Secretary;
Angus P. McDonald;
Mose Delaware;
Peter Magpie.

There being a quorum present, the meeting was called to order.

Supt. Fred C. Morgan read to the Committee the letter dated December 22, 1916, Ed-L&O 91496-16, 128353-16, RCG, relative to the question of permitting a rod and gun club of St. Ignatius, Montana, to stock certain reservoirs of the Flathead Reservation with fish.

The superintendent also called the attention of the Committee to the activities on this reservation recently of two men who it appears had been inducing certain of the Indians to sign an agreement to enter into contract with a firm of attorneys, to pay said firm a certain per cent of the tribal moneys for assistance in securing said moneys for the Indians.

Regarding the stocking of the reservoirs with fish the Committee unanimously agrees in recommending that the Department cooperate with the Federal Bureau of Fisheries in having the stocking done, with catfish and Chinook salmon. As to issuing of permits, it is agreed that none should at this time, or until long enough for the fish to grow large enough for food purposes, be issued; and that before any permits at all are issued that the matter be again be brought before the attention of the Business Committee for disposition at that time. It is also further recommended that the reservoirs be established as game or bird preserves, and that hunting on the same be prohibited.

It is further the opinion of the Committee that the members of the reservation should be encouraged to observe or respect the state game and fish laws in so far as hunting and fishing on the reservation is concerned. In other words, that fishing and hunting be done in the same periods as the open season provided by the state laws, to the end that the fish and game of the reservation be conserved.

As to the Indians who left on the 2d instant for Washington, the Committee protests against any agreements or contracts entered into by them on behalf of the Indians of Flathead Reservation, as said Indians do not represent the Flathead Reservation, and should not be recognized as representing this reservation in any way. And the Committee unanimously protest against the approval by the Department of any contract or agreement providing for the payment to any attorney or attorneys, or any other person or persons, of any per cent or portion of the tribal moneys.

The Committee also unanimously requests that the entire membership of nine members be authorized to visit Washington, the expenses of the trip to be reimbursed from the tribal fund "Indian Moneys, Proceeds of Labor, Flathead Indians," for the purpose of preventing the entering into of contracts or agreements by the Indians who have heretofore gone unauthorized to Washington, or to protest against any other measures they or any parties influencing them may attempt to adopt that that [sic] are detrimental to the interests of the Flatheads. The Committee also desires that the authorization for visit Washington be immediately granted, as they can best leave their ranches and businesses on the reservation during the winter season and before spring opens up and their work demands their presence here. It is also the opportune time for such a visit while Congress is in session, in order that they may be represented in any proposed legislation which may adversely affect the Flathead Indians. And for the welfare of the Flatheads it is the opinion of the Business Committee that they should visit the Department and the Bureau of Indian Affairs and become acquainted with the officers and officials in charge of the work, familiarize themselves with the records and work in said Department and Bureau connected with Flathead Reservation. Any expenditure for such a visit would be more than repaid by the benefits that would accrue to the Flathead Indians from the knowledge obtained by the Committee.

The Committee also authorizes and requests the superintendent of Flathead Reservation to telegraph the Commissioner of Indian Affairs protesting against the recognition of the Indians who have heretofore left for Washington as representing the Flathead Indians, and protesting against the approval of any agreements or contracts that may be entered into by them.

Duncan McDonald, Chairman
Charles Allard, Secretary
Moses Delaware
Angus P. McDonald
Peter Magpie, his mark.

Document 82

Flathead Delegation to D.C. Opposes Reclamation Policy January 10, 1917

Source: "Flatheads On Warpath," *The Daily Missoulian*, January 10, 1917, page 10, col. 2.

Editors' note: In 1916 Congress reimbursed the Flathead tribal funds which had been used to pay for the construction of the Flathead Irrigation Project, but that left the charges as liens against the allotments and homesteads in the project. Mary Lemery helped organize the Flathead Tribal Council to oppose the irrigation project. Apparently most of the traditional chiefs supported the Flathead Tribal Council in preference to the Business Committee.

Flatheads On Warpath

Six Chiefs of Nation Start for Washington to Tomahawk Senate.

The Flatheads are on the warpath!

The chiefs of the Selish nation, ordinarily so peaceful as to be scorned by strenuous tribes, have taken up their tomahawks and nerved themselves to battle.

The United States senate is their game. They hope to cow the upper house of the national congress into acquiesence in a plan for a modification of the reclamation policy in the Flathead country.

It cannot be said that the warring Selish left a bloody trail behind them. In fact, they didn't even make any noise. They started for Washington so silently that no one in Missoula knew of their going. Today they should reach the capital.

In the war party are Chief Baptiste Kakashe, Chief Antoine Moiese, Chief St. Pierre Michel, Chief Andrew Bullhead, Chief Dominick Antez and the Chief George Riley. With them is "Princess" Eluwhisimshi, a young Indian girl who serves as interpreter.

The Indians interrupted their journey at Kansas City, where it is said, they entertained the natives and were themselves made merry. They danced for the Missourians and were feted in return.

The Indians do not like the way in which the government funds for reclamation of Flathead lands are being spent. They hope to convince the senate that a better way of handling the Flathead projects is possible.

"We are on our way to Washington to plead for a people which are oppressed," is the way the Indians have put it.

Document 83

Malcolm McLeod Ran Various Ronan Businesses

January 26, 1917 — June 13, 1919

Source: *The Ronan Pioneer*, January 26, 1917, page 8, col. 2; "Harness & Shoe Repairing Shop," *The Ronan Pioneer*, April 25, 1919, page 5, col. 6; *The Ronan Pioneer*, June 13, 1919, page 4, col. 2.

Editors' note: Tribal member Malcolm McLeod sold firewood, operated a leather shop, and ran an auto bus in Ronan in the late 1910s.

For the best dry wood on the market, at $2 per rick delivered, see Malcolm McLeod or leave orders at the hardware department of Scearce's store. adv.

— January 26, 1917

* * * * * * * * * *

Source: "Harness & Shoe Repairing Shop," *The Ronan Pioneer*, April 25, 1919, page 5, col. 6

****

Malcolm McLeod announces that he runs a regular auto bus to and from trains. Those wishing to go to the depot can get him by calling phone 482. adv.

— June 13, 1919

Malcolm McLeod
Source: Photograph Archives, Montana Historical Society, Helena, Montana, photo PAc 85-91.02121

Document 84

Tribal Council Delegation Opposes Dixon Irrigation Plans February 1917

Source: "The Flathead Insurrection," *The Daily Missoulian*, February 18, 1917, page 4, col. 1-2; "Attorney Is Stuck for Indian Victims," *The Daily Missoulian*, February 22, 1917, page 1, col. 2-3; "Indians Received with Enthusiasm," *The Daily Missoulian*, February 22, 1917, page 1, col. 3; Excerpts from "Revel at Hunt Ball," *The Washington Post*, February 21, 1917, page 4, col. 1-3.

Editors' note: In February 1917 Senator Joseph Dixon still owned *The Daily Missoulian* and the paper was upset that the Indians were not happy that the money being used to construct the irrigation project was a lien against the individual Indian allotments and white homesteads. The Flathead Tribal Council delegation opposing the construction appropriations was assisted by Victor J. Evans, a Washington, D.C., attorney. Evans was a wealthy Washington patent attorney who, among other interests, also represented a number of Indian tribes seeking legal redress for government wrongs. The Montana Senators vigorously fought the Tribal Council delegates in order to continue the irrigation appropriations to benefit the white Montana economy.

The Flathead Insurrection.

It is rather amusing to their neighbors here at home to read the latest story from Washington, telling how "Chief" Moiese and "Chief" Sam Resurrection and other malcontents from the old Flathead reservation country are making their annual pilgrimage to the capital to spread the usual lurid stories of incompetent administration of their affairs.

Every year these pilgrimages take place from most of the Indian reservations of the west. Usually it is found that some Washington claim attorney, with the assistance of a local partner, has financed the trip in the hope of getting a "contract" out of the Indians, payable out of their tribal funds.

In the old days these contracts with Washington claim attorneys were prolific of more scandal and intrigue than all the mistakes of the Indian office and its agents put together.

The illiterate red man readily listens to all the impossible stories afloat about untold riches that properly belong to him. The average reservation Indian delights in "investigations" and trips to Washington to "get his rights."

When boiled down, his vague ideas of "getting his rights" usually means an immediate division of tribal funds. The average reservation Indian does not take much stock in bank accounts. He wants cash in hand for quick investment in top buggies, talking machines and second hand automobiles.

As a matter of fact the modern Indian has been better treated than any other of Uncle Sam's children. Schools, hospitals, rations, farming implements and irrigation ditches have been provided for him at government expense.

The Indian himself must learn the painful lesson that his white brother is still learning, that work and not government subsidy is the basis of all prosperity for the individual.

We are not advised as to the source of supply of railroad tickets and boarding house fare for the present delegation headed by "Chief" Moiese and his compatriots, but it is a perfectly safe guess that back behind the scenes is some claim attorney, who wants a contract payable out of Flathead tribal funds.

****

Attorney Is Stuck for Indian Victims

Tried to Work Up Case for Reds; Now He's Out Their Expenses.

Washington, Feb. 21. — (Special.) — When it developed today that Victor J. Evans, a Washington attorney, prepared the charges against agency employes which nine Flathead Indians have been reciting before the senate Indian committee for six days, the committee declined to proceed further with the hearing.

Senators Walsh and Myers, who conducted cross-examinations of the Indians, believe that if the committee takes any action on the complaints it will be to direct the Indian office to investigate specific charges and correct any wrongs found to exist.

At the hearing today the committee decided not to report the Myers bill proposing the sale of Crow reservation lands. This kills the bill for the present session.

Evans, the attorney who was behind the Indians' charges, is in sorry straits as a result of the discovery of his part in the affair. Evans, it was shown, employed George Wasson, a half breed, to work up the case. Wasson spent three months on the reservation, collecting affidavits charging agency employes with embezzlement, immorality and general dishonesty. Then he secured for

Evans a contract to represent the Indians. Evans was to get a commission upon sums he might collect or save for the reds.

But the validity of this contract was not established and Evans will probably lose not only his expected commissions, but the expenses of the Indians as well, for the committee today refused to accede to demands that the nine Indian witnesses and the two half-breeds, Wasson and Marie Bemoire, be paid $500 each for their expenses.

Appropriation Safe.

The complaints cannot under any circumstances affect this year's appropriation of $750,000 for the Flathead reclamation project, included in the Indian appropriation bill.

* * * * * * * * *

Indians Received with Enthusiasm

Washington, Feb. 21. — (Special.) — The 16 Flathead and Sioux Indians who are visiting Washington from Montana while presenting complaints to the senate Indian committee took a prominent part in the Washington Hunt club's Mardi Gras ball last evening. Under the direction of Dr. Hopkins and Victor J. Evans they represented a group entitled, "Daniel Boone and American Indians."

A war dance given by the Indians was well received. The ball was the most brilliant function Washington has seen this season and was attended by over 1,000 people prominent in official and resident society.

* * * * * * * *

Revel at Hunt Ball

Marti Gras a Brilliant Close for Capital's Social Season.

Washington's social season went out in a blaze of glory last evening at the Mardi Gras hunt ball, in the large ballroom of the Willard. . . .

Indians Are Spectacular.

The most spectacular and interesting feature of the pageant was the seventh group, Daniel Boone and American Indians, a band of Blackfoot [Flathead] Indians who happen to be spending some time in Washington. They were picturesque to a degree, and their clothes were more than ordinarily handsome in color and elaborate beading. They were in charge of Victor Evans. Chief Ka Ka She, 93 years old, is the chief of the Flathead tribe. The others were Chief Bullhead, Chief Mosese, Chief Machelle, Chief Antez and Chief Grizzly Bear, Coming-up-the-Mountain, Marie Lemery, Flathead Indian maiden, with a costume over 100 years old; Louis Lantow, Louis Pellew, Joe Pierre and George B. Wassam.

They did a war dance, seemingly enjoying it as much as the company, which was by this time grouped in informal little parties on the floor, standing in the boxes and at various vantage points. After their grotesque and interesting performance they retired to one side of the hall, where Gen. and Mrs. Hugh L. Scott went to greet them. Gen. Scott kept up a lively conversation with them, apparently a witty one, too, all in the sign language, which Gen. Scott appears to handle fluently. Many others of the guests were presented to the Indians, who held a court of their own for some little time. . . . .

Document 85

Flathead Tribal Council Complains About Indian Policies February 21, 1917

Source: Chief Ka Ka She, et. al., to Assistant Commissioner of Indian Affairs, February 21, 1917, and enclosure [Chief Ka Ka She, et. al.}, to Chairman and Members Senate Committee on Indian Affairs, February 16, 1917, from file 18,530/1917 Flathead 056, Central Classified Files, RG 75, National Archives, Washington, D.C.

Editors' note: These letters laid out the complaints against Flathead Agency policies made by the Flathead Tribal Council. Tribal funds were no longer being used to fund construction of the Flathead Irrigation Project, but agency expenses were still being paid by the tribe and the agency was not giving the tribal members an accounting of the money. The Flathead Tribal Council felt the forced opening of the reservation in 1910 was a great injustice to the tribe through which the tribe lost many of their assets. They also wanted legislation that would allow the Flathead tribes to sue the government in the U.S. Court of Claims for damages resulting from past government policies.

Washington, D.C.,
February 21, 1917.

Honorable E. B. Merritt,
Assistant Commissioner of Indian Affairs,
Washington, D.C.
Dear Sir:

At one of the recent hearings of the Flat Head delegation before the Senate Indian Committee you were good enough to invite the delegation to come to your office after the Senate Committee hearings were finished, and to present to you a statement of our needs.

As you were present at all the sessions of the Committee hearings on Flat Head matters and listened to the discussions, it will not be necessary, perhaps, in this letter, to go very fully into details about matters already presented to the Committee and we shall only set out briefly a list of the things that the Indians desire to submit and discuss.

In view of what is said in a memorial presented by us to the Senate Indian Committee, a copy of which is attached hereto, we respectfully ask your consideration of the things therein itemized.

Nothing more need be said with reference to the hesitation or reluctance of the delegation to present itself at your office upon arrival in Washington, save only this, that the Flat Head Indians now assure you that they are, and will always be willing and glad to come directly to the office with their appeals for assistance and protection if they are made to feel that the office is in sympathy with them rather than with those against whom they justly complain, and that their requests for assistance and relief are worthy of your serious consideration.

The Flat Head Indians look upon the opening of their reservation as a great wrong; they have always so regarded it. They did not know that they had the power to prevent it. They have felt up to this time that they had little or no approach to any power that could or would assist them in postponing such action by Congress. Their effort at securing favorable hearings from government officials from time to time had not been successful. They felt that they had no-one to whom they could appeal with confidence and they yielded to a power which seemed beyond their influence or control.

The Flat Head irrigation project, which we regard as merely a part of the plan of opening the reservation for the benefit of the white settler, we consider the second step in our undoing. At the beginning it seemed a bold attempt at what might almost be called (respectfully) the robbing of our tribal fund. This wrong was by its very boldness brought relief, from the Indian Bureau, as we now understand, and we are glad to know that the recent legislation correcting the injustice to the Flat Head Indians, restoring to our tribal fund the money wrongfully taken from it for this reclamation project, received your approval and was accomplished with your cooperation.

In order that this delegation may know the attitude of the Indian Office towards the Indians in regard to the several matters that are involved in their present endeavors on behalf of the tribe, we ask for an official expression from the Indian Bureau on the matters specified in the enclosed memorial to the Commissioner and in addition thereto the following:

1. The Indian police force on the Flat Head Reservation should be reorganized in the interest of the Indians on the reservation.

2. Members of the tribe who have not received allotments should be given allotments on the Public Domain equal in extent to what is allowed as a homestead to a white man, such allotments to be selected by the parents of all allottees who are under age.

3. An itemized account showing the amount of money realized from the sale of surplus lands and the disposition made thereof is requested; also a statement

showing the disposition made of the annual appropriation by Congress for the Indians on the Flat Head Reservation; also an itemized statement of the amounts received and the disposition of the money accruing, from the grazing privileges on the reservation.

4. That saw-mills and grist-mills be established at suitable points on the reservation for the convenience of the members of the tribe and that three (3) threshing machines be furnished for their use; also that (5) cows be furnished to each allottee.

Very respectfully.
The Flat Head Delegation
Chief Ka Ka She [thumb print]
Chief Anton Moiese [thumb print]

Judge Baptiste Kakashe, Pend d'Oreille
Source: Photograph Archives, Montana Historical Society, Helena, Montana
detail from photo 954-528

Chief Charley Machelle [thumb print]
Chief Antiste [thumb print]
Andrew Bullhead [thumb print]
George Rilley [thumb print]
Louie Pellew [thumb print]
Louis C. Lantow
Joseph Pierre
Mary Lemery
George Bundy Wasson

* * * * * * * *

[Enclosed:}

Washington, D.C.,
February 16, 1917.

To the Honorable The Chairman
and Members of the Senate Committee
on Indian Affairs.
Gentlemen:

The undersigned delegation, representatives of the Flathead Nation of Indians, by way of concluding their presentation to your Committee of their statement of conditions on the Flathead Indian Reservation, which it has been their duty to offer and which you have so patiently heard, we submit the following by way of a summary of our matters; and we beg leave to add only such items as will serve, if possible, to make simple and clear the principal reasons for our presence in Washington and our appeal to your Committee for consideration of the Flathead Indians' cause.

The Flathead Indian Reservation is far removed from the seat of Government. The Flathead Indians cannot but feel that they have been very remote in point of consideration received at the hands of that Department of the Government to the care of which they and their property are committed.

From the time of the opening of their reservation to white settlers, and before, it has been the policy of the Government to destroy their tribal organization, and it has seemed to them that this policy results in destroying their prosperity, their happiness, their manhood. These things the Flathead Indians believe. The belief has been forced upon them, grounded in them, and fastened to their minds. They accept the conviction unwillingly, they know the name of "Great Father." It had as much meaning to them as to other tribes. The idea conveyed by "Great Father" has induced them often to send their chiefs and headmen thousands of miles to the City of Washington to present and plead their cause. These Flathead leaders came to Washington, we believe, in exactly the spirit that this Committee would want them to come. They were ever friendly, kind-hearted and earnest; if sometimes they were complaining, surely there was justification. But they came to Washington as upright, honest men in the interest of their tribes, to lay before the Commissioner of Indian Affairs and the Secretary of the Interior true statements of what it was the duty of the Government officials to find out for themselves.

These chiefs and representatives of the Flathead Nation, gentlemen of the Committee, never received at the hands of the officials of this Government the consideration and the treatment that the dignity of their mission entitled them to. We think it charitable to suggest that those to whom they appealed had but a poor conception of the heart and mind planted within the rough exterior of the Indian form; otherwise the consideration which has been shown to these honest people by your Committee during the last week would have been shown to them during the recurring years of the last decade when they came to make their natural appeal to the Commissioners of Indian Affairs and the Secretaries of the Interior that have been their guardians during that period.

We venture this much of preface, gentlemen, because of the fact that a complaint has been lodged before your Committee by the present Commissioner of Indian Affairs that our delegation did not immediately present itself to the Commissioner and there plead a cause. The truth is that before the weariness of the journey of 3,000 miles had been overcome by the old men of this delegation, one of whom is almost a centenarian, a gratuitous message was brought to us from the Commissioner that he wanted it distinctly understood that the expenses of the Flathead Delegation would not be paid by the Indian Bureau. While the old men in the delegation did not regard this message, perhaps, as an insult, it did offend and wound them deeply; and we submit that it was only natural for them to await from the Commissioner another message that would indicate that a visit from them to his office would be acceptable.

The Flathead Indians have shown your Committee that their reservation was to them a home, sufficient in all respects for their comfort, welfare, happiness. They were prosperous, contented, self-supporting people. They were intelligent, respected, independent. While their knowledge was not the knowledge of the white man, it was a knowledge adequate for their necessities, and they were the cause of no anxiety and virtually no expense to the Government of the United States.

When, against their will, under the urgent demands of the surrounding white population and the politicians of the State, their tribal home was destroyed, and what they loved and wanted was taken from them by the strong arm of the Government, and there was given in exchange what they did not want, the last great wrong was imposed upon an unoffending, peaceful people.

The recurring ills and injuries to the Flathead Nation, following year by year since the date of the disruption of their tribe and tribal rights, may have been accidents; the Indians feel and believe they have the right to feel that they were not accidents, but only the natural development of a well laid plan, not only to open an Indian Reservation; not only to destroy a tribal organization; not only to annihilate a happy community, but illegally and clandestinely and surreptitiously to absorb for the benefit of the white man as rapidly as could be done under guise of law of the value that the coveted property of the Indian possessed; and this delegation respectfully submits to your Honorable Committee that an honest survey of the conditions, a careful calculation of the losses to the Indians, will justify the prophecy that the length of one generation will nearly suffice to destroy all evidence of Indian ownership in a majority of this property.

1. That as far as possible all Agency employees be Indians and that the white persons now holding government positions on the reservation be superceded by such Indian employees; and that this include the office of Superintendent.

2. That an investigation be made forthwith into the methods employed by all Indian traders on the Flat Head Reservation and that licenses be revoked in all cases where dealings and trading with the Indians are found to be dishonest or oppressive; especially that the practice of compelling the Indians to spend their monthly checks at any given stores be promptly abolished.

3. That all work upon irrigation projects on the Flat Head Reservation be suspended until a thorough investigation has been made and the facts disclosed by public report in furnishing the Indians such information as they are entitled to have regarding the project on their reservation, and thus affording them the opportunity for intelligence, remonstrance and opposition.

4. That the Indian police force on the reservation be re-organized so as to abate present wrongs and oppressive methods from the system.

5. That government schools on the reservation adequate for the needs of the Indian children whose education is at present neglected, be established without further delay; and that a suitable and efficient hospital under government supervision be provided.

6. That an allotment on the public domain be allowed to all members of the Flat Head Nation of sufficient size to make the total amount of land allotted to them on and off the reservation, equal to the amount provided for the white homesteaders under existing laws.

7. That the office of Farmer on the Flat Head Reservation be abolished for the reason that no appreciable advantage is gained by the Indians therefrom.

8. That all power sites and all mineral deposits, including among other things, coal, oil and gas existing on the Flat Head Reservation and not heretofore absolutely disposed of but retained for the exclusive benefit of the Flat Head Nation and that all revenues derived therefrom be credited to and placed in the tribal funds to be distributed per capita among the members of the tribe.

9. That all telephone and telegraph franchises within the Flat Head Reservation be reserved for the Flat Head Nation.

10. That the Indians of the Flat Head Nation be classified as follows: competent, semi-competent and non-competent, and that the rights accorded them with reference to the management of their own affairs be fairly adjusted according to the respective abilities of their classes; that this classification be made by a committee of three persons, one to be selected by the Flat Head Nation, one by the Secretary of the Interior (but not to be the Superintendent or other employee on the reservation) and one by the Governor of the State of Montana; and that the compensation to be paid, such commission to be fixed by the Secretary of the Interior and taken from the tribal fund of the Flat Head Nation.

11. That the tribal funds be apportioned as early as practicable and distributed among the Indians per capita in accordance with the act of March 2, 1907.

12. That power and authority be given the Flat Head Nation to present their claims against the United States through the Court of Claims and the Supreme Court of the United States without further delay.

13. That the Indians having funds deposited to their individual credit be allowed a sufficient amount thereof to build them comfortable homes wherever such funds as sufficient for the purpose.

14. That the present practice of permitting trespass upon Indian lands by white people without interference be discontinued and the Indian owners be protected in the premises.

15. That the Indians believe the Burke Act should be repealed.

Respectfully submitted.

The Flat Head Delegation

[There were no signatures attached to this carbon copy of the letter.]

Document 86

Tribal Council Delegates Oppose Reclamation Project February 23, 1917

Source: "Indians Charge Extravagance," *The Ronan Pioneer*, February 23, 1917, page 1, col. 6.

Editors' note: With the assistance of Senator Harry Lane of Oregon, the delegates from the Flathead Tribal Council were able to get time with the Senate Indian Affairs Committee to oppose the continued funding of the Flathead Irrigation Project. The Montana Senators were much alarmed at this attack on appropriations to benefit the western Montana white population.

Indians Charge Extravagance

Apparently the delegation of Flathead Indians from the Flathead, headed by Chief Moiese and Mary Lemery, are causing considerable trouble in Washington. The following letter received Monday last explains the object and seriousness of their charge:

Washington, D.C.
February 16, 1917.

My dear Mr. Rathbone: — I write hurriedly to say that Chief Moiese and a delegation of eight other Flathead Indians, claiming to have been elected at a tribal council, accompanied by a man from Oregon named Wasson and one Mary Lemere who has an allotment near St. Ignatius, who appear to be their spokesmen and advocates, are here trying to make trouble. Yesterday they appeared before the Senate committee on Indian affairs and made a most violent and virulent attack on the Reclamation service and the Flathead reclamation project, claiming it was a fraud and a failure, that the Indians do not want it, that the white settlers do not want it, and that everybody wants it discontinued and chopped off right where it is. They charge fraud, mismanagement, wastefulness, extravagance and many other things. They claim that the Flathead Indian lands do not need irrigation and that they will raise good crops without irrigation. They claim the Indians are being robbed and all sorts of things. I do not know who is at the bottom of this but it looks like a worked up propaganda to injure the Flathead project.

They also violently attack the Indian bureau and Major Morgan, the Indian agent, and charge dishonesty and criminality. They demand two things, viz., the removal of Major Morgan and that the Flathead project be abandoned forthwith.

This is a great surprise to me. I have been here six years and never before heard that the Indians were dissatisfied with the Flathead project. It looks like somebody is putting them up to this. Senator Walsh and I were in attendance upon the committee all day and vigorously combated their contentions about the reclamation project. I hardly think it will amount to anything. The appropriation of $750,000 for the coming year has already been passed by both house and senate and is not in dispute, and, therefore, confereés can have nothing to do with it. Had this violent attack come a little sooner it might have beaten the appropriation but I think it comes too late. The only way it could beat it now would be for either the house or senate to reject the report of the conferees and beat the entire bill. That is possible but I hardly think probable. Senator Walsh and I will do our best to prevent any such calamity. Many of their statements about the Flathead reservation, the reclamation service and the reclamation project are glaringly false, as I pointed out. I had Mr. Davis, chief of the reclamation service, hurriedly summoned to appear and aid us which he did. I merely write to let you know what is going on. If there should be any disastrous developments, I will let you know.

Yours most cordially,
Henry L. Myers.

Document 87

Tribal Funds for Per Capita

March 9, 1917

Source: "Flathead Money to Be Pro-Rated," *The Ronan Pioneer*, March 9, 1917, page 1, col. 4.

Editors' note: The Flathead Tribal Council was interested in getting tribal money that had been used to pay for the irrigation project and agency expenses paid to tribal members as a per capita.

Flathead Money to Be Pro-Rated

By request the following letter from Assistant Commissioner of Indian Affairs Merritt is published. The letter will be agreeable reading to those who share in the distribution — whenever that may be — and the Pioneer is glad to learn that those who are entitled to this money are to receive it:

Washington, D.C., Feb. 23, 1917.

Miss Marie Lemery
Washington, D.C.
My dear Miss Lemery:

In compliance with your informal inquiry if the funds of the Flathead Indians are being held up because of the presence of the Flathead Indians in Washington, you are advised that this is not the case. The office had in mind the pro rating of the tribal funds of the Flathead Indians under the Act of March 2, 1907, as amended by the Indian appropriation act of May 18, 1916, (39 Stat. L., 141). That legislation, however, provides that the tribal funds of the Flathead Indians theretofore used in connection with the construction of the Flathead irrigation project should be deposited to the credit of the Flathead Indians and held in the treasury of the United States until further authorized by congress. This fund amounts to $440,217.78.

It will probably be necessary to get additional legislation before this fund can be pro rated, and Senator Walsh has already introduced a bill to that effect.

The remaining fund from the proceeds of the Flathead reservation, amounting to $282,449.11, may be pro rated under the existing law, and action to that effect will be taken immediately.

Very truly yours,
E. B. Merritt.
Assistant Commissioner.

Document 88

U.S. Army Recruits Indian Soldiers

April 13, 1917

Source: "Want Indian Recruits for Uncle Sam's Army," *The Daily Missoulian*, April 13, 1917, page 3, col. 1.

Editors' note: In 1917 tribal members who had not received patents in fee were not citizens. The U.S. Army still wanted them to enlist for service in World War I.

Want Indian Recruits for Uncle Sam's Army
Officer Sent from Missoula to Reservation for Red Soldiers.
Not Allowed Before
Hitherto First Americans Have Not Been Allowed to Join Army.

Following directions from the recruiting station at Spokane, Private H. E. Bryant of the local recruiting station, left yesterday for the reservation, for the purpose of encouraging enlistment in the regular army among the Indians, both full bloods and breeds living there. Before the present orders were issued, the noble red man could enlist only after permission had been secured from the adjutant general of the United States army, but now the bars are down and the aborigines will be welcomed into the ranks. It is probable that several regiments composed of full blood Indians exclusively will be formed, if a sufficient number of them enlist. The breeds may be enlisted for service in groups with the pale-face regiments.

The local recruiting station has also been authorized to enlist high school students in groups of 10 for assignment to Fort Worden, Wash., providing the enlistments can be secured at once. If less than 10 enlist in a group, but others signify their intention of enlisting, the local officer is ordered to send the boys that have enlisted in a group, and to send the others to Fort Wright for instructions as soon as they enlist. If a sufficient number of college students may be secured, the recruiting officer is urged to use the same plan, in order to encourage enlistment.

Document 89

Charles Allard to Put on Rodeo in Missoula

May 27, 1917

Source: "Allard Says Big Show in July Will Be Good," *The Daily Missoulian*, May 27, 1917, page 2, col. 1.

Editors' note: Charles Allard, Jr., employed other Flathead Reservation Indians in his program for the 1917 Missoula Stampede. Jackson Sundown, a Nez Perce Indian, was a famous rodeo rider in the early twentieth century.

Allard Says Big Show in July Will Be Good
Stampede to Be Marked by Extraordinary Events, Says Promoter.
Big Stars Coming
Best Wild West Performers in Country to Take Part in Show Here.

Displays of daring and skill in numberless exhibitions will make the Wild West performances which will feature the 1917 Missoula Stampede the best every staged in the west, according to Charles Allard, of Polson, one of the directors of the Wild West shows. Mr. Allard, who is one of the most prominent ranchers on the reservation, and owner of one of the few herds of bison yet alive, is in Missoula conferring with the committee of Missoula men who are making arrangements for the Stampede.

High class performers, who are at the top of their rapidly-thinning profession, will ride and rope and bulldog at the Stampede. Ed McCarthy, who, together with Mr. Allard, is in charge of the Wild West shows, will bring two dozen performers and three score real western horses from Cheyenne. Mr. McCarthy was the originator of the annual Wild West performances which are being staged throughout the country and has for several years been in charge of the Cheyenne Frontier Days shows, which enjoy the reputation of being the best of the kind in the world.

Country's Best Rider.

Jackson Sundown, considered the best rider in the country, is under contract to the managers of the Missoula Stampede, and will ride here. Sundown won the national bucking title by taking first at both Pendleton and Cheyenne, and is reputed to be able to ride any "outlaw" horse in the United States. It will be his first appearance in Missoula.

Many riders who have earned the plaudits of the crowd at former Stampedes will return. Among these will be Ben Oakes, Lee Caldwell, stellar performer at the first Stampede here, Scoop Martin, and others well known to western Montana Stampede fans.

McCarthy will bring with him 24 riders, both men and women, the best known among them being Bill Baker, premier bulldogger of the west, Ray Jones, George Panicke, Jay Miller, Gene McKay, Bob Lee, Billy Wright and Dan Thompson.

Old Winners Coming.

Best known among the men who will bring strings of relay horses here are "Sleepy" Armstrong and "Nep" Lynch, winners in former races.

Ropers of world-wide renown, who will give expert exhibitions of control over their whirling lariats, will provide a feature of the show. Sammy Garrett, the best trick-roper in the country, and George Weir, said to be the champion roper of the United States, will be the headliners of the roping contest.

Women Riders, Too.

Among the best known women riders who will appear at the Stampede, are Bertha Blanchett and Vera McGinnis, both of whom will be entered in feature races, as well as in the chariot races. Allard and McCarthy are in correspondence with several other women riders and performers of fame, and expect to bring the best of them to Missoula on July 3, 4 and 5.

Many New Features.

Features which will be entirely new to Missoula Stampede audiences will be numerous according to Mr. Allard. Stage-coach races, with real old-time stage coaches, will have prominent part of the program. Women's standing races, exhibitions of trick-roping from bridleless bucking horses and fancy riding performances of several varieties will also have a prominent part on the program.

A buffalo chase, in which the bisons owned by Mr. Allard will play a passive part, while Indians in full war-regalia will enact the parts taken by their forefathers centuries ago, is one of the novelties which will be introduced by the managers of the Wild West show. It will be a wild, exciting act, according to Mr. Allard, as the Indians will be armed with blunt arrows and other implements of the chase, and will drive the ancient rulers of the prairie down the field in a wild chase. Bucking bulls and cows, never used before, will have a place on the program.

Longhorn Steers.

Longhorn steers from Texas will be imported especially for the roping and bulldogging contests. The wildest bucking horses or "outlaws" from Cheyenne and Pendleton, will be brought to Missoula, among them being "Yellow Fever," considered the champion bucking cayuse in the country.

American Indians in full war regalia, will take a prominent part in the show. Mr. Allard plans to make the Indian section of the parades which will be held during the Stampede one which will be long remembered. Aboriginal costumes, with plenty of paint and feathers, will abound, and none but the best-costumed will be admitted into the parade. The majority of the Indians will be from the Flathead reservation, though several will come from the Umatilla reservation, near Pendleton. The Indians will be camped near the fairgrounds, and will give war dances every night after the evening show has been concluded.

The managers plan to give snappy, rapid fire shows which last only three hours, instead of dragging through the afternoon. Two of the most competent arena directors in the west have been obtained, and will run the events off in swift succession.

Document 90

Reclamation Fails to Pay for Indian Land

May 28, 1917

Source: Theodore Sharp to Commissioner of Indian Affairs, May 28, 1917, from file 93,389/1918 Flathead 155, Central Classified Files, RG 75, National Archives, Washington, D.C.

Editors' note: The construction expenses of the Flathead Irrigation Project were being charged to Indian allotments and white homesteads, but the project had never paid for the land and other tribal resources they used.

Department of the Interior
United States Indian Service
Flathead Indian School,
Dixon, Montana, May 28, 1917.

Dear Mr. Commissioner:

I am enclosing a formal letter reporting on the appropriation by the Reclamation Service on this reservation, of lands of the Indians for reservoir sites, and timber for the uses of the Reclamation Service, without, so far as I have ascertained, any compensation to the Indians.

This situation seems to have been overlooked and I deem it important that it be reported to you as it seems to me the Indians have a just claim for reimbursement. So far, I think the Indians have not made claim on the account of the appropriation of these lands and timber as many of them do not know the situation, but just at this time there seems to be a gathering of Indian agitators on this reservation who apparently are working with concerted plans to arouse the Flatheads against the Reclamation work and to give these agitators no just grounds for complaint against the work of the Government it occurs to me that it is important that every proper claim of the Indians should be investigated and settled. If this can be done in advance of the outcry of the professional disturbers, it will be far better than to wait until our Service has been forced, apparently, to listen, and will not enable these professionals to claim that *they* are the ones who have brought recognition of the Indians rights, incidentally collecting large sums of money from the Indians for their supposed services.

Just recently a "council" was held at St. Ignatius, on this reservation. I was invited to attend, and did so, as a spectator. The proceedings were dominated by Miss Mary Lemery, a mixed-blood allottee of this reservation, and Mr. Robert Hamilton, a mixed-blood of the Blackfoot reservation. At this meeting a typewritten resolution was presented which recited the opposition of the Indians to the Reclamation work, and contained in a paragraph stating, "Whereas, the Commissioner of Indian Affairs believes this work is imperative on our reservation, Therefore, we ask Congress to investigate our complaints and secure relief for us." This is not the exact wording of the resolution, but it is the sense of it as I recollect it. The idea is, as I see it, to make it appear that the Indian Bureau is at fault and for this fault Congressional investigation is necessary. I was more impressed with this idea after listening to the talk of Mr. Hamilton to the Indians. He first appealed to their prejudices by telling them how happy they were in the old days, before the whites interfered with them; that now the whites have killed the buffalo, driven away the game, restricted the Indians to small reservations, and have broken all the treaties and agreements ever made with the Indians; that formerly the whites came to the Indians and asked them to make treaties, looking up to and respecting the Indians, but now they have the Indians down with the white people's heels on the Indians' necks to keep them down. This is, of course, nonsense, but the ignorant type of Indian does not know it, and at this meeting these statements were received with a loud "Ah-h-h-h" of approval. Having thus secured the interest of the Indians, Mr. Hamilton touched on the Reclamation Service and told how the Indians of the Blackfoot reservation had been deceived and mistreated in connection with this work. He alleged that the cost of the ditches would probably be so great that the Indians would have their lands taken from them to pay for the ditches. He stated that the Blackfoot Indians, the Fort Peck Indians are working against this matter and the Flatheads should join with them. This makes me think there is a concerted effort being made by some one, or some organization, back of Mr. Hamilton, Miss Lemery, and the other agitators to stir up the Indians of these reservations and get a Congressional committee sent to the Northwest.

Miss Lemery was associated with the notorious "Princess Red Feather["] and seems to be apeing her methods, though not so capable. A Mr. George Wasson, a mixed-blood of Oregon also appears to be in the case, and as stated, Mr. Hamilton of the Blackfoot reservation has lately appeared on the scene. I have had no differences with any of these people and do not want any trouble with them, but there is something peculiar about their all coming in here and endeavoring to make sentiment among the Flatheads.

From what I have been able to ascertain in the very short time I have been here, I am led to believe that some of the Indians have cause for complaint about the manner in which the Reclamation Service has disregarded the Indians' claims. At least it appears that the Indians might have been approached more tactfully and much bad feeling avoided.

The big thing, however, as I see it, is the appropriation of thousands of acres of land belonging to the Indians, without recompense, for reservoir sites, and the arbitrary appropriation of timber from the Indians' land without payment, or report to the Indian Service by the Reclamation Service. Since the Indians' lands under the ditches must pay their pro rata share of the expense of the irrigation system, with the whites, there seems no good reason or just excuse why the Indians should in addition have taken from them, without payment, the reservoir sites. I feel certain that the whites would not give up their lands in a similar manner.

My suggestion is, that your Office immediately detail an inspecting official to carefully investigate this matter. I feel that it is so important that this be done that I am presenting the case to you personally. The information regarding the reservoir sites came to me after Inspector W. S. Coleman had left this jurisdiction, or I should have presented the question to him. As Mr. Coleman has become somewhat familiar with the conditions here and is still in the Northwest, if agreeable to you, I suggest that he be returned to take up the questions I have reported on.

Very respectfully,
Theodore Sharp
Superintendent.

The Honorable
Cato Sells,
Commissioner Indian Affairs,
Washington, D.C.

Document 91

Automobiles Confiscated from Bootleggers

June 14, 1917

Source: "Automobiles 'In Jail' For Carrying Whiskey," *The Daily Missoulian*, June 14, 1917, page 2, col. 4.

Editors' note: Suppressing the whiskey trade on the Flathead Reservation was big business in the late 1910s. Offenders lost their automobiles.

Automobiles "In Jail" For Carrying Whiskey
Four Cars Held at Indian Agency Under Provisions of New Law.
One From Missoula
Machines to Be Libelled by Government; Grand Jury Meets Soon.

The automobile's day of immunity from arrest under federal liquor laws is over.

Four automobiles, all alcoholics, are now prisoners of the United States at the Flathead Indian agency at Dixon. One is a Missoula car. The machines will be arraigned before the federal grand jury in Helena this week on bootlegging charges.

"The United States versus a Ford automobile." That is the way the cases will be entered on the docket. The owners of the cars will merely be vicarious defendants.

Carried Whiskey to Reds.

The four machines were captured and interned by federal officers under the provisions of a new law which makes it possible for the government to libel automobiles used in transporting whiskey into the Indian country. Until this year automobiles were not included in the list of carriers subject to arrest for violation of the federal liquor laws. Last year Untied States courts freed an automobile belonging to Louis Pablo, a Flathead Indian, which federal officers had seized on the reservation after a wild all-night pursuit from Missoula. The decision was based on the fact that the law, written before automobiles were in use, applied only to older carriages.

New Law More Modern.

As a result of that decision the law has been extended to cover all carriers — automobiles, submarines, aeroplanes and anything else.

The names of the persons whose car are now held at the Indian agency are being kept secret by the federal officers assigned to liquor-traffic suppression. It is said, however, that one of the cars belongs to a Missoula resident and the others to persons living on the reservation.

The federal grand jury meets in Helena tomorrow. A large number of bootlegging cases from the Flathead are to be heard. The first is set for June 20, it is said.

Document 92

Indians Gather Bitter Root

June 17, 1917

Source: "Indians Come Back to Collect Supply of Favorite Roots," *The Daily Missoulian*, June 17, 1917, Special Features, page 1, col. 3-4, and page 8, col. 3.

Editors' note: By 1917 Indian people harvesting the bitterroot near Missoula had become a novelty. Obviously, the reporter was not able to communicate with the Indian visitors.

Indians Come Back to Collect Supply of Favorite Roots

Out where Missoula dwindles into the prairie, tepees have risen again, like apparitions. A valley ordinarily without sign of its old Indian rulers is now, for a brief season, populated once more.

It is the bitter root season. Down from the Flathead, where the flower is rare, the older Indians have come to harvest their spring crop of roots. One can find them along almost any road, living just as they did 50 years ago; unconscious, apparently, that there are whites in the world.

One will try in vain to learn from them why they have come. Here is an old s...., sitting beside an irrigation ditch near her dirty tepee, washing a great heap of white roots.

"What are you doing?"

"Ugh!"

"What are those skins?" with a gesture toward a line of drying hides that look as they might once have covered dogs.

"Ugh!"

"Making bread?"

"Ugh! Ugh!" (in disgust). "No savvy!"

The Bitter Root does not force itself upon the passer-by as does the sunflower, or the dandelion, but requires some searching. It is a dimunitive plant, flowering close to the ground. The root is small, about the size of a pencil and not very long. It is this root which for decades has been the special delicacy of the Indians of western Montana.

Just how the Indians gather and keep and use the roots is well told by Mrs. Mary C. Ronan, 318 West Pine street. Mrs. Ronan is the widow of Major Peter Ronan, for years Indian agent on the Flathead reservation. It was there, 4 [40?] years ago, that she first became acquainted with the annual migration of the Indians to this valley in search of the Bitter Root.

For though the flowers grow plentifully around Missoula — so plentifully that it has given its name to the river and valley which comes in from the south — yet it is rarely found on the Flathead reservation. In the old days most of the women of the tribe would make the journey to Missoula when the Bitter Root was in flower to gather the precious roots. Nowadays the number of Indians in the city at this season seems large only to the recently arrived easterner. Chiefly the older Indians and the pure bloods pitch their teepees on the flat now. To them the trip is a picnic as well as a harvest. The younger Indians, following the white man's prosaic work of farming.

The root is first washed or scraped by Indians and is then sun-dried. It is gathered in great quantities, each family striving to get a sufficient amount to last them the year. When dried, the roots are stored away in bags just as the white people keep onions. They are made ready for use much the same way. The outer part being peeled off. The inside is used for seasoning soups and stews just as the housewife uses sage. As the name implies, the root has a bitter flavor, intensely sharp.

Another Indian food which would probably appeal more to white people is the common wild sunflower — Balsam orhiza is its real name — which now makes splotches of golden the foot hills. Its stem, if you please, is the Indian celery. They gather and eat it with a little salt while it is fresh and tender. "Chew-ay" is the way their pronunciation of this relish sounds. Just below the flower the outer part of the stem is peeled off. It comes off easily, leaving the inner stem, which is the part eaten.

Mrs. Ronan believes it, with its peculiar flavor, would make a welcome addition to any salad, but advises using only fresh and tender stems.

The stems are plentiful enough now in the foot hills to make "chew-ay" a cheap addition to the home menu, but Mrs. Ronan can remember the time when the flowers practically covered the land on which Missoula now stands. They were the dandelions of that day, for that little blossom had not at that time made its appearance in Missoula. That was 40 years ago and now after an unceasing struggle the dandelion has captured the stronghold of the sunflower and driven it to the hills. And instead of the Indians gathering chew-ey, comes the house-wife with her basket full of dandelion blossoms with which to make wine.

Document 93

Indians in Missoula Jail

June 23, 1917

Source: "Indian's Stomach Prevents Escape," *The Daily Missoulian*, June 23, 1917, page 2, col. 3.

Editors' note: Tribal members came to Missoula to celebrate and ended up in the Missoula jail.

Indian's Stomach Prevents Escape

Antoine is occupying cell No. 1 in the city jail this morning. Antoine is proud possessor of a "corporation," and therefore police officials considered it safe to consign him to this cell, which is famed for the ease with which a slim man makes his exit from it. Antoine was famously drunk when he was picked up yesterday, but he has plenty of company in the city jail. Indeed, Antoine might well imagine himself at home on the reservation, but for the cold bars which separate him from his brethren. For the jail is crowded with drunken Indians, perhaps no longer drunk this morning, but just recovering from the effects.

Joseph Lemoy is there. So is Peter Vanderburg, Peter Lamoose, Louie Swara and Michael Keisser, who is a good Indian, when sober, even though his name is against him. Indians and circusses get along famously, and are accepted as co-incidents, but Indians and whiskey don't mix at all. Two s....s were picked up yesterday after having imbibed too much red-eye, and were taken to the county jail for safe keeping.

Document 94

Tribal Members Scammed by Dentist

July 11, 1917

Source: "Crippled for Life, Man Sues the Modern Dentists," *The Daily Missoulian,* July 11, 1917, page 2, col. 1-2.

Editors' note: Eneas Grandjo and Thomas Wold were reservation residents who suffered from malpractice by a Missoula dental firm.

Crippled for Life, Man Sues the Modern Dentists
Shocking Condition of Eneas Grandjo Reveals Methods of Quack Practitioners Here.

The seriousness of allowing the practice of quack dentistry to exist anywhere in the country has been revealed in Missoula in the shocking condition of Eneas Grandjo. Mr. Grandjo, a resident of the reservation, has been crippled for life as a result of what he alleges to be the malpractice of the Modern Dentists in Missoula.

This firm of "dental surgeons," is owned by a Mrs. Nona Monsch, who is not herself a dentist. Revelations have resulted from investigation conducted for Mr. Grandjo who is about to sue the firm for damages. It has become known that the firm's operatives are of that class of fakes who suddenly appear from nowhere, stay a little while until their true character is known, and then vanish no one knows whither.

Jaw Broken by Quacks.

Mr. Grandjo will probably file his suit against the firm this week. His jaw was badly broken during one of the operations he underwent by the quack dentists employed by Mrs. Monsch. As a result of the injury his face has become terribly swollen for several weeks.

Man's Condition Evident.

Ocular evidence of the evils of quack dental practice have been given by Mr. Grandjo's appearance. Hundreds of persons have noted on the street the condition which has resulted from the "left-handad skill" of the Modern Dentists. As a result of these observations considerable comment as to how it comes about that the state authorities permit a dental firm to be operated by a person who is not and as far as can be learned, never was a dentist. They think this condition even more strange than it would be to have a first class blacksmith or grocer operate a bank.

Hasn't Been Able to Eat.

Aside from the great pain and suffering which the broken jaw has caused him. Mr. Grandjo has paid to competent physicians in the city considerable money to repair, so far as possible, the damages these operators have caused. Maturation set in shortly after the injury was done and as a result, the victim has scarcely been able to eat anything and has lived on liquid foods.

But Mr. Grandjo is not the only sufferer from the incompetence of these operators.

Would Sue for $1,000.

Thomas Wold, who also is from the reservation where Mr. Grandjo lives, already has sued the firm for $1,000 damages as a result of their, "modern methods" in dentistry.

Mr. Wold, in his deposition, stated that the dentists filled several teeth for him without first properly killing the nerve and without cleaning the teeth out before setting the fillings. Several also were crowned without being cleaned properly, he said.

Not only was Mr. Wold made to suffer much and needlessly as a result of the operations, but he was compelled to have the work entirely done over by a reliable dentist, of which there are many in Missoula.

Hotel Clerks as "Cappers."

The filing of Mr. Wold's suit and the preparation for the filing of the suit of Mr. Grandjo revealed one of the methods used by this firm for "getting business." They had established a more or less capper system among the hotel clerks and bartenders in the city.

Whenever a man would complain of his teeth and he was overheard in his remarks by one of these cappers, the latter would suavely inject himself into the conversation and say:

"Pardon me, sir, but I heard you complaining that your teeth need attention. Now, I can tell you of a firm in this city that'll fix you up right and do it at a reasonable price."

The Victim Ensnared.

Whereupon Mr. Victim would be marched over to the Modern Dentists headquarters or would be sent over with a note from the hotel clerk or bartender, and the tooth butchers would get the work.

The Modern Dentists are of the type of operators who ramble from place to place because they are too incompetent to establish a good practice of their own in one place for any length of time. This was revealed when Mr. Wold sought reparation for the damage the concern had done to him.

Bad Teeth Cause Disease.

At the present time, as a result of the great advances of medical science, it has become known that serious diseases originate from bad teeth. Kidney and stomach troubles and even blood poisioning [sic] result if the teeth are not properly attended to.

The demand for men for the army has also given evidence of a striking condition. Hundreds of men, otherwise physically fit for the service have had to be rejected by the physical examiners purely on account of bad teeth conditions.

In view of these facts, it is imperative for the welfare of all the people that no unnecessary damage be done by any dentists. Nevertheless, such firms as the Modern Dentists, headed by a woman who is not and never was a dentist and who apparently is only in the business merely because it provides ample livlihood [sic] at the expense of the public, are allowed to flourish unhindered.

Document 95

Reservation Indians Contribute to War Effort

1917-1918

Source: "Patriotic Indians Buy Liberty Bonds," *The Daily Missoulian*, October 25, 1917, page 2, col. 4; excerpt from "Catholic Indians and the War," *The Indian Sentinel*, vol. 1, no. 9 (July 1918), page 21.

Editors' note: Flathead tribal members contributed to the war effort during World War I. They purchased liberty bonds, complied with rationing, and enlisted in the army.

Patriotic Indians Buy Liberty Bonds
Flathead Redmen Contribute to Fund to Beat Kaiser.

Keenly feeling their allegiance to the United States, Indians of the Flathead reservation enthusiastically contributed to the Liberty loan with the result that more than $10,000 was invested by the redskins of that section during the past week.

This is the report made by H. S. Allen, chief clerk of the Dixon agency, who stopped in Missoula yesterday on his way back to the reservation from Butte.

Mr. Allen declared that Chief Kicking Horse was the first to purchase a bond and afterwards he created interest in the campaign to the extent that many Indians who could scrape together enough money immediately bought a bond or two.

That the Indians are loyal to the United States is indicated in the fact that ten of them enlisted in the army before the draft and that there were very few who claimed exemption when conscripted.

* * * * * * * * *

From St. Ignatius we have splendid accounts furnished by Father A. Sullivan, S.J., who tells that $20,000 was subscribed to the third liberty bond by Indians of the Flathead Agency. Red Cross activities at the Ursuline Convent and the House of Providence have met with only one drawback — insufficient supply of wool. This regrettable condition is frequently mentioned in reports from the various reservations and mission schools. On food conservation,

Father Sullivan writes: "We received and distributed the pledge cards. Some of our people, in fact the majority of them, are very poor, therefore, many of them after learning the meaning of the card remarked that already they were doing more than the Government requires. 'Instead of meatless days or meatless meals,' they said, 'we have meatless weeks.'" "This," adds the writer, "is easy to understand as many of our Indians live in the country far from butcher shops and cannot procure meat even if they had the cash — which, too often, is not at their command. The school children rarely have meat for breakfast; what meat they get at odd times for supper is generally in the form of stews or hash made from meat left from the noon meals. As we are placed, the use of corn and fish, to any extensive degree, would be a costlier proposition than the consumption of the wheat and meat products of our own farm. Fish and corn would have to be shipped to us at expensive rates. Eighty-five of our Indians have enrolled as members of the Red Cross, and twenty-five or more have enlisted in the army.["]

Chapter 4

Documents of Salish, Pend d'Oreille, and Kootenai History Between 1918-1920

Document 96

Priest Described Kootenai New Year's Celebration January 1918

Source: Edward Griva, S.J., "New Year's Day with the Kootenai," *The Indian Sentinel*, vol. 1, no. 7 (January 1918), pages 27-28.

Editors' note: Father Edward Griva did not say which New Year's celebration he spent with the Kootenai Indians on Flathead. This description was published in January 1918, so it probably described a celebration in the middle 1910s.

New Year's Day with the Kootenai

There is a small tribe on the Flathead Reservation known as the Kootenai Indians many of whom live in a town called Layton [Dayton], near Flathead Lake; some are at the Big Arm settlement along the same lake, while the others are scattered throughout the valley that extends between the lake and Warm Springs. These Indians are Catholics. Many of them are very poor and subsist chiefly upon fish. Their language is altogether different from that of the Flathead and is difficult to master. Most of these Indians know the principal prayers and are faithful in the observance of their religious obligations. Some years since, when the writer inaugurated the Temperance Society among them, quite a number of the Indians took the pledge, some for life and others for specified numbers of years. The majority of them have adhered faithfully to their promise.

The Kootenai Indian's commemoration of the New Year is both edifying and interesting. The chief invites all the people of his tribe to his home for the last day of the old year. The invitation is willingly accepted. Fat steers have been killed for the celebration and the women are busy with the bread-making and other preparations for the feast. For two days the Indians are seen arriving at the place of the celebration; the old in big wagons, the young on horse-back — all in their fanciest raiment, their colored blankets, their high bonnets, their best feathers — the young men carrying their best guns. A spirit of good-fellowship prevails, each cordially greeting the other with a hand clasp and the usual salutation: "Kesukuyukuwe," in English: How are you? The better part of the day is devoted to the erection of tents and the preparation of the meals. Nearly all have arrived by the evening of the second day in time for the good hearty supper of meat and bread that is served to the group from oil-cloth stretched on the ground. No tables nor chairs are used; everybody sits on the ground; even the priest, sitting in this Indian fashion to partake of the meal with his red-skinned flock who make this gathering an occasion for communicating news, each to the other; the whole tribe becoming, so to say, like one great family. How friendly the Indians are to one another! If, during the year, there has been any enmity among them, on this occasion they make peace and become reconciled.

Immediately after the supper, the chief demands attention by ringing the bell and then, calling aloud, exhorts all the Indians to go to Confession in preparation for the solemn feast of the following day.

The earnestness of the Indian at such times is remarkable. He has his faults, it is true, but his humbleness and the devotion with which he approaches the tribunal of penance are truly edifying. Only once was the writer privileged to preside at this gathering. Then, more than ever, did he realize the Father's love for his children of his flock and how great is the privilege of ministering to their spiritual needs. Because of the consolations and the happiness that come to him at this time, the priest forgets the fatigue he experiences after hours in the confessional.

Midnight finds the tribe asleep in the cabins or tents or stretched upon blankets on the ground. Early the next morning — New Year's Day — all are up and ready for the summons of the bell rung by the chief. The men, with loaded guns, stand in file before the groups of older men, women and children while the chief rings the bell, and then, in Indian, solemnly says: "The Angel of the Lord declared unto Mary." The tribe answers: "And she conceived by the Holly Ghost." The opening clause of the Angelus is accompanied by a military salute from the men in the front file, each one from left to right discharging his rifle while the people recite aloud the Hail Mary.

Again the bell is sounded, and the chief says aloud: "Behold the handmaid of the Lord," the people answering, "Be it done unto me according to Thy word," and they recite aloud a second time the Hail Mary while each young man in turn again fires a salute. Thus does the chief of the Kootenai, with his people, recite that beautiful prayer — the Angelic Salutation — and there in the open at the dawn of the New Year, by word and deed, they ask the intercession of Mary, Queen of Heaven. Then follow hymns, reverently, joyfully sung as only the Indian can sing his hymn of praise to God. After this the men, then the women, and, finally, the children, approach the chief, shake his hand and wish him a happy New Year. Hymns are again sung by the whole tribe as they surround their chief, and then all assemble for the celebration of the Mass. Being unable to preach in Kootenai, the writer spoke to them in Flathead, a language understood by the chief, who acts as translator for the tribe. Eager to hear the word of God, at least once in a while, these good Indians are very attentive listeners. Prayers are recited aloud during and after the Mass, then all disband for breakfast in the tepees. Later the priest administers baptism — there are always children to be baptized on such occasions. Also he rectifies marriages, distributes medals, pious pictures, rosaries, etc., and, needless to say, does all in his power for the good of these poor Indians. Poor they are, where earthly goods are concerned. Their poverty closely resembles that of our Lord in the Cave of Bethlehem, but they are true and good of heart. The writer will never forget them. That New Year's Day is to him one of happy memory. May God bless these Indians and grant them the grace to remain always as good as they were at that time!

Edward Griva. S.J.

Document 97

Lawyers Fight Over Pablo Estate

January 7, 1918

Source: "Jostled Funeral for Pablo Fees," *The Daily Missoulian*, January 7, 1918, page 2, col. 1.

Editors' note: An Indian as rich as Michel Pablo got the attention of attorneys jockeying for a chance to handle his estate in 1914 and earn generous fees.

Jostled Funeral for Pablo Fees
Engle Says Lawyers Forced Way Up to Mourners' Bench.
To Impress Indians
Deputy Sheriff Testifies in Suit of Dwight N. Mason Against J. P. Swee.

Missoula county lawyers actually "crowded the mourners" at the funeral of old Michel Pablo in order to win favor with the heirs of the rich Indian, according to Deputy Sheriff William Engle of Ronan, a witness in the suit of Deputy County Attorney Dwight N. Mason against John P. Swee for a partnership accounting. Swee handled the Pablo estate, and his fee is the stake in the suit.

Forced Way to Mourners.

Engle testified at the trial that he and John N. Bailey, justice of the peace at Ronan, elbowed a way through the crowded church during the funeral for a few favored attorneys who wanted to get near the mourners' bench. The object, Engle guessed, was that the relatives of the rich Flathead might be impressed and the crowd led to believe that the lawyers were intimates of the Pablo family.

Swee, the witness said, was one of the lawyers. Whether the point of vantage won the Pablo business for Swee or not was not indicated, but at any rate the Ronan attorney secured the plum.

Mason Seeks Part of Fee.

Mason, formerly representative of Missoula county in the legislature and now deputy county attorney, contends that Swee was acting on behalf of the law firm of Mason & Swee, and that he is entitled to a part of the fees, which are said to have amounted to thousands of dollars. Swee, however, asserts that the partnership went out of being before Pablo's death in 1914, and that he handled the estate personally.

The case of the plaintiff has not yet been completed. The evidence probably will not be complete for two or three days.

Document 98

Flathead Tribal Council Protests Agency Policies

January – February 1918

Source; Theodore Sharp to Commissioner of Indian Affairs, January 8, 1918, and Chief St. Pierre Michel, et. al., to Commissioner of Indian Affairs, February 4, 1918, from file 10,804/1918 Flathead 056, Central Classified Files, RG 75, National Archives, Washington, D.C.

Editors' note: Flathead Superintendent Theodore Sharp was very critical of the Flathead Tribal Council and their efforts to present tribal grievances to the federal authorities. Victor Evans, a Washington, D.C. attorney, was assisting the council in advocating tribal complaints. Sharp thought that meant that Evans was responsible for the complaints, but Flathead tribal members had vigorously complained about government policies for years, especially regarding the Flathead Irrigation Project. Before the project, many tribal member farms had private irrigation ditches that were destroyed during the construction of the project or could rely on natural seepage to water their farms. Now the federal government wanted the Indian farmers to pay for the irrigation project which had destroyed their pre-existing ditches. The Flathead Tribal Council wanted decisions affecting the tribe to be made their organization rather than the Flathead Agent and the Flathead Business Committee.

Department of the Interior
United States Indian Service
Flathead Indian Agency,
Dixon, Montana, January 8, 1918.

My dear Mr. Commissioner:

In connection with my letter to you of May 28, 1917, you requested me to keep you advised of the activities of certain factions, especially one headed by Miss Mary Lemery.

This is to advise you that I am informed a party of Indians from this reservation will start for Washington in a few days. The party is headed by Miss Lemery. At a "council" dominated by her, of which she was chairman, Basil Finley, Charles Michel, Dave Couture, Louis Camille Lantow, George Wasson, E. D. Covell, and Mary Lemery were chosen as a delegation to go to Washington.

George Wasson is not of this reservation. He claims to be a mixed-blood Indian from the Coos Bay region, Oregon, I am informed. He has been residing for a large portion of the past year at the home of a brother of Miss Lemery with whom she also makes her home. E. D. Covell is a white man. He has been employed as an engineer with the reclamation service but has not been in the government's service for several years. It is possible that he may not accompany the party to Washington, but they have selected him as one of the number. Dave Couture states that he will not go with the delegation.

The delegation bears with it "resolutions" which Miss Lemery tells the Indians are to be presented to Congress or to a Congressional committee.

In brief, these resolutions represent that many of the Indians' allotments do not need water for irrigation, although such allotments lie within the irrigation projects, and demand that Indians not using water, although their lands lie below reclamation canals and ditches, are not to bear any portion of the construction charges which will be pro rated for the building of the ditches.

I need not say that the idea of not paying anything for the irrigation work is a popular one with the Indians. It has the appearance of bait to interest the approval of the Indians in other demands of the delegation.

The papers carried by the delegation demand that all leases, sales, and other business affecting the tribal property shall be submitted to a tribal council of the Indians for consideration and approval. The Superintendent is directed to call councils for this purpose.

The persons named above as comprising the delegation are also selected as Tribal Agents, and authorized to make contract with Victor J. Evans (now we are getting to it) of Washington, D.C., to act as tribal attorney and counsel. All expenses of the "tribal agents" to Washington and while there, and the fees of Victor J. Evans, are to be paid from the tribal funds.

It is also proposed to establish at Washington, a permanent tribal committee, or representation, "of one or more," with full authority to transact all tribal business, hire attorneys as needed (the attorney will see to it that they are needed) and the expenses of this permanent commission shall be paid for from the tribal funds.

This proposition looks to me to be too raw to need discussion.

The "council" which this delegation represents, in the resolutions it bears, repeals the Act of Congress establishing the Bison Range on the Flathead reservation, and authorizes and directs the Secretary of the Interior and the Secretary of the Treasury to deposit in the public treasury, from tribal funds, the price paid for the Bison Range, with the purpose of having the land revert to the tribe.

The Secretary of the Treasury is further instructed and directed to withhold from the pro rata share in the tribal funds, the sum of $5.00 from each individual Indian of the confederated Flatheads. This money is then to be deposited to the credit of the "Flathead Indian Council" and presumably to be disbursed by the officers of the council. Miss Lemery was chairman of the council making this demand. Approximately $12,500 would be set aside if the demand be acted upon. For what purpose is not clear.

The demand is also made that Dr. J. H. Heidelman be dismissed from the Service as he is not liked "as a physician or as a citizen."

No specific charges are made against Dr. Heidelman. Lacking these, it does not appear necessary to make a statement in his behalf.

I am submitting the foregoing that you may be advised of this delegation and the ostensible purpose they have in visiting Washington. As for myself, I judge the real object is to secure recognition of Mr. Victor J. Evans, and possibly other attorneys, as tribal counselor, and also to, in some manner, get a portion of the tribal funds for the exclusive benefit of the numbers of this committee. The remainder of the demands and resolutions appear to be camouflage.

Very respectfully,
Theodore Sharp
Superintendent.

The Honorable,
Cato Sells,
commissioner of Indian Affairs,
Washington, D.C.

* * * * * * * * *

Washington, D.C.
February 4, 1918.

The Honorable
The Commissioner of Indian Affairs.
Sir:

The Flathead Delegation desire to submit for your consideration these further matters:

1. We ask that the Indian Bureau recognize the authority of the Flathead Tribal Council, which is regularly organized and represents the will, wishes and the power of the tribes occupying the Flathead Reservation in the State of Montana. We especially request that in the future all proposed leases or sales of tribal property and all legislation affecting the tribal rights of the Flathead Nation of Indians be submitted to the Flathead Council in writing upon due

notice to the officers of the Council, who will call a meeting, for the purpose, whenever requested by the bureau or agency officials, such meetings to be held with the Superintendent or other representative of the Indian Bureau present, to explain to the Indians the purposes of any proposed measures and to discuss the same with the members of the tribe in open Council.

The Flathead Tribe of Indians claim the right as the owners of tribal property to have a controlling voice in the leasing, sale or other disposition of the same, subject to the action of Congress.

2. That legislation be enacted to prevent any further appropriation or diversion of the natural flow of waters on or within the Flathead Indian Reservation, where the same have been, or are now, used by the owners of the land on which such streams originate or through which they flow; and, especially, that such waters be not used for any part of the supply to irrigation projects laid out or constructed within the Flathead Indian Reservation.

3. The Flathead Delegation requests the Commissioner of Indian Affairs to assist in the passage of legislation that will restore to the ownership of the Flathead Nation the lands taken from their reservation and converted into what is known as the Bison Range. They desire this property returned to them, that it may be used as a cattle range for the benefit of the Flathead Indians. They show that these lands were withdrawn from their ownership under legislation that disregarded their rights, and that did not justify the withdrawal of the same from their domain. They offer to reimburse the Government, out of their tribal funds, in the sum of $28,955.48, paid by the Government therefor, which they say was a wholly inadequate price, as shown by the appraisement made at the time. They further offer to restore from their tribal funds the present value of whatever improvements have been erected on the property by the Government in the shape of fences or permanent buildings.

4. That provision be made for the employment of three scalers, to be members of the Tribe and selected and appointed by the Tribal Council, to be paid out of tribal funds, and employed in all cases where it is necessary to scale or estimate tribal timber, or timber cut on individual allotments within the Flathead Reservation; and that no timber shall be sold from the said Flathead Reservation without the employment of such scalers.

5. The Flathead Delegation protests against the further retention and employment of Dr. John Heidelman as agency physician for the Flathead Indians, for the reason that there is wide-spread and general dissatisfaction with him, due to his neglect of official duties and the insufficient service rendered by him to the Indians.

6. The Flathead Delegation report that, pursuant to the directions contained in the resolutions under which they were appointed, they have confirmed and

ratified the employment, heretofore made by the Flathead Indians, of Victor J. Evans, of Washington, D.C., whom they have in open Council selected as their attorney to represent them at Washington, D.C., in all matters pertaining to their tribal interests, and to provide for their benefit the services of such attorney or attorneys from time to time as may be necessary or beneficial in the protection and enforcement of their rights.

The Flathead Delegation, on behalf of the Flathead Nation of Indians, respectfully requests the Commissioner of Indian Affairs, the Secretary of the Interior and all other departmental officials, to recognize the selection, appointment and employment of Victor J. Evans and those whom he may provide as attorneys and counsel for the Flathead Indians.

7. The Flathead Delegation request the Commissioner of Indian Affairs approve and allow payment of a bill heretofore filed in favor of Victor J. Evans, in the sum of $2,500.00, for money advanced to, or expended for, the Flathead Nation in meeting the expenses of the Flathead Delegation which attended the 65th Congress, 1st Session; and the Commissioner of Indian Affairs is hereby assured that it is the urgent request of the Flathead Indians that this bill be paid, for the reason, among other things, that the Flathead Nation realizes that the generous action of Victor J. Evans in providing the means which made it possible for this delegation to appeal to the authorities at Washington in behalf of their tribal interests, have accomplished more than had been done before by the tribe through the efforts of all the delegations previously sent to Washington in behalf of the Flathead Nation. This debt the Flathead Indians consider a debt of honor, and they are disappointed that it has been allowed to go a year unpaid.

8. The Flathead Delegation requests the enforcement and approval of legislation providing for the setting aside, out of tribal funds of the Flathead Nation, of a sum equal to Five Dollars ($5.00) for each member of the Tribe, to be used disbursed and disposed of as the Flathead Indians in Council may decide, provided that the money shall be used for expenses incurred for the benefit of the tribe in general.

Very Respectfully.
Chief St. Pierre Michel [thumb print]
Louis C. Lantow
Dave Couture
Mary Lemery
Basile Finely
George Bundy Wasson
Delegates of the Flathead Nation of Indians.

Document 99

Citizen Indians Ask for Per Capita Payment

January – April 1918

Source: "Indians Seeking Funds of Tribe," *The Daily Missoulian*, January 29, 1918, page 2, col. 5; "May Segregate Tribal Funds," *The Ronan Pioneer*, April 26, 1918, page 1, col. 5.

Editors' note: Citizen Indians on the reservation in January 1918 were asking for a per capita payment from all the funds and assets of the tribe. The Flathead Agent pointed out a provision in congress to pay out the cash portion of the tribal assets. The local banks must have been thrilled at the possibility that the per capitas of many tribal members would be deposited in reservation banks who would control how the money was spent.

Indians Seeking Funds of Tribe
Reds Want Money Disbursed at Once; Petition Is Circulated.
Will Help Flathead
Backers of Movement Point Need of Reservation for Cash.

Members of the Flathead Indian tribes who have already received their patents to the allotments of land, are anxious to have the government estimate the value of the tribal lands and all of the other property rights that may belong to the tribe, and make an early distribution of whatever money may be coming to each individual. A petition is already being circulated on the reservation for the signatures of the Indians who favor this plan. This petition is meeting with general favor.

There is an influence on the reservation working to keep the government from making any distribution of money, say supporters of the petition. This influence will, it is charged, tend to keep back the progress of the reservation. Influence is being brought to bear in Washington to this effect, but the secretary of the interior will have the other side of the story when he receives the petition of those that want an early valuation and distribution.

The majority of the Indians are said to be anxious to get their money as soon as possible. The petition that is being circulated is a follows:

Want Money Apportioned.

We, the undersigned, members of the Flathead Indian reservation, Montana, who have received patents in fee to the allotments made us on said reservation and are therefore citizens of the United States, respectfully petition that estimates be made of values of all tribal lands, timber, power sites, Camas Hot Springs, all reserves, including lands held by the reclamation service for power and reservoir sites or other purposes, and of any other tribal property, and these estimates be added to the sum of all moneys now held by the United States for the Indians of Flathead reservation; that the sum so determined be used in determining the pro rata share each member of the reservation is entitled to, based on the total population of the Flathead reservation; and that the full amount each individual is found entitled to, be paid to each and all of us who have received patents in fee to our allotments, thus releasing us from all claims upon the government or further interest in any tribal property or tribal benefits.

* * * * * * * * *

May Segregate Tribal Funds

That Superintendent Theodore Sharp is sympathetically cognizant of the needs of citizen Indians on the Flathead reservation is evidenced by a provision written into the pending Indian appropriation bill, which, if enacted into law, should prove of no little benefit to the allottees directly affected and influence to a corresponding degree commercial progress in the Mission valley.

The provision in question which is contained in the annual appropriation bill now before congress bears the approval of the Secretary of the Interior and the Indian Office and its subject matter is manifested from the following letter of Theodore Sharp to Harry Burland of this city:

Flathead Agency, Dixon, Mont.,
April 10, 1918.

Mr. Harry Burland,
Ronan, Montana,
Dear Sir:

With respect to the petition made recently by Indians of this reservation who have received patents for their own allotments, and forwarded by myself at their request to Washington for the consideration of the Indian Office and the Secretary of the Interior, in which petition the citizen Indians ask for a pro rata division of the tribal funds and property, I wish to state that I am now in receipt of a letter from Washington from which I quote as follows:

"You are advised that at this time there is pending in the Indian bill a provision which directs that all tribal funds be segregated and the shares of competent Indians paid directly to them, and the shares of non-competents and minors be deposited in local banks to their credit for expenditure under Indian money regulations. If this provision is in the bill upon its final passage, prompt steps will be taken to effect the segregation of all tribal funds as stated above."

From the above, the prospect of securing legislation which will obtain the result requested in your petition seems to be good. I will advise you further when I ascertain definitely what action has been taken with respect to the passage of this bill.

Respectfully,
Theodore Sharp, Supt.

Document 100

Indians Oppose Appropriations for Irrigation Project February 1918

Source: "Indian Delegates Oppose $750,000 Appropriation," *The Ronan Pioneer*, February 1, 1918, page 1, col. 6; "Vote $250,000 for Flathead; Fight Goes On," *The Daily Missoulian*, February 14, 1918, page 1, col. 5; "Indians' 'Friends' Not Always Genuine," *The Daily Missoulian*, March 3, 1918, Special Features, page 4, col. 7.

Editors' note: Western Montana whites were very upset over Indian objections to further appropriations for the Flathead Irrigation Project. Montana Senators and officials and businessmen were frustrated that tribal members did not appreciate how much the Indians needed the indebtedness from the irrigation construction. In 1918 the construction costs were a lien against the Indian allotments and white homesteads. See the letter from Chief St. Pierre Michell, et. al., to the Commissioner of Indian Affairs, March 6, 1918, reprinted below, for more detail about the tribal complaints.

Indian Delegates Oppose $750,000 Appropriation

Much speculation and excitement has been aroused in reservation circles over the action of a duly accredited delegation of Indians of the Flathead tribe who are now in Washington with petitions to be [the] Indian department asking that all reclamation work on the Flathead project be suspended and that no further appropriations be made for continuing the project, contending that irrigation is unnecessary and charging the reclamation service with undue extravagance in the expenditure of appropriated money. The appropriation of $750,00[0] passed upon by the last session of congress is also protested and it is estimated that this appropriation will be sufficient to complete the project upon which many thousands have already been expended.

In response to a telegram from Senator Myers to Coker F. Rathbone of Ronan, asking that the people of the reservation take some action and cooperate in an effort to offset the effects of the propaganda, a meeting was held Thursday night attended by Indians and whites alike, and as a result of the meeting it is the concensus [sic] of opinion that the majority of the Indians are not in favor of the action of the Indian delegation, believing it to be to a great extent due to agitation on the part of a few, and chiefly, it is alleged, on the part of one Victor Evans, a Washington attorney, through whose efforts and at a nominal charge of $5.00 each from members of the Flathead tribe, the delegation became duly accredited in Washington.

A committee composed of I. M. Brandjord, Coker F. Rathbone, H. H. Burland, Mose Delaware and John N. Bailey was appointed to draft a resolution to the department asking that action on the matter be suspended until petitions could be circulated and forwarded to Washington expressing the sentiment of the people in regard to the reclamation work, and the petitions will be circulated tomorrow. Other reservation towns are busy on the matter, and judging from opinions expressed by educated and intelligent Indians, very little difficulty will be met in securing an almost unanimous petition to the department to postpone definite action on the petitions of the delegation in Washington.

****

Vote $250,000 for Flathead; Fight Goes On
Governor Stewart Promises Support to Irrigation Campaign.
Indian Employed to Oppose Grant
Head of Delegation Admits Washington Attorney Hired Him.

Although the senate committee on Indian affairs yesterday allowed only $250,000 for reclamation projects on the Flathead reservation instead of the $750,000 asked and needed, western Montana's fight for the full amount will be continued with the support of Governor S. V. Stewart and President J. M. Hamilton of the State College.

Senator H. L. Myers yesterday sent word that the Indians opposing the reclamation work had injured themselves at the senate committee's hearing by admitting their connection with Victor J. Evans, a Washington attorney, under contract to stop the project. Simultaneously came the announcement that Governor Stewart, President Hamilton and officials of the Great Western Sugar company will back up the appeal of the Flathead farmers for better irrigation facilities.

Food Output Threatened.

Governor Stewart yesterday informed D. D. Richards, secretary of the Missoula Chamber of commerce, that he approved the request of the Flathead people and had telegraphed his indorsement to Washington. Restriction of the reclamation program will reduce Montana's output of food, the governor said, at a time when food is most needed. As head of the state council of defense the governor will appeal to the senate again today.

President Hamilton also sent a telegram to Washington approving the $750,000 appropriation. Two representatives of the college have been on the Flathead recently as investigators, and their findings indicate the need of irrigation.

Sugar Company Interested.

"If the Flathead country is to produce the sugar beets which the country needs so badly the farmers there must have water," said F. A. Wilson, local manager for the Great Western Sugar company yesterday. Mr. Wilson took the matter up with President Petriken of the company, who will appeal to the sugar commission for its influence.

Meanwhile the Missoula Chamber of Commerce and other western Montana organizations prepared for an intensive campaign to last until the $750,000 appropriation shall have been granted or beaten in the senate. Senator Myers promised to continue the fight for a larger allowance.

* * * * * * * *

Indian Hired by Attorney.

Washington, Feb. 13. — Special. — The climax in the hearing before the committee on Indian affairs came today when George Wasson, an Indian from Oregon, admitted under cross-examination that he was employed by Victor J. Evans, an attorney of this city, to work among the Flathead Indians and persuade them to come to Washington and oppose the appropriation of $750,000 for the Flathead reclamation project.

In the previous hearings the Indians had made a favorable impression on the committee, but after the Wasson admission the good faith of their opposition was questioned, and the committee finally voted for an appropriation of $250,000.

During his testimony Wasson said that he had secured the position of counsel for the Indians for Evans, and that he was acting for and at the instance of the attorney in the missionary work he had done among the tribe.

* * * * * * * * *

Indians' "Friends" Not Always Genuine.

The Flathead Indian Progress, the semi-monthly paper published at the Flathead Indian Agency, has some pertinent things to say about "friends" of the Indian in its current issue. The remarks apply well to the recent protests against an appropriation for reclamation work on the reservation. Says the Progress:

The gunners of this battery are mostly "white attorneys from Washington" introduced to the Indians by some "prominent native of the tribe."

The latter seek to persuade their "dear people" that this lawyer can overthrow the government or at least the Indian department; also that it will require some ammunition like "powers of attorney" and a royal "percentage" of the tribal funds and a little "divvy" with the dear son-of-the-tribe in order to succeed.

The hotels in Washington are enjoying the patronage of these gunners, who are spending much time in "hard labor" lobbying the hotels. After congress is over, the period of explaining why they did not succeed begins back home and more money must be collected to pay the hotel chefs during another session of congress. These batteries are called by wonderful titles like "Brotherhood" of the Isolated Conifer, or the "Great Sachem" of the Sublime-Order-of-the-Nocturnal-Luminant. They all cover the tracks of the Stalker after the Indian's money. If anyone wants more light they are referred to the congressional records and some earlier history of these gunners.

Document 101

Flathead Delegates Defend Opposition to Appropriations March 6, 1918

Source: Chief St. Pierre Michell, et. al., to Commissioner of Indian Affairs, March 6, 1918, from file 21,980/1918 Flathead 056, Central Classified Files, RG 75, National Archives, Washington, D.C.

Editors' note: See U.S. Senate, Committee on Indian Affairs, *Indian Appropriation Bill, 1919: Hearings, June 30, 1919.* Sixty-fifth Congress, Second Session. (Washington, D.C.: U.S. Government Printing Office, 1918) for the full record of the hearings. The delegation from the Flathead Tribal Council objected because the cost of the irrigation construction would be a substantial lien against the Indian allotments and reduce the value of the land for possible sale. White homesteaders and local businessmen were desperate for the appropriations, though in later years the homesteaders insisted they could not afford their share of the construction costs either.

National Hotel,
Washington, D.C.,
March 6, 1918

The Honorable
The Commissioner of Indian Affairs,
Sir:

The Flathead Delegation has just received a printed copy of the Hearings before the Committee on Indian Affairs, United States Senate, Sixty-fifth Congress, Second Session, on H.R. 8696, in which publication appear numerous letters, petitions, protests, etc., that seem to require an answer from us. This answer would have been made in writing at the time and submitted to the Committee if we had had access to the letters and petitions referred to.

It appears that on January 30, 1918, a telegram was sent by Senator H. L. Myers to a lawyer at Polson by the name of Sawyer, saying that a "delegation of misguided Indians had arrived in Washington to fight appropriations for the Flathead reclamation project," and asking Mr. Sawyer to "get busy and get letters, petitions and affidavits of whites and Indians setting forth true conditions and needs and true desires of whites and Indians."

The telegram adds:

"Especially show that Indians need and want water on land. Get substantial Indians back of you and as many as possible. Mail all papers to me."

It would seem that in response to this appeal a "**Petition**" was prepared, signed and transmitted to Senator Myers.

On January 31, 1918, Mr. Sawyer wired Senator Myers as follows:

"Polson, Mont., January 31, 1918.

Hon. Henry L. Myers,
United States Senate, Washington, D.C.:

Dispatch received. Business men are busy getting affidavits and petitions. Try to have Senate Committee postpone hearing a few days to allow papers to reach you. Call on Hon. E. B. Merritt, Indian Office, for dispatch sent by Indians protesting against Indian committee now in Washington; also preparing petition Ronan Stignatius [sic].

C. M. Sawyer."

The petition, in two parts, is found on pages 456, 457, 458 and 459 of the Hearings, and the first paragraph of the same is a protest against our representing the petitioners at Washington before the Interior Department or the Indian Bureau; against the payment of any money to us for the reason that we have not been delegated by the Indian Committee to go to Washington on behalf of the Indians of the Flathead Reservation; against the claim that the Indians of the reservation do not want the lands irrigated, etc.

We believe that the Indian Office should have evidence of the facts involved in this matter, and we beg leave to present them as briefly as we can in this letter.

This delegation was regularly selected, appointed and authorized by a full Council of the Flathead Nation, held at St. Ignatius, on November 28, 1917, after due notice; the action of the Council was practically unanimous; the Superintendent of the reservation was notified and invited to attend the Council, but informed the Chairman of the Council that business in the court at Helena prevented his attending the Council.

Some of the more prominent Indians whose names appear on the petition were present at the Council, including George Riley and Chief Thomas Antiste, who were, themselves, members of the delegation in 1917 that came to Washington with credentials similar to those given the delegation in 1918.

If the delegation is "misguided," the Indian Council that sent them here must have been also misguided, because we bring credentials from the Indians in the form of resolutions adopted at the Council, and those resolutions are on file in your Office and speak for themselves.

With reference to the signatures found on this petition, we call your attention to the fact that very few, if any, of the persons whose names are signed to this petition have allotments located on a part of the reservation affected by the irrigation project; some at or near Nirada may have irrigable lands. For this reason these particular petitioners have nothing to lose, because their lands will not be subjected to the lien of $4,000.00 to an eighty.

Note: Let us say here and now that this delegation is not fighting appropriations for irrigation projects, but is only trying to protect the Indian's allotment against a lien that the Indians consider illegal and unjust. The Flathead Indians will not be found opposing the irrigation project if their legal and equitable rights in the land are respected.

In the next place, some of the names signed to this petition are there by mistake or fraud, being in some cases the names of dead persons and in others the name or names of persons not on the reservation at the time, as, for instance, that of Antoine Stasso, who is serving a term of thirty years in the Federal prison at Leavenworth, Kansas, having been convicted and sentenced for murder of a member of the Flathead Nation. A member of this delegation now in Washington has received two letters from Stasso, written in Leavenworth, since our arrival here.

A number of the names appearing on the petition seem to be the names of children, and an investigation is now being made to determine how many names have been fraudulently signed, how many are the names of dead persons and how many are the names of children. We shall be glad to furnish your Office the facts on these points when they are fully ascertained.

As said above, this delegation is not opposing the irrigation project on the Flathead Reservation; they are only opposing the injury and injustice that follows the present system of taxing their lands. They have asserted to you and to the Senate Committee that the allottees on the reservation are opposed, generally, to this project, if it fastens a lien of $4,000.00 on each of their eighties. Of course, we know that there are some lands that might be benefited for selling purposes by the mere fact that they could be said to be irrigated lands. We have tried to show, and we believe it to be true, that the lands not under the ditch and, therefore, not subject to the indebtedness that the lien would create, will sell on the average for a better price than the lands under the ditch with the lien fastened upon them.

Likewise, we believe it is true, that the Indians owning lands under the ditch, generally, do not want the irrigation project. In some cases, certainly, it is true that the lands under the ditch would bring, and do bring, better crops without the use of water than with its use. But, in our view of the matter, the main point is that the Indians do not want the irrigation, and we believe that the wishes of the Indians should have recognition before the wishes of anyone else, because the land is Indian reservation land, and the irrigation project is not the Indians' project; it was not begun at their request nor with their consent. As soon as they learned what the effect would be to fasten a great debt upon their lands, they began the protest that the delegation of 1917 and the delegation of 1918 have tried in a fair and honest way to present to Congress. The letters addressed to Senator Myers and published in the Hearings, the petitions accompanying the same, and the printed evidence elsewhere developed on this subject, show that the efforts in behalf of the irrigation project are being made not by Indian allottees and Indian farmers, but mainly by persons who are not farmers at all. It would seem that the real persons interested in promoting the project are those that benefit most largely by the expenditure of the large sums of money appropriated for carrying on the work; and, if you will examine into the facts, we believe it will be found that even those white homesteaders who are being induced to protest against us and our work are persons interested, directly or indirectly, very much more in the money that is spent on the project than on the improvement of any lands that they may have taken up, possibly for bona fide homesteads, possibly for speculation.

Bearing upon this subject the delegation refer, in passing to the communication from the "St. Ignatius Commercial Club," "The Ronan Commercial Club" and any other commercial club or Chamber of Commerce that may have adopted resolutions in the matter. The population of St. Ignatius, is perhaps, from two to three hundred persons, including schools and hospital; the population of Ronan is probably less; the commercial clubs and the Chambers of Commerce in these smaller towns would probably not include many farmers or bona fide homesteaders on the reservation. The names of the individuals signed to the published letters show interest on the part of a class of person who are chiefly concerned otherwise then as owners of the land, and it is, perhaps, only natural that they should oppose any action that might delay or diminish the size of appropriations of money to be distributed in their section.

On January 31, 1918, Mr. Andrew B. Beckwith, replying to Senator Myers' telegram of the 30th, says that we "represent a very small part of allotted Indians." This statement is not true; this delegation represents the whole of the allotted people on the Flathead Reservation, being delegated by the unanimous vote of a full Council held for the purpose of sending a delegation to Washington. Moreover, we believe that we represent the individual views, wishes and purposes of a very large majority of the Indians, and that they would all so report to you, if given a fair opportunity to do so, and not misguided by persons seeking to confuse their minds with other conflicting questions. Mr. Andrew Beckwith was present at the three days' council held by Inspector Linnen on the Flathead Indian Reservation in the summer of 1917, and the record of that council will show that not a single Indian testifying there expressed a desire for irrigation privileges, whereas all of them who spoke on the question protested against it, so far as we now remember.

This delegation respectfully asks you to find out what truth there is in the statement contained in Mr. Beckwith's letter:

> "The farmers who used water received on an average twenty bushels per acre, while their neighbors who did not use water got from six to nine bushels per acre."

As against this statement, we ask you whether a report by the farmers who did the actual threshing on the Flathead Reservation will not show that the 1917 crop of wheat raised on the irrigated lands was less to the acre than the wheat raised on the lands not irrigated.

Mr. Andrew Beckwith, who signs this letter, is a brother of the George Beckwith referred to in the affidavit of William H. Sabin filed with the Senate Committee on Indian Affairs at the Flathead Hearings in 1917, and he, Andrew B. Beckwith, is actively employed, as is Mr. Addison K. Lusk, by the Beckwith Mercantile Company, of St. Ignatius.

> William H. Sabin, being first duly sworn, deposes and says: That he is a white man, 41 years of age, and a homesteader residing upon the Flat Head Indian Reservation in the State of Montana, where he has resided for the last six years.
>
> That from June 1910, until March 1911, he was employed by the Beckwith Mercantile Company, a corporation organized under the laws of the State of Montana, and doing business upon the Flat Head Indian Reservation in the State of Montana, being in charge of its lumber department.
>
> That during the time he was so employed by such company, the United States Reclamation Service, frequently made purchases of lumber for its use in construction work. That said Reclamation Service advertised according to law for such lumber, stating that sealed proposals would be received for the same, said bids to be opened on a certain date, at a certain time, and from the bids submitted, one would be accepted for furnishing such lumber.
>
> That such sealed proposals were received at the office of the Reclamation Service, and turned over to the Chief Clerk, Mr.

> Charles W. Donnelly, to be kept by him unopened until the date specified in the advertisement.
>
> That before the time set for the opening of such bids, generally one day, George H. Beckwith, President of the Mercantile Company, came into the office of the said William H. Sabin, (who had charge of the lumber department of such company) bringing with him the lowest bid submitted up to that time, which bid was opened, but by whom it is not known, and figured with said William H. Sabin, on a bid that would just come under that bid, so that the bid of the Beckwith Company would be the lowest one submitted and it awarded the contract for furnishing the lumber, which was in most instances always awarded to the Beckwith Company.
>
> That further, that the same methods were employed by the Beckwith Company and Chief Clerk Donnelly in connection with the contracts for furnishing the Reclamation Service with beef.
>
> That the said Charles W. Donnelly, is at the present time, connected with the Alaskan Railroad in Alaska, under the supervision of the United States Government, holding a position of trust in the office of the purchasing agent.
>
> (Signed) Wm. H. Sabin.

Mr. Beckwith's letter says that individual farmers who are using the water are growing fine stands of alfalfa and cutting three crops a year. This is true of a few farmers, some years; the same thing is true of a good many farmers who have non-irrigated lands. But the fact is that the raising of alfalfa is a very unimportant industry on the Flathead Reservation.

Mr. Beckwith's letter also says that a great many of our farmers are going into the dairy business. We know of no Indian who has gone into the dairy business or wants to go into it, and we know of very few white men that have gone into the dairy business. The fact is that about four years ago some farmers on the Flathead Reservation, Indians and white men, were induced to buy stock in a creamery at Missoula, about fifty miles or more from Mission Valley, and we think you will find, if you care to investigate the matter, that these farmers have been trying hard during the last year or two to get rid of their holdings at a large discount.

Mr. Lusk, testifying at the request of Senator Myers, ventures the statement on page 342 of the Hearings that out of (the last) nine years four years produced total failure of corps on non-irrigated lands. The knowledge and experience of this delegation lead them to say to you that there has not been a total failure of crops on non-irrigated lands on the Flathead Reservation in forty years, and that the nearest approach to a failure was last year, when it was due not to the lack of water, but to the fact that the ground froze on the 8th of November, 1916, and stayed frozen until the spring rains began, after which the ground was kept so wet from rain that the farmers were not able to plow the lands in time to put in their seed early enough to raise a crop of grain. The crops for that year on the non-irrigated lands was about a half crop, while the crops on the irrigated lands were practically a failure. So the most charitable construction to place on Mr. Lusk's testimony is that he must have meant irrigated lands and not the non-irrigated lands.

The irrigation project was and is only one of a large number of important matters that the Flathead Indians have in hand and for which they sent their delegation to Washington. We do not think it is right to let this one subject overshadow everything else, and we are soon to return home for the purpose of trying further and harder to induce a more liberal disposition towards us in our efforts on behalf of the Flathead Indians, and especially to induce more favor towards the Flatheads in recognizing their right to be heard in the matter of managing their tribal affairs.

The irrigation problem to the Flatheads is this, the Flathead Reservation is essentially a wheat growing region, the most desirable grade of wheat is raised on non-irrigated lands, and the lands for wheat raising purposes are, as a rule, more valuable without irrigation than with it. That is the only matter to which this delegation asks your attention, and they do that, as said above, not for the purpose of interfering with Government appropriations for reclamation projects, but only for the purpose of avoiding an injustice to the Indian allottee, whose lands, in his opinion, do not need irrigation but do need to be protected against the injustice of a tremendous lien which must be paid off by him or his descendants.

Mr. C. M. Sawyer, the Polson lawyer, seems to have employed one Ben Cramer, who describes himself as an American born citizen, fifty-two years of age, twenty-one years resident on the Flathead Reservation; one of its most successful farmers, who knows the conditions of the soil and climate, and whose success does not need to be proved because he is willing to admit it under oath.

Some members of this delegation are well acquainted with Ben Cramer and, inasmuch as he assumes the responsibility of saying that the delegation are without any authority and are a part of a small group of dissatisfied Indians, who have been unsuccessful at farming, even on the best lands and with fine opportunities, and that he believes the delegation is incited by one of its members, who had called a meeting last year and failed in securing even a vote by the Indians on a resolution introduced by her, it is proper for them to put on record at your Office the facts.

The resolution referred to is as follows:

> At the meeting of the Flathead Tribe of Indians, held on the 19th day of May, A.D. 1917, at St. Ignatius, Montana, the following resolutions were duly passed and adopted:
>
> Whereas, it has been the experience of the pioneers and new settlers as well, to raise hard wheat without irrigation, and
>
> Whereas, the irrigation system constructed by the United States Reclamation Service have damaged the best lands, whether allotted, inherited, sold, or surplus unallotted entered lands, because of superfluous seepage and actual damage to the land through which it passes, and
>
> Whereas, it is, in the opinion of the Honorable Commissioner of Indian Affairs, that further construction of the said irrigation systems is imperative; therefore, be it
>
> Resolved: That it is the consensus of opinion of this tribe of Indians and white settlers to ask the Congress of the United States to investigate the irrigation situation, with a view to eliminate the objectionable features which jeopardize the best interests of all concerned.

It was introduced by a member of this delegation at a Council where there were probably three hundred Indians in attendance. The resolution was adopted unanimously. Superintendent Sharp was present. Ben Cramer, a white man and not a member of the Tribe, was present at the Council and did everything in his power to defeat the resolution.

It might be of some interest to know that this man's character is notoriously bad; that he has been chased off the reservation by the Indians numerous times; that he is commonly spoken of as a horse thief; that he is a notorious bootlegger and gambler, and that in the summer of 1917 he was arrested and convicted for introducing liquor on the reservation, at which time his car containing six or seven cases of whiskey were confiscated by Government Officials, and that he is now at large on bond.

While it is not a matter of great importance, perhaps, to the Indian Bureau whether Ben Cramer is a man of good or bad habits, we do think that the opinion of the Officials of the Indian Bureau should not be formed solely upon representations made by such a man or by those who employ him to present their cases at Washington.

A recent publication in the Kalispell Bee names Joe Bonaparte, of the Kootenai Tribe, on the Flathead Reservation, as "Chief Bonaparte," and tells of his patriotic action in buying war stamps and in opposing the action of this delegation at Washington.

It is reported to our delegation that "Chief" Bonaparte was very active in assisting Ben Cramer to secure the signatures to the petition above referred to.

Joe Bonaparte is enrolled as a member of the Flathead Nation it is true; that, unfortunately, cannot be denied. Joe is a good natured fellow; he is a good talker; he is well known to the members of this delegation; when not in jail he is for the most part living from house to house with his relatives on the reservation; when in jail (and during the last year he has been in at least three times) he is employed largely as interpreter at the Agency. We think that Joe would not be regarded as a man on whom the Government would like to rely for its information about as serious business as that which is entrusted to this delegation by the Flathead Nation.

The delegation, in taking leave of your Office before returning home, assure you that they will have further communications to submit at a comparatively early date on the foregoing matters and trust that there will be favorable action on the same.

Very respectfully,
Chief St. Pierre Michell [thumb print]
Louis C. Lantow
Dave Couture
Mary Lemery
Basil Finley per. Irene Lemery
George Bundy Wasson
Delegates of the Flathead Nation of Indians.

Document 102

Kootenai Chief Misled by Petition

April 8, 1918

Source: George Bundy Wasson to Chief Coostata, April 8, 1918, from file 39,951/1918 Flathead 121, Central Classified Files, RG 75, National Archives, Washington, D.C.

Editors' note: Kooostata's name was on a petition opposing the Flathead Tribal Council delegation in Washington, D.C., but he did not support all that was in the petition. Organizing on the reservation was a challenge with all the competing interests. In 1918 the government used tribal funds to pay the expenses and salaries of the Flathead Agency, without tribal consent.

April 8, 1918.

Chief Coostata,
Dayton, Montana.
Dear Friend:

I have at hand your letter of March 31, 1918, addressed to Miss Marie Lemery, in which you state that you wish to protest against having your name attached to the petition presented to the Committee on Indian Affairs, United States Senate, by Senator Henry L. Meyers; you also state that you were deceived by the two men who called upon you, Joe Bonaparte and Abraham. You state that they made you understand that $5.00 was asked from every Indian of the tribe, even children; and you also state that you thought $5.00 was too much, and that was the reason why you gave your name. You also stated that you are surprised to know that your name appeared on the petition twice, and that you are going to call your tribe together for the purpose of straightening out this matter, which you say seems to you to be a piece of crooked business.

As directed by Miss Lemery, when she left here about a week ago, I am reading her mail, and as a delegate, elected by the tribe for the purpose, I am answering this letter.

I am very glad to know that you have taken that stand, as stated in your letter, because I always knew that you had the interest of your people at heart and was willing to help them. I know that you had the people's interest at heart when you objected to the paying of $5.00 from every member of the tribe, even children, because you did not understand fully what this $5.00 was to be used for and, no doubt, Joe Bonaparte and Abraham knew of your objections to this item in the council proceedings of last November, so they used that in order to get your name on the petition; and, if that is so, you have stated well when you said you would endeavor to straighten out that piece of crooked business.

Such work as that goes to prove that the Indians ought to organize and stick together, and not sign any paper or petitions of any kind until such petition has been thoroughly talked over and interpreted so that the Indians would understand the meaning of every word before they signed. That is why you should hold council meetings in every district, so that all matters of business could be read over by competent interpreters who are trustworthy and the Indians allowed to discuss the merits of each measure in their own language, and instruct the delegates who are elected to vote at the grand council as to the wishes of each District. The Indians have a hard fight before them, and the only way they can accomplish anything is by pulling together.

The salary and expenses of the employees, policemen and liquor traffic men on the Flathead Reservation and also the employees of the Reclamation Service amounts to many times more to each individual Indian than the $5.00 asked for in the minutes of their council held on the 28th of November, 1917.

The object of the Indians is to do away with all of this unnecessary expense, and in order to do that they will have to put themselves in the position to transact their own business, and in order to transact their own business it is necessary for them to have a little fund to work on.

The delegation that was here in Washington drafted a bill asking for $5,000.00 to be used by the Flathead Indian Council for the purpose of defraying the expenses of the Council. This $5,000.00 would amount to something like $2.50 from each member of the tribe, to be taken out of their individual share of the tribal fund, the same to be used by the Council and not by any individual Indian.

At the present time, under the Indian Bureau system, the Indians funds derived from the lease of tribal lands and the sale of tribal timber are placed in the Treasury under the head of "Proceeds of Labor, Flathead Indians," and this money is used to pay the expenses of employees on the Indian Reservation such as foresters, timber scalers, cruisers, whiskey traffic men and any other expenses that may be incurred on the reservation. You are paying out your children's money and your own money and you do not know it. They do not even ask your consent to allow it to be paid. They merely just take it without saying a word to you, and the only way the Indians can beat them out of it is to prove to Congress that the Indians are capable of living upon their own reservation and farming their own lands, selling their own cattle and selling their own grain and hay, without the assistance of Government employees. You know very well that you can do this, and I know that you can do it, and we believe that the Indian Bureau knows that you can do it, but it is not the policy of the Bureau to decrease the number of its employees; in fact, the number of employees in the Indian Bureau have increased immensely in the last six or seven years.

Now, it is your duty to instruct your people to be law abiding people on the reservation; it is your duty to instruct them not to try to carry whiskey on the reservation, and it is your duty to instruct them to use every effort to catch such men as Ben Cramer when they carry whiskey on the reservation.

If you will do that, it will not be necessary for the Government to employ whiskey traffic men at your expense to keep down the liquor traffic on the

Kootenai Chief Koostatah
Source: Photograph Archives, Montana Historical Society, Helena, Montana, detail from photo 954-573

Flathead Indian Reservation. That is one way to do away with some of the officers on the reservation whose salaries are paid out of the Indians funds, and that was the efforts of the delegation here in Washington, to reduce the appropriation bill as much as possible, so as to save money for the Indians. You cannot expect your delegation to accomplish everything in one year. It takes a long time.

I believe that the Indians on the Flathead Reservation have accomplished a great deal in the last year. Two years ago the Indians were not allowed to hold any meetings. Now they can hold their meetings unmolested to discuss their own business. Two years ago the Flathead Delegation would come on to Washington and the Indian Bureau would not recognize them. If they did not have their own money to pay their own expenses, they would have to starve and send home for money to return home on. This year the Flathead Delegation came on to Washington; the Indian Office recognized them as delegates representing the Flathead Nation of Indians; Congress recognized them as delegates representing the Flathead Nation of Indians; the Flathead Delegation this last year did not have to go hungry; the Indian Office paid their hotel bills; the Indian Office paid for their ticket coming on here; and the Indian Office paid their fare home then they got ready to go. The commissioner of Indian Affairs discharged Dr. Heidelman because the delegates asked that he be discharged.

These facts will prove that the Falhead [sic] Indians have accomplished much the last year, and if they will all stick together and pull the same way, they will accomplish much more in the future, and that is what you want to instruct your people, is to stick together and not sign petitions until those petitions have been fully explained at a council meeting by some competent interpreter, who is trustworthy.

No doubt, Miss Lemery is home by this time and she will explain to you more fully what has been accomplished by the delegation and what steps are to be taken to accomplish more. I expect to be going West in a few weeks and would be pleased to stop off on your reservation for a short time, and anything that I could do at any time to help your people along, I will always be glad to do it.

Thanking you very much for the interest you have taken in your people, I am,

Very truly yours,
(signed) George Bundy Wasson
(Little Chinook)

Document 103

Two Indians Arrested for Stealing Wheat

May 1918 — January 1919

Source: "Two Wounded in Gun Fight," *The Ronan Pioneer*, May 31, 1918, page 1, col. 1; "James Grinder Pleads Guilty," *The Daily Missoulian*, January 15, 1919, page 2, col. 1; "Matt Receives Heavy Sentence," *The Daily Missoulian*, January 21, 1919, page 6, col. 6.

Editors' note: Two Indians from the reservation were arrested for stealing grain from a field near Pablo.

Two Wounded in Gun Fight

In making the arrest of Peter Matt and James Grinder, half breed Indians, charged with stealing wheat from the grainary [sic] of John J. Rogers living on Mud creek, U.S. Officer W. G. Brown was shot in the arm and Pete Matt is in the Missoula hospital with a gunshot wound in his hip.

Upon being notified of the activity of Matt and Grinder in the wheat business last Friday night, Officers W. G. Brown and J. C. Curtis proceeded to the Rogers ranch and waited until they were leaving the grainary with a full load of wheat. When commanded to surrender, Grinder threw up his hands and gave up, but Matt slid off the wagon with a shot gun and fired at Brown, striking him in the left forearm. Both Brown and Curtis fired at the same time and it is thought that Curtis' bullet was the one taking effect in Matt's hip. He dropped to the ground with a loud howl of pain and let himself be taken and disarmed. They were brought to Ronan along with the wagon load of wheat and Dr. A. K. Resner attended to the wounds of the two men. Sheriff Green was notified and came out from Missoula Saturday morning to take Matt and Grinder to Missoula where one was lodged in jail and the other in the hospital.

Officers Brown and Curtis went to Missoula also and while there Mr. Brown was operated on and had the shot and particles of clothing removed from his arm, and while the wound is serious and painful he is expected to recover in due time. Matt's injuries are more serious and it will be some time before he will be able to walk.

Matt and Grinder are both well known on the reservation and have been in trouble several times before. The present case against them is serious and they will probably get a heavy sentence, particularly Matt.

* * * * * * * * *

James Grinder Pleads Guilty
Judge Lentz Will Sentence Confessed Burglar on Thursday.

James Grinder, half breed Indian, accused of burglary, admitted his guilt when brought before Judge Theodore Lentz yesterday. He will be brought into court for sentence on Thursday morning.

Court attaches [watchers?] are convinced that stiff a sentence awaits the man, in view of the fact that he jumped his bond in *[line of text missing]* penitentiary convictions which are the outstanding features of his record. The penalty provided by law is from two to fourteen years in the state penitentiary.

Grinder was arrested in Butte by the sheriff of Silver Bow county, after his whereabouts had been learned by Under Sheriff Higgins, who, with other members of the sheriff's force had been seeking him for several days as the time for his trial approached.

The charge against Grinder was based on the theft of grain on the Flathead reservation, and as the result of this fact, the residents of the reservation were much interested in the case. Many of the ranchers in that locality have tracts of land widely scattered and to store the crop granaries are built and the grain stored on the premises. It is said that from one of these granaries the grain was obtained by Grinder.

James Grinder and Peter Matt were arrested May 25, charged with theft of wheat. United States Officer Brown and another officer came upon them shortly before daylight while they were driving along with a load of wheat near Pablo. The officers commanded the men to throw up their hands and Grinder surrendered. Matt showed fight and jumped to the opposite side of the wagon, seized a shotgun and fired at close range at Brown, inflicting a wound in the arm. Brown returned the fire and dropped Matt with a wound in the leg and the side.

The Matt trial on an assault charge will be held before Judge Asa L. Duncan next month.

* * * * * * * * *

Matt Receives Heavy Sentence

Pleads Guilty to Assault in First Degree and Gets 5½ to 11 Years.

Yesterday afternoon Judge Asa L. Duncan sentenced Peter Matt to serve five and one-half to 11 years in the state penitentiary. This closes the chapter in a crime which has been of more than ordinary interest to residents of the reservation. James Grinder, who was with Matt at the time the assault was committeed [sic] was recently sentenced to serve a term of from seven to 14 year.

Matt and Grinder were driving along the road near Pablo with a load of grain alleged to have been stolen. Federal Officer Brown ordered them to surrender. Grinder gave up, but Matt showed fight. Matt shot Brown, who returned the fire, but before Matt could shoot again, he was shot twice by Deputy J. C. Curtis, who was assisting Brown make the arrest.

Matt first pleaded not guilty, but later changed his plea to guilty. He was taken to Deer Lodge yesterday by Undersheriff Arthur Higgins.

Document 104

Tribal Members Attend Circus in Missoula

August 24, 1918

Source: "Reds and Circus Keeps Cops Busy," *The Daily Missoulian*, August 24, 1918, page 5, col. 1.

Editors' note: Some Indians and Irishmen attending the circus in Missoula used alcohol to grease the celebration.

Reds and Circus Keeps Cops Busy
Many Indians Come to Town and Trouble Ensures for Some.

Circus day brought to town the usual crowd of Indians, who sought a good time and some of the white man's liquor and incidentally the city jail sounded like an Indian camp just at powwow time last night.

Philip Piere [sic] became intoxicated and was going to "clean out" Delonico's restaurant on West Front when Patrolman Fred Burks arrested him and took him to the city jail. Policeman Bishop put a stop to a threatened riot by Peter Matt at the Pollard rooming house on West Pine street yesterday afternoon. Matt is now at the city jail.

J. O'Donnell, a white man, maddened with too much whiskey, started a fight on West Front street. Patrolman Phelps arrested O'Donnell, but his fighting blood was up and he refused to go to jail. A blow from the fist of Phelps sent O'Donnell to the mat, but he came up looking for more and went down again when the policeman caught him on the jaw. He kept on battling, however. Night Chief McDonnell and Policeman Bishop arrived on the scene and the prisoner was finally subdued. He is confined at the city jail.

Document 105

Alcohol Fueled Reservation Brawl

October 28, 1918

Source: "Indians Battle and 2 May Die," *The Daily Missoulian*, October 28, 1918, page 2, col. 3.

Editors' note: Newspaper reports of drunken brawls on the reservation were common, but the peaceful everyday activities of most tribal members did not make the papers.

Indians Battle and 2 May Die

Whiskey, Cards and a Brawl Result in Stabbing at the Mission.

St. Ignatius, Oct. 27. — Special. — Big Thomas and Ed Finley, halfbreed Indians, are near death here as the result of whiskey, cards, a brawl, and a stabbing affray early Sunday morning. Bootleggers, operating near the Mission Saturday night, are blamed by the local authorities.

Several Indians, eager for booze, procured it of them and made off to a dirty little hut to gamble and enjoy their purchase. There were about 15 or 20 of them, it is said.

Nothing was heard from them until about 2 o'clock this morning. At that hour, Dr. T. A. Matthews was awakened by a loud hammering at his door, and he was summoned to administer to two wounded Indians.

The story, as pieced together today, follows:

Fight Over Card Game.

The card game was progressing nicely when a dispute arose. Big Thomas, it is said, drew a knife on Ed Finley. A fight followed in which it is reported, that Thomas with one swift dive, planted the knife in Finley's ribs, penetrating the latter's lung just over the heart. Thomas in the meantime had received only a slight wound in the arm from Finley. At this time, the crowd witnessing the fight, interferred and separated the two bucks.

A second chapter began.

Frank Lomar, a friend of Ed Finley, seeing that his companion was badly wounded, is reported to have grabbed a club, swinging it over Thomas' head, landed it with a blow that fractured his skull and sent him to the floor, where he lay unconscious, following the Indian custom of trying to get revenge.

Thomas has not yet regained consciousness, and only moans and groans. He and Ed Finley are both in a very serious condition. Theodore Sharp, superintendent of the Flathead agency, was notified at once. He came this afternoon and took away two auto loads of prisoners to the reservation headquarters.

Document 106

Charles Allard Sued

December 22, 1918

Source: "Charles Allard Sued by Bankers of Ronan," *The Daily Missoulian*, December 22, 1918, page 2, col. 1.

Editors' note; Charles Allard, Jr., was an active promoter of rodeos and Indian celebrations, but this time he made the newspaper for a less positive development.

Charles Allard Sued by Bankers of Ronan

Charles Allard, promoter of Missoula Stampedes and well known as a cowpuncher throughout the northwest, is being sued by the First National bank of Ronan for the collection of $1,480.65 alleged debt. His wife, Lulu Allard, is also a defendant in the case.

The suit was filed yesterday in district court, and in order to collect the sum, the plaintiff has issued a foreclosure of mortgage and asks for a sheriff's sale of land.

According to the complaint, Charles Allard and Lulu Allard on July 15, 1918, in Ronan, executed a promissory note to the bank, in exchange for which was given $1,301.60, with interest at 10 per cent. In order to secure payment, a mortgage on land owned by Allard was delivered at the same time. Through its attorney, Coker T. Rathbone of Ronan, the bankers are asking sale of the land, from which to collect $1,480.65, which they claim is the amount due on the note, the interest and the attorney's fees.

Document 107

Death of Chief Moiese

December 29, 1918

Source: "Moiese, the Friend of the White Man, to Hunting Ground," *The Daily Missoulian*, December 29, 1918, page 3, col. 2.

Editors' note: Apparently Salish Chief Moiese was a casualty of the 1918 influenza epidemic.

Moiese, the Friend of the White Man, to Hunting Ground
Medicine of the Tribe Fails When Fatal Illness Comes.

Another connecting link between the past and present has been snapped.

Chieftain Moiese, friend of the white man, sub-chief of Charlot, enemy of the Nez Perce, is dead.

It wasn't right that he died as he did. Chieftain Moiese deserved a better end. He was a good Indian, possessed of the ideals of Charlot — wise in council, proud in demeanor, cognizant of civilization.

Moiese died because he placed his faith in a medicine man of his tribe — one Poker Jim. It happened Friday night. The details bring regret. Yet, beneath it all lies the romance of Indian lore. Poker Jim is the medicine man. Moiese was 79 years of age. He was sick unto death. And the keen-edged mind was dulled. He believed in Poker Jim.

The Curse of the Paleface.

It was the curse of the white man that did it. Poker Jim was drunk. In fact he was very drunk when Chief Moiese was brought to his camp west of Missoula Friday night, with his life threatened by pneumonia.

The medicine man ordered his aged chief to be wrapped in blankets and laid without the tepee upon the ground.

Then Poker went to sleep.

And early yesterday morning, when Albert Matt, nephew of the chief, went to the camp of the medicine man he expected to find his chief and uncle wholly cured. He, too, believed in the incantations of Poker Jim.

Instead, he found the medicine man still helpless with whiskey. And when he lifted the blanket from the face of his chief Moiese was dead.

Chief Antoine Moise and family
Source: National Anthropological Archives, Smithsonian Institution,
Washington, D.C.
photo 09939900

The exposure during the night had taken the life from that chieftain who served the settlers when he was young — and who placed faith in Poker Jim when he was old.

It was the medicine man's brother, Joe Poker, who told Coroner Lucy how it happened. So influenza is named as the cause of death — with neglect entering in.

Chief Moiese was noble. There was none of the modern jaded breed in him. He belonged to that race that is fast disappearing from the old west. He was a sub-chief to Charlot, friend of the white man.

The history of Moiese dates back to the days when Missoula was young. It was because of him and Chief Charlot that Chief Joseph of the Nez Perces changed his course in 1877. Those two met the marauders at Lolo. Charlot called Chief Joseph "cousin." But they ended entreaty with a threat. They told him that the Bitter Root Indians would unite with the settlers if the Nez Perces placed foot upon their soil. The battle of the Big Hole followed. How that fight at the end of the benchland near Gibbons resulted is known to all.

In 1884 the tribe split. Some remained in the Bitter Root. Others, among them Moiese and Arlee, went to the Flathead. Those were trying times for Charlot, for the government wished him to move from Bitter Root land. And on October 17, 1891, he did so. He went to the new home of his people on the Jocko.

And that was told yesterday by A. L. Stone of Missoula, who knew Moiese and followed old trails. The death of the chief grieved him — as it did others who have known Missoula when houses were far apart.

"I thought Moiese had better sense," he said.

Document 108

Flathead Tribal Council Petition

February 11, 1919

Source: Mary Lemery, et. al., "Proceeding of General Council," February 11, 1919, from file 14,747/1919 Flathead 054, RG 75, Central Classified Files, National Archives, Washington, D.C.; "Indian Powwow Held at Mission," *The Daily Missoulian*, February 18, 1919, page 1, col. 3 and page 2, col. 3.

Editors' note: This petition presented the complaints and requests of the Flathead Tribal Council led by Mary Lemery to Congress and the Indian Office. The two resolutions which are struck through here, seem to have been crossed out before the petition was sent to the Flathead Agency and Washington, D.C., in 1919.

Proceeding of General Council

Flathead nation at St. Ignatius, on Flathead Reservation in the State of Montana, February 11th, 1919.

That whereas on this day and date first above written, the council of the Flathead Indians of the State of Montana, convened according to the usual manner and custom of the tribe for the purpose of considering the various matters affecting the tribal affairs of this nation of Indians, the enjoyment of our rights in securing a remedial legislation for our relief, in development of our resources and advancement in civilization.

That whereas on the 11th day of February 1919, at a General Council meeting of the Flathead Nations and several confederated tribes or bands composing the same duly called and assembled, pursuant to notice regularly given according to tribal customs and held at St. Ignatius, on the Flathead in the Stare of Montana the following resolutions were adopted to-wit:

Whereas we have reason to believe that our timber fails to bring enough revenue for the support of those who need help and special attention:

Whereas the cost of construction of irregation [sic] systems has cost to June 30th, 1918 $3,103,935.08, and estimated additional cost to complete $3,000,000, total $6,103,935.08, therefore we do hereby strongly protest against such expenditure if assessed against our allotments, and also protest against the $40,000 item in the Indian Appropriation Bill as relates to Flathead matters.

Whereas we have reason and cause to believe that our affairs are in such a state as to warrant a thorough investigation and therefore it is a consensus of opinion of this tribe of Indians that every department under this agency be investigated and that accounting be made to ascertain every cent and dollar of our lease money, the proceeds from the sale of timber and other funds held in trust by the Government of the United States:

Whereas Congress of the United States on April 23rd 1904, passed an act for the survey and allotment of lands now embraced within the limits of the Flathead Indian Reservation in the State of Montana, and the sale and disposal of all surplus lands after allotment now therefore be it Resolved that so much of the said Act be amended as relates to allotment of lands so as to rpovide [sic] allotment of land for those who have not heretofore been alloted [sic] which are 618 or more:

Whereas this tribe of Indians have produced competent and qualified timber cruisers who who [sic] can be employed by the Government should be strongly advocated by this tribe:

~~Whereas we realize nothing from the water power embraced within this reservation that such possibilities be developed and utilized by lease or otherwise and proceeds therefrom expended for the benefit of the said Flathead Tribe of Indians:~~

Whereas deceased and other allotments have been sold without our knowledge and consent and consequently such sales are made to the detriment of the heirs and allottees whose interests should be protected and safeguarded therefore, we ask that hereafter no more such sales be made:

~~Whereas additional school facilities for our children are needed because about 300 of our children are without adequate educational advantages, therefore we most urgently request that $40,000 be appropriated for the tuition of those who attend Catholic Mission Schools of St. Ignatius, Montana:~~

Whereas all destitute Indians have no means to procure their needs, they should be provided with rations and other necessaries of life:

Whereas the jurisdictional act conferring upon the court of Claims authority to consider and determine all legal and equitable claims of the Flathead and other tribes of Indians of Montana against the United States Government be enacted into a law at an early date:

Whereas our grazing lands are very much limited, we ask that all such grazing lands be conserved for the benefit of the Indians who have not adequate range for their live stock:

Whereas we strongly protest against the lease or sale of the Camas Hot Spring located within this reservation the property of this tribe. Resolved further that the enrollment of this tribe of Indians shall be closed finally on

Feb. 6th, 1919 when the tribal funds now in the Treasury of the United States, to the credit of Flathead tribe of Indians shall be segregated and paid to the several Indians who are entitled to the same.

Resolved further that it is the sentiment and opinion of this tribe that the said abuses and grievances shall be the basis of this Councils action against the abnormal conditions of our affairs and be it further resolved that a copy of these resolutions be sent to the Indian committee of Congress and department having to do with Indian affairs.

Respectfully submitted,
Mary Lemery, Chairman
Baptist Marengo, Secretary.
Dave Couture
Baptist Ki-Ki-She, [thumb print]
Sapiel Michell, [thumb print]
Martin Charlo, [thumb print]
Andrew Bullhead, [thumb print]
Sam Finley, [thumb print]
Jerome Lumpry
Eneas Adams, [thumb print]
Michel Keiser, [thumb print]
John Charley, [thumb print]
Martin Michell, [thumb print]
John Vallee
Louie C. Lantow
Alphonse Courville
Eneas Michel

Those authorized by the Council, under this date to execute a foregoing proceedings have signified their names by thumb marks and signatures.

Superintendent's Certificate.

I, Theodore Sharp, Superintendent and Special Disbursing Agent at the Flathead Agency on the Flathead Reservation in the State of Montana, hereby certify that the foregoing minutes of the general council of the Flathead Tribe of Indians held at St. Ignatius, Montana on the 11th day of February 1919 are correct and true copies of the said council adopted in my presence by the said Tribe of Indians.

Theodore Sharp

Certificate of Interpreters.

We the undersigned, do hereby certify that we are members of this tribe of Indians and acted as interpreters in the general council of this tribe of Indians held at St. Ignatius in the State of Montana on the 11th day of February 1919, that the same is true and correct.

(Interpreters) Louie C. Lantow
[one signature only]

* * * * * * * * *

Indian Powwow Held at Mission
Flatheads Meet with Four of Their Chiefs Present to Make Demand.
Manage Own Affairs
Major Sharp Indorses Desire of Indians to Have Self Government.

St. Ignatius, Feb. 17. — Special. — Resolutions which are to receive the indorsement of Major Sharp, agent of the Flathead Indian reservation, and asking that the affairs of the Indians be administered by themselves without the help of any organization, were drawn up at a historic meeting of the Indians held at the Mission last week.

The Indians kept the affair a profound secret, and only today were sufficient of the details obtainable to give an account of what happened. All during the fall and winter there have been small gatherings of the Indians, until finally they got together in one mass meeting, following which they laid their resolutions and plans before Major Sharp and secured his promise of co-operation, and appointed a committee to have charge of the expression of their desires to Washington.

First Council in Years.

The meeting included representatives from all over the reservation, even from as far away as Browning. It is said to be the first real council of the Flatheads for the discussion of a tribal policy since the white man settled in western Montana.

The official representatives included four chiefs, and numerous other members of the tribe as follows:

Chief Kakashea, St. Ignatius; Chief Martin Charlo, Arlee; Chief Charlie Michel, Ronan; Chief Andrew Bullhead, Camas; Felix Medore, Pascal Antone, John Charlie, Basil Philip, Alphonse Courville, Polson; Basil Finley, Eneas Conco, Blind Michel, Antoine Finley, John Valley, Ronan; Dave Couture, Perma; Louis Camille, Camas; Jerome Longpre, Alex Matt, Michel Kaiser, Sam Ressurection and Michel Louis, Arlee.

Chiefs Add Dignity to Session.

The presence of the four chiefs added a note of dignity and seriousness to the meeting which began in the morning when Indians swarmed in on every road leading to the Mission, until 8 o'clock the next morning, when the same roads were thronged with the tribesmen, tired with a night of dancing and pow-wowing, and satisfied with a successful meeting.

February 12 will be long remembered by the Flatheads. After the business session of the evening, there followed a mighty celebration, a war dance, in which one hundred Indians, who had come prepared for the occasion with elaborate costumes and war paint, took part, while at least two hundred more stood by and watched. The gray-haired chiefs made the dance much more spectacular, and put into the affair the necessary spirit. The Flathead War dance, the Smoke dance and the regular S.... dance, whose chief feature is the exchange of gifts were the principal events of the evening.

Miss Mary Lemery was the presiding officer, and Batiste Marengo of Polson was secretary. Robert Hamilton, an Indian lawyer who is a very conspicuous figure, took a prominent part in the meeting.

Indians Are Dissatisfied.

Despite the cloud which hovers over the exact proceedings of the "business" session of the council, the evident dissatisfaction of the Indians at their condition could not be concealed, and it is embodied in the resolutions which were drawn up. That their hearts are heavy and their minds sad is due to the system under which they live, and so the resolutions, it is declared, described the system which they ask to be adopted. It is said to be a plan which may be carried out without any red tape, and it is based upon the funds which the Indians receive from the government.

The resolutions express the Indian belief that the timber lands sold by the government amounted to several million dollars instead of the $100,000 which came to the reservation, $60,000 going to the agency direct and the rest divided among the Indians. The sum to the agency is devoted to the payment of the agency officials, and the general management of the Indian affairs.

Can Manage Own Business.

The document states the confidence of those who prepared it that the Indians are able and qualified to manage their own affairs without the help of any agency or similar organization. The money then could be sent to them direct from Washington without any intermediary. They object too, to having the land of deceased Indians sold and the returns used for schools which they claim are not up to the standard. There was also a plea for more grazing land for their herds, which are being shut out with the steady stream of farmers who fence up the once open plains.

The resolutions are to be signed by Major Sharp, who is inclined to let them try their schemes and see what will result, and then sent to the commission on Indian affairs, which has been approached several times before but with no result. As soon as the commission at Washington has taken action on this, there is to be another meeting similar to this one, to go further into the affair.

Document 109

Duncan McDonald Opposes Changes in Policies

March 9, 1919

Source: "Duncan M'Donald Here for Health," *The Daily Missoulian*, March 9, 1919, page 3, col. 1-2.

Editors' note: Duncan McDonald had long been chairman of the Flathead Business Committee which worked closely with the Flathead Agent. He opposed the new policies proposed by Mary Lemery and the Flathead Tribal Council.

Duncan M'Donald Here for Health
Famous Montana Pioneer Opposes Pensioning of the Indian.

Duncan McDonald, a famous Montana pioneer, arrived in Missoula yesterday to consult physicians in regard to his health, which has been failing lately. Mr. McDonald is 70 years of age and has been a resident of this county longer than any other person. He was born on Post creek on the reservation.

"A man who favors a bill to pension the Indian ought to be pensioned himself," said Mr. McDonald. "He isn't able to take care of himself. As soon as you begin to pension a person that is where you fail. How can you expect the Indian to amount to anything when you make him feel that he will be taken care of for the rest of his life."

"Then you think the Indian should not be treated as a ward of the government?" he was asked.

"Most decidedly," was the abrupt answer.

"I tell you we have I. W. W. [Industrial Workers of the World] in our tribe. There are some big strapping fellows who work a few days and then spend the rest of their time in the poolrooms. The poolrooms are as bad as the saloons.

"The lawyers at Washington are robbing the Indians. You can put that in.

"When the officials come from Washington the Indians go to them and say they want an axe, a shovel, or a plow. But if there was a barrel of whiskey they would soon pay for it. You can put that in. It is a cut for my people.

"They gave the negro emancipation. They set him free without pensioning him. Why can't they do the same with the Indian?"

Mr. McDonald says that there will not be good crops next season unless there is a big storm.

"I remember a winter back in 1878 or '79 we had fine weather in the early part of the season. Old November was warm. In December the roads on the reservation were dusty and in February the green grass was high. There were thousands of birds. The flowers were blooming and it was just like summer. And then all of a sudden in March there came a terrible blizzard. The birds were killed and I found hundreds of them scattered about in various nooks and crevices where they had sought shelter. I won't look for spring until the first of April. Old March is a bad month."

Document 110

Indians Charged With Gambling

March 28, 1919

Source: "Arlee Men Nabbed Gambling Charge," *The Ronan Pioneer*, March 28, 1919, page 1, col. 2.

Editors' note: Gambling was still popular among tribal members, despite the law.

Arlee Men Nabbed Gambling Charge

In a raid on the Barnaby pool hall in Arlee late last Saturday night, five men were arrested by Deputy Sheriff J. C. Curtis and taken to Missoula where a hearing was held Monday and they were charged with gambling. Wm. Rairdon plead guilty and was fined $100. The other four, Tony Barnaby, Many Bear, Antoine Finley and Pierre Joseph, entered pleas of not guilty and have retained attorneys to defend their cases.

Document 111

Homesteader Wants Charlo's Widow Evicted

April – May 1919

Source: [Theodore Sharp] to Commissioner of Indian Affairs, April 16, 1919, and C. F. Hauke to Messrs. Mulroney & Mulroney, May 10, 1919, from file 62,247/1918 Flathead 310, Central Classified Files, RG 75, National Archives, Washington, D.C.

Editors' note: Sometimes the letter of the law was not able to accommodate the wishes of an elderly woman to live out her life in the house where she had stayed for many years.

Department of the Interior
United States Indian Service
Flathead Agency — Dixon, Mont.
April 16, 1919.

Commissioner of Indian Affairs,
Washington, D.C.
Sir: —

This is to acknowledge receipt of letter of Mulroney & Mulroney, Attorneys-at-Law, dated March 26th, 1919, and referred to this office for report.

The letter referred to asks that action be taken by the Superintendent of the Flathead Reservation or by the U.S. Government, through proper officials, to secure the ejectment of Isabel Charlo from land purchased by Mr. H. H. Francis, and described at the $S^{1}/_{2}$ $SW^{1}/_{4}$ $SE^{1}/_{4}$, and the $SE^{1}/_{4}$ $SE^{1}/_{4}$ $SW^{1}/_{4}$ of Section 16, Twp. 16 North, Range 19 West.

The attorneys of Mr. Francis represent that he has conferred with this office, and that he has been advised from this office that "nothing can be done, and that it would be best for Isabel Charlo to remain upon the property."

The land described above is a portion of the allotment of Mary Finley, Flathead Allottee No. 1222. This land was duly advertised for sale at an appraised value of $750.00, and Mr. H. H. Francis made an offer of $902.00 under sealed bids. The sale was forwarded through the usual channels to your Office, and was approved by the Commissioner of Indian Affairs September 18, 1918, and by the Department October 10, 1918, and from the letter of

Mr. Francis' attorneys, it appears that patent has been issued to him for the land. The circumstances in this case seem to be as follows:

Under date of July 16th, 1855, a treaty was entered into with the Flathead Indians, which treaty was ratified by the Senate March 8th, 1859. Article 5 of this treaty provides in part that the head chiefs of the Confederated Tribes of Indians were to be paid $500.00 per year each for a term of 20 years, after the ratification of the treaty, as a salary, and there was to be built for them — at suitable points on the reservation, a comfortable house which should be properly furnished, and that for each of them, 10 acres of land were to be plowed and fenced, "the salary to be paid to, and the said houses to be occupied by, such head chiefs so long as they may be elected to that position by their Tribes, and no longer." Under the provisions of the above treaty, I am informed that a house was erected for one of the leaders of the Tribe, known as Chief Charlo. This house was built on land near the site of the Indian Agency, as at that time, located at Jocko. This house, I understand, was occupied by Charlo until his death in 1910, and this same house has been occupied by his widow, Isabel Charlo, since his death. This woman, Isabel Charlo, is, as I understand it, the person referred to in the letter of Mulroney & Mulroney. At the time the house was built, it should be understood that this was not a reservation on which any allotments had been made, but was what is termed as a "closed reservation." Later, about the year 1908, when lands on the Flathead Reservation were segregated into allotments, and individual Indians were designated certain allotments for their particular use and occupancy, the land where the house occupied by Charlo is located, was allotted to Mary Finley, Flathead Allottee No. 1222, and no reservation of the house or any of the land surrounding it for the use of Charlo appears to have been made. I understand that Mary Finley did not secure possession of the house at any time, but that she did have the use of the land, — at least she negotiated a lease or leases on the land, and secured the rentals from such lease.

To this office, it appears that Mrs. Isabel Charlo has no lawful right to occupy the house in question, as whatever title was vested in her deceased husband, Chief Charlo, it would seem has expired with his death according to the language of the treaty, which says that said houses are to be occupied by such head chiefs so long as they may be elected to that position by their tribes and no longer. Chief Charlo having been dead nine years, his right of occupancy seems to have terminated, and no provision seems to be made for the passing of this right to his heirs. Furthermore, the fact that Charlo did not receive this land as a portion of his allotment when the allotments were made, but that the land was allotted to Mary Finley, would seem to carry with it any buildings or improvements on the land. This doubtless was an oversight of the allotting agent at that time, but seems to be the facts of the matter, nevertheless.

I cannot find any communication or record in the files of this office, that has been had with Mr. Francis relative to his occupying this property, or anything to indicate that that this office ever told him that he should permit Isabel Charlo to remain upon the land. I did, at one time, write to Mr. Fred R. Angevine, Deputy County Attorney, with respect to the matter, in reply to an inquiry of Mr. Angevine's. A copy of this letter is enclosed herewith, and it will be noted that in this letter, I make the suggestion that in view of the extreme age of Mrs. Charlo — about 87 years — some arrangement might possibly be made between Mr. Francis and herself by which she might occupy the house the remainder of her life period. This, however, was not given as advice to Mr. Francis, but was a suggestion made to Mr. Angevine.

It is the opinion of this office that Mr. Francis has a perfect legal right to take action in the courts to dispossess Mrs. Charlo from the premises in question, if he cares to do so. It also appears that instead of executing this right, he is seeking, through his attorneys, Mulroney & Mulroney, to secure the action he desires by having the U.S. authorities do it for him. I do not feel this office is under obligation to undertake the matter for Mr. Francis, as he has been granted a fee patent and full title to the premises, and Mrs. Charlo does not appear, in the view of this office, to have been granted any rights on the premises by the Government. If she is wrongfully there, and Mr. Francis thinks she should immediately be dispossessed, it is a matter for him to take into the proper courts, jurisdiction over this land by the Government having been released on the issuance of patent in fee.

Very truly yours,
[Theodore Sharp]
Superintendent.

* * * * * * * * *

May 10 1919

Messrs, Mulroney & Mulroney,
Attorneys at Law,
Missoula, Montana.
Gentlemen:

I have to state as follows with reference to your letter of March 26, 1919, concerning the occupation by Isabel Charlo of part of the allotment of Mary Finley sold to H. H. Francis.

Before the lands were allotted Mrs. Charlo's husband, who was chief of the tribe, was, under treaty provisions, given a right to occupy the land now in controversy as long as he represented the tribe as chief. He occupied the land until his death and his wife was not disturbed in her occupancy after that time. There is nothing to show that the allottee or the present lessee objected to Mrs. Charlo's presence.

The Indian is very old, and to leave what she has always considered her home, would be such a hardship that the Government would not care to take any steps toward her removal. There is little doubt that if the facts concerning Mrs. Charlo were known to Mr. Francis he would be lenient toward this old Indian woman, whose case will soon be settled out of court.

Very truly yours,
(Signed) C. F. Hauke
Chief Clerk.

Document 112

Vulcanizing Shop

The Ronan Pioneer, April 25, 1919, page 5, col. 1.

Document 113

Duncan McDonald Talks of the Old Days

May 11, 1919

Source: "Indian Colony Is Paid Visit," *The Daily Missoulian*, May 11, 1919, page 7, col. 1-2.

Editors' note: Duncan McDonald was always willing to talk to reporters. He lamented the loss of the traditional Indian ways and especially the loss of the Indian names for geographic features in western Montana. The reporter made some mistakes with quotation marks, but they are reproduced here as printed.

Indian Colony Is Paid Visit

Bitter Root Diggers Watched by Duncan McDonald and Reporter.

"Step into the taxi," said Duncan McDonald.

The Missoulian reporter saying [seeing] the venerable citizen of the Flathead, and knowing that always he has a story, complied. Southward through the city they travelled and out toward Fort Missoula. As they crossed the big city bridge, McDonald pointed to the bank opposite the Milwaukee railroad station.

"We rode down the trail and forded the river there in 1858. We camped on that island. That was many years ago."

McDonald for seventy summers and winters has lived on the Indian reservation. Then the buffalo were more numerous west of the divide than to the east.

"I have sold my home," announced McDonald, as the machine sped along.

"And you will retire and take it easy?" asked the reporter.

"I will fish, gather berries and dig the bitter root," was the reply.

The machine approached a flock of sheep being driven along the roadway. A lamb, but a few hours old, lagged behind, and finally fell by the highway. The old Indian looked sorrowfully at the little one.

"Poor little thing," he said. And he made you know he meant it. On sped the machine until finally —

"There they are," he exclaimed, his eyes alight.

Silhouetted by the ray of the setting sun over the western mountain range, they made a picture never to be forgotten. Smoke spirals floated upward and drifted toward the city and the civilization that was so near and yet seemed so far and unreal. It was strange to step into a machine in a modern city and he [be] whisked away in ten minutes into a scene that Remington or Paxson portrays of the days before the white man came.

There, ten minutes from the city, was a scene of 1860. S....s in variegated blankets were seated about the tepees. McDonald and his companion approached leisurely. One of the s....s looked up, and her face lighted with a smile of greeting. McDonald extended his hand and spoke to the woman in the Indian tongue.

"She says," he interpreted, "that they have just arrived and have not gathered any of the bitter roots. We will visit other tepees."

"Do you know them?"

"Know them?" he laughed incredulously. "I know every man, woman and child on the reservation by name. The younger woman is Anne, the elder is Mrs. Harriett Nine Pipe."

They approached another tepee and McDonald exclaimed:

"Why, there's my uncle's wife, Mrs. Alexander Big Knife." And he shook hands with a good natured s.... who was busily fashioning a spoon from a cocoanut shell. They conversed a moment, and the reporter peeped into the tepee.

The evening meal was cooking. Meat was roasting on an upright stick jabbed into the ground near the fire, and from time to time the meat was turned about. A coffee pot, seeming out of place in those surroundings, bubbled on the coals. A pappoose played near the blaze. Near the fire and reclining on an Indian blanket, an attractive Indian girl lazily puffed a cigarette.

"She says," spoke McDonald to his companion, "there is not going to be much bitter root this [y]ear because of lack of rain. But come, I will show you where they dig it, and how it looks."

Behind the tepee, several pounds of the Indian staple were spread on a white cloth drying in the sun. And Mrs. Big Knife gave a demonstration in home economics. With an instrument of elk horn, T-shaped, the flower was quickly pried out of the ground and with a deft motion, the skin of the root was peeled off, leaving the root white and clean.

"Here," said the old man, "is a bitter root you have seen gathered and prepared for drying. The average family in a good year picks and dries about 50 pounds of it."

"They use it for medicine I suppose," said the reporter.

"You use oatmeal don't you?" asked McDonald. Answered in the affirmative he continued:

"You don't use it every day, do you?"

"No, of course not. We would get tired of it."

"Well, that's the way with the bitter root. It is a food. It is cooked in various ways and is sometimes eaten with milk and sugar. It is used as a food and not as a medicine, although it contains medicinal properties."

Leaving the tepee McDonald returned to the taxi.

On the trip back to the city McDonald expressed his resentment because so many of the names of towns and rivers and landmarks had been changed from the original Indian names.

"This is the Bitter Root country right here," said McDonald.

"The name of the stream that is called Bitter Root is not correct. The Indian name translated is Red Willow."

"The name of that mountain over there," po[i]nting to Jumbo, "is Sinemko," meaning an obstacle between two mountain ranges. That is its proper name. Some day I am going to have the word "Sinemko" displayed on the side of the mountain as a memorial to our people. The letters will be half as large as the "M" on Mount Sentinel."

As the city drew near the mountain sides north of the city could be seen resplendent with the sun-flowers.

"Our people are getting too high-toned," said McDonald, as he pointed to the sun flowers, "that is the reason they are decaying. They at one time used the sun-flower for food. They gathered the tender stems and roots which make excellent food. They like canned and shelf-goods now. The roots of the sun-flower are cured and when cooked swell like dried fruit and are nice and sweet.

"You have seen nothing strange," said McDonald. "Our people have their harvest times the same as you do. Some of our foods ripen in the fall. There is the native onion, the camas and certain moss from trees that make excellent food. They used to get the camas near Potomac, but it is all fenced in now. They obtain it now at Camas, but that is getting also fenced rapidly.

"How is it prepared? A hole is dug, and a layer of rocks is placed and covered with wood, the stones are heated red hot. They are allowed to cool a little then covered with clean leaves. On the leaves are placed a layer of the moss, also some native onions and camas. This is then again covered with leaves. The hole is filled with dirt and a hot fire is built and the mixture is baked for 24 hours. The dope is mixed into leaves. When it is taken out it is dried in the sun. It will keep for months. It is very good to eat."

"This has been a pleasant day," said McDonald as he alighted at the Shapard hotel and entered the lobby taking his accustomed seat in the corner by the window. My visit started this morning. Frank D. Brown, better known as "Sand Bar," Sam Ritchey of Garnet and J. W. Blair of Helmville, all whom I have known for years, got together in the lobby and we talked all morning."

"Talked?" said Harry Shapard "sound more like the robbing of a stage-coach. You fellows certainly did enjoy yourselves."

Document 114

Plans for Fourth of July at St. Ignatius

May 30, 1919

Source: "Mission to See Big Celebration," *The Daily Missoulian*, May 30, 1919, page 3, col. 1

Editors' note: Indians and whites at St. Ignatius made plans for a big Fourth of July celebration at the Mission. Activities included Indian dances, speeches, baseball, wrestling, horse races, and other events.

Mission to See Big Celebration

Indians From All Over the Northwest Will Attend Fourth Doings.

St. Ignatius, May 29. — Special. — By far the biggest thing in the near future for St. Ignatius is the splendid Fourth of July celebration now on foot. The committee in charge of the day is busy, and has been busy for two weeks, making plans more definite and more satisfactory to the ones most vitally interested in the event, namely, the Indians. The grounds must be the best and biggest in the surrounding country, and every detail be perfectly satisfactory to the dancers, or the enthusiasm wanes and the Indians fail to respond.

Besides the Indian dances which will last for a week after the Fourth of July festivities, there will be a baseball game for a $100 purse, a wrestling match for a $250 purse, a tug-of-war and other customary sports for such a day. All this is set for the grove on the Isidor Woodcock allotment, but may be changed on account of the slight dissatisfaction on the part of the Indian committee. The committee has made an effort to offer special inducements to the contestants in order that they might keep the attractions at home and not have the day lacking in any detail. The horse races will not be any small feature of the day, for the ponies here are not wanting when it comes to speed.

The Mission has been for years the natural meeting place for the Indians in their dances and ceremonies, and although several neighboring towns bid high for this special attraction, they could not offer so suitable a location as many around the Mission, and so the valley again will be the scene of festivities, and messages are being sent to all the tribes in northern Idaho and all over Montana to gather at the accustomed meeting place for another year of festivities.

The following is the program arranged for the several days:

July Fourth.

10:00 a.m. — Flag raising and speech. Parade of Indians through streets of town. Everybody follows parade to grounds.
11:00 a.m. — Small sports at grounds.
12:00 noon — Basket dinner.
1:00 p.m. — Fourth of July oration.
2:00 p.m. — Baseball game.
4:00 p.m. — Wrestling match; small sports.
5:00 p.m. — Everybody up town.
7:00 p.m. — Tug-of-war, up town.
7:30 p.m. — Picture show, dances, etc.

July Fifth.

1:00 p.m. — Foot races, horse races, etc., at picnic grounds.
2:30 p.m. — Baseball game.

July Sixth.

1:00 p.m. — Foot races, horse races, etc., at picnic grounds.
2:30 p.m. — Baseball game.

Document 115

Alex Pablo Was Partner in Auto Company

June 13, 1919

Source: "Notice of Dissolution," *The Ronan Pioneer*, June 13, 1919, page 4, col. 3.

Editors' note: No details were available, but tribal member Alex Pablo had been a partner with a white man in the Central City Auto Company in Ronan

Notice of Dissolution

Notice is hereby given, that the co-partnership heretofore existing by and between Alex Pablo and L[l]oyd I. Wallace under the firm name of Central City Auto Company is hereby dissolved by mutual consent by the said Alex Pablo withdrawing from the firm. The said Lloyd I. Wallace will continue the business under the firm name and designation of Center City Auto Company and will pay all debts owing by the firm and collect all debts and bills owing to said firm.

Alex Pablo.
Lloyd I. Wallace.

May 23 — June 13.

Document 116

University Presents Salish History Pageant

July 31, 1919

Source: "Real Indians Tell Their Views About Missoula's Pageant," *The Daily Missoulian*, July 31, 1919, page 2, col. 2.

Editors' note: On July 30, 1919, students at the State University of Montana Summer School presented a pageant-masque based on Salish history, St. Mary's Mission, and Father Pierre DeSmet. The text of the pageant was published as Margaret P. Ganssle, director, *The Selish: A Pageant-Masque* (Missoula, Mont.: Missoulian, 1919). The "Historical Material Committee" consisted of Paul C. Phillips, M. J. Elrod, A. L. Stone, and Mrs. Peter Ronan. Some Salish tribal members danced at the performance.

Real Indians Tell Their Views About Missoula's Pageant

"It was jake with me."

That was the comment of one of the Selish Indian dancers after the pageant. He had taken off his brilliant finery of feathers and beads and was putting on the ordinary street costume of the white man. And he was talking of his automobile ride down from the reservation and whether he would take the train back. All in the English of the street.

Truly the "show" was over. Masque and pageantry and make believe were fading quickly into matter-of-fact tomorrow. The days of Clark and Cox and Father De Smet and the Coyote were slumbering in history again — and only five minutes after the last "Hi-yi!" had been given around the tom tom.

But They Liked It.

The real Indians were still Indian enough, however, to be rather uncommunicative in their comments on the make-believe Indians. But most of them understood what the pageant was about, and they liked it. What did they like the most?

"It like it all. All the same to me," said Louis Nine Pipe. And he added, "It was a happy gang. I like that."

The grunts and smiles of the other Indians showed that they shared his sentiments.

"And the dances of the white girls?"

"Very good." But one Indian couldn't see why they should dance with shawls.

Dr. Morton J. Elrod of the biology department of the university explained the pageant to some of them as it progressed.

"Now they are in St. Louis," he remarked.

Not Really St. Louis.

"Hmm. . . That's no St. Louis. St. Louis is city. Not like that."

"Oh, but that was St. Louis 80 years ago. You never saw St. Louis then," explained Dr. Elrod.

"Now, see! They're back here again from St. Louis."

"Hmm. . . . Pretty quick," was the Indian's only comment.

The Selish Indians who took part in the pageant and danced afterwards were: Paul Ashley, Joe La Moose, Sam Resurrection, Mike Charlot, Louis Nine Pipes, Adolph Luke, Peter Pichette, Benny Whiterabbit, Paul Charley, Jerome Vanderburg, his wife and three children: Louise Irvine and child, Cecile Tillier, Christine Tillier, and Chief Kabashi [Kakashi].

Paul Ashley was with Al G. Barnes' circus for some time. Joe La Moose was the Indian with the long headdress of feathers.

Talking now in English, now in Selish, the group finished putting the garments of other days away in suitcases, and refreshed themselves at a bubble-fountain.

Yes, the old days are gone.

Document 117

Flathead Tribal Claims in U.S. Senate

August 13, 1919

Source: Excerpt from U.S. Congress, Senate, *Relief of the Flathead Nation of Indians: Hearing before the Committee on Indian Affairs, United States Senate, August 13, 1919*, Sixty-sixth Congress, First Session. (Washington, D.C.: U.S. Government Printing Office, 1919), pages 4-6.

Editors' note: The Flathead Tribal Council testified in favor a bill to allow the Flathead Reservation tribes to sue the government for failure to fulfill treaty promises and mismanagement of tribal affairs by the Flathead Agency. They did not want to have the Secretary of the Interior and Commissioner Affairs controlling their choice of attorneys. The tribes finally declined to file a claims case under the provisions of the law that passed this congress, but waited until another law that was more favorable to the tribes was passed. The Chairman of the Senate Indian Committee in 1919 was Charles Curtis, the part-Indian Senator from Kansas.

Statement of Miss Mary Lemery.

The Chairman [Charles Curtis, Kansas]. Miss Lemery, you are a member of the Flathead Tribe of Indians?

Miss Lemery. Yes.

The Chairman. Do you live on the reservation?

Miss Lemery. Yes.

The Chairman. In what capacity do you appear here?

Miss Lemery. As a delegate of that tribe, representing the Flathead Indians.

The Chairman. How large a delegation was sent here?

Miss Lemery. There were four of us.

The Chairman. You are speaking now for the entire delegation?

Miss Lemery. Yes, sir.

The Chairman. We will take up first the bill S. 2298, and I will present for the record at this point a letter from the Secretary of the Interior. . . . .

[S. 2298 allowed the Flathead Nation of Indians to submit their claims against the government to the United States Court of Claims. Secretary of the Interior Franklin K. Lane recommended that the bill be amended to require that the

Secretary of the Interior and the Commissioner of Indian Affairs approve the tribe's contract with their attorneys in the claims suit and that the attorneys' fee could not exceed 10 percent of the award or $25,000.]

The Chairman. What statement have you to make in regard to S. 2298, Miss Lemery?

Miss Lemery. The first two amendments proposed to the bill I have no objection to.

The Chairman. Then take up the third proposed amendment. What is your objection to the third?

Miss Lemery. I object to having the Secretary of the Interior and the Commissioner of Indian Affairs choose the attorney for the tribe. It is not only my objection, but it is the objection of the tribe, as there has been discussion before the Flatheads at different times. They object to it because they fear that it will —

The Chairman. You say that you object to the Secretary selecting the attorney. This bill does not mean that he is to select the attorney. The bill reads that the attorney to whom you give a contract must have that contract approved by the Secretary of the Interior and the Commissioner of Indian Affairs — by the department. It does not mean that the department will select your attorney, at all. What do you say to that?

Miss Lemery. I do not want him to approve. I do not want the Bureau of Indian Affairs to have any jurisdiction over our bill.

The Chairman. You mean over the selection of your attorney?

Miss Lemery. Over the selection of our attorney; and I do not want it provided that they must approve our contract.

The Chairman. You think that is a matter that ought to be settled wholly by the tribe?

Miss Lemery. By the tribe; because I think this is just to defeat the purpose of our legislation.

The Chairman. This question has been raised, Miss Lemery, on a number of bills, and it is the intention of the chairman to refer all bills asking that Indian claims be sent to the Court of Claims to a subcommittee of this committee, and the question as to whether or not the attorneys selected shall be approved by the Secretary of the Interior will be considered as general policy by the subcommittee and settled by the full committee at a later date. Now, go on.

Miss Lemery. The next amendment proposed is in regard to the fee — the determining of a reasonable fee, not to exceed 10 per cent, or $25,000. We have no idea, no knowledge, what the claims will involve.

The Chairman. Do you not know the amount of your claims? Have you no idea as to that?

Miss Lemery. We have no idea. We may have more than one claim; $25,000 may cover just one claim.

The Chairman. That does not mean the amount of your claim; that refers to the amount of the attorney's fee. This provides that the fee shall not exceed $25,000. Do you understand that?

Miss Lemery. I understand; but we do not know what it will cost to determine this claim.

The Chairman. Then you object to a limitation of the fee by the Secretary of the Interior in a contract?

Miss Lemery. I do.

The Chairman. You want the amount to be unlimited, do you?

Miss Lemery. No; we want the limit stated in the bill — not more than 15 per cent. We would rather have the court fix the fee.

The Chairman. Do you not know that 15 per cent is an exorbitant fee in Indian claims?

Miss Lemery. It says "not to exceed 15 per cent." Setting the fee at not less than 15 percent, or more than 15 per cent would not justify us in one way. I do not see where it would justify us.

The Chairman. As representing the Flathead Tribe of Indians, you want to get the fee down to what is a reasonable and fair charge?

Miss Lemery. I would not want any fixing of the fee to interfere with getting a good attorney.

The Chairman. Certainly not. I know, from 25 years' experience, that 10 per cent is an exorbitant fee in an Indian claim. Is that all that you have to say on that subject?

Miss Lemery. That is all.

The Chairman. Is there anything else that you want to say on that bill?

Miss Lemery. If we can not get a favorable report on these two last provisions in this bill, we would rather not have a report, because I feel that this is to defeat our legislation.

Document 118

Flathead Tribal Leader Flies in Plane

September 19, 1919

Source: "Chief Big Hawk Flies in Plane at Fair Grounds," *The Daily Missoulian*, September 19, 1919, page 3, col. 2.

Editors' note: Big Hawk, a Salish Indian from the reservation, was treated to an acrobatic ride over the Missoula Valley in the new invention, an airplane.

Chief Big Hawk Flies in Plane at Fair Grounds
Flathead Warrior Lives Up to His Name, and Gets "Deezy."

What's in a name?

Nothing, some people will tell you, but yesterday afternoon Chief Big Hawk of the Flathead tribe demonstrated that he hadn't been labeled wrong when he soared over Missoula in the Watkins' airplane. What aviator could hope for a better cognomen?

But that isn't all, Lieutenant Hoyt gave the chief a few of the thrills of aviation, looping-the-loop, side slipping and nose-diving. And when the chief came down he said ["]it was great."

"Only when he do trick my head get deezy and I hold it down," he told bystanders when he stepped from the 'plane.

The chief also volunteered the information that it had everything beat, was better than a horse and that he would get one of his own some day if he ever got enough money.

It is said that Big Hawk is the first full blooded Indian to ride in an airplane. At least he is the first Flathead Indian to view Missoula from the sky.

"My name is Big Hawk and I want to ride in big hawk," he said in making arrangements for the flight.

A novel advertising stunt will be put on by Barney's Fashion shop this morning with the aid of the Watkins' airplane. At 11 o'clock the machine will fly low over Higgins avenue, dropping a number of bills. One of the bills will bear the numerals 913, the number of the 'plane. The person who finds this bill and presents it a Barney's Fashion Shop will be given a free ride in the airplane.

Persons at the fair grounds yesterday were disappointed because Sergeant Cadden, the parachute jumper who travels with the airplane was unable to make the flight, but atmospheric conditions were such that it was impossible without extreme danger to the jumper.

The warm sun which shone through the day removed all the moisture from the air, which became very light on account of the heat, the company officials explained. As a result, it was difficult to climb high, and Lieutenant Hoyt had to make many wide circles before he was able to get high enough to do his stunts with Chief Big Hawk.

Because altitude such as is needed for the parachute jump could not be reached, that part of the thrill in the program, had to be given up for the day.

A number of passengers took flights during the day, but on none of them was the altitude of the previous day's flight reached. It was impossible for the aviator to get more than 1,500 feet above the ground.

Lieutenant Hoyt, who is piloting the airplane, received his training as an aviator with Lieutenant James Conlan, well known here. The two entered the army ground school at Berkeley, California, at the same time and were in the same class to finish. They became intimately acquainted there. From Berkeley they were both sent to the finishing school at Mather Field, California. Th[e]y were granted commissions practically at the same time. Lieutenant Conlon is now traveling salesman for the John's-Manville company, with headquarters at Billings. Lieutenant Hoyt speaks most highly of him.

In addition to Chief Big Hawk, yesterday's passengers in the airplane were: A. Garard, George C. Smith, M. Gerrif, Edith Greenough and E. C. Hardesty. Mrs. G. W. Barnhill and *[missing text]* passengers today.

Document 119

Indian Student at St. Ignatius

October 1919

Source: Excerpt from "Students' Chapter," *The Indian Sentinel*, vol. 1, no. 14 (October 1919), page 43-44.

Editors' note: Agnes Redhorn was a student at the Ursuline school at St. Ignatius. Among other things, she noted that none of the students at the school had gotten sick during the recent influenza epidemic.

Ursuline Convent,
St. Ignatius, Montana.

Dear Editor:

I belong to the Flathead tribe, have been attending this mission school for three years, and am now in the fifth grade. I feel it is a great privilege for me to be allowed to give an account of our school and surroundings. We are located in a beautiful valley with lofty, snow-capped mountains all around us. The church is not far from our school. I think this church must be one of the grandest in the West. A short time ago, we learned that the good, saintly Jesuit Brother, whose work of art this is, had gone to his reward.

With the coming of the fall season and its bright-colored leaves our surrounding country grows very beautiful, day by day. In the school grounds there is a Grotto of Lourdes that is almost covered, at times, with the Virginia creeper and baby ramblers. Near by, there is a long hedge of roses. In the summer time these flowers are used to adorn the altars in the convent chapel. About two miles from here there is another shrine of Our Lady where we often stop, in our rambles in the woods, to pay a little visit to the Blessed Virgin.

There were many pupils at our school last year, in spite of the dreadful epidemic that was all around. We did not have one case of influenza in our school. We can never thank God enough for this. Good St. Roch must have interceded for us. There is a statue of this saint in the front hall. Every morning, after Mass, for many months, we recited a prayer to St. Roch to ask his help.

We march in and out of school to the sound of the drum played by one of the boys. Sometimes a girl plays the drum, but she does not beat it as well and regular as the star drummer boy. We sing several songs. The patriotic one that we like best is, "Keep the Home Fires Burning." We have three sodalities, the Infant Jesus, the Guardian Angel, and the Blessed Virgin Sodality that meet every Sunday. Although we have catechism every day, there is one day that we all look forward to with joy — this is Thursday morning when Father Hubert Post gives us the instruction. He tells us so many interesting stories! We have a set of sixty-nine great big, beautiful colored pictures that represent the different subjects in the life of our Lord, from His Birth in a Stable to the Coming of the Holy Ghost. They show us the Sacraments, the Four Last Things, the Commandments, a Soul in Grace and one in Sin, a Good Death and the Death of the Sinner, and many more subjects. We have learned the Sunday Vespers, and we sang them for the first time last year at Easter. I am sure Father Superior was pleased. We sing the *Missa de Angelis* every Sunday.

Your little friend,
Agnes Redhorn.

Document 120

Chief Kakashi Complains About Divorces

November 11, 1919

Source: Kakashi to Great White Father, November 11, 1919, from file 107,469/1919 Flathead 743, Central Classified Files, RG 75, National Archives, Washington, D.C.

Editors' note: As the church chief at St. Ignatius, Kakashi complained about divorces being granted to tribal members by the state courts. He wanted more effort made to reconcile couples who were having disputes.

St. Ignatius Nov. 11, 1919.
Mont.

To the Great White Father
Washington, D.C.
Sir:

I have been for over fifty years chief of the Flathead associated tribes. Today I have called my tribes together to consider how we could take back our good old ways. You surely have heard what all know that the Flathead Indians have not only been friendly to the whites and to their great Chiefs, but also have always been one of the most moral tribes of the red men. But unfortunately since so many white men have invaded our cherished lands, a great number of our young people have taken the wild ways of many of your wild white children. Among these ways the one which we detest the most because it drags us down to the lowest degree of mankind is the breaking of marriage by divorce. Our friends, both white and indain, tell us that no other nation or tribe has so many divorces in proportion as our own. Therefore we come to ask you for power to remedy this evil by allowing three or four of us instead of the county court to settle disputes that might cause these divorces.

Thanking you in advance for a prompt and favorable reply I am

Respectfully,
Kakashi
his [thumb print] mark.

Document 121

Flathead Tribal Council Objects to Agency Expenses December 26, 1919

Source: Washington J. Endicott to Commissioner of Indian Affairs, December 26, 1919, from file 13,396/1920 Flathead 054, Central Classified Files, RG 75, National Archives, Washington, D.C.

Editors' note: Washington Endicott, an Indian Inspector, did not approve of the efforts of the Flathead Tribal Council to reduce Flathead Agency expenses that were being charged to tribal funds or their opposition to agency policies.

Department of the Interior
United States Indian Service
Flathead Indian Agency,
Dixon, Montana, December 26, 1919.

Honorable Cato Sells,
Commissioner of Indian Affairs,
Washington, D.C.
My dear Mr. Commissioner:

In regard to my telegram of December 24, and as justification therefor, I respectfully beg leave to state:

That Mary Lemery pretended to have called a "general council" of the Indians of the Flathead reservation at St. Ignatius for December 24, and that it had been more or less generally stated that Robert Hamilton was to be present; that one of the principal matters to be discussed would concern reservation boundaries, and that Mr. Hamilton had acquired, and would present, a copy of the Stevens map in substantiation of the claim that Indians have been wrongfully, and without compensation, deprived of certain lands.

Robert Hamilton did not appear at the "council," which was not called, nor recognized, by the superintendent, the business committee or by any government official or responsible body of Indians. The meeting was, in fact, a rump caucus. There was no organization and no parliamentary rules were observed. Mary Lemery assumed the chairmanship and appointed Max Barnaby, Indian, secretary and interpreter. No minutes of the proceedings were taken.

At no time were more than sixty (60) persons present in the hall while the caucus was being conducted.

Max Barnaby did not truly interpret speeches made in opposition to the plans of Mary Lemery, but, on the contrary, substituted his own comments and opinions.

Max Barnaby declared adopted a "resolution" asking that Ten Thousand ($10,000) Dollars be set aside from money due the Indians of the Flathead reservation to pay the expenses of a "committee of four" to go to Washington and there to represent the Indians of Flathead reservation, and to liquidate some Two Thousand Five Hundred ($2,500) Dollars in claims incurred for committees, attorneys, and other alleged expenses in time past.

That the motion for this resolution was not correctly put, nor properly considered; that only eight persons raised their hands to vote in the affirmative, and the motion was declared, by Max Barnaby, to have been carried, when no call had been made for the negative vote; that no negative vote was allowed, counted, or considered.

At the time the alleged vote was taken there were probably forty persons in the hall where the caucus was being held.

By similar means a committee of four, two of whom are Mary Lemery and Max Barnaby, was selected to represent the Indians of Flathead reservation in Washington, and that your inspector overheard Mary Lemery instruct Max Barnaby, before the committee was selected, that she wished it understood that she was "in on that."

Throughout the caucus Mary Lemery and Max Barnaby were uniformly antagonistic to the Indian Bureau, the plans of the Honorable Commissioner and of the Honorable Secretary of the Interior, and the administration of Honorable Theodore Sharp, superintendent, his farmers, matrons, police, and other assistants.

Max Barnaby further disgraced the uniform of the United States army, already defiled by personal contact with him, by publicly attacking the work of matron Mrs. McCoy of St. Ignatius, as representing extravagance and useless expense. He declared that money paid to the matron should be saved in the interest of economy. At various times Mary Lemery has personally abused Mrs. McCoy, and has personally and by overt acts interfered with the ministrations of Mrs. McCoy to the sick. Of some of these offenses Supervisor West, who has visited St. Ignatius, is believed to have knowledge. Of others, Dr. Patterson, your physician in charge, could give information.

Your inspector does not pretend to have positive proof, but he believes that there is, with its center at Washington, D.C., among certain attorneys, a conspiracy which generally affects the votes in Congress and the administration of Indian reservations in the State of Montana and that Mary Lemery is a tool to whom is intrusted certain work to be done on the Flathead reservation in behalf of these conspirators and the individuals and interests they represent.

Respectfully submitted,
Washington J. Endicott
Inspector.

Robert Hamilton, Sr.
Source: National Anthropological Archives, Smithsonian Institution, Washington, D.C.
photo BAE neg. 411, Blackfeet, Robert Hamilton, Sr.

Document 122

Agent Complains About Tribal Council Delegation January 20, 1920

Source: Theodore Sharp to Commissioner of Indian Affairs, January 20, 1920, from file 109,764/1919 Flathead 056, Central Classified Files, RG 75, National Archives, Washington, D.C.

Editors' note: The Flathead Tribal Council working to force changes in agency policies on the reservation was not looked upon favorably by the agent or the Business Committee which supported the agent. Robert Hamilton was a Blackfoot who encouraged a number of protests against government Indian policies and was a general thorn in the flesh of the Indian Office in Washington, D.C. For more information about Hamilton see Thomas R. Wessel, "Political Assimilation on the Blackfoot Indian Reservation, 1887-1934: A Study in Survival," in Douglas H. Ubelaker and Herman J. Viola, eds., *Plains Indian Studies,* Smithsonian Contributions to Anthropology, No 30 (1982), pages 59-72.

Department of the Interior
United States Indian Service
Flathead Indian Agency,
Dixon, Montana, January 20, 1920.

Honorable Cato Sells,
Commissioner of Indian Affairs,
Washington, D.C.
My dear Mr. Commissioner:

In connection with my letter of January 14, forwarding a letter from Mr. Duncan McDonald, chairman of the Flathead Business Committee, protesting against a party of Indians headed by Miss Mary Lemery representing themselves as an authorized delegation to Washington on tribal business, I now forward for your information a clipping from the Browning Review.

It appears that some of the Indians, headed by Miss Lemery, have held a meeting at which they "adopted Mr. Robert J. Hamilton into the tribe" and Mr. Hamilton thereby, it appears, claims to be representing the Flathead tribe at Washington with Miss Lemery.

I understand that Mr. Hamilton is a member of the Blackfoot tribe of Indians and received an allotment on the Blackfoot reservation and is enrolled with the Blackfoot tribe. It would seem that he could not hold tribal relations with both the Blackfeet and the Flatheads, even were the alleged adoption a regular one. As a matter of fact there has been no proper adoption of Mr. Hamilton into the Flathead tribe, and it would appear that there could not be under existing conditions. No general council of the tribe has been held to consider the question of Mr. Hamilton's adoption, nor has any meeting of the tribal business committee been held on the question. It is understood that a meeting of some of the friends of Miss Lemery was held at which Miss Lemery was chairman and purported tribal business was transacted including the "adoption" of Mr. Hamilton, but this irregular assemblage could in no sense be termed a tribal council.

The clipping enclosed also states over the signatures of Miss Lemery and Max Barnaby, that her delegation is leaving for Washington "at the expense of the tribe." This is what Mr. McDonald in his letter heretofore transmitted to you, protests against and what this office has called attention to. Much harm results if these irregular, unauthorized, and unnecessary parties of Indians can go to Washington on their own responsibility, and after arriving there secure allotments of the tribal funds to pay their expenses and per diem for their time while absent from the reservation. When they can do this, it undoubtedly lends color to their claims that they are recognized by the authorities as duly qualified representatives of the tribe, and lays the foundations for other and additional trips by themselves and other self-elected delegations who may desire "a trip to Washington."

Very respectfully,
Theodore Sharp
Superintendent.

Document 123

Kootenai Chief Complains About Agency Policies January 21, 1920

Source: Theodore Sharp to Commissioner of Indian Affairs, January 21, 1920, from file 107,469/1919 Flathead 743, Central Classified Files, RG 75, National Archives, Washington, D.C.

Editors' note: The traditional chiefs opposed divorces being granted by state courts, but the Flathead Agent felt that was out of his jurisdiction. The remainder of the letter summarized the conflict between the traditional chiefs and the Flathead Agent and Indian court. Unfortunately, the letter gave very little explanation of the views of the chiefs.

Department of the Interior
United States Indian Service
Flathead Indian Agency,
Dixon, Montana, January 21, 1920.

The Commissioner of Indian Affairs,
Washington, D.C.
Sir:

Receipt is acknowledged of Office letter dated January 16, 1920, which quotes a telegram sent to Hon. Thomas J. Walsh, ostensibly by Koostatah and other Indians.

Replying, I will note the several statements made in the telegram separately and in detail. I quote:

> "He arrests and imprisons our people for minor offenses despite our vigorous protests, but leaves at large and unmolested notorious offenders against our home life and matrimonial obligations."

The records of this office relating to arrests of Indians is kept up to date. For the fiscal year ended June 30, 1919, which I assume will be sufficient as an illustration, Indians were arrested on the following charges:

Assault on government officer	1
Introducing intoxicants	10
Drunkenness	29
Gambling	44
Adultery	26
Disturbing the peace	5
Wife beating	2
Desertion of family	1
Interfering with Indian police	3
Petty larceny	1
	122

It will be noted that the majority of the cases in which Indians have been arrested by this office is for gambling, drunkenness, and adultery. In each and every one of these cases, the accused has been given a hearing by a judge of the court of Indian offenses, a member of the same race as the accused, and not by the superintendent. The sentences imposed are those of the Indian judge, although they receive the approval of the superintendent. Sentences are commuted by the superintendent, and this is done when the good behavior of the prisoners entitle them to such action. It is to be noted that most sentences are commuted.

In a sense, gambling is a minor offense; so is drunkenness, and petty larceny, and many other transgressions, if they are compared with rape, assault with a deadly weapon, or murder. But these so-called minor offenses exist, and there are more of them than of the greater crimes. If order is to be maintained on the reservation, police powers must be exercised. If the Indians are to be led to habits of industry, and to make some progress in civilization, these offenses cannot be ignored. Every one who has lived on an Indian reservation knows that gambling is one of the most wide-spread and one of the most demoralizing vices practiced among the Indians. Indians have purchased farming equipment and this office has helped them to obtain horses, vehicles, seed, and tools to start farming, and started them. They meant well, and made an effort until they got into a gambling game. Then everything they had was lost. All of their money, horses, tools, and even personal clothing was gambled away. No progress can be made while this vice is ignored. I have not ignored it. At the same time no one can say that I have any mania for the prosecution of this class of offenses to the neglect of greater ones. At all times I have endeavored to use discretion and fair judgment in these matters.

I have no hesitancy in saying that the statement made in the telegram quoted, that I leave at large and "unmolested notorious offenders against our home life and matrimonial obligations," is simply an untrue one. This is a flat statement and I am willing to have it checked up. I think I know what Koostatah means. I believe it is this: Some of the Indians who have been married by religious rites have gone into court and secured divorces, and have again married, under the law, by the civil authorities to other partners. Koostatah desires me to arrest such persons and put them in jail until they agree to return to their first spouses. I cannot find where I have authority to act in this way. Koostatah ignores the law in the matter entirely, as also does his advisor in this attitude, and holds that while these Indians continue living with the partners to whom they are married under the civil law, they "are notorious offenders against our home life and matrimonial obligations.["]

My position in this matter is a neutral one. I neither tell the Indians that they have to secure divorces, nor do I try to place an Indian in jail for having secured one. The matter of divorce is one for the courts, and I have told the Indians who asked me that the authority lies with the civil court judges, and that I lacked jurisdiction. It seems to me that this is only a sane and proper position. I do not undertake to direct the religious belief of the Indians, and as an official to enforce the laws of the federal government in my particular field, it would be highly improper for me to assume to myself the authority of the civil courts. Koostatah has said to me that he proposes compelling Kootenai Indians of his tribe who have secured divorces, to abandon their spouses, in cases where they have remarried, and return to those to whom they were married prior to the civil divorce. Should he do this, without the formality of another divorce and another marriage, there will be several persons guilty under the laws, and it will be necessary for some one to exercise authority on these points.

"His policy encourages divorce and the breaking of home ties."

As above stated, divorces among the Flathead confederated tribes must be by legal process, in the proper courts. I cannot undertake to compel Indians who have made their appearances in the courts and have been granted divorces by qualified authority, to ignore the decrees rendered in their cases. But this is what Koostatah asks. I have advised Indians against divorce on trivial matters, and have attempted to adjust their family differences when they come to my notice. It must be understood, however, that the Indians do not always advise or consult with the superintendent about these matters, and whether they do consult with him or not, after the courts have heard their pleas, and rendered their decisions, it is improper for me to ignore the decrees and demand of the Indians that they do so also. But this is exactly what Koostatah thinks I should do. If, as he says, divorces are against the laws of his tribe, and his religion, his complaint is against the laws of the state of Montana, and the judges of the civil courts who grant them, and not against the superintendent.

> "Further his policy weakens the authority of the chiefs and he assumes authority that has always been vested in the chiefs. We want our tribal laws and rights respected and maintained. The chiefs are not and will not be mere servants to any Agent."

Evidently the one composing the telegram for Koostatah ignores the fact that the days of tribal government among the Indians has long since passed. With the passing of those days, also passed the authority which a chief once exercised over the persons and property of the Indians. Once a chief punished whom he would among his people. His rule was one of might and fear. He rewarded those who found his favor. Chiefs no longer can do these things. Once a chief ordered stripped, bound, and flogged unmercifully an individual who violated his commands, or if it so pleased him, had him put to death. Although this authority no longer exists, Koostatah wishes it resumed. Reference to a request made to your Office under date of January 15, 1919, by Koostatah, George Riley, and some others, that the tribal customs once prevailing be restored, shows the idea suggested by Koostatah, — and perhaps suggested to him. Office letter of February 5, 1919, (6114-15) advises Koostatah that the plan is not consistent with the endeavor of the government to prepare Indians for citizenship, and place each individual on his own responsibility.

The superintendent is far from arrogating to himself authority. He endeavors to step carefully, and at the same time firmly and with good judgment in carrying out the principles of the law, with the idea always of training a people who not many years ago were wandering nomads, something of the civilized life. The reference to the chiefs not being servants for an Agent is not understood. It seems to be inserted for rhetorical effect. It is enough to state that they are not servants, and never have been called on to be such.

> "Let the treaty of 1855 be observed."

If there is any failure on the part of the government to carry out the treaty of 1855, more particular statement should be given. I do not know what this means. I do notice, however, in the treaty of 1855 a provision that the tribes making the treaty, and Koostatah's tribe is one of them, "agree not to shelter or conceal offenders against the laws of the United States, but to deliver them up to the authorities for trial." It is suggested that this be brought to the attention of Koostatah and his advisors.

> "We protest against the practice of Mr. Sharp in calling large groups of our people to Dixon, a distance of 45 miles, to answer his questions when he could easily come to us at Elmo or Dayton for this purpose."

Of the above statement, I have to advise that no such practice exists. The Indians in large numbers are not called to Dixon to answer questions. There have been occasions when arrests of a number of Indians have been made by properly designated employees, acting under instructions. I assume that this is what is meant, although the statement seems to carry a false impression to one not conversant with the facts.

In December last, Koostatah came to my office and reported that some of the Indians were gambling. He named two and asked that they be arrested, saying that if they were placed in custody they would tell who the remainder of the gamblers were. Acting on this suggestion, Lookingglass and Lame Joe were placed under arrest. They made pleas of guilty in the court of Indian offenses, the charge being having rented their houses to gamblers for the purpose of conducting games. They named the Indians who gambled in these houses and I directed Mr. B. D. Wolfinger to arrest eleven Indians and bring them to Dixon. On these instructions Mr. Wolfinger placed the individuals under arrest but on their own request that they be permitted to delay coming to the agency for several days, Mr. Wolfinger agreed to delay matters. On January 8, most of the Indians notified came to the agency and accompanying them were Koostatah, George Riley, and Pierre Paul (Abrahams), who came without invitation and entirely of their own volition. These three men informed me that the Indians arrested for gambling ought not to be tried before the Indian court, or punished, although they had not denied gambling, for the reason that Koostatah had told the Indians they should not be held for any penalties. Koostatah declared that he was empowered to decide such matters and that he had told the Indians they would be permitted to go home. Pierre Paul claimed to be a chief, and said a chief's authority regulates these matters, although he has himself served time for offenses at the agency jail and knows better. With two exceptions, all of the Indians arrested when brought before the Indian court made pleas of guilty. One of these two was exhonorated by the judge and the other one was proven guilty by the testimony of a number of witnesses. On returning to Polson, on their way home, I am informed, Koostatah, George Riley and Pierre Paul sent the telegram to Senator Walsh which is the subject of this letter.

It is to be noted that the arrests of these gamblers grew out of the request made by Koostatah himself, and from all evidence obtainable and the admissions of the ones arrested, the action taken was entirely proper. That outside influences are at work on the Indians is quite plain. For years the Indians have had officials in charge of the reservation who have enforced the laws, including laws against what is termed the minor offenses and the result of violations of these laws is well known to every Indian. Now, it appears, the Indians are being led to think, by suggestion, that the so-called chiefs should direct affairs; that the superintendent is without authority, and that he is usurping rights and authority which properly belongs to the so-called chiefs, with the result, naturally, that the Indians be led to resist the enforcement of the laws by the superintendent and the employees. This is shown by the fact that one of the Indians notified by Mr. Wolfinger of his arrest, went from his home near Dayton to Polson with the other Indians, on their way to the agency, but when he reached Polson, for some reason he suddenly changed his mind, and informed Mr. Wolfinger that he was not going and that no one could take him. This statement was made in the presence of Mitch Michel, an Indian policeman, and Samuel Andrews, forest guard. After putting up considerably resistence he was handcuffed, and then agreed to come along. One Mrs. Gravelle did not appear as agreed and on a second visit by Mr. Wolfinger to her home she pointed a loaded rifle, fully cocked, at Mr. Wolfinger and declared she would not go. The rifle was secured and is at this office and on account of being a woman, Mrs. Gravelle was sentenced by the Indian judge, rather than being taken into the federal court for her attitude. But these two instances show the result of the ill-advised suggestions to Koostatah and the Indians of his tribe by persons seeking to influence them against the enforcement of the laws. It might be well to state that the sentences imposed by the Indian court in these gambling cases, varied from 13 to 35 days, and a commutation of sentence for good behavior is made of one-third of the time. It will be noted that these sentences are not harsh or excessive.

> "We, chiefs, need our authority to rule our people and we want it respected."

Here again appears the idea that the Indians are subject to chiefs, who have authority to direct individual Indians what they must do, or cannot do, and to enforce these commands. Among the Indians are men who call themselves chiefs, but it is now more or less a designation by courtesy, and in fact is a tinsel title in these days, — something like the calling of superintendents "Major," which prevails on some reservations. This office has not opposed the so-called chiefs in their views, so long as these views have not interferred with the administration of business. And it is noteworthy that it is only recently that the idea has sprung up and been advanced by the so-called chiefs themselves that the old days of authority, when Indians roamed the plains and mountains, was again in effect.

Respect for proper authority is necessary for good government. It is suggested that Koostatah and the other Indians interested with him, properly might be advised to recognize the laws of the State and of the Federal Government, and not to listen to the poor advice of individuals who seek to create dissension and array the Indians against officials for their own purposes.

Very respectfully,
Theodore Sharp
Superintendent.

Document 124

Tribal Council Opposes Irrigation Appropriation January 30, 1920

Source: "Indians Oppose Irrigation Fund," *The Ronan Pioneer*, January 30, 1920, page 1, col. 4.

Editors' note: A continuation of the efforts of the Flathead Tribal Council to prevent further construction appropriations for the Flathead Irrigation project as long as they would result in liens on tribal allotments.

Indians Oppose Irrigation Fund

Special correspondence from Washington to the Missoulian on Jan. 21, says that one more attempt to obtain an appropriation of $100,000 for the Flathead irrigation project was made when Senators Myers and Walsh of Montana appeared before a sub committee of the house committee on Indian affairs, to urge an adequate appropriation for the project.

At the same time, Mary Lemery of the Flathead reservation, and Robert Hamilton of the Blackfeet reservation, both part Indian, appeared before the committee and asked that no appropriation of any kind be made for the Flathead project. They argued that the whole project should be abandoned, saying that the whites instead of the Indians were getting all the benefits.

Document 125

Missoula Sheriff Declares War on Arlee

February – March 1920

Source: "Drunken Debauch Ends in Murder on Reservation., *The Daily Missoulian*, February 6, 1920, page 1, col. 4; "Green Declares War on Arlee," *The Daily Missoulian*, February 8, 1920, page 3, col. 4; "Arlee Pool Hall Ordered Closed," *The Daily Missoulian*, March 16, 1920, page 2, col. 3.

Editors' note: The Missoula sheriff was busy trying to enforce state law at Arlee on the reservation. In one case an Indian named Michel Parker was killed.

Drunken Debauch Ends in Murder on Reservation
Adele Gabeau at County Jail Charged with Killing Michel Parker.

Adele Gabeau, an Indian woman, is under arrest charged with killing Michel Parker, another Indian, at Arlee last evening. According to reports brought to Missoula at an early hour this morning by Deputies Hughes and Curtis of the sheriff's force, the woman shot Parker near Barnaby's poolroom at Arlee. The shooting was witnessed by a number of Indians.

First reports received here were that Parker had committed suicide after being jilted by the woman, but upon an investigation made by the deputies the decision was reached that it was a murder case and not a suicide and the woman was placed under arrest and brought to Missoula.

Parker and the Gabeau woman had spent yesterday in Missoula and had returned to Arlee on No. 3. It is said that they had been drinking together during the day. The woman refused to discuss the shooting and all that she would tell the officers was that she was sorry she had done it.

* * * * * * * * *

Green Declares War on Arlee
Sheriff Announces He Will "Clean Up" Town, Scene of Parker Tragedy.

Aroused by the recent shooting and the frequent arrests of gamblers at Arlee, officials at the sheriff's office have declared their intention of putting a stop to the lawlessness there.

"I'm going to clean out gambling from Arlee if I have to raid the place every night," said Sheriff James T. Green last night. Sheriff Green had just returned from Arlee, where he investigated the shooting of Michel Parker. Accompanying him were Deputies Hughes and Curtis who had arrested three men for gambling in the reservation town.

The men were taken while in game in an old house there and the building was crowded with spectators when the officers walked in. Michel Plant and Abel Combas, a boy of 19, are in trouble with the officers for the first time and were released on their promises to appear Monday morning. Eneas Grandgo, however, is an old offender, according to the officers, and was released on a $75 bond to appear at the same time.

According to Sheriff Green many people around Arlee are not satisfied with the verdict of the coroner's verdict which found that Michel Parker had shot and killed himself Thursday.

A number of those in Arlee at the time of the shooting are inclined to believe that the shooting was done by Adele Gebeau, an Indian woman, who is now being held in the county jail pending the action of the county authorities.

The tragedy occurred outside of a poolhall in Arlee Thursday night, when Parker and the woman returned from Missoula, where they had obtained a supply of denatured alcohol. They were both under the influence of the liquor when they returned to the reservation and in a struggle between them Parker was shot by a pistol which he carried.

* * * * * * * * *

Arlee Pool Hall Ordered Closed

Barnaby Place Has Been the Scene of Many Drunken Disturbances.

A temporary injunction closing the Felix Barnaby pool hall in Arlee was ordered yesterday by Judge Theodore Lentz in department two of the district court.

The action was taken in connection with the abatement proceedings filed a few days ago by Deputy County Attorney Fred Angevine against the pool hall. In the complaint, it is charged that the pool hall has been implicated in the numerous disturbances of the peace in Arlee recently. It is charged that the pool hall has been the scene of the drunkenness and disorderliness which has occasioned Sheriff J. T. Green many raids upon the town of Arlee within the past few weeks.

The injunction issued by Judge Lentz will close the pool hall until further notice. It is believed that the hearing in the case will come before Judge Lentz within the next two weeks.

According to Deputy County Attorney Angevine, this is the first abatement proceeding to be brought in Missoula county. The case is said to come under the new 1917 law which allows a place of business to be closed which has been used for illegal purposes. According to Deputy County Attorney Angevine, it is also possible under the new law to seize the fixtures of a place of business and sell them. In such a case the money so received goes into the school funds of the county.

"I want to serve notice on the places of business which might come under this new law," said Deputy County Attorney Angevine, "that in the future I shall investigate complaints of the infraction of this law. In case of such complaints, we shall take action similar to this in the Barnaby pool hall."

Document 126

Tribal Council Delegate Asks Uncle for Support

February – March 1920

Source: Washington J. Endicott to Commissioner of Indian Affairs, March 22, 1920, and enclosed Max J. Barnaby to Felix Barnaby, February 27, 1920; from file 31,780/1920 Flathead 155, Central Classified Files, RG 75, National Archives, Washington, D.C.

Editors' note: Inspector Washington Endicott and most Indian Office officials resented the efforts of the Flathead Tribal Council to force changes in Flathead agency policies. Max Barnaby asked his Uncle Felix Barnaby to support the Tribal Council delegation to Washington, D.C.

Department of the Interior
United States Indian Service
Reno Indian Agency
Reno, Nevada,
March 22, 1920.

Honorable Cato Sells,
Commissioner of Indian Affairs,
Washington, D.C.
My dear Commissioner:

The enclosed letter, as you will note, was written by Max J. Barnaby, concerning whom I have already informed you, to his uncle Felix Barnaby, Orlee [Arlee], Montana.

Mr. Felix Barnaby being more friendly to the Honorable Commissioner than is his nephew Max, placed the letter in such a channel that it has reached me here. You will note by the contents that the purpose of Max Barnaby, Mary Lemary and Robert J. Hamilton are distinctly hostile toward yourself and toward the Indian Bureau in general. Of this condition of affairs I became aware while on the Flathead Reservation. Enos Conko and John Chorlie [sic] are merely the tools of Mary Lemary and Max Barnaby is her creature. The Lemary clan and Hamilton have been assiduous in sewing [sowing] seeds of dissention throughout the Flathead Reservation as has already been indicated in my report and previous correspondence.

I am submitting this letter to you for what it is worth.

Most Respectfully,
Washington J. Endicott
Inspector.

* * * * * * * * *

[Enclosure:]

National Hotel
Washington, D.C.
2/27/20

Mr. Felix Barnaby
Arlee Mont.
Dear uncle: —

Every thing is moving along nicely for the delegation. our activities in D.C. is worrying the Indian Bureau, and they are anxious for us to go home.

As soon as we have our hearings, Eneas Conko, John Charlie and myself will leave for home, leaving Miss Lemery and Hamilton to finish up. We understand Sharp has been very active with some false statements, for which he will have to answer when we get home. his conduct will be looked into by congress, when the proper time comes. Secretary of the Interior Lane is vacating and so will Cato Sells. getting to hot for them. the Indians are getting after the Interior Dept. and the Indian Bureau. they don't like it, but they will have to take there medicine.

The Indian Bureau system is sure rotton as I saw with my own eyes, and here after I will have the no mercy for any Indian Bureau official, which I made very plain to Merett during one of our pleasant calls at the Bureau. Yes we Indians are sure very rich — in promises only — as far as the Bureau is concerned.

Congress is going to help us, and its up to every Indian to support the contention of the Delegation.

Kindest regards to you all.
Your nephew.
Max J. Barnaby.

Document 127

Flathead County Taxed Kootenai Indians

March 19. 1920

Source: Chief Koostatah to Indian Department, March 19, 1920, from file 26,540/1920 Flathead 302, Central Classified Files, RG 75, National Archives, Washington, D.C.

Editors' note: Chief Koostatah could not see any justice in being forced to pay taxes to Flathead County when he was not a citizen and got no services from the county.

Dayton, Montana,
March 19, 1920.

Indian Department,
Washington, D.C.
Gentlemen,

The writer is Chief of the Kootenai Indians living on the Flathead Indian Reservation in western Montana.

I am a full blood Indian; I have never applied for my patent, and do not intend to. I am a ward of the Government; not a citizen.

The treasurer of Flathead County, Montana, — the county in which I live, — is trying to make me pay taxes on a few head of horses and cattle that I own. And they are charging me for horses and cattle that I do not own.

I have no rights as a citizen. How then have I any of the obligations of a citizen?

The Government treats us as children. It holds our money; and gives it out to us in very small sums, — just enough to live on. Now must we take the food money we get, give it back for taxes, and go without food?

If we are mere children, and incompetent to handle our own business, by what means do we become competent as soon as there is a war to fight, or money to be paid? In the treaty of 1855 nothing is said about taxes. We Indians have lived up to that treaty. Is the government going to let the County impose obligations on us that are not specified in that treaty?

As wards of the Government we ask immediate protection from these County men.

I am sending you the paper I received from the County. It says that if we do not pay these taxes soon the County will sell our cattle. Can the County do this without first asking the Government? And is the Government going to allow this crime?

For three years we have not had much rain. We have lost many of our horses and cattle because there was no hay. Now if the Government is going to let the County take away from us what few we have left, then we might as well kill then off right away and eat them.

If my people have to take their food money for taxes, then they will not farm or raise cattle; but they will go back where they were many years ago.

Please tell me right away whether the County can take our cattle for taxes. I am asking this question for all my people. They are all waiting for your answer.

Very respectfully,
Chief Koostatah, his x mark.

Document 128

McLeod's Stage

The Ronan Pioneer, March 19, 1920, page 5, col. 5-6.

McLEOD'S STAGE

ROUND TRIP TO MISSOULA DAILY

Leaves Ronan 8:30 Arrives Missoula 11:30
Leaves Missoula 4:00 Arrives Ronan 7:00

MAKE ALL MISSOULA HOTELS

Headquarters Sterling Hotel

Document 129

Auto Theft Results in Arrest

March 26, 1920

Source: "Auto Theft Lands Three in Hoosgow," *The Ronan Pioneer*, March 26, 1920, page 1, col. 3-4.

Editors' note: Three young men took a joyride in a stolen automobile.

Auto Theft Lands Three in Hoosgow

Sam McDougall, James Deuchan and Antoine Matt, three half-breed Indians, were taken to Missoula Tuesday and lodged in jail on a charge of stealing a Studebaker automobile from O'Brien and Raitor at Ronan.

As nearly as could be learned the car was stolen about 2 o'clock Monday morning. They drove the car north to Big Arm, where they stole a barrel of gasoline. Turning at Big Arm, they took the road leading to Hot Springs and got ctuck {stuck] in a mud hole. They were pulled out and continued until the gears on the car were stripped. In the meantime they took the wrong road and came back almost to Sloan's Ferry. Here they had to abandon the car, and when officers traced them around on their ride, they were found at that point and arrested. John Nadrau went out from Ronan and took charge of the three and brought them to Ronan and on to Missoula.

In a statement to the county attorney, Deuchan tried to fasten the guilt of stealing the car on the other two men, saying that he waited in the alley while they got the car out of the garage. According to the two he was on watch in the alley. His home is near Havre. McDougall is from Polson and Matt's home is Ronan.

The car was a Studebaker Six and was brand new. O'Brien and Raitor having had the car only a few days. In making the ride the car was considerably damaged, none of the three evidently being able to drive or take care of the machinery. The barrel of gas stolen at Big Arm was carried in the tonneau and badly damaged the upholstering, and one door was broken loose, besides the damage to the gears and overheating the motor.

Document 130

Business Committee Two-Year Term Expired

April – May 1920

Source: Mary Lemery to Commissioner of Indian Affairs, April 22, 1920; Theodore Sharp to Commissioner of Indian Affairs, May 11, 1920, from file 109,764/1919 Flathead 056, Central Classified Files, RG 75, National Archives, Washington, D.C.

Editors' note: A Flathead general council in 1909 elected a Flathead Business Committee for a two-year term. Since the agent liked who had been elected, the members were continued in office until 1920 without a new election. Other tribal members thought regular elections should be held for the Business Committee or it should be replaced with the newer, more radical Flathead Tribal Council. The Flathead Agent feared that any new election would result in a Business Committee which opposed agency policies.

National Hotel
Washington, D.C.
April 22, 1920.

To the Commissioner,
Bureau of Indian Affairs,
Department of the Interior,
Washington, D.C.
Dear Mr. Commissioner:

About ten or twelve years ago the members of the Flathead tribe elected a council or business committee to represent the tribe in matters pertaining to their tribal affairs.

The Department for the last ten or twelve years has continued that council or business committee in power and has denied to the Flathead people the right to, from time to time, hold elections and select members of their tribe as members of said council or business committee who were in sympathy with the desires, objects and aims of the great mass of the tribe. This situation became so pronounced that in 1916, without official authority therefor, the Flathead people assembled and voluntarily held a council of their own. The Department has refused to officially recognize the representatives selected by the Flathead people at said general council. The result is that the members of the tribe refuse to recognize the council recognized by the Department, and the Department refuses to recognize the council recognized by the Indians. My people desire only fair treatment and the Department certainly can desire only a dependable expression of my people.

In order that this may be brought about, I respectfully request, on behalf of all the members of the Flathead tribe, that an election be called and held about the 1st of June, due notice thereof to be given to all the members of the tribe; that at said general council the members of the tribe be afforded an opportunity to select a council or business committee composed of a definite number to be by your Office determined. The present council or business committee organized ten or twelve years ago consists of nine members. The council or business committee organized by the Indians themselves in 1916, consists of 15 members. We are desirous of minimizing the number of the members of the council so as to prevent excessive costs, and I suggest a council or business committee of nine members, one member to be selected from each of the five respective districts, and four to be selected from the tribe as a whole.

I make this request in the belief that if it is granted, it will inure to the benefit of both my people and the Department. It will enable my people to select representatives who are in harmony with their views and it will enable the Department to obtain the real views of the Indians.

I respectfully request early and favorable consideration of this matter, particularly in view of the fact that if an election is to be held in June, sufficient time should be given for proper notice to all the interested parties.

Very truly yours,
Mary Lemery
Delegate, Flathead Council,
elected in 1916 by the members of the tribe.

* * * * * * * * *

Department of the Interior
United States Indian Service
Flathead Agency — Dixon, Mont.
May 11, 1920.

Commissioner of Indian Affairs,
Washington, D.C.
Sir: —

Receipt is acknowledged of Office letter dated April 29, 1920, enclosing a copy of a letter from Mary Lemery concerning the Flathead Business Committee.

In compliance with the request of your Office for information as to when and how the present members of the Business Committee were selected, and term of office for which they were elected, I would advise that after searching the files of this office, the information obtainable indicates that this Committee was elected by a general council of Indians on May 10, 1909. The following is a copy of a notice calling the general council for the purpose of electing a Business Committee, — this notice being issued by Superintendent Fred C. Morgan, at that time in charge of this jurisdiction:

> Flathead Agency, Jocko, Montana.
> February 17, 1909.
>
> **Notice.**
>
> A General Council of the Indians of the Flathead Reservation is hereby called to convene at St. Ignatius, Montana, on Wednesday, March 10, 1909, at 9:00 a.m., sharp.
>
> There will be presented to this Council for its action a number of applications for enrollment.
>
> The council will also be called upon to elect a business committee, whose duty it will be to transact tribal business at the call of the Superintendent. The different tribes will be represented on this committee as follows: Flatheads — 2; Kootenais — 2; Pend d'Oreilles — 2; Kalispells — 1; Spokanes — 1. The ninth member will be selected by the Superintendent. The business committee will consist of nine members. Any other business of general interest to the Flathead & Confederated Tribes may be brought before this council.
>
> Fred C. Morgan,
> Supt. & Spl. Dis. Agt.

The proceedings of the general council, held according to the terms of the notice above given, indicate that at that time enrollments of various Indians were received, and other business transacted. The minutes of the meeting, referring to the election of the Business Committee, are as follows:

> "A motion to elect for two years a business committee composed of nine members, to transact for the tribes all business of a tribal nature, voted upon by all present at the council, carried by 140 to 13. The motion also gave the Superintendent the power to remove from the committee any member who violated the rules and regulations, becoming drunk, etc. Nominations were made and submitted to the council and the following persons chosen:

Duncan McDonald and Mose Delaware, for the Flatheads;
Angus McDonald, sr., & Chas. Allard, for the Kootenais;
Peter Paul and Eneas Concow for the Pend d'Oreilles;
Magpie for the Kalispells;
Joe Peon for the Spokanes;
Chief Charlo, member at large; unanimous choice of council."

The above seems to be all the information I can find in the files concerning the selection of the Business Committee. I would advise that Joe Peon, one of the members originally elected, has since died, and Peter Paul is no longer a member of the Business Committee, — my information being that he was dropped as a member of this Committee on account of misdemeanors in conduct, more particularly drunkenness. The Business Committee is now composed of Duncan McDonald, Chairman, Moses Delaware, Angus McDonald, Charles Allard, Eneas Michel (Conco), Magpie, Charlo and John Matt. John Matt was appointed to succeed Peter Paul, who was relieved for the reasons as above indicated, and a resolution was passed by members of the Business Committee at the meeting held September 3, 1919, that Eneas Conco be requested to withdraw as a member of the Business Committee for the reason that he is a leader among the gamblers. This resolution is embodied in the minutes of the Business Committee held September 3, 1919, at which time the applications of various individuals for enrollment was considered in connection with the preparation and closing of the final roll of the Tribe. A copy of these minutes was transmitted to your Office.

Note is taken of request made by Miss Lemery that a general council be convened about June 1st for the selection of a new Business Committee, and it is suggested that one member in this Committee be selected from each of the five districts, and four from the Tribe as a whole.

With respect to these suggestions, in case the Office believes it advisable to order a general council for the purpose selecting a new Business Committee, I would advise that June 1st will not be an appropriate time, as I have received information from Honorable H. P. Snyder, Chairman of the House Committee on Indian Affairs, that the sub-committee, which is visiting the reservations in the west will probably visit this reservation about June 1st, and for this reason, that date will not be a good one for the election of a Business Committee, since this office will be engaged with the sub-committee about that time.

If your Office considers it proper that a new Business Committee should be selected, I suggest June 15th as a better date for the calling of a general council for the purpose indicated.

With respect to the distribution of the members of the Business Committee, I believe that it would be better, instead of selecting one member from each of the five districts and four at large, to select the Business Committee with respect to the different tribes of this reservation. It should be remembered that this jurisdiction is termed The Confederated Flathead and it is composed of fragments of a number of tribes. The larger number of the Indians are of Flathead, Kootenai and Pend d'Oreilles blood, and I therefore recommend that should a new Business Committee be selected, it be on the basis of two members for the Flatheads, two for the Kootenais, two for the Pend d'Oreilles, one for the Kalispells, one for the Spokanes, and one member at large.

Any council of the Indians for the purpose of selecting a Business Committee should be at the call of the Superintendent, after proper notice is given to the Indians in all parts of the reservation, and at least two weeks' notice should be given. For this reason, the suggestion is made that should a new Business Committee be authorized, a meeting for the purpose of selecting it should be on or subsequent to June 15th.

Very truly yours,
Theodore Sharp
Superintendent.

Document 131

Land Patents Are Forced on Tribal Members

May 7, 1920

Source: "Indian Board's Work Near Done," *The Daily Missoulian*, May 7, 1920, page 8, col. 2.

Editors' note: In 1920 the government forced some tribal members to accept patents to their allotments which made them citizens but also liable for taxes. Many of the newly "freed" Indians lost their land because they could not pay that taxes and water charges.

Indian Board's Work Near Done

Government Officials Are Investigating Competency of Redskin Wards.

The work of the special competency board on the Flathead reservation regarding the issuance of patents to members of the Indian tribes there, and their ability to become citizens, is nearly completed, according to Major Theodore Sharp, superintendent of the Flathead Indian agency, who was in Missoula yesterday.

The board, which is composed of Major Sharp, Inspector D. E. Smith of San Francisco, and Supervisor C. E. Coe of the department of the interior at Washington, has been at work on the reservation for several weeks.

"The policy of the government," said Major Sharp, "gradually is becoming more liberal than it has been in the past as regards the Indian wards of the government. This is evidenced by the fact that the office of Indian Commissioner Cato Sells at Washington has issued more fee patents to Indians, which has the effect of making them citizens, in the last two years, than were issued in the 10 years prior to that time."

The work of the commission has been to visit the Indians in their homes, observe their character and industry, and judge whether they are competent to have fee patents issued to them.

Document 132

Indians Complain About Irrigation Project

June 1, 1920

Source: Excerpts from U.S. House of Representatives, Subcommittee of the Committee on Indian Affairs, *Indians of the United States: Investigation of the Field Service, Volume 3,* Sixty-sixth Congress, Second session. (Washington, D.C., U.S. Government Printing Office, 1920), pages 1277-1284 and 1292-1294.

Editors' note: These statements were made at a hearing at Dixon, Montana, held by a subcommittee of the House of Representatives Committee on Indian Affairs. Most of the complaints revolved around the construction funding for the Flathead Irrigation Project. Martin Charlo, Kaikaishe, and Duncan McDonald pointed out that before the project was constructed they had private irrigation ditches which the project destroyed. Now the government wanted them to pay for water from the new ditches.

Statement of Mr. Martin Charlo.

The Chairman [Homer P. Snyder, New York]. What is your name and whom do you represent? What tribe of Indians do you represent?

Mr. Charlo (interpreted by Max J. Barnaby). Martin Charlo. I represent the Flathead Nation of Indians and the chiefs.

The Chairman. You are here to make a statement of conditions?

Mr. Charlo. Yes, sir.

The Chairman. We will give you 10 minutes to make a statement in your own way.

Mr. Charlo. I have protests to make against the conditions of my water rights. I am paying for water than I do not get any benefit from. Several Indian members of the tribe have had their money taken away from them for supposed water charges. That is a point of view that is not right. The previous water that was my private water right has been taken away from me and I am being charged for the same. The Reclamation Service cut into my ditch and diverted my stream of water into the canal and is charging me for that same water. A treaty was made with me by the white men that I was to have this water, and in that treaty I was given to understand that the water was mine. All the waters within the boundaries of the Flathead Reservation were to belong to me. I am sure that was the agreement made at that time.

I would like relief to get these water rights straightened out. At this time I have no water for my crops and am being charged for water I do not get on the crops, and the pro rata share of my money has been taken to pay for the supposed water charges. This statement I am making is true to the best of my knowledge.

The Chairman. Have you paid any actual money for water?

Mr. Charlo. I have not paid for water myself; my son is charged.

The Chairman. Do you know any Indian who has paid for water?

Martin Charlo
Source: Photograph Archives, Montana Historical Society, Helena, Montana
photo 954-501

Mr. Charlo. I know of one Indian who is blind and could not see and could not work out on the farm, and $60 of his money has been taken for water, and I know about other Indians who are present here.

The Chairman. Does this man who is blind use water from the ditch?

Mr. Charlo. I do not think he has any water from the ditch or any connection.

The Chairman. Do you have land on the ditch?

Mr. Charlo. I have no water from the reclamation on my land.

The Chairman. Could you get water on your land from the Reclamation Service?

Mr. Charlo. The water can not be put on the land from the reclamation.

The Chairman. How do you know that there is a charge against your land if you can not get water from the ditch?

Mr. Charlo. The law, as I understand it — if the stream is above my land, where it could be used on my land, they are going to charge me for it.

The Chairman. Then the water could be used on your land if you wanted to use it?

Mr. Charlo. If I wanted to use it.

The Chairman. Are you opposed to the Reclamation Service here as a whole?

Mr. Charlo. I am opposed to the reclamation activities, because my money is being used for this project and I am being charged for the water.

The Chairman. Then you would prefer that no further work on the project be done?

Mr. Charlo. I can see for myself that the money that has been used is money squandered. I do not want a dollar of my money, or any further money, to be put into this irrigation project from past experience.

The Chairman. Do you understand that the tribal funds now are being used for this irrigation project?

Mr. Charlo. Two years ago I heard that they were going to use the tribal funds for construction of the ditches by the Reclamation Service.

The Chairman. Do you know that any of it has been used?

Mr. Charlo. I do not know of any instances lately, but back when the Reclamation Service began they used the Indian money when they made and built canals, which have never been used from the time they were built.

The Chairman. I understand from your statement that you are opposed to the reclamation scheme and that you feel that you have been injured by reason of the fact that water that you had on your own has been taken away from you and nothing has been supplied you to take the place of it.

Mr. Charlo. Yes; that is why I am opposed. My private individual water has been taken away from me.

The Chairman. But your land is still where you could get water from the ditch if you wanted to?

Mr. Charlo. I would have water if the Reclamation would give me back my stream to my lands.

The Chairman. Would you be satisfied if you were assured that you and the other Indians were to have sufficient water to have the project continued and completed?

Mr. Charlo. From what I gather it is agreeable to me, but I would not be able to pay for that water.

The Chairman. Does the Indian have to pay for that service here?

Mr. Barnaby. Yes.

Statement of Mr. John B. Finley, St. Ignatius, Mont.

(The witness was duly sworn by the chairman.)

The Chairman. State your name and residence.

Mr. Finley. John B. Finley, St. Ignatius, Mont.

The Chairman. Do you desire to give testimony at this hearing?

Mr. Finley. Yes, sir.

The Chairman. St. Ignatius is in this project?

Mr. Finley. Yes, sir.

The Chairman. You appear as opposed to the irrigation scheme?

Mr. Finley. Well, in some ways; yes.

The Chairman. Are you an Indian?

Mr. Finley. Yes, sir; supposed to be.

The Chairman. What tribe?

Mr. Finley. Kootenai.

The Chairman. Half breed or what?

Mr. Finley. About three-quarters.

The Chairman. Briefly and in five minutes you may go ahead and state your objections and tell us why you are opposed. That will leave us five minutes in which to ask questions.

Mr. Finley. According to the records of the ditches, we do not hardly object to the ditches, only that we do not want to have any debts to the ditch proposition. We want to be cleared of this lien against our land for the water. We think the water is ours, and we do not feel like paying for any irrigation when it is our own property.

The Chairman. Of course, the ditches are in and somebody has to pay for them.

Mr. Finley. That may be true, but when the treaty was made no such thing was done.

The Chairman. When the treaty was made nobody ever conceived that any such project as this would ever be started.

Mr. Finley. That might be so; but there was no kind of agreement made for our water.

The Chairman. Do you believe that the Indians are not benefited, and will not be benefited eventually, by this project?

Mr. Finley. The majority will never be benefited; that is, the old ones; it may do good to the younger ones.

The Chairman. They had originally some 80,000 acres of this irrigable land, and much of it is disposed of; and, of course, they have been benefited to that extent on account of this irrigation scheme here, whether holding or disposing of their lands here.

Mr. Finley. That may be all right, that part, for some of them; but we are looking for the biggest majority of them.

The Chairman. There is only a small number of Indians actually farming, and a small acreage being farmed by them?

Mr. Finley. They have no way to farm when they have money held back and issued a little at a time; I do not see how they can farm.

The Chairman. Now you are getting to the question of the per capita payments. You think the bureau is slow in distributing tribal funds that are collected from the reservation lands here?

Mr. Finley. Yes; that goes to the farming proposition.

The Chairman. What other proposition?

Mr. Finley. To the farming, and water, of course. They have to do something to make a living when they have got money and can not get it.

The Chairman. I understand that the money has been pretty thoroughly distributed — the money raised off the land by the sale of timber has been distributed all to the Indians per capita, and most of them have disposed of it in various ways.

Mr. Finley. The breeds may be all right, but I am talking for the full bloods.

The Chairman. What is the objection of the full bloods as to the project?

Mr. Finley. That lien on the land for the water is their objection.

The Chairman. The Indian wants his land free of charge for the development of the scheme?

Mr. Finley. Yes, sir; no lien.

The Chairman. Is he willing to pay for the water that he uses after the scheme is completed?

Mr. Finley. That I do not know exactly if they do or not, but they have it coming.

The Chairman. If there was any guaranty that the full blood would continue always to occupy the land and cultivate it successfully, there might be some justification in your argument, but when we come up here and find that out of all of the allotments of the Indian, out of 80,000 acres, that there are only 2,500 acres actually being operated by Indians, and most of them are half breeds, it would seem as though if the full blood got what you ask that he would not keep it long; he would simply turn it over to somebody else.

Mr. Finley. That is what I am telling you, how could they operate when they have not got the means of operating? When we have got money we can not get the employment of our own money to buy anything like that to operate the ranch.

The Chairman. I do not think I quite get your idea. How much money do you understand that this tribe has on deposit now that is due them from the Government?

Mr. Finley. I could not tell about that.

The Chairman. Your income for the last year was reported at $135,000. How much of that has been distributed. I do not know.

Mr. Finley. I mean about this, that you state that there are only about 2,500.

The Chairman. Two thousand five hundred acres of this project under ditch being cultivated by Indians of all bloods.

Mr. Finley. That is what I say. There would be more than what you name, providing they all get their money at once.

The Chairman. Where is this money they would get?

Mr. Finley. From the heirs of lots of Indians who have money tied up and only get $25, $50, or $100 a month, just enough to live on.

The Chairman. Of course, this committee does not know what amount of money there is on deposit from these sales that might be distributed to certain Indians.

Mr. Finley. That is what I am explaining right now.

The Chairman. You do not know how much there is. You know there is some, but you do not know how much.

Mr. Finley. Yes, sir.

The Chairman. You think if that money was distributed to the Indians up here that they would go and farm more acreage?

Mr. Finley. They could buy implements and horses, and something to work with. You could not buy but one horse with $100.

The Chairman. I think the committee would be glad to recommend that that money be distributed and that the Indians have the opportunity to get more land. Are you opposed to the irrigation project and believe that it does not benefit the Indians?

Mr. Finley. Well, it only benefits in some dry seasons for hay and such things as that.

The Chairman. When you have a dry season the water would be a good thing for you?

Mr. Finley. Providing it is in hay.

The Chairman. Do you mean to say that if an Indian has money to his credit over here in the agency and he wants to buy a horse or a team of horses, a plow or a wagon, that the agent will not buy it for him?

Mr. Finley. Yes, sir.

The Chairman. Do you have any money there in the agency yourself?

Mr. Finley. No, sir.

The Chairman. They gave you all of yours?

Mr. Finley. Yes.

The Chairman. Do you know of any Indian who had money enough to buy a team of horses and they would not buy it for him?

Mr. Finley. There is quite a few here that I know they still have money.

Mr. Carter. Do you understand that you have any tribal funds undistributed? I do not mean sales of inherited lands, dead Indian lands, but tribal funds at Washington. Do you understand that the Flatheads have any that have not been distributed; per capita payments, I mean?

Mr. Finley. Yes; but I do not know exactly how much.

Mr. Carter. Have you made any effort to try and find out just how much it was?

Mr. Finley. That the delegate is supposed to know.

Mr. Carter. Have you ever asked your agent?

Mr. Finley. No. sir.

Mr. Carter. Does your agent make any statement, public statement at all, as to the amount of funds that each Flathead Indian has?

Mr. Finley. No, sir.

Mr. Carter. Do you want that done?

Mr. Finley. Yes, sir.

Mr. Carter. You would like to have a statement two or three or four times a year showing exactly what is coming to you?

Mr. Finley. Yes, sir.

Statement of Chief Kaikaishe, Flathead Indian.

The Chairman. Proceed in your own way.

Chief Kaikaishe (Interpreted by Max J. Barnaby). I do not agree with the operation or the activities of the Reclamation Service.

The Chairman. Why?

Chief Kaikaishe. In that treaty that was made the reservation was made of the streams within this reservation to be the property of the Indians themselves. To-day he is at a loss to know where he stands relative to the water rights. It is my water, yet I am paying for it, being charged for it.

The Chairman. Have you ever paid any money for the water?

Chief Kaikaishe. I have not paid for any water myself. I would like information definitely, relative to the water. I understand that a tunnel or something was built this side of Polson and no doubt you did not go to see that. About four or five hundred thousand dollars of the Indians' money has been appropriated there and has disappeared; no one seems to know where that went to.

The Chairman. Some members of the committee did go to the spot and are familiar with it, and they understand that only $100,000 was spent there, and that money was replaced in the tribal fund.

Chief Kaikaishe. I am supposed to see you members of the committee of the House and give this information to you directly.

The Chairman. Are you a farmer now? Do you farm any land yourself?

Chief Kaikaishe. I am getting too old now.

The Chairman. I appreciate that. I did not mean that you worked on the farm yourself, but have you any land that is worked for you by your own people — your family?

Chief Kaikaishe. I have no children and nobody to work my land.

The Chairman. When you were 25 years younger than you are now, did you work any land then?

Chief Kaikaishe. I raised big crops in those times, 25 years ago.

The Chairman. Was your land then on any old irrigation scheme or did you just have the rain that came from the heavens to help you?

Chief Kaikaishe. I had a stream to irrigate from when I raised the crops.

The Chairman. You irrigated yourself, then, in that way.

Chief Kaikaishe. Yes, sir.

The Chairman. You believe that the water is a good thing for the land?

Chief Kaikaishe. I like the water if I can get it.

The Chairman. Of course, you know that the general agricultural development here has been a good thing for the country?

Chief Kaikaishe. I do not go out to see any of those agricultural activities. I stay at home.

The Chairman. Your principal grievance is that somebody else is using the water that you claim under some old treaty was given wholly for the use of the Indians here?

Chief Kaikaishe. Yes.

Mr. Tillman. I understand the chief claims, and so do other members of the Indian tribe, that this water is theirs and that they ought not to be charged for it if their land is irrigated by it. That is the position of a great many Indians here.

Chief Kaikaishe. Yes, sir.

Mr. Tillman. If you were 5 miles away from the Flathead River and very thirsty and unable to get there and get a drink of water and a white man should go there and bring the water to you in a bucket, so you could drink it, do you think you ought to pay the white man for that trouble?

Chief Kaikaishe. I would pay the white man to bring water to me.

Mr. Tillman. What is the difference if the white man, by his energy and capital and by intelligence, irrigates your land from the Flathead River and puts it on there, why should he not be paid for the water, if you would pay the white man for bringing you a drink of water. It is still your water. There ought to be no distinction.

Chief Kaikaishe. I would pay for the water if the water was the white man's water, but if it is the Indian's water I would not pay for it.

Mr. Tillman. It is the Indian's water when the white man brings it to you in the bucket, and yet you would pay the white man for it. I would like to know the distinction between the water in the bucket and the water in the ditch, assuming it is your water.

Chief Kaikaishe. I would pay for the water, pay the white man for getting the water for me, but not for my water. The water is mine.

Mr. Carter. Do you understand that you have some tribal funds to which you are entitled?

Chief Kaikaishe. I understand I have some funds.

Mr. Rhodes. Is it not a fact that before the Government ditch was put here that most of the Indians got what water they wanted from ditches of their own?

Chief Kaikaishe. We made ditches of our own and had our own irrigation project before the white man ever came into this country, and used plows and pick and shovel to dig these ditches.

Mr. Rhodes. Did you get an allotment of land on this reservation?

Chief Kaikaishe. I have an allotment.

Mr. Rhodes. Was it on or near the ditch?

Chief Kaikaishe. There is no ditch near my land.

Mr. Rhodes. Was there a ditch there, and did you get water before the project started?

Chief Kaikaishe. Yes; I had water before the irrigation came in.

Mr. Rhodes. Then irrigation, instead of giving you water, has cut you out of water?

Chief Kaikaishe. Yes; it took water away from me.

Mr. Rhodes. Can you get water from the ditch at all now?

Chief Kaikaishe. I do not think I can get water from this ditch now.

Mr. Rhodes. What have you done with your allotment? Do you still own it?

Chief Kaikaishe. I have my allotment.

Mr. Hayden. Do you lease it now?

Chief Kaikaishe. The fathers have my land; leased to them.

Mr. Hayden. Now much do they pay you?

Chief Kaikaishe. I think I get $500 a year from the lease; I am not sure.

Mr. Hayden. You said you had all the water you wanted before the project was started. Did all the Indians have all the water they wanted before the project started?

Chief Kaikaishe. There were a lot of Indians that had water, and I had water myself, before the reclamation project came into the country.

Mr. Hayden. Did all of them have all the water they wanted every year?

Chief Kaikaishe. Everybody had plenty of water, and there was no kick.

The Chairman. This man's time has gone much beyond the limit. Have you some others that want to be heard?

Mr. Barnaby. We want to introduce our spokesman next.

The Chairman. Let him come ahead, then. We thank Chief Kaikaishe for the information he has given us.

Chief Kaikaishe. For the last seven years I have been going to Washington trying to get some of the funds for the Indians. Now, recently a pro rata payment has been made. The money came to the agency here and the superintendent has hold of that money to-day. A lot of that money has not been paid at all yet. This money should be distributed to every man, woman, and child.

The Chairman. We will take that up with the superintendent immediately, when we get through with this hearing, to see what can be done. That is as far as we can go with this witness. . .

Statement of Mr. Duncan McDonald.

The Chairman. Do you speak English?

Mr. McDonald. I speak American.

The Chairman. Do you live here on the reservation?

Mr. McDonald. I was born about 14 miles from here, in 1849.

The Chairman. What do you do for a living?

Mr. McDonald. Everything.

The Chairman. Tell us some one thing.

Mr. McDonald. Horticulture, mining, trading, stock raising.

The Chairman. What do you work at?

Mr. McDonald. Just now?

The Chairman. Yes.

Mr. McDonald. I am living on the interest of my money.

The Chairman. I congratulate you.

Mr. McDonald. Thank you. I am the oldest Indian in this crowd right now.

The Chairman. Tell us what you have to say with regard to whether or not this irrigation project should be continued. That is what we are up here to hear about.

Mr. McDonald. Why stand here like the dog in the manger? The white man is in debt to the Indian for the land. The white man he gets his land on a dry place, Indian land. By working hard he gets some money to pay what he owes to the Indian. Now, the white man says I can not raise grain without water. The Indian says, you will pay me but I will not give you the water. I want the Indian and the white man here equal. For heaven's sake, talk about n......s, you are treating these white people on the reservation worse than n......s. Help these white men to get out of debt. The Indian says, I must have my water. I tell my friends, go to the head man of the Reclamation and don't go to quarreling. But it seems to me their whole attention is to jump on the superintendent.

Here is a letter from the commissioner. I go to the commissioner. Here is one from the Secretary of the Interior. Then I go to the Secretary of the Interior. Well, here is Congress and there is where we land. The chairman of this business committee. I refer you to the superintendent; he is the representative of Uncle Sam, duly authorized. There was a council elected and recognized by the Indian Office. Now, as I understand, there are a lot of agitators. You know we have Debs — he wants to run for President — and Townley. You would have Gompers and everybody running for President. If I had a vote, I would vote for Billy Sunday, as far as I am concerned.

Now, I say that I am not kicking at reclamation, because I raised the biggest orchards on this reservation, raising fruits for 30 years, and now you send pamphlets about farming, to save everything, so I did. My fruits, apples, from my orchards were in perfect order. The newspapers gave me a blow-out for the condition that I had this orchard in. If I go and make a little cider to give my friends a little, then you put me in the penitentiary.

The Chairman. Not me.

Mr. McDonald. When I say you I mean Uncle Sam; you represent Uncle Sam.

The Chairman. I did not vote to put you in jail for making cider.

Mr. McDonald. I had a ditch there years and years through my orchard. What did they do? People above me were helping themselves to my ditch and my water, and my poor old wife packing water in a bucket to water her little corn. Now, is it fair, when here is a man got a garden drowned out with water and my wife packing water with a bucket? I went and shut off that water. He comes to me and says, "Here, I am not afraid of you. I will use all the water that I want from that ditch." But here I am without the water and there is my ditch. I had a notion to kill that man right there, but something prevented me from doing that. I came mighty near committing murder right there. That is the way I was treated, and there is no man, Indian or white man, on the reservation that is harder working than I am, and I am just as good as any white man or Indian to work; I was not depending on Uncle Sam to feed me on rations. If the white man wants water to pay his debt to the Indian, give it to him. If there is a million dollars to be had, what is the use of my kicking. That is the way I look at it. Get if finished and completed.

Mr. Carter. Then there will be enough water for all.

Mr. McDonald. Then we will be Americans. [Applause.]

The Chairman. You have given us some very valuable information, and we are very glad to know you feel that way about it, and we believe you represent the better sentiment of the people up here.

Mr. McDonald. My sentiment is, pay the Indian his just dues.

The Chairman. But give the white man his water first?

Mr. McDonald. I say both.

The Chairman. One follows the other.

Mr. McDonald. If the Indian has got water and the white man has got dry land, while the white man owes that Indian for that land, he say I can not pay for water.

The Chairman. I think we understand your statement fully. We can not give you any more time.

Mr. McDonald. I am sorry. I could give you guff here for a whole week.

Document 133

Statements at Flathead Business Committee Meeting June 2, 1920

Source: "Particulars of the Business Committee...," June 2, 1920, from file 55,158/1920 Flathead 154, Central Classified Files, RG 75, National Archives, Washington, D.C.

Editors' note: Some of these statements are not easy to follow. Most of the complaints by tribal leaders involve the construction and operation of the Flathead Irrigation Project. Some complaints refered to access for grazing now that homesteads had been located on much of the former open grazing range.

Particulars of the Business Committee continued from June 2, 1920, met at the agency office at 1 o'clock, Duncan McDonald chairman. Angus McDonald's statement.

I propose that since the project has been started at a great expense to the Government and in part an expense to the tribe, damages, etc., that it would be poor policy to discontinue it. It is more beneficial to continue the unfinished project. Any waste that has been expended by the Government or its Project Manager, of moneys for the construction of these projects should be borne or eliminated from the final cost that is to be charged or proposed to be charged to the tribe since the tribe is the owner, rightful, legal owner of the water as well as the land through which the canals are constructed. The tribe should not be charged to the full the same as the settler, and especially those that are not benefitted by the ditches should not be charged at all. As we understand — my information may be wrong — the Government in some way has a lien on our allotments, it is presumably to be supposed that all allotments, but we object to being charged with any costs that we are not liable to, and where we are not getting any benefit from as a tribe.

The question of reservoir sites, completed and uncompleted, leased and unleased, under what jurisdiction are those sites? Are they still within the jurisdiction of the Indian Bureau or are they within the jurisdiction of the Reclamation. Does the money from leasing those lands go to the project or does it go to the tribe? Those lands under those reservoir sites are still tribal lands not paid for. What are the statutes [status?] of those tribal lands unpaid for? Personally, I am opposed to the tribe demanding pay or acquiring money for projects already completed with water in them except the individual who may be damaged by such reservoir, he probably or they probably would have some damage, but I am opposed to the tribe demanding money for the reason that if it is sold it would probably become state, and if such is the case the Indian could not go on it and hunt and fish as he pleases. If the project is not sold the tribe will get more benefit than it would from the money derived from the sale of the project, for having the right to go on it when he pleases is great. I am speaking for reservoir sites that are actually in use not power sites.

I understand the Indians, the Kootenais especially, would like to have a sort of check put on timber. We ask the Indian Department to appoint one two or three, or more, but three will be sufficient, members of the tribe — all those of Indian blood that could be appointed by the Indians — to check over timber that is being cut, logged, or give the Indians an idea of how nearly correct the official estimators work is, or in other words to check up Mr. Sharp and his deputies in their timber operations.

Charles Allard's statement.

Referring to the reservoir sites, as far as the benefit we have, take the Ninepipe Reservoir as an illustration, to take and give it to the Reclamation — there is probably 250 acres of land to take it over to the Reclamation — the white man is the one who has the benefit and for the Indians not to be paid for it when the white man uses it, I can see no reason for that at all. This Ninepipe Reservoir is leased by some Missoula people now and I know lots of people who get a permit from the man farming it.

This reservation is the same as an allotment. We own this just the same. Now they come along and take it for reservoirs. Take for instance if you have a big ranch and someone below you wants to put an irrigation project there to irrigate his land and yours. He comes up and wants this done. There are more whites that will be covered by the project than the Indians, and why should the Indians give them the benefit? and I think we should be paid for all these reservoirs but the power sites we want kept for their value. We want to take up this matter and see if we are going to get paid.

Referring to Mr. Crowe's statement the other day, he said the charges on the Jocko Project will be about $35 an acre; the Pablo Project $60 an acre; the Camas Project $150 an acre. It averages at any rate about $65 an acre. They proposed to take and throw them all in one unit, and to average this up with the Jocko Project will cost about $130 an acre. In the Camas district there are very few allotments that will be in that project. There is none that is good without any water and they take that land and this up here as a lot of it with private water rights. The Jocko district which is $35 and there are more Indians up here, and they want them to stand half of the Camas district's expenses, and it is just the same as helping the white man up there as to help the Reclamation Project. I want the units to stand their charges separately. They are asking us to pay for the white man's. Another thing we should put in a complaint about it trying to irrigate the places that are not practical — trying to get water on sandy places which do not justify having it. I should think the Reclamation should make the appropriation and have it through with.

Pierre Magpie's statement.

I am in favor of the Indians paying for water, but I am opposed to the lien as referred to by Mr. Angus McDonald. The water was taken by the white men when they came on the reservation, by reservoirs, ditches, etc. which they put in, and the Indians never were consulted in that matter, and the settler was to be a farmer and not a stock-raiser. Should the white men bring the water from the outside — from off the reservation, and then charge The Indians for that water? If the Reclamation makes a ditch on the Indians' land let him get the water free of charge, and any damages let him pay for.

Duncan McDonald's statement.

That Jocko Project that comes within a few miles of Ravalli — about three miles from Ravalli — what is the use of making ditches which will cost $100 when you can get them for $10. The Department wanted to send an engineer out here when this project was to be made but the Superintendent said he would get a miner with a spring level and would run the ditch. The Indians made the ditch with miners' level from the old Government mill. This Reclamation outfit, they fooled around there surveying, spending thousands of dollars on the same old ditch. The Reclamation outfit come along and fooled around for a year or two surveying that same ditch. That was unnecessary. They then came along with that ditch and stopped. They can continue that if they want some water in the Jocko. Now they figure to get the north fork of the Jocko into the St. Mary's Lake. Here is a ditch about eight miles. It has cost thousands of dollars and yet the place is dry. These people could bring the water about a mile and a half and have it, but they go fooling round and still have no water. What is the sense of that when they can bring the water down. They have wasted at least $150,000 by the railroad company, for I know the ground. And the Jocko district is estimated at $35. I do not want the water but what is the use of spending a hundred dollars when you can do the work for five dollars.

Eneas Conclow's statement.

I want to know if the Reclamation has a right to dam up the original creeks and damage them so that the people below are dried out entirely without any water for domestic purposes.

Ducharme's statement.

I am pretty sure that water will do lots of damage on my place. When my water was flowing to the lake it damaged Mr. Bell and he could not work his land for a while so if the ditch is above us it will damage our land and I do not want to damage my neighbor. The water on my place is used for the benefit of the schoolhouse more than anything else.

Baptiste Marengo's statement.

I do not feel that we ought to have that ditch up there or we will be drowned out. Two members of my family have allotments there. If that ditch should break out there we would be swamped. This sub-irrigation is going to do us a lot of harm.

Mr. Bell's statement.

I am a neighbor of Mr. Ducharme and my land is under his ditch. I threshed 25 bushels of grain on my place during the past three years. I was damaged by Mr. Ducharme's ditch and had to get him shut off his ditch before I could cut my grain.

Max Barnaby's statement.

In that connection, let the Tribal Council pick out these men and come here and qualify before the Superintendent for the work of checking over the work of timber operations such as cutting and logging. The Indian Bureau would want something to say to that and would have to approve it. Let them come here and sort of take an examination.

Statement by Angus McDonald.

The subject of grazing has been brought up; settlers fencing tribal lands for their special use to the seclusion of tribal stock; also driving tribal stock from tribal lands, grazing lands, into lanes whereby such stock are compelled from their nature to roam in the lane where there is no feed, no water; hence the objection here both in the human, so far as I am concerned, as well as owners. The stock is abused, dogged, and killed. The question is if there is any right for such people to monopolize tribal grazing lands. It is a known fact that they have no rights, no treaty rights, no lawful rights. Is the Indian Bureau or the Secretary of the Indian Bureau to issue permits to these settlers to graze stock within certain described lands, knowing from the nature of the animal to graze there would wander on other lands from the nature of the animal would not remain on the land but would wander, interfere with tribal rights of the Indians. Though the whole tribe, as a whole may derive a small benefit perhaps 25 cents may save that much and have per capita derived from such permits. The loss of individual Indians is so great that the Department should see that those permits are withdrawn. (Bruns and Bierman are the names of the men who leased from me.) The wish that the permits be discontinued as I say the nature of the animals is such that they will not remain under specified tracts of land where the animals are permitted to graze, but will roam wherever nature calls them; hence, that is to roam on unprotected allotments that are not fenced. In addition to that the so called stockman will ramble into the woods at will when and where he pleases. He may take his cow or he may take an Indian's cow. It gives him a right to title when and where he pleases. The Indian has no protection as compared with this man. He has no knowledge whether the man is honest or not. I have found that they are not all honest. They will take cattle, horses, sheep. I understand that settlers have an organization called the Settlers' Protection Association. How true this is I do not know. Their aim is to defend one another against the Indian and against the stockmen.

The question of jurisdiction over Indians and settlers has been proned to put most of the cases, if not all, within the jurisdiction of the State whereas it should legally or rightfully have belonged to the Federal Court. I want the permits cancelled now.

The other complaint I have against the Superintendent is this: The timber cruisers, I do not know on this side of the river, east of the river, but I know west of the river that their permits to settlers whereby they are to cut three or

Angus P. McDonald
Source: Toole Archives, Mansfield Library, University of Montana, Missoula, Montana, photo MS 562, 12-24

four cords of wood are violated and the settlers take 15 or 20. The timber men never consult the settler and he cuts wood wherever he pleases. My contention is that Mr. Flower, the field man on the west side of the river, have this practice stopped. Where a settler wants wood, green timber especially, let him take what he wants, pay for it, but the foresters must see what he takes. We don't object to them getting the wood. I would suggest that the Department give these settlers, poor or otherwise, the timber, the dead timber, freely.

With reference to the Hot Springs, we respectfully but earnestly demand the withdrawal of the permit. We want to withdraw the permit, — a part of it set aside for the exclusive use of the Indians. The other part, the Department can do with as it pleases. It can lease, rent, or whatever it sees fit but not sell. It is large enough to supply all the wants of the inhabitants of the state of Montana. We asked the Department to appropriate of the tribal funds, $5,000 to erect a building at those springs for the exclusive use of the Indians. The surplus use of the water to be rented to the settlers but not to be monopolized by anyone, if settler or townsman. Sell it by the gallon. The Indian does not require $5,000. The Indian wants the exclusive use of all the water he wants for his use, when and how he pleases. The Indian, being sensitive, doesn't want too much publicity, but likes to have private ownership. The only drawback to our standing is the sanitation. My contention is to withdraw the present lease, set aside for the specific use of the Indians a certain part of the Springs, and you may lease, convey or whatever you please except to deed. If the Department of the Interior sees whereby the tribe can get any financial benefit by leasing the surplus let it do so; otherwise, I would be willing after our own water is set aside, to give it to the State free. The benefit derived now is not enough to justify the tribe of monopolizing. Let the state do it for its citizens. There is sufficient water. The hotel, banks, private houses, can be supplied at a small rental price, still the state would have plenty of water for the poor.

Referring to irrigation matters, I would add in addition that the allotments under the Reclamation project or bordering same, should be examined and injury or damages to allotments affected by irrigation ditches, be reconsidered after having been examined. I also suggest that rights of way be considered, and the allotments compensated for what damages are done. It is necessary to damage allotments some times for the purpose of improving them. The difference between the benefit caused to the allottees and the benefit given to such allotment because of ditches should be considered.

Statement by Charles Allard.

Regarding the lease with Bierman and Bruns, I should think there should be someone appointed to look after that for the benefit of the tribe. All of them as far as that goes. I do not believe in revoking any of those leases unless by so doing it benefits the tribe.

Regarding Indian water rights where an Indian has already taken water, should he not be allowed to take the water from the ditch and just pay the maintenance. There are a few instances on the reservation like that where the Government can use water and not infringe on their rights, instead of them building when there already is a ditch.

The Business Committee opposes the Indian Office from paying transportation and salaries of Indian delegates that are going to Washington such as Mary Lemery, John Charley, Max Barnaby and Martin Conclow.

Statement by Duncan McDonald.

The white farmers come here to take up an 80 or a 160 acre tract of land for farming, and instead of farming they have started in stock-raising. They want to raise stock on the range and run off our own stock, the Indians' stock, from the ranges. The Indians, and one of our members here and another there of the Business Committee, are losing their stock for the simple reason that the farmers are taking our grazing away, and what are we going to do? We have no range, no grass. These ranges belong to us. The section lines put up by the white farmers prevent the Indians from having any way of getting out on the public roads. One day I travelled for five miles and could not get out. Now, I say I want to give back what belongs to us and let Mr. Farmer attend to his own business and go into stock-raising. Let him raise his fruit or stock or anything else. But the farmers drive our cattle, the Indians' cattle, which really belong to the Indians, off the ranges. Why should the Indian be dispossessed. We want somebody to look after these people so as to give any of these men or any other men a place to put their cattle after buying them at auction sales. Now, what are we going to do? Uncle Sam says he wants us to be in good circumstances and now it seems he is helping these settlers while we are getting poorer. It looks to me that way. You will see the position of the Indian, if you are a responsible man, and see if the Indian has any rights. We have no objection for the whites to go ahead and plow and raise all they can, but they shouldn't buy stock and go to work and raise hay for next winter and dispossess us of the mountains that we own. Regarding this grazing question, it seems some of the Indians here have been threatening to go to Washington and have our Superintendent fired. I would go to the United States Commissioner; then, of course, the Commissioner must use his judgment. If you are liable he will send the United States Commissioner and gobble you up. He certainly can put you in jail or anyone else in the pen. Why go to all this unnecessary expense while we have a United States Commissioner. Isn't that right to go to the United States Commissioner?

I have never seen a white man yet hung for killing an Indian. You cannot get a jury here to decide against a white man. The white people are always talking about the "dirty old Indians."

Statement by Pierre Magpie.

I am grieved the way I have been treated by my white neighbors. I have lost a good many head this winter. Sheep men around there on his place have taken all his grass. He says we don't want any sheep on this Indian claim. He is not complaining about the public domain but the Indian ranges that are broken onto by the white people. His place is always molested by settlers cattle and horses. The Indians are losing all the time and they lose cattle. All these men have stock, — the members of the tribe. We raise our stock on our own reservation and we would like to put a stop to these trespassers. You know these people impose on our rights.

Referring to the treaty about 66 years ago held at Hellgate Canyon, Governor Stevens, Alexander Victor and Michel and Paul Antoine were connected with the council and Governor Stevens was sent from Washington. And there they selected to have an agent and from your agent you will get your instructions for a better view of the Indians. And that is why I have great faith in my agent because he is my protector, selected by this Committee held at Hellgate Canyon. And for that he is our protector our overseer on the reservation, and supposed to investigate any complaint presented to him. We have this Committee to discuss what we want to have done. Now I am glad if these things are done which we have been discussing and I feel proud. We make our resolutions and forward them to the Commissioner of Indian Affairs and he returns the report either accepted or rejected, and that is the reason we are discussing that thing today.

Regarding the allotments of the children. We do not know anything, have never heard nor do not know what they are going to do.

There is another thing I would make an objection against. People come from other parts of reservations and we don't want them.

Regarding the water rights of my son-in-law, Joseph Vanderburg, I would like to state that I believe they are taking his water away, that is the white people. It is Mr. Gladden who is using all this water. I have another contract made with Gladden for a ditch. I made out the papers here and want to ask what can be done. It is my private water right. They have built a ditch through my land. I want to protect myself. I think we made the ditch through contract here at the agency and we both were to use the water. Under the laws of the whites, after five years, he is afraid they will take it away from him and he wants to be protected. Gladden will secure the water right from the creek and in order to get it across Magpie's allotment he has contracted with Magpie to furnish water for a given number of years. Vanderburg has always had trouble with Gladden and he wants to be supported by the agent so he will be protected.

Henry Matt's Statements.

I came before the agent here and made a complaint about my water. Our Superintendent, Major Bellew, gave my check for payment of water; that is before the Reclamation had any claim on my water. A lien judgment was secured against me and I came to my superintendent to make this complaint and am glad to make this statement to you. They seem to have a charge against me on water on our own allotments, my wife's and children's, and I want this matter taken up by the superintendent. There are 32 allotments besides those that have water rights. I live at the old Jocko agency. We need all the surplus water but it is being taken away from us. My crops have not been good because of insufficient water. The head gates are closed, preventing my getting water. I have been burned out two years now, and am a hard-working man and have always before made a success. I cultivate my wife's and children's allotments. We have a private ditch for the children, and a hearing was held in Missoula to prove the water belonged to the children.

Statement by Father O'Malley.

Mr. Traylor, there are two items of $2,000 that are being badly confused in this matter. Item No. 1 refers to House Joint Resolution No. 321, in which the Indians pray for an appropriation of $10,000 with which to prosecute, test suits in the District Court of Montana with the hope of recovering what they think are their proper rights in Montana.

The second appeal, let it be understood I am not vouching, I am merely stating facts, for $10,000 is for a lump sum of $10,000 to be placed at the disposal of the Tribal Council from which they may draw funds with which to send delegates to Washington whenever, by a vote of the Tribal Council, it is decided that delegates ought to be sent and the idea is precisely to prevent what has happened this year where those who think they have represented the tribal delegates, and contracted that they must now be paid, and I want to state that I understand this is past history, history that was made before I was connected with this at all; that some few years ago, they sent and I cannot define who the "they" are, but I understand that it was a tribal council, real or fictitious, that went to Washington and an indebtedness of $2500 was incurred, $500 of this $2500 has been paid and the party advancing the other $2000 has not been paid, and in their tribal council held recently they promised the $2000, as an honest debt, that they would leave discharged, — that is within the $10,000. I do not know the personnel of that delegation. I believe Finley was in that delegation. I believe also that Riley was in that delegation.

Document 134

Proposed Election of New Business Committee

June 1920

Source: Theodore Sharp to Commissioner of Indian Affairs, June 16, 1920; enclosures Chief Bull Head to Commissioner of Indian Affairs, June 17, 1920; Chief Sapiel Michel and Eneas Conko to Commissioner of Indian Affairs, June 15, 1920; Chief Martin Charlo to Commissioner of Indian Affairs, June 15, 1920, from file 109,764/1919 Flathead 056, Central Classified Files, RG 75, National Archives, Washington, D.C.

Editors' note: The Indian Office was dragging its feet about having a new election for the Business Committee on the Flathead Reservation. Many tribal members, including some of the chiefs, wanted an election to select new members for the committee.

Department of the Interior
United States Indian Service
Flathead Agency — Dixon, Mont.
June 16, 1920.

Commissioner of Indian Affairs,
Washington, D.C.
Sir: —

Under date of June 8th, at the request of some of the Indians of this reservation, I wired your Office as follows: "My letter May 11th concerning business committee. Indians ask information regarding proper manner electing new members. This office suggests a general council. Wire." No reply having been received, on June 14th I again wired you Office: "My telegram eighth. Indian council called for tomorrow. Please wire immediately proper manner electing members of business committee." I received in response to my telegram the following reply: "Your telegram eighth. Office sees no need for disturbing present business committee as a whole. Hence general council unnecessary."

The intention of my telegrams was to inquire what procedure should be followed in electing new members to vacancies which now exist in the tribal business committee. There are at present two vacancies in the committee, — the original committee having consisted of nine members. I am advised by several members of the committee that they desire to resign or withdraw from the duties of committeemen, and in case they should take this action, there would be additional vacancies to be filled. The intent of my inquiries by telegraph was to ascertain the method of filling the vacancies on this committee, which would be in accordance with the procedure recognized by your Office in such cases. Your telegram of June 14, however, does not indicate the manner which should be followed in filling vacancies; accordingly the committee, as it now exists, is incomplete.

It will be noted that the committee originally was elected for a period of two years, — this election having been made in the year 1909, and the two-year period has long since expired, — no new election having been held as seems to have been the original plan was to be done each two years. Certain Indians, instigated by individuals not members of the Flathead Tribe, have organized what they term a "Supreme Council" of the Flathead Tribe. This so-called council is an organization designed to supplant and take over the work of the business committee and the general councils of the Indians which have heretofore been called when matters of tribal interest were to be considered. The "Supreme Council" is composed of President, two Vice-Presidents, Secretary, Treasurer, three trustees and sixteen delegates, together with, I am informed, nine chiefs. the delegates are supposed to be two from each of eight localities on the reservation, — four of these localities, or in other words, half the delegates being from territory in and adjacent to Polson. The Secretary of this planned organization is a white man, not a member of the tribe, and at least one of the trustees is also not a member of the tribe, and has no tribal rights here. The white man who is the secretary has publicly claimed tribal rights by adoption as a member of the Kootenai Indians. As a matter of fact, there has been no such adoption, and so far as this office is advised, no recognition of any alleged adoption has ever been made by your Office.

The business committee being a recognized organization for conducting tribal business, it is believed that it should continue in force and effect. The members of this business committee were originally selected from different districts on the reservation, and comprise representative men of the tribe. This office fails to see any necessity for additional organizations, which would only seek to handle the same class of business which has heretofore been conducted through the general councils of the tribe and the business committee. It is also believed inappropriate that any organization for the transaction of tribal affairs should contain among its members — and especially as officers — men who have no tribal affiliations. At a meeting of this so-called "Supreme Council," the appropriation of $10,000 from the tribal funds was recommended, and it seems that action is sought to secure the appropriation or allotment of this

$10,000 to be used by the "Supreme Council" for the payment of expenses of this organization, and in the payment of attorneys for services to be rendered and heretofore rendered, and such other matters as the council finds expedient. In explaining this item, the Secretary (the white man heretofore referred to) stated that several years ago, some of the Indians went to Washington at their own expense, and were advanced funds by some one — just whom, the Secretary alleges he does not know, and that this indebtedness has never been paid, and that the Indians now, through the "Supreme Council," desire to refund the money which was advanced, amounting — I understand — to $2,000 or $2,500. While I do not have positive information on this point, my understanding is, from advice I have received, that the claim for reimbursement is for money advanced by Mr. Victor J. Evans, Washington, D.C.

As stated in my telegram of June 14th, a council of Indians was called for June 15th, at which time they desired to consider the matter of filling vacancies in the business committee. The plan of the organization termed the "Supreme Council" is to elect to the business committee from the delegates or officers of the so-called "Supreme Council" only, thereby making the business committee a branch or subsidiary adjunct of the "Supreme Council." Lacking definite instructions from your Office as to the manner of choosing members to fill vacancies on the business committee, no action was taken at the council held yesterday, and in fact no council proceedings were held, but the matter was deferred to a future date, and it was agreed that the Superintendent would by letter ask for information regarding definitely the status of the business committee, and the manner of electing members to fill vacancies that have occurred, and which may hereafter occur, on this committee. In this same connection, I believe it advisable that the Office should instruct me whether, in view of the fact that the original business committee was elected for two years only, and no election has been held for 11 years, a general council should be called to elect an entirely new business committee, or re-elect the members now in office, or just what procedure should be taken to place the business committee on a better footing. It seems inappropriate that the committee should continue in office for so long a period, when it was chosen for a definite time of two years, although I believe it would be difficult to secure a more representative committee, or one with better men as composed in its personnel.

The Indians have decided to await full instructions by letter from your Office, and I request that consideration of these matters be given early attention.

Very truly yours,
Theodore Sharp
Superintendent.

* * * * * * * * *

Camas District,
Perma, Mont.
June 17th, 1920.

Hon. Cato Sells,
Commissioner Indian Affairs,
Washington, D.C.
Dear Sir: —

As the question of electing of a business committee, on the Flathead Reservation has been taken up with you by our delegation while in Washington, the tribe wishes you to request the Superintendent to call a general meeting for an election on the 27th of June, 1920, in Ronan, Montana, which will be the most convenient for the tribe.

Will you kindly acknowledge receipt of this stating what action you have taken on same.

Yours truly,
Chief Bull Head.

****

Ronan, Mont.
June 15, 1920

Hon.' Cato Sells Com.'
Indian Affairs.
Dear Sir

As the question of electing of a business Commette On the Flathead Reservation has been taken up with you by our delegation While in Washington.

The tribe wishes you to request the Sup't.' to call a general meeting for an election on the 27 of June in Ronan Mont; which will be the most coneveint for the tribe. an's at once.

Chief, Sapiel Michel
Eneas Conko

****

Arlee, Mont.
June 15, 1920

Hon Cato Sells, Commissioner of Indian Affairs
Dear sir

As the question of electing of a business Committe on the Flathead Reservation. Has been taken up with you by our delegation while in

Washington. The tribe wishes you to request Supt. Sharp, to call a general meeting for an election on the 27th of June. in Ronan, Mont. Wich will be the most convenient for the tribe. Answer at once.

Very cordially your.
Chief Martin Charlo.

Document 135

Young Indian Killed in Railroad Accident

June 18, 1920

Source: "Find Indian Was Killed by Train," *The Daily Missoulian*, June 18, 1920, page 5, col. 4.

Editors' note: The accidental death of a young tribal member was a tragic event for his family and the St. Ignatius community.

Find Indian Was Killed by Train
Sheriff and Major Sharp Agree That Lad Was Not Victim of Foul Play.

Sheriff J. T. Green accompanied by Major Sharp, the Indian Agent, made a thorough investigation yesterday of the facts surrounding the death of Moses Tellier, 16, of St. Ignatius, who was struck and instantly killed on the track of a branch railroad running from Spokane into the Coeur d'Alene country, early Tuesday, according to the story told by his two Indian companions, Vincent Curley and Eneas Badroads, who accompanied the body when it was brought to St. Ignatius yesterday.

Some doubt as to the facts as given by Curley and Badroads were expressed after they had given it, but the officials, after investigation, found nothing that would indicate that death had resulted from other sources than that to which the accident had been attributed. The body was examined carefully and there were no traces of violence. The body was badly bruised where it had been struck by the train.

All three of the young men are well known on the reservation. The young victim is the son of Isaac and Cecile Tellier, well know Indian residents. Cecille Tellier had a prominent part in the pageant presented at the State University here last year.

According to the story as told to the officials by Badroads and Curley, the trio went to Spokane early in the week. Arriving there, their money gave out, and, fearing lest they be arrested, they decided to "hike" into one of the Indian reservations in Idaho. They started their hike on Monday, after following the line of one of the railroads for some distance.

After a time, becoming weary, the three decided to lie down and rest. The grass was wet, the two said, and so they went to the railroad track and lay down there, where the ground was dry. There, the three all went to sleep.

Some time later a train approaching on the railroad awoke Curley. He declares that he aroused so late that he had only time to grab the boy nearest to him and pull him from the track, as the train dashed by. It happened to be Badroads, and the result was that Tellier was instantly killed.

The mother of the dead youth was notified and she went to get the body, bringing it to St. Ignatius today.

The story as told by Curley and Badroads was not clear in detail, and it was at once determined that a rigid investigation should follow. The two were not sure of the railroad where the accident occurred, and there were other things that the officers desired to look into.

An early report that Tellier was kicked off a moving train while stealing a ride, was denied.

Document 136

Mary Lemery's Political Activism Gets Notice

July 17, 1920

Source: "First Indian Girl to Be the Head of a Tribe," *The Dearborn Independent* (Dearborn, Mich.), July 17, 1920, page 14.

Editors' note: Mary Lemery got some national publicity for her work as the chairman of the Flathead Tribal Council.

First Indian Girl to Be the Head of a Tribe

Many persons still entertain the romantic impression that the Indians of the United States fondly and reverently refer to the Commissioner of Indian Affairs at Washington as "The Great White Father."

Possibly that was the case in bygone years before the North American Indians had become as modernized as in recent years.

Miss Mary Lemery, one of the brightest and most charming Indian girls to be found among the 325,000 members of the various tribes, says the Indians long ago discontinued the high-sounding, but meaningless, "Great White Father" expression, and now both jokingly and seriously refer to the ultra-sedate, serious and solemn commissioner as "The Great White *Bother*."

Miss Lemery, who is a member of the Flathead tribe, of Montana has the honor and distinction of being the first Indian woman in the history of the country to be made president of the Tribal Council. She has held this exalted position of authority for four years.

There are almost 3,000 members of her tribe. With due ceremony the leading men of the Flatheads conferred the Eagle feather upon Miss Lemery, which is their solemn manner of manifesting unlimited trust and esteem.

In addition to superintending the business affairs of her people, this talented Indian girl owns and manages a farm of 300 acres. She manages every detail, from hiring and firing the laborers to marketing the crops. She has made a thorough study of agriculture. Her garden is said to be the show-place of her community. Any man in her section of Montana will tell you that the horse she fears does not exist.

Most of the Flathead Indians are members of the Roman Catholic faith, and Miss Lemery is a well-known graduate of the Holy Name College, of Oregon.

Mary Lemery

Source: "First Indian Girl to Be the Head of a Tribe," *The Dearborn Independent* (Dearborn, Mich.), July 17, 1920, page 14. From The Henry Ford, Dearborn, Michigan.

This hustling and determined girl spent most of the winter in Washington, in an effort to persuade Congress to give the Indians fairer treatment in the management and disposal of their property.

When asked to state what changes were desired by her people, Miss Lemery with deep earnestness replied: "We want freedom and citizenship; we want our own money and property prorated among the individuals now, not in the dim distant years of the future. We feel that we are perfectly capable of handling our own property in our own way, and that we do not need a governmental bureau at Washington to kindergarten us as though we were a lot of kids.

"Much of our property is comprised of timber land, which is very valuable. The government has been cutting timber, off and on, from our lands since 1855. At the present time sixteen sawmills are busily engaged in sawing up our beautiful white pine, spruce and tamarack trees, and they are doing this at a terrific rate. But up to this good hour not a single Flathead Indian — man, woman or child — has received a five cent piece of the proceeds of the sale of this timber. Fifteen million dollars of our money is tied up through the Indians Bureau in timber lands.

"We feel that the time is about ripe for us to have an opportunity to get a look at our own funds.

"Much of our other property is just as badly tangled up in seemingly endless skeins of Indian Bureau red tape and idiotic paternalism on the part of officials who know as little about our needs and desires as King George of England or the Duke of Iceland, and who foolishly insist that we are still an aggregation of irresponsible children who must be nursed and coddled."

Anyone who looks into the keep, calm eyes of Mary Lemery, and listens to her serious and intelligent conversation cannot fail to be convinced of the fairness and righteousness of her claims.

Surely, Indians of the Mary Lemery type are better able to look after their own affairs in far-off Montana, than is a government official in a swivel chair in the Interior Department at Washington.

Why not give the Indians a chance?

Document 137

Charles Allard Takes Flathead Indians to Bozeman July 24, 1920

Source: "Allard to Take Flathead Indians to Bozeman Roundup," *The Daily Missoulian*, July 24, 1920, page 6, col. 5.

Editors' note: Allard's rodeo promotions in Bozeman and other Montana towns gave employment to a number of Flathead Reservation tribal members in 1920.

Allard to Take Flathead Indians to Bozeman Roundup

Bozeman, July 23. — Charlie Allard of Polson, who last year had charge of the band of Flathead Indians at the Bozeman roundup, has again contracted to bring the Indians to Bozeman for the big roundup on August 5, 6, and 7. Last year the Flatheads amazed even the old timers of Bozeman by the richness and magnificence of their dress and Allard writes that they have been working all winter on even more gaudy costumes for this show. In addition to the Indians and their string of horses, Mr. Allard recently made a trip to Pendleton, where he contracted for the tops of the Oregon bucking horses and several relay and roman strings. This will make at least five different relay strings in the relay races at Bozeman. In the Pendleton stock will be Fox, the most famous bucker in the coast state, a horse that has a reputation on a par to Coyote, the famous little Bozeman sorrel. Several of the Flatheads have sent in their entries in the bronch [sic] riding contest and others will take part in the wild horse race.

The Indians added so much to last year's roundup in Bozeman that more money has been appropriated for them by the association this year and an even better Indian display is expected. The beautiful white buckskin robes worn by the s....s in the parade aroused the comment of the Bozeman women as well as the tourists from the east, who are less familiar with such rappings. About 100 Indians are expected for the roundup.

Document 138

Duncan McDonald Relates Tales of His Life

July 28, 1920

Source: "Old Timers Talk of Pioneer Days," *The Daily Missoulian*, July 28, 1920, page 3, col. 4-6.

Editors' note: Duncan McDonald was always anxious to relate stories to the newspaper reporters he met.

Old Timers Talk of Pioneer Days
Duncan MacDonald Gives History of War Dances.

Never a word did Duncan lose as he listened intently to Fred S. Edwards, who told him of his visit to the blood-stained battlefields of France, and of the social conditions now existing in England. And Duncan MacDonald, the seer of the Flathead reservation, gave something in return; he told of the happenings covering a period of 70 years, of which he spoke authoritatively, and of other events he had been told by his father, a Scotchman of renown.

Three old timers, all of whom have resided in Montana for more than 30 years, and others, to whom the stories were not entirely new, were present during the narration of historical events. There was John Swanson, a prominent Blackfoot rancher; Dan Mahoney, a stock buyer known from one end of the state to the other, and Fred S. Edwards, a prominent stockman.

"That's how I learn," said Duncan. "I have learned more from Edwards in this short time than I could by reading 50 books, and I know what he says is true."

Edwards owns a large ranch in the Ross' hole country, and an argument started as to how that locality got the name.

It had been said, and believed, that a s.... man from Elk City was the man Ross' hole was named after, but Duncan exploded that theory with the presentation of facts in his possession.

"Alexander Ross, a Hudson Bay factor, went through Montana in the early 70s [sic] with a party of 52 men," he said. "It was a bad winter and for days they battled with the snow in that portion of the country named after this factor — the Ross' hole. Wolfe and Ryman have a book descriptive of their trip."

Following a discourse concerning the various pieces of sculpture displayed in Washington, D.C., under the guise of what Mr. McDonald sarcastically calls art, which does not meet with his approval, Duncan leaned back in his chair, deftly rolled a cigarette, and then the story, which his hearers knew was forthcoming, was told.

"Yes, those were some dances we had in those days," he said. "Someone had informed the government that the dances should not be permitted and they were prohibited by law, until Secretary of the Interior Garfield visited the reservation some years ago [in 1907]. I believe he was accompanied by Senator Dixon.

Duncan McDonald in later years
Source: Manuscripts and Special Collections, Holland Library, Washington State University, Pullman, Washington,
Historic Photo Collection, PC2 box30, folder 52

"I was dressed in my warrior costume, eagle feathers and all, and he approached me and asked me about the Indian dances — a dance was in progress at the time for his benefit.

"'What about these dances?'" asked Garfield. 'What means this paint and feathers?'

"I looked at him for a moment, then I said. The red woman paints her skin red. Your white woman paints her skin white. Is there any harm in that?

"Your young man goes to a dance. He goes first to the barber shop and gets shaved and powdered. Then he borrows a white shirt and a diamond ring, and a dress suit and goes to the dance. When he puts his arm around a beautiful, attractive young lady, do you think he is thinking about killing anybody then?"

"With a sweep of my hand toward the dancing Indians, I said:

"Look at them. Look at their faces. Do they look like they want to kill? (And every darned Indian was a hoeing it down like the devil)," chuckled Duncan.

"Garfield took in the situation and understood what I was trying to convey to him, and from that time on we were not molested with our Indian dances.

"I have a new war bonnet I made recently," said Duncan. "Those feathers of the golden eagle! They are wonderful. Everyone of your women ought to have one.

"Your bald-headed eagle on your currency, he's an I.W.W. and I'll prove it.

"The golden eagle is a sport. He will fly for miles to seek his prey and lives upon game. Your bald-headed eagle will watch for a fish hawk to seize a fish from a lake or stream, then he will follow him and take the fish away. Your grizzly bear is also an I.W.W. He will follow a panther or mountain lion whom he knows is on the trail of a deer. He will let the panther kill the deer, then he will slip up and drag the deer away and bury it and eat until he can eat no more, and until it is gone.

"The golden eagle is the only true eagle. His feathers are white tipped with black, which grows darker the older the bird gets. These feathers were greatly prized. Many years ago, they were obtained in large numbers. We hunted the golden eagle like you folks do the ostrich for its plumes. In a fight, the warrior picked out his man according to the value of his war bonnet of feathers. If he wanted to marry the prettiest girl in the tribe he would kill the warrior and present her with the war bonnet."

Then the scene shifted to local and national politics, with which Duncan MacDonald is probably as conversant as any man not actively engaged in politics in the northwest.

Document 139

Drunken Flathead Indians Arrested in Missoula

October 2, 1920

Source: "Too Much Booze Causes Trouble," *The Daily Missoulian*, October 2, 1920, page 2, col. 1.

Editors' note: Indians from the Jocko Valley came to Missoula and celebrated with alcohol.

Too Much Booze Causes Trouble
Jerome Vanderberg and Agnes Arlee Fight With Police.

Jerome Vanderberg and Agnes Arlee, Indians, who imbibed too freely of moonshine, and resisted arrest were arraigned yesterday before Police Judge Bonner charged with disturbing the peace. Vanderberg was fined $100 and given a sentence of 30 days in jail, while Agnes was given the alternative of paying $50 fine or serving 25 days in jail. Vanderberg's jail sentence will be suspended if he pays the fine.

Jerome and Agnes didn't give up without a struggle. It took three strong policemen to drag them to the city jail. Night Chief Morris, Patrolman Flammer and Special Officer Tompkins battled with the pair before they were subdued. Patrolman Flammer was kicked in the head by the woman. At the station Jerome became violent and unsheathed a knife. He didn't get an opportunity to do any carving for a "Jack Dempsey" to the jaw put him down for the count.

Agnes Arlee will be remembered by the thousands who attended the fair this week as the Indian woman who rode in the women's relay races.

Index